Rorschach Assessment of Psychotic Phenomena

Rorschach Assessment of Psychotic Phenomena takes the reader beyond where James H. Kleiger's original work, *Disordered Thinking and the Rorschach*, left off. This new book offers readers a number of conceptual bridges between Rorschach characteristics commonly associated with psychotic phenomena and a range of psychological, neurocognitive, and psychoanalytic constructs that help psychologists move beyond static, test-bound interpretations of scores and indices.

Beginning with a broad-based understanding of disordered thinking and reality testing, Kleiger provides an updated review of the contributions of past Rorschach luminaries and contemporary figures who have helped make the Rorschach a robust tool for assessing aspects of psychotic-level experience. The contributions of major figures are highlighted and assessed in terms of their empirical, conceptual, and practical implications. In addition to providing a balanced, respectful review of each of these leading figures and the systems they developed, Kleiger offers a new way of organizing and conceptualizing what is currently understood about Rorschach scoring variables pertaining to psychotic phenomena. Kleiger's aim is to help Rorschach practitioners not only consolidate their grasp of key scoring variables and what each means about an individual's thought processes and internal experiences, but also expand their clinical understanding of the psychotic phenomena being assessed. He includes a wide range of psychotic phenomena, like negative symptoms, cognitive impairment, magical thinking, and impairment of insight, all of which are subjects of diagnostic interest when using the Rorschach with psychotically prone individuals.

The final section on psychopathology looks at how the Rorschach is useful in differential diagnosis of primary psychoses and those conditions that may include secondary psychotic phenomena. In step with contemporary DSM-5 standards, Kleiger organizes his discussion of severe psychopathology in a manner consistent with how psychotic phenomena are currently understood in the clinical and scientific literature. In addition to reviewing key clinical characteristics of these conditions, along with Rorschach contributions to the diagnosis of these disorders, he also focuses his lens on the Rorschach assessment of malingered psychosis and psychotic phenomena in children and adolescents.

Written with the same well-researched attention to detail and integrative style as Kleiger's earlier work, *Rorschach Assessment of Psychotic Phenomena* will prove invaluable to clinical psychologists, psychiatrists, and psychoanalysts interested in understanding and assessing psychosis.

James H. Kleiger is a psychologist-psychoanalyst in private practice in Bethesda, Maryland. He is a Fellow in the Society for Personality Assessment and Board Certified in Clinical and Personality Assessment Psychology. Kleiger has written *Disordered Thinking and the Rorschach* (1999) and was senior author of *Assessing Psychosis: A Clinician's Guide* (2015), both by Routledge.

Rorschach Assessment of Psychotic Phenomena

Clinical, Conceptual, and Empirical Developments

James H. Kleiger

LONDON AND NEW YORK

First published 2017
by Routledge
2 Park Square, Milton Park, Abingdon, Oxon OX14 4RN

and by Routledge
711 Third Avenue, New York, NY 10017

Routledge is an imprint of the Taylor & Francis Group, an informa business

© 2017 James H. Kleiger

The right of James H. Kleiger to be identified as author of this work has been asserted by him in accordance with sections 77 and 78 of the Copyright, Designs and Patents Act 1988.

All rights reserved. No part of this book may be reprinted or reproduced or utilised in any form or by any electronic, mechanical, or other means, now known or hereafter invented, including photocopying and recording, or in any information storage or retrieval system, without permission in writing from the publishers.

Trademark notice: Product or corporate names may be trademarks or registered trademarks, and are used only for identification and explanation without intent to infringe.

British Library Cataloguing in Publication Data
A catalogue record for this book is available from the British Library

Library of Congress Cataloging in Publication Data
Names: Kleiger, James H., 1952– author.
Title: Rorschach assessment of psychotic phenomena: clinical, conceptual, and empirical developments / James H. Kleiger.
Description: Abingdon, Oxon; New York, NY: Routledge, 2017. | Includes bibliographical references and index.
Identifiers: LCCN 2016035284 | ISBN 9780415837675 (hardback: alk. paper) | ISBN 9780415837682 (pbk.: alk. paper) | ISBN 9781315271385 (e-book)
Subjects: | MESH: Rorschach Test | Psychotic Disorders—diagnosis | Diagnosis, Differential
Classification: LCC BF698.8.R5 | NLM WM 145.5.R7 | DDC 155.2/842—dc23
LC record available at https://lccn.loc.gov/2016035284

ISBN: 978-0-415-83767-5 (hbk)
ISBN: 978-0-415-83768-2 (pbk)
ISBN: 978-1-315-27138-5 (ebk)

Typeset in Times New Roman
by codeMantra

For my loving parents, Ann and Ralph

Contents

List of figures ix
List of tables x
Acknowledgments xi
Foreword xiii

Introduction 1

PART I
Understanding and assessing psychotic phenomena 7

1 Psychotic phenomena: Toward a conceptual understanding of reality testing and disordered thinking 9

2 Assessing disordered thinking and psychotic phenomena 27

PART II
Rorschach assessment of psychotic phenomena 35

3 Hermann Rorschach's experiment 37

4 Contributions of Rapaport and Holt 42

5 The Thought Disorder Index 65

6 The Comprehensive System and Rorschach Performance Assessment System 82

7 Alternative Rorschach approaches for assessing disordered thinking 103

8 Integrated model of Rorschach signs of disordered thinking 108

PART III
Dimensions of disordered thinking   123

9. Disorganization: Problems in focusing, filtering, and language usage   125
10. Illogicality: Problems in reasoning and logic   145
11. Impoverishment in thinking and language   168
12. Awareness of perceptual and reasoning errors   182

PART IV
Differential diagnosis of psychotic phenomena on the Rorschach   191

13. Primary psychoses and the Rorschach   193
14. Secondary psychotic phenomena and the Rorschach   227
15. Malingered psychosis and disordered thinking   248
16. Rorschach indications of psychotic phenomena in children and adolescents   260

Final Thoughts: Empirical, conceptual, and practical considerations   280

Index   287

Figures

3.1	Hermann Rorschach	37
4.1	David Rapaport	42
4.2	Robert Holt	52
5.1	Philip Holzman	65
6.1	John Exner	82
6.2	Irving Weiner	82
6.3	Greg Meyer	94
6.4	Don Viglione	94
6.5	Joni Mihura	94
6.6	Robert Erard	94
6.7	Phil Erdberg	94

Tables

4.1	Rapaport's Deviant Verbalizations	45
5.1	Principal component (empiric) classification of TDI categories	75
9.1	TLC categories of formal thought disorder reflecting disorganization	132
16.1	Sampling of Darleen's Rorschach responses	275

Acknowledgments

There are so many significant individuals without whose support, patience, guidance, technical assistance, and intellectual inspiration this work would not have been possible. First, I acknowledge the love and guidance provided by my family, especially my wife, children, sister, and parents. I have a long list of teachers and mentors, each of whom was knowledgeable about subjects that I found fascinating and took a keen interest in my eagerness to learn. Here, I would like to offer my profound thanks to Nelson Jones, Irwin Rosen, Martin and Lui Leichtman, Leonard Horwitz, Bob Athey, Don Colson, and Deborah Levy.

A huge debt of gratitude is owed to Ali Khadivi, who has provided innumerable conceptual and clinical insights, equaled only by the solid friendship we have established. Together we wrote *Assessing Psychosis: A Clinician's Guide*, which served as a valuable resource and intellectual fermentation for this book. Thank you, Ali.

As always, I have relied heavily upon and learned so much from my friends and colleagues in the Society for Personality Assessment and the International Rorschach Society. I especially want to acknowledge, in no particular order, Jed Yalof, Don Viglione, Tony Bram, Irv Weiner, Charles Peterson, Bruce Smith, Marvin Acklin, Barton Evans, Joni Mihura, Phil Erdberg, Greg Meyer, Virginia Brabender, Barry Ritzler, Paul and Howard Lerner, Bob Erard, Pekka Koistinen, Thomas Rosen, Heikki Toivakka, Odile Hussein, Tefika Ikiz, Lily Rothschild-Yakar, Liza Lacoua, and Piero Porcelli.

I am grateful to Drs. Urs Germann and Anne Andronikof for permission to publish a photograph of Hermann Rorschach. My appreciation also goes to the Kansas Historical Society for supplying a photograph and giving permission to include a picture of David Rapaport. Thank you to Drs. Robert Holt, Irving Weiner, Robert Erard, Philip Erdberg, Gregory Meyer, Joni Mihura, and Donald Viglione for permission to use their photographs as well. I also am grateful to Andrea Metts for permission to publish a photograph of her father, John Exner, and to Paul and Ann Holzman for permitting me to include a photograph of Philip Holzman.

Special homage goes to Robert Holt, who generously offered to review my chapter on Rapaport and his contributions. I feel fortunate to have had his input and editorial suggestions.

I would also like to extend a special thanks to Joanne Freeman for her superb editorial assistance. Thank you also to Kate Hawes, Charles Bath, and all at Routledge, UK for their patience and support in making this book a reality.

Finally, to the anonymous legion of patients I have had the privilege of knowing and learning from over the past 40 years of practice, I offer my gratitude. I thank them especially for their patience and their tutelage.

Foreword

Martin Leichtman

From its inception, the Rorschach test has been inextricably bound to the study of thought disorder. Hermann Rorschach did his doctoral research on hallucinatory phenomena under Eugen Bleuler at the time the latter was completing his classic study, *Dementia Praecox or the Group of Schizophrenias* (1911). After obtaining his degree, Rorschach, like other young Swiss psychiatrists such as Jung and Ricklin, sought to find ways of adapting psychological tests to the assessment of personality and psychopathology. Advancing his inkblot "procedure" with this purpose in mind, he was particularly concerned with its application to psychoses and noted a number of test signs of disturbed thinking (e.g. DW responses, confabulatory-combined whole responses, and contaminated whole responses).

Dying shortly after the publication of *Psychodiagnostics* (1921), Rorschach could not have anticipated that his test would become the preeminent psychological instrument for the assessment of thought disorder. Over the next century innumerable clinical psychologists, including some of the finest minds in the discipline, highlighted a wide variety of ways in which Rorschach's test revealed multiple facets of disordered thinking, advanced numerous systems for their measurement, and engendered a massive body of research on the topic. As a consequence, a recent standard psychiatric textbook described the Rorschach as "the test most widely used in examination of thought disorders" (Clarkin, Howieson, & McClough, 2008) and even its harshest critics concede its usefulness in this regard (Wood, Nezworski, & Garb, 2003).

The power of the Rorschach as a diagnostic instrument derives from the nature of the test task and its distinctive features. The task requires that subjects use an unfamiliar, exceptionally plastic medium to create any of an almost infinite number of images. They must then explain and justify their representations to an authority figure about whom they know little except that he or she will use this information to form an impression of their personalities and make recommendations that may have a profound effect on their future. Thus, how subjects handle the task generates a remarkable array of information about their modes of representation, the content of their thoughts, their language, their reasoning, and the ways in which they experience themselves and others. Moreover, because of the stress attendant on the enterprise, the Rorschach yields data on the manner in which different forms of severe psychopathology enter into these processes whose richness and novelty are unmatched by that derived from any other test.

However, the very richness of this data, the many ways in which it has been codified and analyzed, the sheer volume of the resulting clinical and research literature, and the relative neglect of basic theory about the nature of the Rorschach test and the rationale for test signs have posed formidable challenges for those seeking to appreciate the full potential of the instrument. For these reasons, not only students struggling to master the test, but also the most experienced clinicians and researchers have been deeply indebted to James Kleiger for his landmark work, *Disordered Thinking and the Rorschach* (1999). In addition to providing the best and most comprehensive overview of three-quarters of a century of research and theory, the book included judicious discussions of both familiar and often-overlooked scoring systems, a conceptual foundation for understanding thought disorder scores and patterns of disordered thinking, and a practical clinical guide to differential diagnoses of psychoses and borderline conditions based upon the distinctive patterns of disordered thinking encountered in each.

With the publication of the present volume, we are even more indebted to Dr. Kleiger for the single best introduction to a century of theory and research on applications of the Rorschach to an understanding of disordered thinking. Of particular importance in this regard is his inclusion of recent, cutting-edge applications of the technique such as the Rorschach Performance Assessment System (R-PAS) and abbreviated card set methods. Yet what is most significant about the book is that it is not simply an updated, second edition of his earlier work. Rather, it has been an occasion for reexamining and deepening his analyses of a host of critical issues. For example, he offers readers a multidimensional conception of disordered thinking, moves beyond a focus on Rorschach scores to an appreciation of their linkage to a host of psychological, psychoanalytic, developmental, and neuropsychological concepts, and suggests more sophisticated clinical applications of the Rorschach to the diagnoses of psychotic conditions. Supplanting its predecessor, Dr. Kleiger's new work is now the essential reference for researchers and clinicians with a serious interest in the Rorschach and the study and treatment of disordered thinking.

References

Bleuler, E. (1911). *Dementia Praecox or the Group of Schizophrenias* (J. Zinkin, trans.). New York: International Universities Press, 1950.
Clarkin, J., Howieson, D. B., & McClough, J. (2008). The role of psychiatric measures in assessment and treatment. In H. E. Hales, S. C. Yudofsky, & G. O. Gabbard (Eds.).

The American Psychiatric Publishing Textbook of Psychiatry (5th ed., pp. 73–100). Washington, DC: American Psychiatric Publishing.

Kleiger, J. (1999). *Disordered Thinking and the Rorschach.* Hillsdale, NJ: Analytic Press.

Rorschach, H. (1921). *Psychodiagnostics* (5th ed.). Bern: Hans Huber, 1942.

Wood, J. M., Nezworski, M. T., & Garb, H. N. (2003). What's right with the Rorschach? *The Scientific Review of Mental Health Practice, 2,* 142–146.

Introduction

Why write this book? Twenty years have passed since I began writing *Disordered Thinking and The Rorschach* (Kleiger, 1999). At the very least, that span of time has justified producing a second or revised edition to incorporate the many developments that have occurred in the field. When I embarked on this project, I did so with the intent of writing just such a second edition; however, I quickly encountered a number of difficulties. What was the best way to acknowledge significant changes in diagnostic concepts, major developments in Rorschach psychology, and, most important, my own evolving interests and understanding of disordered thinking and psychotic phenomena? So, what began as *Disordered Thinking and The Rorschach, Second Edition*, soon changed to *Disordered Thinking and The Rorschach: A Second Look*, as a way to capture two decades of changes. Though clearly related to its predecessor, the current volume is more like a younger cousin than the direct offspring I had first intended—similar ideological DNA but with enough newness and novelty to distinguish it from the first book. Thus, the title evolved to *Rorschach Assessment of Psychotic Phenomena*.

Psychotic phenomena and disordered thinking

The title reflects an essential change in this book. The term "psychotic phenomena" is meant to connote a broader range of psychotic-like symptoms or features that can be thought about as dimensions that exist along a continuum. This is consistent with how psychosis is currently regarded, less in terms of discrete categories of disorders and more as a series of symptom dimensions that can be placed along a continuum of severity. Although the Rorschach is less useful in identifying the presence of key symptom dimensions like hallucinatory phenomena or delusional beliefs, it does provide an excellent method for assessing problems in thinking, reality testing, and insight or awareness, all of which may reflect psychotic or psychotic-like symptoms and experiences.

The term "psychotic phenomena" encompasses a broad definition of problems in thinking and perceiving. However, most would agree that the Rorschach makes its chief diagnostic contribution in capturing oddities in thinking. In *Disordered Thinking and The Rorschach*, I argued that the term "disordered thinking" offers advantages over the older, more traditional term "thought disorder." In the current book, I extend this distinction. I reserve the term "thought disorder" for the narrower diagnostic concept originally called "formal thought disorder." Essentially a categorical term, "thought disorder" is regarded as a diagnostic concept that describes a symptom dimension of psychosis in the DSM-5 (American Psychiatric Association, 2013), which is now referred to as Disorganized Speech (Thinking). In contrast, "disordered thinking" is a broader, multidimensional psychological concept, less categorical and diagnostic in scope but including multiple dimensions of disturbed thinking that occur along a continuum of severity. Thus, in Chapter 1, I introduce a way of conceptualizing five dimensions of disordered thinking, which can be useful for diagnosticians trying to understand the vulnerabilities that exist in their patients (Kleiger & Khadivi, 2015). However, let me issue a caveat for the reader. Although I have tried to distinguish between the concepts of thought disorder and disordered thinking, there are times that I may use them interchangeably. When I do this, I am using the term "thought disorder" more generically, as a way of referring to what has traditionally been regarded as a psychotic-level symptom. Hopefully, I will not confuse the reader with these fluid terminology changes.

An interest in history

Like its older cousin, this volume pays homage to seminal contributors to the Rorschach assessment of psychotic phenomena, in particular disordered thinking. As before, I include chapters in Part II summarizing the contributions of Rorschach giants who pioneered methods for assessing disordered thinking with the Rorschach. It seemed fitting to begin this section with a brief chapter devoted to Hermann Rorschach's original contributions. This is followed by chapters addressing the contributions of David Rapaport, Robert Holt, Philip Holzman and the TDI, John Exner, Irv Weiner, and Greg Meyer, Donald Viglione, Joni Mihura, Philip Erdberg, and Robert Erard, the developers of the R-PAS. Obviously, the synthesis of R-PAS contributions is new; however, chapters on the other leading contributors have been rewritten. In places, I borrow from my earlier book; but, for the most part, each chapter has been revised and reorganized.

The contributions of Rapaport and Holt are included in a single chapter (Chapter 4), as are the contributions from the Comprehensive System (CS) and R-PAS (Chapter 6). Chapter 5 associates the Thought Disorder Index (TDI) principally with Philip Holzman; however, many key contributors such as Deborah Levy and Michael Coleman, not to mention Mary Hollis Johnston, contributed mightily to the development of the TDI. Each of the chapters in Part II concludes with a summary of the empirical support, conceptual contributions, and clinical or practical utility of each system. I have also included in Chapter 7 a group of alternative Rorschach methods for assessing disordered thinking. I did so not only because I am a history buff when it comes to the Rorschach, but also because of the novelty of some of the ideas in these lesser, and in some cases unknown, contributions.

Conceptual bridges

As was the case with my 1999 book, I continue to be interested in moving beyond a cataloging of scores to understanding more about what the scores mean. From a conceptual perspective, I am interested in developing a deeper understanding of what Rorschach Special Scores (CS) or Cognitive Codes (R-PAS) might signify about an individual's internal world in terms of cognitive functioning, typical modes of reasoning, and experiences of self and others (Kleiger, 2016). Too often, we become stuck at the level of test scores or indices. We have difficulty linking these test-based metrics to broader conceptual and clinical reference points concerning the nature of disordered thought or broader aspects of the patient's functioning. The scores themselves become reified, and we often settle for the knowledge that a patient gives Deviant Responses (DRs), Fabulized Combinations (FABs), or Incongruous Combinations (INCs). In my 1999 book, I may have contributed to this test-bound mode of thinking when I wrote about "combinative, confabulatory, paleological, and contaminatory thinking." Although my intention was to deconstruct each of these categories and move beyond specific scoring categories, the focus still remained on these Rorschach-based concepts. Too often these broader Rorschach-based categories, like the specific scores themselves, can become endpoints in our thinking instead of serving as starting points for trying to understand the psychological, developmental, clinical diagnostic, and even psychodynamic concepts that might be associated with the test scores or categories. In this sense, typical approaches of assigning different "thought disorder scores" to Rorschach responses often lead to the circular conclusion that the respondent has a thought disorder (Kleiger, 2016). More useful diagnostic questions such as what these scores might reveal about the nature of the individual's psychopathology or more specific functional questions about an individual's abilities to focus, filter, organize, monitor, and apply logic to his or her thoughts are left unexplored.

There are essentially two types of "bridges" I am interested in constructing. The first follows the trend in my initial book—namely, to try to bridge Rorschach scores with a broader range of meaningful concepts. To achieve this aim, I have tried to broaden the lens and look at myriad of ways that Rorschach scores might link up with traditional psychological, developmental, psychoanalytic, and neurocognitive concepts. The second type of bridge I want to erect is between Rorschach Special Scores or Cognitive Codes and the ways in which disordered thinking is thought about clinically and in psychosis research. The basis for some of this thinking originated in discussions with Ali Khadivi in 2014. Thus, in Chapter 8, I introduce an integrated model for organizing Rorschach Special Scores or Cognitive Codes in a manner that is not only conceptually meaningful but also more consistent with how disordered thinking and thought disorder are regarded beyond the borders of the Rorschach itself.

Furthermore, to move beyond static categories of Rorschach-bound scores, Part III includes four chapters that focus on four overlapping dimensions of disordered thinking: disorganization, illogicality, impoverishment, and disturbances in awareness of disturbed thinking and reality testing. The disorganization dimension provides a way of understanding deviant verbalizations (DVs) and deviant responses (DRs). Illogicality reflects the inferential and reasoning process that takes place silently as the patient tries to form conclusions and attribute meaning to the inkblots. Essentially, illogical thinking involves errors in reasoning and/or perception, which are represented by combinative responses (INC and FAB) and certain types of embellished or overinterpreted DRs, Autistic Logic (ALOGs)/Peculiar Logic (PECs), and Contamination responses (CON). Finally, impoverished thinking, though more elusive and not as clearly represented by specific Rorschach scores, can signal the presence of psychotic phenomena in patients suffering from negative symptoms or cognitive impairment.

Psychotic phenomena and psychopathology

Part IV focuses on psychotic phenomena and disordered thinking associated with primary psychoses (Chapter 13) and secondary psychotic phenomena (Chapter 14). The distinction between these chapters has to do with Rorschach manifestations of psychotic phenomena in those disorders for which psychosis is a primary distinguishing feature versus those conditions in which psychotic symptoms or experiences may, under certain conditions, emerge. Thus, Chapter 13 includes the broad schizophrenia spectrum and related conditions (schizophrenia, schizotypal personality, schizoaffective disorder, and delusional disorder) as well as affective psychoses (bipolar and depressive psychoses). I have also included material about attenuated psychoses and drug-induced psychotic disorders. In Chapter 14, the focus turns to psychotic phenomena and disordered thinking associated with borderline psychopathology, trauma, and dissociative disorders. Additionally, I have added a briefer discussion of Obsessive–Compulsive Disorder (OCD)-spectrum conditions, although clinical, research and Rorschach literature are less extensive in these areas. Because malingered psychosis on the Rorschach is an increasingly important concern for diagnosticians, I devote Chapter 15 to this diagnostic conundrum. Finally, no Rorschach book of this sort would be complete without attention to psychotic phenomena in children and adolescents. Thus, the final substantive chapter in Part IV concerns psychotic manifestations and Rorschach literature pertaining to children and adolescents suffering from a range of diagnostic conditions similar to those in adults, which are discussed in Chapters 13 and 14.

In the final analysis, what began as a modest update to an existing book became a larger project. Although clearly related to its 1999 cousin, *Rorschach Assessment of Psychotic Phenomena* offers a broader, more current, and finely nuanced overview of Rorschach contributions to assessing individuals whose thinking is disordered, whose reality testing is disturbed, and who may lack the ability to step back and recognize that others have difficulty understanding their thinking.

References

American Psychiatric Association. (2013). *Diagnostic and Statistical Manual of Mental Disorders* (5th ed.). Washington, DC: Author.
Kleiger, J. H. (1999). *Disordered Thinking and The Rorschach*. Hillsdale, NJ: The Analytic Press.
Kleiger, J. H. (2016). Thinking about thought disorder on the Rorschach. *Rorschach Training Programs Inc. Newsletter,* 8. New York: Rorschach Training Programs, Inc.
Kleiger, J. H., & Khadivi, A. (2015). *Assessing Psychosis. A Clinician's Guide.* New York: Routledge.

Part I

Understanding and assessing psychotic phenomena

Chapter 1

Psychotic phenomena
Toward a conceptual understanding of reality testing and disordered thinking

Consider this familiar scenario. One of the interns in your practicum has completed an outpatient testing on a 25-year-old male, J. D. You have supervised the Rorschach and agreed that J. D. had a high number of minus-form-level responses and gave three Level 2 Special Scores, or Cognitive Codes as they are now described in the Rorschach Performance Assessment System (R-PAS; Meyer et al., 2011). The severity of these scores indicates a disturbance in reality testing, along with both a severe lapse in J. D.'s logic and disorganization in how he verbalized his responses. Although there were no accompanying clinical signs of psychosis and no one on the team has raised questions about this possibility, your intern is certain that we have evidence that J. D. must be psychotic. Do you agree? Before you answer, it might be useful to review the relationship between reality testing, thought disorder, and psychosis.

Psychosis, reality, and reality testing

In many ways, the concept of "reality" is incompatible with the "world of psychosis" (Parnas, 2015). According to Parnas, reality, in a "Newtonian" sense, is that which exists objectively, materially, and independently of acts of consciousness. Psychosis may be thought of as an experiential state in which one stands outside of the real world. As a construct, reality can be parsed into separate, but related, psychological processes: the experience of reality and reality testing.

The experience of reality has to do with one's immediate sensory perception of the world and involves a shared sense of the world around us. Parnas noted how both Jaspers (1913/1963) and Janet (1926) distinguished between this primary sense or awareness of reality, on the one hand, and a judgment about what is real, on the other. The sense of reality is more of a sensory and affective experience of the world and less of a reflective cognitive judgment about one's experience (Parnas, 2015). Weiner (1966) contrasted reality sense with reality testing, linking impaired reality sense to perceptual disturbances in self or ego boundaries.

Reality testing, one's judgment about reality, is a more familiar concept that we employ diagnostically. Unlike the immediate sensory awareness or perception of reality described above, reality testing is a judgment one makes about this experience: Does what I am sensing, perceiving, seeing, and hearing originate in my mind or in the world outside of my mind? In other words, reality testing is a conscious, but sometimes implicit, judgment one makes about the locus of a stimulus.

One's experience of reality may be impaired while one's reality testing remains intact. For example, one may hear voices or see other figures in a room when no one else is present yet judge correctly that this experience of reality is inaccurate, that these are hallucinatory experiences. Conversely, one may perceive reality correctly but interpret its source or meaning incorrectly. An example would be an individual who accurately perceives people whispering in the hallway and concludes that they must be conspiring against him. The concept of insight is related to reality testing. In the first case, the individual is not psychotic. He or she is experiencing a perceptual symptom usually associated with psychosis; however, the person's insight into the locus and source of the anomalous perceptions remains intact. In the second case, the individual's sense of reality, his sensory perception of the immediate world around him, is intact but the meaning he ascribes to the experience is inaccurate. The judgment of conspiracy resides in the individual's mind, not the outside world. It is a failure in reality testing and may signal the potential or presence of psychotic experience.

Psychosis implies the loss of reality testing, where one is unable to discriminate between what is "inside" and what is "outside" one's own mind. However, poor reality testing, by itself, does not automatically constitute psychosis. Many individuals have difficulties establishing an objective frame of reference. They imbue their experiences with too much subjectivity and fail to distinguish between their own thoughts and feelings and those of others. It is only when the capacity to make this distinction becomes sufficiently impaired, when the individual fails to distinguish between what is "real" and what is "imagined," that we speak of psychosis. At this point, we cannot be sure that this is the case with our intern's patient, J. D. We still have not addressed the question of thought disorder.

Psychosis and thought disorder

Psychosis is a superordinate construct understood in two different, but overlapping, ways (Parnas, 2015). First, it represents a class of severe mental disorders, based on clinical descriptions of signs and symptoms. Second, the term "psychosis" is used descriptively to define acute, episodic, and sometimes enduring states characterized by the presence of hallmark features such as hallucinations, delusions, thought disorder, severely disturbed behavior, and negative symptoms.

Along with hallucinations and delusions, "thought disorder" is a key symptom dimension associated with psychosis. Hallucinations without insight and/or delusions are typically sufficient conditions to assume the presence of psychosis. However, in the absence of either of these, thought disorder alone is usually insufficient (and unnecessary) for establishing a diagnosis of psychosis. In other words, patients may hallucinate and harbor delusional beliefs with impaired insight but not exhibit thought disorder. Such patients would certainly be considered psychotic. Conversely, a patient such as J. D. may demonstrate signs of thought disorder on a procedure like the Rorschach while not having hallucinations, delusions, or behaving bizarrely. In the absence of critical, insight-impairing symptoms, such patients may not be considered psychotic. Thus, we cannot conclude that a patient like J.D. has a clinically diagnosable psychosis. Our intern has discovered something of vital importance about this patient's mental functioning; however, we cannot make formal diagnoses on the basis of test findings alone. Okay, the intern accepts your counsel that indications of thought disorder on J. D.'s Rorschach do not mean that this patient *is* psychotic; but J. D. has a "thought disorder," right? However, before responding, reflect on this deceptively simple question and ask yourself: What is "thought disorder" after all?

Thought disorder or disordered thinking: An elusive concept

A recent review of the phenomenology of thought disorder provides clarity for what has been a confusing concept (Roche et al., 2015). Unlike its sibling concepts, hallucinations and delusions, a precise understanding of the meaning of "thought disorder" has proven to be somewhat elusive. Disagreement regarding the scope of the definition, the underlying mechanisms, and the degree of diagnostic specificity associated with the presence of what has traditionally been referred to as "thought disorder" has contributed to the haze surrounding the concept and confusion about what to call it (Kleiger, 1999; Kleiger & Khadivi, 2015). Disagreements among psychologists, psychiatrists, and linguists over whether it is speech or thinking that is "disordered" have muddied the conceptual waters and contributed to the dissatisfaction with the traditional terminology. Unfortunately, as is often the case in social sciences, when new terminology is introduced, underlying concepts often become fluid and meaning begins to drift. Terms begin to be used interchangeably without recognizing the conceptual distinctions. Such is clearly the case with the term "thought disorder." Because of the absence of a clear and unambiguous definition, a number of new terms have rushed to fill the conceptual vacuum. Terms such as disorganized thinking, cognitive disorganization, disorganized speech, language disorder, disordered thinking; or a more inclusive and cumbersome expression, disorders of thought, language, and communication (Andreasen, 1978) are but a few of the more common terms used to capture this phenomenon.

How did we arrive at this point of conceptual confusion and such a clinician-confounding proliferation of terminology? A brief historical review helps set the stage for understanding the sources of confusion and for beginning to disentangle the resulting knots in our conceptual understanding and terminology.

A brief look back

Over 100 years ago, Kraepelin (1896/1911) and Bleuler (1911/1950) focused on disturbances in thought processes as a critical symptom in dementia praecox (Kraepelin's term) or schizophrenia (Bleuler's term). Kraepelin emphasized deterioration in intellectual processes, which in turn disrupted the ordering of thoughts and created a "derailment" in the flow of ideas. Bleuler identified a "loosening of associations" between thoughts, a fundamental feature of schizophrenia. Thus, the stage was set for subsequent generations of mental health professionals to conceptualize thought disorder according to definitions of luminaries like Kraepelin and Bleuler. However, there were two somewhat paradoxical problems with the Kraepelenian and Bleulerian definitions of thought disorder. One concerned the narrow scope of the definition. The other had to do with overemphasizing thought processes, per se, while ignoring the function of language or speech.

The narrow definition: Thought disorder as loosening of associations

On the one hand, the traditional definition of thought disorder became narrowly wedded to an associational model. Thus, thought disorder was equated with a loosening of associations or disruptions in the flow or connectedness of ideas. For example, *The Comprehensive Textbook of Psychiatry* (Vol. 2) (Freeman, Kaplan, & Saddock, 1976) defined formal thought process disorder in terms of "irrelevance and incoherence of the patient's verbal productions. It ranges from simple blocking and mild circumstantiality to total loosening of associations, as in word salad" (p. 1333). In discussing symptoms of schizophrenia, the DSM-IV (American Psychiatric Association, 1994) used the term "disorganized thinking," instead of "thought disorder" to describe a patient's tendency to "'slip off track' from one topic to another ('derailment' or 'loose associations'); answers to questions may be obliquely related or completely unrelated ('tangentiality')" (p. 276). The DSM-5 (American Psychiatric Association, 2013) further narrowed the terminology by emphasizing the speech component, placing most emphasis on loose associations, disorganization, and incoherence. In the paragraph defining "Disorganized Thinking (Speech)," illogical thinking is not mentioned at all (p. 88). What is missing in these narrower definitions is attention to the "thinking component" and the complexity and multidimensional nature of the cognitive processes that could underlie thought disorder.

Thought, speech, or communication disorder?

On the other hand, as researchers attempted to broaden the definition of thought disorder beyond a simple associational model (Cameron, 1938; Goldstein & Scheerer, 1941; von Domarus, 1944), they overemphasized the realms of thinking and logic and minimized the importance of the language production system. According to Bentall (2003), "Bleuler's identification of thought disorder with thinking led researchers to neglect what psychotic patients were actually saying" (p. 381). Researchers assumed that language is simply "the light of the mind" (Mill, 1963) and viewed speech as representative of thought processes (Harrow & Quinlan, 1985; Lanin-Kettering & Harrow, 1985; Holzman, Shenton, & Solovay, 1986). Holzman, probably the clearest spokesman for this group, asserted that language is a transparent medium through which thought is expressed. According to Holzman, since deviant verbal productions of psychotic patients reveal disturbed thought processes, the peculiarities in psychotic communication should be labeled "thought disorders" and not speech or language disorders. Harrow and Quinlan (1985) acknowledged that speech and thought are not necessarily isomorphic with each other and that bizarre communication may, in some cases, be a product of impaired expression of reasonable ideas. However, like Holzman, they believed that their research supported the conclusion that faulty language or speech is generally a result of strange thinking; hence, they, too, favored the term "thought disorder."

Linguists challenged the assumptions of psychological researchers and disputed the empirical basis for equating speech with thought. Chaika (1990), who introduced the term "speech disorder," accused psychological and psychiatric researchers of circular reasoning when they claimed that disturbed thinking underlies disturbed speech. She said that there was no empirical evidence demonstrating that disordered thinking always produces disordered speech. Although thought is expressed through language, it is a logical fallacy, according to Chaika, to conclude that language is a direct expression of thought. Chaika's view, echoed by others (Rochester & Martin, 1979; Harvey & Neale, 1983), is that language, speech, and thought cannot be equated and that all that we can study are observable disturbances in speech. Making inferences about the nature of underlying thought processes based on the quality of an individual's verbal productions is not always warranted.

To summarize this debate, linguists study the formal qualities of deviant speech and entertain a range of possible causative explanations, whereas traditionalists assume that DVs reflect disturbed thinking. In essence, the approach of these researchers is consistent with psychiatric and psychodiagnostic methodology, in which one assumes that inferences about underlying psychological structures and organization can be made on the basis of observable behavior. In contrast, linguists challenge these assumptions and question the validity of inferring the nature of that which is not available for direct observation.

The dialectical nature of the thought-versus-speech question does not require one to take sides with either the psychological researchers or the linguists. Concerns regarding both the narrow definition of thought disorder, on the one hand, and the issue of thought processes versus speech can be addressed by incorporating both perspectives into a comprehensive model of thought disorder. This is what Andreasen (1978) had in mind when she developed the Scale for the

Assessment of Thought, Language, and Communication (TLC) to provide a comprehensive and consistent set of reliable definitions that could be used clinically. As evident from the name of her scale, she increased the conceptual span of thought disorder to include disturbances in both speech and thought.

Despite the significance of Andreasen's contributions to the understanding and measurement of thought disorder, one can identify a couple of important shortcomings in her approach. First, rightly or wrongly, Andreasen (1982) advocated relinquishing the traditional term thought disorder and substituting terms such as communication disorders, dysphasia, or dyslogia. Despite her empirical studies and thoughtful rationale, these terms are cumbersome and confusing. Although flawed conceptually, the traditional term "thought disorder" is more familiar and enables clinicians to communicate with each other more effectively. The second limitation in Andreasen's approach to defining and studying thought disorder (discussed in greater detail later) is that despite the equal billing of thought, language, and communication, her scale focuses more on what the individual says and less on how the person reasons, forms concepts, and makes inferences about his or her experiences—namely, how one thinks.

Factor structure of thought disorder

Moving beyond the narrow, associational definition and the speech-versus-thought dichotomy, the clinical nature of thought disorder can be parsed into various components, leading to a richer and more meaningful conceptualization of disordered thought.

Positive and negative thought disorder

Just as general features of psychosis can be classified in terms of positive versus negative symptoms, this same distinction can be applied to thought disorder. Positive thought disorder includes formal features of speech, thought content, or underlying reasoning processes that are bizarre, illogical, and confusing to the listener. Harrow and Quinlan (1985) used the term "bizarre–idiosyncratic thinking" to capture the broad category of positive thought disorder manifest in confusing speech and illogical thinking. Most of the Schneiderian first-rank symptoms—such as thought broadcasting, thought withdrawal, and thought insertion (Schneider, 1959)—are prime examples of positive thought disorder content that implicitly reflects underlying illogicality in reasoning processes.

Unlike positive thought disorder, which is characterized by the presence of bizarre and idiosyncratic form and content, negative thought disorder is understood as an impoverishment of thought and speech. Here, it is the absence of normal rate, fluency, rhythm, and flow of thoughts/speech, as well as a constriction in the range of content that defines negative thought disorder. Typical categories are (1) poverty of speech, which includes responses that are brief and unelaborated; (2) poverty of thought content, which reflects empty speech, devoid of meaningful information; and (3) perseveration of ideas, in which ideas and themes are repeated regardless of changes in circumstances. Poverty of speech is noted by restriction in the amount of spontaneous speech. Replies to questions are brief, contracted, and concrete, requiring frequent prompting from the interviewer.

Andreasen (1979a) also discussed positive and negative thought disorder, but, once again, her focus remained on formal qualities of speech (i.e. variables described as "formal thought disorder") and not on underlying cognitive processes, which may produce either illogical or impoverished thought processes. For Andreasen, positive thought disorder is characterized by derailment, disorganization, and disconnectedness of the thought processes and is represented by circumstantial thinking, tangentiality, derailment, distractible speech, clang associations, and incoherence. Andreasen used the term "derailment" to capture the disorganization reflected in positive thought disorder, as opposed to older terms like "loosening of associations" and "flight of ideas." In contrast, Andreasen indicated that negative thought disorder is characterized by peculiar and restricted thought processes, including features like neologisms, thought blocking, illogicality, poverty of speech, and poverty of speech content. In these types of disorders, the individual's speech is delineated by highly idiosyncratic or markedly improvised thinking.

Further contributing to the distinction between positive and negative forms of thought disorder, Liddle and colleagues (2002) factor analyzed thought disorder responses in patients with acute and chronic forms of schizophrenia using their Thought and Language Index (TLI). They found three nearly independent factors that capture characteristics of positive and negative thought disorder: (1) impoverished thought and language (poverty of speech and speech content); (2) disorganized thought and language (looseness, peculiar word usage, poor syntax and logic); and (3) nonspecific dysregulation of thought (perseveration and distractibility).

Form, content, reasoning, and social perspective

Well before Andreasen developed her broader measure of thought, language, and communication disorders, Schilder (1951) widened the narrow Kraepelinian/Bleulerian definition of thought disorder by distinguishing between disturbances in the form versus the content of thought. Taylor (1981) sharpened this dichotomy and defined disorders in form as disturbances in rate, fluency, rhythm, flow, filtering, word usage, and associational linkage. These became known as constituents of "formal thought disorder." In other words, disorders in form represented *how* the individual said things. Thus, these formal features of thought are dimensions of speech that reflect executive and attentional variables (focusing, filtering, and shifting) and aspects of the language production system (fluency in word retrieval and pace of expression, cohesive linkage, and discourse coherence). This conforms to current symptom definitions of "formal thought disorder" (frequently referred to as FTD) in the DSM-5 and supports a change in terminology from "disorganized thinking" to "disorganized speech."

In contrast, disorders of content involve *what* the individual is talking about. Traditionally, disordered thought content has been restricted to beliefs such as overvalued ideas, ideas of reference, bizarre beliefs, and, ultimately, delusions. Each of these disorders of content is ultimately the end product of the individual's cognitive operations, or more precisely, how he/she forms concepts and reasons. While in this broad sense, beliefs reflect what the individual thinks and are the result of reasoning processes, factor- analytic studies of the dimensions of psychotic symptoms have shown that bizarre beliefs and conceptual disturbances load on different factors (Reininghaus, Priebe, & Bentall, 2013).

Grebb and Cancro (1989) broadened the content category of thought disorder to include not just ideas and beliefs but how stimuli are thought about, reasoned with, and interpreted. This broader definition of disordered thought content includes not simply *what* the person is thinking (i.e. "beliefs") but *how* he or she thinks (i.e. the "reasoning" behind this thinking). As such, disordered thinking not only includes the form of a person's speech or the content of his beliefs, but it may also include the less visible or audible capacities to reason logically, form concepts, think abstractly, make inferences, and maintain perceptual and conceptual boundaries.

Weiner's (1966) simple formulation of disturbances in thought processes presented another way of integrating dimensions of form and content, or speech variables and thinking variables. According to Weiner, thinking problems can be analyzed in terms of disturbances in focusing, conceptualizing, and reasoning. His first dimension includes problems establishing, maintaining, and shifting attention, which may lead to disturbances in formal features of thought or speech, which include scanning, focusing, filtering, pacing, flowing, and associative linkage. The second and third dimensions, concept formation and reasoning, are content-specific variables, associated with abstract thinking and inference making. Concept formation includes the ability to interpret experience at appropriate levels of abstraction and reflects the continuum of concreteness and overinclusiveness.

Caplan (1996) summarized her research on the development of thought disorder in children, which investigated cognitive, linguistic, and social mechanisms in deviant communication processes. Caplan interpreted thought disorder more broadly and operationalized the more inclusive DSM-III (American Psychiatric Association, 1980) definition of thought disorder in her Kiddie Formal Thought Disorder Rating Scale (K-FTDS; Caplan et al., 1989). Included among the thought disorder signs in her research were illogical thinking, loose associations, incoherence, and poverty of content of speech. Thus, her more comprehensive definition incorporated linguistic and cognitive variables and reflected the presence of both positive and negative aspects of thought disorder.

In addition to loose associations and verbal incoherence, researchers have studied the construct of "bizarre-idiosyncratic thinking" (BIT; Harrow & Quinlan, 1985). BIT occurs along a continuum from nonpsychotic to psychotic individuals. It is a broad construct that refers to a strange, peculiar, or illogical component in an individual's thinking.

Berenbaum and Barch (1995) factor analyzed various thought disorder scoring systems, along with ratings from clinicians and linguists, expecting that two dimensions (disturbed form and content) would account for the range of thought disorder subtypes. However, their study showed that subtypes of thought disorder could not be simply dichotomized into disorders of form and disorders of content. Instead, their findings yielded four factors: (1) disturbances in fluency; (2) disturbances in discourse coherence; (3) disturbances in content; and (4) disturbances in social convention. Disturbances in fluency and discourse coherence included examples of tangentiality, derailment, looseness, grammatical lapses, neologisms, incoherence, and loosely connected associations. The researchers hypothesized that disturbances in fluency and discourse coherence reflect disturbances in the language production system, which relies on attentional and executive resources and is responsible for the planning, monitoring, editing, as well as the grammatical and phonological encoding, of linguistic information. On the other hand, disturbances of content and social convention reflect problems not in language, per se, but in thinking and "impaired perspective" (Harrow, Lanin-Kettering, & Miller, 1989), which reflect a failure in one's ability to judge the social appropriateness of one's verbal productions. According to Harrow and colleagues, thought-disordered individuals fail to discern whether or not they will sound bizarre or comprehensible to others.

Holistic model of disordered thinking: How, what, where, when, and why

Recently, Kleiger and Khadivi (2015) proposed a broader, psychological approach to conceptualizing thought disorder. Their multidimensional approach extends the concept of disordered thinking beyond narrow definitions of formal thought disorder or disorders of form versus content. The five components of their model include (1) *How* things are said; (2) *What* is said; (3) *Where* the conclusions or beliefs come from or how they are cognitively formulated; (4) *To Whom and When* one's thoughts and words are shared; and (5) *Why*, or under what conditions, does one think or speak in disorganized and illogical ways.

The *How* dimension refers to the traditional term "formal thought disorder"—the way individuals express their ideas—and includes what Andreasen (1979a) referred to as derailment, disorganization, and disconnectedness of thought processes in positive thought disorder. Examples include circumstantiality, tangentiality, derailment, flight of ideas, distractible speech, clang associations, and incoherence. Negative thought disorder includes impaired flow, thought blocking, inadequate language production, and odd word usage. Thus, we can refer to the positive thought disorder features of the *How* dimension as disorganization, or disorganized speech as it is now called in the DSM-5. Negative aspects of the *How* dimension are best described as impoverished speech.

The *What* dimension encompasses thought disorders of content (i.e. bizarre beliefs). Although it is true that bizarre beliefs and delusions load on a separate dimensional factor from conceptual disturbances (Reininghaus et al., 2013), delusions are ultimately a product of underlying errors in thinking and reasoning processes. From this broader perspective, bizarre ideas and delusions are positive symptoms that reflect how a person has reasoned or thought about his/her observations and experiences. Conversely, negative thought disorder reflects restricted, impoverished, or vacuous ideational content.

The next component in our holistic model is to consider the thinking or reasoning processes that lead to the ideas and conclusions that make up our beliefs. Here, our attention turns to *Where* those ideas come from or, more precisely, the way in which the processes of concept formation, inductive and deductive logic, and reasoning underlie illogical inference making and ultimately lead to bizarre and idiosyncratic beliefs. Some individuals may verbalize their illogical reasoning and express their bizarre beliefs in disconnected and disjointed ways, while others may do so while not sounding disorganized at all. Thus, the positive aspect of the *Where* dimension is referred to as illogicality. Negative thought disorder may reflect rigid, concrete, and perseverative thought processes. Here, individuals may reveal their difficulties with mental flexibility, concept formation, and representational thinking. If we look at the patient from a neuropsychological perspective, the *Where* dimension might also include deficits in underlying cognitive and executive functions. As seen below, both positive and negative thought disorder can be understood in terms of impairment in underlying neurocognitive functions.

Broadening our viewpoint even further, we may add an often-overlooked social perspective related to thought disorder. Typically not included in a comprehensive definition of disordered thinking, the *To Whom and When* component is a function of social cognition and includes related concepts of awareness of one's disturbing ideas, cognitive insight, and theory of mind (ToM). The essential issue in the social dimension is one of filtering, censoring, timing, and awareness of appropriate social context. In other words, can the individual consider how others might hear what he or she is saying? In both positive and negative forms of thought disorder, there may be no indication of communication reciprocity, self-monitoring, or awareness of the perspective of the listener.

Finally, we can also incorporate a *Why* component, namely trying to understand *Why* an individual verbalizes or thinks in an illogical or disordered manner. Questions of *Why* someone might demonstrate disordered thinking or speech, and under which conditions this might occur not only concern the neurobiology of thought disorder but may also involve questions about, anxiety, affect, motivation, conflict and defense, shifting self-experience, and object relational paradigms. Thinking about dynamics underlying disordered thinking adds an important dimension in humanizing individuals who demonstrate thought disorder. It helps broaden our focus beyond taking an inventory of symptoms to trying to understand what the individual is saying (no matter how disconnected, illogical, impoverished, or inappropriate it may seem) and why we are having a difficult time understanding them. It helps us, as clinicians, not to limit our attention only to sets of symptoms but instead to reorient ourselves to the struggling individuals whose symptoms may, among other things, serve various functions and represent solutions to overwhelming problems in their lives.

Dichotomous or continuous variable: Thought disorder or disordered thinking?

Contrary to Kraepelinian tradition, which viewed psychoses categorically and symptoms as discrete, unitary phenomena, contemporary researchers view psychotic phenomena along a continuum from subthreshold symptoms, on the one hand, to full-blown, diagnosable disorders, on the other (see Kleiger & Khadivi, 2015). In keeping with this trend, researchers and practitioners agree that thought disorder fits along a continuum from normal to psychotic thinking (Harrow & Quinlan, 1977, 1985; Johnston & Holzman, 1979; Andreasen & Grove, 1986; Holzman et al., 1986; Liddle et al., 2002). The Magical Ideation Scale (Eckblad & Chapman, 1983) and the Community Assessment of Psychic Experiences (CAPE) (Stefanis et al., 2002) were developed to measure subthreshold forms of disorganized and illogical thinking.

Researchers (Harrow & Quinlan, 1977; Marengo & Harrow 1985) have demonstrated that mild levels of thought disorder occur frequently, both in patients who have schizophrenia and those who do not. However, the most severe levels of thought disorder occur less frequently among all groups of patients, except for those who are acutely psychotic. Even within the same diagnostic group or individual, there is variability in the degree of thought disorder between individuals and even within the same individual depending on the phase of illness (Harrow & Quinlan, 1977).

If we accept the existence of a continuum of thought disturbances, the term "thought disorder" becomes somewhat misleading in that it implies a distinct and unique entity dichotomous with normal thinking. For this reason, Harrow & Quinlan (1977) proposed that the term "disordered thinking" be substituted for "thought disorder." The term "disordered thinking" is consistent with the concept of action language (Schafer, 1976) and one that helps avoid reification of constructs by remaining closer to the raw data of observable behavior.

Differential diagnosis and pathognomonic signs

From a historical perspective, the psychiatric and psychodiagnostic study of thought disorder has been inseparable from the evaluation and diagnosis of schizophrenia. Up to the mid-1970s, the centrality and specificity of thought disorder to schizophrenia was largely unquestioned (a fact that will be echoed repeatedly throughout this book). Until relatively recently, the work of the Andreasen group (Andreasen, 1979a, 1979b) and the Harrow group (Harrow & Quinlan, 1977; Harrow et al., 1980, 1982; Rattenbury et al., 1983) demonstrated convincingly that disordered thinking is as prominent in manic psychosis as it is in schizophrenia. Harrow and Quinlan (1985) found not only that high levels of thought disorder occur in both manic and schizophrenic patients but that there is no difference in the extent of thought disorder between the two groups. This issue will be examined in more detail in subsequent chapters.

Having established that disordered thinking is not specific to schizophrenia and that it is also associated with manic psychosis, Marengo and Harrow (1985) wondered whether thought disorder is simply a general function of psychosis as opposed to being a manifestation of any particular diagnostic syndrome. They found that even though psychotic patients were more thought disordered than nonpsychotic patients, severely disordered thinking was not just a basic function of psychosis but occurred significantly more frequently among manic and schizophrenic patients than it did in other psychotic conditions. They observed that the thought disorder occurred most frequently in mania, followed in descending order by schizophrenia, schizoaffective disorders, other psychotic conditions, nonpsychotic disorders, and depression. Thus, while severe thought disorder is not specific to and pathognomonic of one diagnostic entity in particular, it is more frequently observed in mania and schizophrenia (in acutely psychotic and nonpsychotic manic patients alike) than in other types of psychotic and nonpsychotic disorders.

In their factor-analytic study of the Positive and Negative Syndrome Scale (PANSS; Kay, Fiszbein, & Opler, 1987) items, Reininghaus et al. (2013) found their thought disorder dimension, called "disorganization," occurred most frequently among schizophrenia spectrum and other psychotic disorders. Specific symptoms included conceptual disorganization and difficulties in abstract thinking. Furthermore, negative symptoms were also more common in this family of psychotic disorders. Positive symptoms—including delusions, grandiosity, and unusual thought content—were found most among bipolar and schizophrenia spectrum disorders.

Using the Rorschach, Holzman's group further refined the specificity issue by demonstrating that schizophrenia, mania, and schizoaffective conditions can be distinguished by qualitative aspects of their disordered thinking (Shenton, Solovay, & Holzman, 1987; Solovay, Shenton, & Holzman, 1987). Although they found certain types of thought disorders were nonspecific and occurred in each psychotic group, they discovered that each psychotic condition had a "signature" thought disorder, characterized by different patterns of disordered thinking that could play an important role in differential diagnosis.

Over the last two decades, additional studies have documented the presence of disordered thinking, previously associated at first exclusively with schizophrenia and later with mania, in a greater variety of patient groups. Psychological test findings demonstrated a range of thought disorder phenomena in borderlines (Singer, 1977; Kwawer et al., 1980; Carr & Goldstein, 1981; Armstrong, Silberg, & Parente, 1986; Edell, 1987) and eating-disordered patients (Small et al., 1982). Other studies have established the presence of varieties of disordered thinking in depression (Ianzito, Cadoret, & Pugh, 1974; Silberman, Weingartner, & Post, 1983; Carter, 1986);

in schizoid personality disorders (Wolff, 1991); among the nonschizophrenic relatives of schizophrenic individuals (Shenton et al., 1989); and, occasionally, in normal subjects (McConaghy & Clancy, 1968).

Neuropsychological approaches: Executive functions by another name?

Increasingly, researchers have tried to understand disordered thinking from a cognitive neuroscience perspective (McGhie & Chapman, 1961; Nuechterlein & Dawson, 1984; McGrath, 1991; Elvevag & Goldberg, 2000; Goldberg & Weinberger, 2000; Barch, 2005). From this point of view, disturbances in thinking are investigated in terms of impairments in cognitive functions such as attention, memory, verbal fluency, executive functioning, and processing speed. It is somewhat surprising that both Kraepelin and Bleuler paved the way for later efforts to examine the neurocognitive underpinnings of thought disorder psychologically by highlighting the attentional deficits in schizophrenia. Nuechterlein & Dawson (1984) concluded from their studies that impairments in attention may be more of a "trait" variable for subjects with schizophrenia than they are for those with mania. In another series of investigations, Braff and his colleagues demonstrated that individuals with schizophrenia exhibit abnormal information processing when compared to nonpatient controls (Braff & Saccuzzo, 1981; Braff & Geyer, 1990; Braff, Saccuzzo, & Geyer, 1991; Braff, Grillon, & Geyer, 1992). When attention and information-processing functions are impaired, individuals with schizophrenia may become more distractible in response to a flood of poorly inhibited internal and external stimuli, leading to cognitive fragmentation and markedly disordered thinking.

Deficits in working memory have also been found to be associated with the attentional vulnerabilities found in patients suffering from schizophrenia. The working memory system enables the individual to hold relevant information in mind, while utilizing it to solve a problem. Several studies found a link between working memory deficits and thought and communication disturbances and how emotional arousal may further disrupt working memory in vulnerable individuals (Oltmanns & Neale, 1978; Goldberg & Weinberger, 2000; Bentall, 2003).

Impairment in the semantic memory may play a role in disrupting associative links between related ideas (Bentall, 2003). The semantic memory system, which stores ideas and knowledge, is a complex network of concepts linked by association. Thus, impairment in semantic memory can disrupt associative linkages between ideas, leading to looseness and disconnection between one idea and the next.

Impaired executive functions like self- and source monitoring may also contribute to disordered thinking. Executive planning and editing are viewed as common denominators of disordered thinking (McGrath, 1991). Editing, or self-monitoring, refers to an individual's ability to monitor and adjust his or her speech to the communication needs and perspectives of the listener. The ability to comprehend that others have separate minds and needs distinct from one's own represents the capacity for a ToM. Deficits in ToM might prevent individuals from recognizing that other people might not be able to comprehend what they are trying to say, resulting in an impaired perspective.

Deficits in source monitoring (similar to the older concept of reality testing) may prevent an individual from identifying the source of a particular stimulus. The individual may be uncertain whether he/she *said it* or simply *thought it*. Source-monitoring deficits may make an individual susceptible to leaving out important segments of information when speaking to others, which, in turn, may make his or her speech confusing or unintelligible to others.

Bentall (2003), an outspoken critic of traditional concepts of psychosis and thought disorder, hypothesized an integrated model of neurocognitive deficits that could lead to speech that is loose and incomprehensible to others. According to his tentative model, vulnerable individuals respond to emotional arousal with deficits in working memory, which then lead to poor source monitoring and eventually to unintelligible speech. Deficits in self-monitoring may also make these vulnerable individuals unaware of how they sound and what impact their speech is having on others.

Final thoughts on the elusive concept of disordered thinking

Considering disordered thinking from a variety of perspectives guards against simple, reductionistic formulations that either overlook or exaggerate subtler manifestations of this concept. A more comprehensive definition of disordered thinking includes multiple aspects of cognitive and language functioning. It addresses the form of thoughts (as expressed through speech), the content of the thoughts, conceptual and reasoning processes that give rise to these thoughts, and social-cognitive features that reflect when and how one shares his or her unusual thoughts. An expanded definition of disordered thinking includes the dimensions of disorganization, illogicality, and impoverishment, each of which may be manifested in an individual's speech, thoughts, and/or behavior.

A broader understanding of disordered thinking appreciates the links between disorders in thought and communication and disturbances in fundamental cognitive processes that govern attention, memory, reasoning, and self-monitoring. Only with this more comprehensive perspective, can we capture the multidimensional nature of disordered thought.

At this point, we can respond to our intern's questions with greater clarity. As noted previously, evidence of severe thought disorder scores on the Rorschach or any testing procedure do not equate to a diagnosis of psychosis. No test scores or responses by themselves are pathognomonic for establishing a clinical diagnosis. However, the presence of Level 2 Special Scores or Cognitive Codes is indicative of a potential fracture in J. D.'s ability to organize his ideas and employ logic when dealing with complexity and uncertainty, along with the possible risk for psychosis. Evidence of J. D's fractures might only become apparent under conditions in which he is left on his own to play with possibilities and construct meaning in the absence of external direction (Peterson & Maitland, 1983). Whether we choose to call this "thought disorder" or "disordered thinking" seems less important than communicating to J. D.'s treatment team that he may be highly vulnerable to thinking in severely disorganized and/or illogical ways under specific conditions and, as such, may be a considerable clinical risk.

References

American Psychiatric Association. (1980). *Diagnostic and Statistical Manual of Mental Disorders* (3rd ed.). Washington, DC: Author.

American Psychiatric Association. (1994). *Diagnostic and Statistical Manual of Mental Disorders* (4th ed.). Washington, DC: Author.

American Psychiatric Association. (2013). *Diagnostic and Statistical Manual of Mental Disorders* (5th ed.). Washington, DC: Author.

Andreasen, N. (1978) *The Scale for the Assessment of Thought, Language, and Communication* (TLC). Iowa City, IA: University of Iowa Press.

Andreasen, N. (1979a). Thought, language, and communication disorders: I. Clinical assessment, definition of terms, and evaluation of their reliability. *Archives of General Psychiatry, 36*, 1315–1321.

Andreasen, N. (1979b). Thought, language, and communication disorders: II. Diagnostic significance. *Archives of General Psychiatry, 36*, 1325–1330.

Andreasen, N. (1982). Should the term "thought disorder" be revised? *Comprehensive Psychiatry, 23*, 291–299.

Andreasen, N., & Grove, W. M. (1986). Thought, language, and communication in schizophrenia: Diagnosis and prognosis. *Schizophrenia Bulletin, 12*, 348–359.

Armstrong, J., Silberg, J. L., & Parente, F. J. (1986). Patterns of thought disorder on psychological testing: Implications for adolescent psychopathology. *Journal of Nervous and Mental Disease, 174*, 448–456.

Barch, D. M. (2005). The cognitive neuroscience of schizophrenia. *Annual Review of Clinical Psychology, 1*, 321–353.

Bentall, R. P. (2003). *Madness Explained: Psychosis and Human Nature*. New York: Penguin Group.

Berenbaum, H., & Barch, D. (1995). The categorization of thought disorder. *Journal of Psycholinguistic Research, 24*, 349–376.

Bleuler, E. (1950). *Dementia Praecox or the Group of Schizophrenias*. (J. Zinkin, Trans.). New York: International Universities Press (Original work published in 1911.).

Braff, D. L., & Geyer, M. A. (1990). Sensorimotor gating and schizophrenia: Human and animal model studies. *Archives of General Psychiatry, 47*, 181–188.

Braff, D. L., Grillon, C., & Geyer, M. A. (1992). Gating and habituation of the startle reflex in schizophrenic patients. *Archives of General Psychiatry, 49*, 206–215.

Braff, D. L., & Saccuzzo, D. P. (1981). Information processing dysfunction in paranoid schizophrenia: A two-factor deficit. *American Journal of Psychiatry, 138*, 1051–1056.

Braff, D. L., Saccuzzo, D. P., & Geyer, M. A. (1991). Information processing dysfunctions in schizophrenia: Studies of visual backward masking, sensorimotor gating and habituation. In S. Steinhauer, J. H. Grizelier, & J. Zubin (Eds.), *Handbook of Schizophrenia: Neuropsychology, Psychophysiology, and Information Processing* (Vol. 5, pp. 303–334). Amsterdam: Elsevier.

Cameron, N. (1938). Reasoning, regression and communication in schizophrenics. *Psychological Monographs, 50,* 1–340.

Caplan, R. (1996). Communication deficits in childhood schizophrenia spectrum disorder. In J. H. Beichtman, N. Cohen, M. Konstantareas, & R. Tannock (Eds.), *Language, Learning, and Behavioral Disorders* (pp. 156–177). Cambridge, UK: Cambridge University Press.

Caplan, R., Guthrie, D., Fish, B., Tanguay, P. E., & David-Lando, G. (1989). The kiddie formal thought disorder rating scale: Clinical assessment, reliability, and validity. *Journal of the American Academy of Child & Adolescent Psychiatry, 28,* 408–416.

Carr, A., & Goldstein, E. (1981). Approaches to the therapy of borderline condition by use of psychology tests. *Journal of Personality Assessment, 45,* 563–574.

Carter, M. L. (1986). The assessment of thought deficit in psychotic unipolar depression and chronic paranoid schizophrenia. *Journal of Nervous and Mental Disease, 174,* 336–341.

Chaika, E. O. (1990). *Understanding Psychotic Speech: Beyond Freud and Chomisky.* Springfield, IL: Thomas.

Eckblad, M., & Chapman, L. J. (1983). Magical ideation as an indicator of schizotypy. *Journal of Consulting and Clinical Psychology, 51,* 215–225.

Edell, W. (1987). Role of structure in disordered therapy in borderline and schizophrenia disorders. *Journal of Personality Assessment, 51,* 23–41.

Elvevag, B., & Goldberg, T. E. (2000). Cognitive impairment in schizophrenia is the core of the disorder. *Current Reviews in Neurobiology, 14,* 1–21.

Freeman, A. M., Kaplan, H. I., & Saddock, B. J. (1976). *Comprehensive Textbook of Psychiatry* (Vol. 2). Baltimore, MD: Williams & Wilkins.

Goldberg, T. E., & Weinberger, D. R. (2000). Thought disorder in schizophrenia: A reappraisal of older formulations and an overview of some recent studies. *Cognitive Neuropsychiatry, 5,* 1–19.

Goldstein, K., & Scheerer, M. (1941). Abstract and concrete behavior: An experimental study with special tests. *Psychological Monographs, 53,* 1–151.

Grebb, J. A., & Cancro, R. (1989). Schizophrenia: Clinical features. In J. I. Kaplan and B. J. Sadock (Eds.), *Synopsis of Psychiatry: Behavioral Sciences, Clinical Psychiatry* (Vol. 5, pp. 757–777). Baltimore, MD: Williams & Wilkins.

Harrow, M., Grossman, L. S., Silverstein, M. L., & Meltzer, H. Y. (1980). Are manic patients thought disordered? *Scientific Proceedings of the American Psychiatric Association.* Washington, DC: American Psychiatric Association.

Harrow, M., Grossman, L. S., Silverstein, M. L., & Meltzer, H. Y. (1982). Thought pathology in manic and schizophrenic patients. *Archives of General Psychiatry, 39,* 665–671.

Harrow, M., Lanin-Kettering, I., & Miller, J. G. (1989). Impaired perspective and thought pathology in schizophrenic and psychotic disorders. *Schizophrenia Bulletin, 15,* 605–623.

Harrow, M., & Quinlan, D. (1977). Is disordered thinking unique to schizophrenia? *Archives of General Psychiatry, 34,* 15–21.

Harrow, M., & Quinlan, D. (1985). *Disordered Thinking and Schizophrenic Psychopathology.* New York: Garden Press.

Harvey, P. D. & Neale, J. (1983). The specificity of thought disorder to schizophrenia: Research methods in their historical perspective. *Progress in Experimental Methods of Personality Research, 12*, 153–180.

Holzman, P. S., Shenton, M. E., & Solovay, M. R. (1986). Quality of thought disorder in differential diagnosis. *Schizophrenia Bulletin, 12*, 360–371.

Ianzito, B. M., Cadoret, R. J., & Pugh, D. D. (1974). Thought disorder in depression. *American Journal of Psychiatry, 131*, 703–707.

Janet, P. (1926). *De l'angoisse à l'extase (From Anguish to Ecstasy)*. Paris: Felix Alcan.

Jaspers, K. (1963). *General Psychopathology*. Chicago, IL: University of Chicago Press. (Original work published in 1913.).

Johnston, M. H., & Holzman, P. S. (1979). *Assessing Schizophrenic Thinking*. San Francisco, CA: Jossey-Bass.

Kay, S. R., Fiszbein, A., & Opler, L. A. (1987). The Positive and Negative Syndrome Scale (PANSS) for schizophrenia. *Schizophrenia Bulletin, 13*, 261–276.

Kleiger, J. H. (1999). *Disordered Thinking and the Rorschach*. Hillsdale, NJ: The Analytic Press.

Kleiger, J. H., & Khadivi, A. (2015). *Assessing Psychosis. A Clinician's Guide*. New York: Routledge.

Kraepelin, E. (1919). *Dementia Praecox and Paraphrenia*. (R. M. Barclay, Trans.). Chicago, IL: Chicago Medical Books. (Original work published in 1896.)

Kwawer, J., Lerner, H., Lerner, P., & Sugarman, A. (Eds.). (1980a). *Borderline Phenomena and the Rorschach Test*. New York: International Universities Press.

Lanin-Kettering, I., & Harrow, M. (1985). The thought behind the words: A view of schizophrenic speech and thinking disorders. *Schizophrenia Bulletin, 11*, 1–7.

Liddle, P. F., Ngan, E. T. C., Caissie, S. L., Anderson, C. M., Bates, A. T., Quested, D. J., White, R., & Weg, R. (2002). Thought and Language Index: An instrument for assessing thought and language in schizophrenia. *The British Journal of Psychiatry, 181*, 326–330.

Marengo, J. T., & Harrow, M. (1985). Thought disorder: A function of schizophrenia, mania, or psychosis? *Journal of Nervous and Mental Disease, 173*, 35–41.

McConaghy, N., & Clancy, M. (1968). Familial relationships of allusive thinking in university students and their parents. *British Journal of Psychiatry, 114*, 1079–1087.

McGhie, A., & Chapman, J. (1961). Disorders of attention and perception in early schizophrenia. *British Journal of Medical Psychology, 34*, 103–116.

McGrath, J. (1991). Ordering thoughts on thought disorder. *British Journal of Psychiatry, 158*, 307–316.

Meyer, G. J., Viglione, D. J., Mihura, J. L., Erard, R. E., & Erdberg, P. (2011). *Rorschach Performance Assessment System: Administration, Coding, Interpretation, and Technical Manual*. Toledo, OH: Rorschach Performance Assessment System.

Mill, J. S. (1963). In J. M. Robson (Ed.), *Collected Works of John Stuart Mill*. Toronto: University of Toronto Press.

Nuechterlein, K. H., & Dawson, M. E. (1984). Information processing and attentional functioning in the developmental course of schizophrenic disorders. *Schizophrenia Bulletin, 10*, 160–203.

Oltmanns, T. F., & Neale, J. M. (1978). Distractibility in relation to other aspects of schizophrenic disorder. In S. Schwartz (Ed.), *Language and Cognition in Schizophrenia* (pp. 117–143). Oxford, UK: Lawrence Erlbaum Associates.

Parnas, J. (2015). Philosophical and phenomenological perspectives on psychosis. In F. Waters & M. Stephane (Eds.), *The Assessment of Psychosis. A Reference Book and Rating Scales for Research and Practice* (pp. 17–43). New York: Routledge.

Peterson, C. A., & Maitland-Schilling, K. M. (1983). Card pull in projective testing. *Journal of Personality Assessment, 47,* 265–275.

Rattenbury, F. R., Silverstein, M. L., DeWolfe, A. S., Kaufman, C. F., & Harrow, M. (1983). Associative disturbance in schizophrenia, schizoaffective disorder and major affective disorders: Comparison between hospital and one year follow-up. *Journal of Consulting and Clinical Psychology, 51,* 621–623.

Reininghaus, U., Priebe, S., & Bentall, R. P. (2013). Testing the psychopathology of psychosis: Evidence for a general psychosis dimension. *Schizophrenia Bulletin, 39,* 884–895.

Roche, E., Creed, L., MacMahon, B., & Clarke, M. (2015). The epidemiology and associated phenomenology of formal thought disorder: A systematic review. *Schizophrenia Bulletin, 41,* 951–962.

Rochester, S. & Martin, J. R. (1979). *Crazy Talk: A Study of the Discourse of Psychotic Speakers.* New York: Plenums.

Schafer, R. (1976). *A New Language for Psychoanalysis.* New Haven, CT: Yale University Press.

Schilder, P. (1951). On the development of thoughts. In D. Rapaport (Ed. & Trans.), *Organization and Pathology of Thought* (pp. 497–518). New York: Columbia University Press.

Schneider, K. (1959). *Clinical Psychopathology.* (M. W. Hamilton, Trans.). New York: Grune & Stratton.

Shenton, M. E., Solovay, M. R., & Holzman, P. (1987). Comparative studies of thought disorders: II. Schizoaffective disorder. *Archives of General Psychiatry, 44,* 21–30.

Shenton, M. E., Solovay, M. R., Holzman, P., Coleman, M., & Gale, H. J. (1989). Thought disorder in the relatives of psychotic patients. *Archives of General Psychiatry, 46,* 897–901.

Silberman, E. K., Weingartner, H., & Post, R. M. (1983). Thinking disorder in depression. *Archives of General Psychiatry, 40,* 775–780.

Singer, M. T. (1977). The Rorschach as a transaction. In M. Rickers-Ovsiankina (Ed.), *Rorschach Psychology* (pp. 455–485). Huntington, NY: Krieger.

Small, A., Teagro, L., Madero, J., Gross, H., & Ebert, M. (1982). A comparison of anorexia and schizophrenia on psychology therapy measures. *International Journal of Eating Disorders, 2,* 17–36.

Solovay, M. R., Shenton, M. E., & Holzman, P. S. (1987). Comparative studies of thought disorders: I. Mania and schizophrenia. *Archives of General Psychiatry, 44,* 13–20.

Stefanis, N. C., Hanssen, M., Smirnis, N. K., Avramopoulos, D. A., Evdokimidis, I. K., Stefanis, C.N., Verdoux, H., & van Os, J. (2002). Evidence that three dimensions of psychosis have a distribution in the general community. *Psychological Medicine, 32,* 347–358.

Taylor, M. A. (1981). *The Neuropsychiatric Mental Status Examination.* New York: Spectrum.

von Domarus, E. (1944). The specific laws of logic in schizophrenia. In J. S. Kasinin (Ed.), *Language and Thought in Schizophrenia* (pp. 104–114). New York: Norton.

Weiner, I. B. (1966). *Psychodiagnosis in Schizophrenia.* New York: Wiley.

Wolff, S. (1991). Schizoid personality in childhood and adult life: I. The vagaries of psychology labels. *British Journal of Psychiatry, 159,* 615–620.

Chapter 2

Assessing disordered thinking and psychotic phenomena

Whether one employs clinical interviews, rating scales, or psychological testing methods, assessing a complex and elusive dimension like thought disorder remains a key challenge in diagnostic work. Which definition of thought disorder do we accept, and which methods should we utilize? Can we rely on a patient's self-report when trying to determine the presence of disordered thinking, or do we need a more direct measure of how the individual thinks? Should we only test patients while off medication? These are only a sampling of the questions that make the assessment of disordered thinking a perplexing, yet fascinating challenge for clinicians (Kleiger, 1999; Kleiger & Khadivi, 2015).

Controversial issues in assessing thought disorder

Because the construct itself has been called into question (Rochester & Martin, 1979; Bentall, 2003), instruments that purport to measure disordered thinking instead of disordered speech are vulnerable to the criticism that they lack sufficient construct validity to justify claims of their effectiveness as diagnostic tools. Despite this conceptual controversy, psychologists are often called upon to assess ways in which patients process and organize information, apply logic to problem solving, and express their ideas cohesively and coherently. Rightly or wrongly, clinicians share a practical language and use familiar terms to communicate with one another about the patients that we evaluate and treat. The construct of "thought disorder" (versus speech or language disorder) has gained ascendancy in the fields of psychopathology and psychodiagnostic testing and continues to be an accepted variable that clinicians and researchers seek to measure with instruments and techniques of all sorts.

Assessment efforts can be hampered by the lack of consensus on what constitutes disordered thought. If thought disorder is construed narrowly as "disorganized speech," then assessment may overlook other important elements of investigation—for example, the *How*, *What*, *With Whom*, *When*, and *Why* of thought disorder, as discussed in the last chapter. As we have seen, there is agreement that disordered thinking exists along a continuum of severity and reflects a number of different anomalies in language processing, cognitive functioning, and social perception. However, the methods for assessing these elements vary widely in availability, practicality, reliability, validity, and clinical usefulness. Although there may be overlap in many of the variables studied by different assessment approaches, comparison between the various techniques is often difficult. Different assessment methods may employ different names for similar variables or use the same name for essentially different types of disordered thinking. The obvious solution is to adopt a multi-method approach that employs an adequate sampling of empirically valid methods in order to achieve a convergence among inferences from different methods.

Achieving sufficiently high inter-rater reliability, clinical sensitivity, and specificity with the instruments is a challenge since many of the rating or scoring systems themselves are quite intricate, difficult to learn, and subject to interpretation. Research on the most prominent interview systems, rating scales, and performance methods demonstrates that high inter-rater reliability is possible; however, learning many of these assessment techniques requires training that goes beyond simply familiarizing oneself with the manuals.

Many of the categories of disordered thinking are not independent of one another and occur together in more severely disturbed cases. Scoring the presence and discerning the meaning of one particular type of thought disturbance may be obscured by the presence of several other types. Just as the simultaneous mixing of several different colors together can produce an impenetrable blackness, the concurrence of multiple types of disordered thought in one sample of speech or Rorschach response makes for a similar kind of obscurity in scoring and interpretation. Should all examples of disordered thinking in a given sample (e.g. a single response) be scored or just the most significant process? If one scores each subtype separately, how does one then make sense of the contribution of each subtype in the presence of others? Can each be understood separately, or does the simultaneous presence of several subtypes of disordered thinking simply suggest severe confusion and disorganization characteristic of an acute disturbance? On the other hand, since some subtypes of disordered thinking have more specificity to certain types of disorders than others, the presence of these subtypes with other subtypes may have special diagnostic significance.

The impact of phase of illness, medication, and context must be taken into consideration when assessing disordered thinking. The degree to which an individual's thinking is disorganized will depend on whether he or she is in an acute phase or in a partial or complete remission from the active disturbance. Positive signs of thought disorder are generally episode-dependent variables. And just as neuroleptic medication reduces positive symptoms like delusions and hallucinations, so does it attenuate the emergence of more florid signs of thought disorder on psychological testing (Hurt, Holzman, & Davis, 1983; Spohn et al., 1986).

Valid measurement of disordered thinking also requires one to evaluate the subject's motivation, attitude, and the context in which the idiosyncratic thinking is revealed. Awareness of disturbed thinking is an increasingly important variable. Is the subject aware of the bizarreness of his or her speech or ideas—and if so, what is his or her attitude toward it? Is idiosyncratic thought used to shock, control, or entertain? As Johnston and Holzman (1979) pointed out, the presence of odd and difficult-to-understand material does not constitute immediate grounds for inferring the incursion of a psychotic process.

Methods and techniques for assessing thought disorder

Chapman and Chapman (1973) reviewed methods of measuring thought disorder in schizophrenic patients, which included (1) informal description of spontaneous verbalizations; (2) description and interpretation of verbalizations made to standardized stimuli; and (3) standardized scoring of verbalizations on standardized tests. Koistinen (1995) divided assessment techniques into two broad categories: those using structured or semi-structured interview techniques and those based on psychological testing instruments. Kleiger and Khadivi (2015) devoted attention to three assessment methods employed in clinical and research settings, represented by interviews, rating scales, and psychological testing. The narrower focus of this book centers on the third category of assessment, with special emphasis on performance-based methods, the Rorschach in particular.

Performance-based psychological assessment methods

In addition to conventional broadband, multi-scale personality inventories such as the MMPI-2 (Butcher et al., 1989a; 1989), the MMPI-2-RF (Ben-Porath & Tellegen, 2008), and PAI (Morey, 1991), which contain scales related to self-reported psychotic phenomena, performance-based methods assess what patients *do* rather than what they can or decide to *tell* us. Miller (1987) compared methods of inquiry and concluded that when individuals respond to the performance requirements of the testing situation, they display their ego functioning, behavioral, and response potentials. Although we are always interested in what patients, their family members, and other raters might tell us about their functioning, a comprehensive assessment remains incomplete without an assessment of actual functioning based on performance measures. Ultimately, through performance testing, we seek to determine what it is that the patient *cannot* tell us.

Performance measures include a wide range of psychological and neuropsychological testing procedures in which what the patient does is as important, if not more so, than what he says. For example, it is one thing to ask someone about his memory, reality testing, and ability to think in an organized manner and form mature concepts; it is another matter to assess these functions directly by having the person engage in a performance task constructed to measure these variables. Empirically valid neurocognitive instruments are based on a standard and explicit set of instructions that specify what the person must do to perform the task. Thus, the individual is provided with a structured problem-solving task that is presented with clear-cut directions and expectations. Neuropsychological testing assesses cognitive functions associated with thought disorder, such as working and semantic memory, attention, executive functioning, processing speed, verbal fluency, and social cognition. Neuropsychological evaluations help identify the degree of cognitive impairment associated with psychotic symptoms and assist with planning for treatment and cognitive rehabilitation (Reichenberg et al., 2009).

Historically, researchers and clinicians have used other performance instruments to measure disturbances in concept formation and abstract thinking associated with thought disorder. Object Sorting Tests (Vygotsky, 1934; Goldstein, 1939; Goldstein & Scheerer, 1941; Hanfmann & Kasanin, 1942) and the Proverbs Test (Benjamin, 1944; Gorham, 1956) have been used to measure concreteness and overinclusion, two of the early concepts that were viewed as central deficits in schizophrenic thought disorder. Marengo and colleagues (Marengo et al., 1986) constructed a comprehensive measure of bizarre-idiosyncratic thinking based on two brief verbal tests, the Gorham Proverbs Test (Gorham, 1956) and the Comprehension subtest of the Wechsler Adult Intelligence Scale (WAIS) (Wechsler, 1955). This has proven to be a reliable technique that provides a measure of the presence, severity, and type of disordered thinking.

In some performance tasks, the instructions given to the individual are clear, and the object of the task is apparent. Other sets of performance measures are based on briefer, open-ended, and more opaque instructions. Typically referred to as "projective tests," these instruments present individuals with an ambiguous stimulus and, with little direction, ask them to respond. "Projective testing" is no longer the preferred term because it is thought to minimize the cognitive and perceptual problem-solving aspects of these procedures. However, no other projective, performance-based methods have rivaled the Rorschach in its utility for assessing disordered thinking.

Rorschach: The gold standard

Although a variety of projective procedures may be useful in assessing aspects of psychosis (Kleiger, 2004), the best example of a projective performance test for addressing questions about the potential for psychotic functioning is the Rorschach. The Rorschach has a long history of use as a psychodiagnostic instrument in the assessment of psychosis and thought disorder (in particular, Rorschach, 1921/1942; Rapaport, Gill, & Shafer, 1946/1968; Johnston & Holzman, 1979; Solovay, Shenton, & Holzman, 1987; Kleiger, 1999; Holzman, Levy, & Johnston, 2005).

Since the Rorschach was developed more than 70 years ago (Rorschach, 1921/1942), researchers and clinicians have devoted enormous attention to identifying signs of schizophrenia and other forms of serious psychopathology. Although early psychodiagnostic studies with the Rorschach mirrored general psychiatric diagnostic trends, which assumed an isomorphic relationship between schizophrenia and disordered thinking, clinicians and researchers have gradually developed more sophisticated ways of conceptualizing and measuring thought pathology with the Rorschach.

The patient is handed ten inkblots, one at a time, and asked little more than "What might this be?" Due to its unstructured and ambiguous nature, the Rorschach is uniquely suited for assessing a patient's thought organization and reality testing. Peterson and Maitland-Schilling (1983) challenged the long-held belief that the Rorschach inkblots were inherently unstructured or ambiguous. They viewed the procedure as a forum in which the patient is invited to "reveal the inner world in the process of modifying, misperceiving, and elaborating a controlled sample of reality, i.e., the test stimuli" (p. 272).

Using the Rorschach to study disordered thinking does not depend on the projective hypothesis, which holds that a subject projects idiosyncratic conflicts and other aspects of his or her internal world onto the ambiguous inkblot stimuli. Likewise, one does not need to make symbolic interpretations of response content to make inferences about underlying thought processes. On the contrary, Rorschach responses, as samples of verbal behavior, remain closely tied to actual phenomena that the investigator studying disordered thinking is trying to measure. Rorschach responses reflect consistent properties of an individual's style of perceiving, thinking, and communicating and, as such, can provide a basis for making representational inferences (Weiner, 1977) about how an individual perceives, thinks, and communicates in other settings that are unstructured, open-ended, and not clearly defined.

Mihura's meta-analysis of Rorschach research further solidified the role of the Rorschach in assessing psychotic phenomena and thought disorder in particular (Mihura et al., 2013). For example, Mihura found robust support for the validity of Level 2 Special Scores (indicators of severe thought-disordered codes), WSUM6, and X-%.

The Rorschach has been used to assess thought disorder in a broad range of patients and in a variety of assessment contexts. Holzman and colleagues (2005) summarized a vast body of Rorschach research that highlighted the effectiveness of the TDI (Johnston & Holzman, 1979) in assessing thought disorder in different groups of psychotic patients, in children and adolescents, and in patients with right hemisphere cortical damage. Leichtman (1996) has written about developmental underpinnings of thought disorder. Forensic psychologists have documented the utility of the Rorschach for evaluating thought disorder in criminal cases (Acklin, 2007). More recently, psychologists have used the Rorschach to investigate indications of emerging thought disorder in individuals who may be at high risk for developing psychotic disorders (Kimhy et al., 2007; Ilonen et al., 2010; Inoue, Yorozuya, & Mizuno, 2014; Kleiger & Khadivi, 2015; Lacoua, Koren, & Rothschild-Yakar, 2015; Rothschild-Yakar et al., 2015).

Finally, even those who have long criticized the Rorschach acknowledged the solid empirical basis for using the Rorschach to assess psychotic phenomena (Wood et al., 2003). According to these critics, who at one point called for a moratorium on the clinical use of the test, "A few Rorschach scores are useful for the evaluation of thought disorder ... For this reason, they can provide useful information for the diagnosis of schizophrenia, bipolar disorder, borderline personality disorder and schizotypal personality disorder" (p. 259).

References

Acklin, N. W. (2007). The Rorschach test and forensic psychological evaluation: Psychosis and the insanity defense. In C.B. Gacono, & F. B. Evans (Eds.), *The Handbook of Forensic Rorschach Assessment* (pp. 157–174). New York: Routledge.

Benjamin, J. D. (1944). A method for distinguishing and evaluating formal thinking disorders in schizophrenia. In J. S. Kasinin (Ed.), *Language and Thought in Schizophrenia* (pp. 65–90). New York: Norton.

Ben-Porath, Y. S., & Tellegen, A. (2008). *Minnesota Multiphasic Personality Inventory-2-RF* (MMPI-2-RF). Minneapolis, MN: University of Minneapolis Press.

Bentall, R. P. (2003). *Madness Explained: Psychosis and Human Nature*. New York: Penguin Group.

Butcher, J. N., Dahlstrom, W. G., Graham, J. R., Tellegen, A. M., & Kreammer, B. (1989a). *The Minnesota Multiphasic Personality Inventory-2, Manual for Administration and Scoring*. Minneapolis, MN: University of Minneapolis Press.

Butcher, J. N., Graham, J. R., Williams, C. L. & Ben-Porath, Y. (1989b). *Development and Use of the MMPI-2 Content Scales*. Minneapolis, MN: University of Minnesota Press.

Chapman, L., & Chapman, J. P. (1973). *Disordered Thought in Schizophrenia*. New York: Appleton-Century-Croft.

Goldstein, K. (1939). The significance of special mental tests for diagnosis and prognosis in schizophrenia. *American Journal of Psychiatry, 96*, 575–588.

Goldstein, K., & Scheerer, M. (1941). Abstract and concrete behavior: An experimental study with special tests. *Psychological Monographs, 53*, 1–151.

Gorham, D. R. (1956). Use of the proverbs test for differentiating schizophrenics from normals. *Journal of Consulting Psychology, 20*, 435–440.

Hanfmann, E., & Kasanin, J. S. (1942). Conceptual thinking in schizophrenia. *Nervous and Mental Disease Monograph Series, 67*, vii–115. New York: NMDM.

Holzman, P. S., Levy, D.L., & Johnston, M. H. (2005). The use of the Rorschach technique for assessing formal thought disorder. In R. F. Bornstein and J. M. Masling (Eds.), *Scoring the Rorschach: Seven Validated Systems*. New York: Routledge.

Hurt, S. W., Holzman, P. S., & Davis, J. M. (1983). Thought disorder: The measurement of its changes. *Archives of General Psychiatry, 40*, 1281–1285.

Ilonen, T., Heinimaa, M., Korkeila, J., Svirskis, T., & Salokangas, R. K. R. (2010). Differentiating adolescents at clinical high risk for psychosis from psychotic and non-psychotic patients with the Rorschach. *Psychiatry Research, 179*, 151–156.

Inoue, N., Yorozuya, Y., & Mizuno, M. (2014). Identifying comorbidities of patients at ultra-high risk for psychosis using the Rorschach Comprehensive System. Paper presented at the XXI International Congress of Rorschach and Projective Methods, Istanbul, Turkey.

Johnston, M. H., & Holzman, P. S. (1979). *Assessing Schizophrenic Thinking*. San Francisco, CA: Jossey-Bass.

Kimhy, D., Corcoran, C., Harkavy-Friedman, J. M., Ritzler, B., Javitt, D. C., & Malaspina, D. (2007). Visual form perception: A comparison of individuals at high risk for psychosis, recent onset schizophrenia and chronic schizophrenia. *Schizophrenia Research, 97*, 25–34.

Kleiger, J. H. (1999). *Disordered Thinking and The Rorschach*. Hillsdale, NJ: The Analytic Press.

Kleiger, J. H. (2004). Disordered thinking and projective testing. In M. Hilsenroth & D. Segal, (Eds.), *The Handbook of Projective Psychological Assessment*. New York: Wiley & Sons.

Kleiger, J. H., & Khadivi, A. (2015). *Assessing Psychosis. A Clinician's Guide*. New York: Routledge.

Koistinen, P. (1995). *Thought Disorder and the Rorschach*. Oulu, Finland: Oulun Yliopistd.

Lacoua, L., Koren, D., & Rothchild-Yakar, L. (2015). Poor awareness of problems in thought and perception and risk indicators of schizophrenia-spectrum disorders. A correlational study of nonpsychotic adolescents in the community. Paper presented at the annual meeting of the Society for Personality Assessment, Brooklyn, NY.

Leichtman, M. (1996). *The Rorschach: A Developmental Perspective*. Hillsdale, NJ: The Analytic Press.

Marengo, J. T., Harrow, M., Lanin-Kettering, I., & Wilson, A. (1986). Evaluating bizarre-idiosyncratic thinking: A comprehensive index of positive thought disorder. *Schizophrenia Bulletin, 12*, 497–509.

Mihura, J. L., Meyer, G. J., Dumitrascu, N., & Bombel, G. (2013). The validity of individual Rorschach variables: Systematic reviews and meta-analyses of the Comprehensive System. *Psychological Bulletin, 139*, 548–605.

Miller, S. B. (1987). A comparison of methods of inquiry: Testing and interviewing contributions to the diagnostic process. *Bulletin of the Menninger Clinic, 51*, 505–518.

Morey, L. C. (1991). *The Personality Assessment Inventory Professional Manual*. Odessa, FL: Psychological Assessment Resources.

Peterson, C. A., & Maitland-Schilling, K. M. (1983). Card pull in projective testing. *Journal of Personality Assessment, 47*, 265–275.

Rapaport, D., Gill, M., & Schafer, R. (1968). *Diagnostic Psychological Testing* (Rev. ed.). R. R. Holt, Ed. New York: International Universities Press. (Original work published in 1946.)

Reichenberg, A., Harvey, P. D., Bowie, C. R., Mojtabai, R., Rabinowitz, J., Heaton, R. K., & Bromet, E. (2009). Neuropsychological function and dysfunction in schizophrenia and psychotic affective disorders. *Schizophrenia Bulletin, 35*, 1022–1029.

Rochester, S., & Martin, J. R. (1979). *Crazy Talk: A Study of the Discourse of Psychotic Speakers*. New York: Plenum.

Rorschach, H. (1942). *Psychodiagnostics* (5th ed.). Bern, Switzerland: Hans Huber. (Original work published in 1921.)

Rothschild-Yakar, L., Lacoua, L., Brener, A., & Koren, D. (2015). Impairments in interpersonal representations and deficits in social cognition as predictors of risk for schizophrenia in non-patient adolescents. Paper presented at the annual meeting of the Society for Personality Assessment, Brooklyn, NY.

Solovay, M. R., Shenton, M. E., & Holzman, P. S. (1987). Comparative studies of thought disorders: I. Mania and schizophrenia. *Archives of General Psychiatry, 44*, 13–20.

Spohn, H. E., Coyne, L., Larson, J., Mittleman, F., Spray, J., & Hayes, K. (1986). Episodic and residual thought pathology in chronic schizophrenics: Effect of neuroleptics. *Schizophrenia Bulletin, 12*, 394–407.

Vygotsky, L. (1934). Thought in schizophrenia. *Archives of Neurology and Psychiatry, 31*, 1063–1077.

Wechsler, D. (1955). *Wechsler Adult Intelligence Scale Manual*. New York: Psychological Corporation.

Weiner, I. B. (1977). Approaches to Rorschach validation. In A. Rickers-Ovsiankina (Ed.), *Rorschach Psychology* (pp. 575–608). New York: Krieger.

Wood, J. M., Nezworski, M. T., Lilienfeld, S. O., & Garb, H. N. (2003). *What Is Wrong with the Rorschach? Science Confronts the Controversial Inkblot Test*. New York: Wiley & Sons.

Part II

Rorschach assessment of psychotic phenomena

Chapter 3

Hermann Rorschach's experiment

As suggested in the previous chapter, trends in the Rorschach assessment of disordered thinking have mirrored broader psychiatric trends in the diagnostic conceptualizing of psychopathology, psychosis, and thought disorder, in particular. Like their psychiatric counterparts, early Rorschach contributors did not consider thought disorder separately from schizophrenia. Such was true of Hermann Rorschach.

Figure 3.1 Hermann Rorschach.

Well before the publication of his inkblot experiment, Rorschach had a keen interest in schizophrenia and had developed his own theoretical position distinct from those of Bleuler, Freud, and Jung (Akavia, 2013). In his novel experiment, Rorschach discovered that his inkblot creations were sensitive to fault lines in a subject's thinking. He coded several types of responses that reflected thought disturbances, signaling the vulnerability to, or presence of, schizophrenia. Rorschach conceived of his inkblot experiment as a test of perception. As such, he considered deviant response processes in terms of perceptual anomalies as opposed to disturbed linguistic or ideational phenomena. Without using the term "thought disorder" or the like, Rorschach (1921/1942) introduced three types of perceptual anomalies that became forerunners of the major thought disorder scoring categories in all Rorschach scoring systems that followed.

When discussing the "mode of apperception," or location scores, Rorschach presented several atypical ways that subjects could deliver whole responses. In comparing his various patient samples, he noticed that certain test scores or "signs" appeared most often in psychotic records. He used the term "confabulated whole answer" (to which he gave the symbol DW) to describe how "a single detail, more or less clearly perceived, is used as the basis for interpretation of the whole picture, giving very little consideration to other parts of the picture" (1921/1942, p. 37). Rorschach gave as an example of a confabulated whole answer: "A crab," on Card I when it was based solely on the small claw-like figures in the center top portion of the blot. He went on to state that the Form Quality (FQ) of such confabulated whole responses, the DWs, would be poor.

Rorschach contrasted imaginative subjects with confabulating ones. He found that imaginative subjects could produce an integrated response without distortion of the individual elements of the blot, while confabulators took two elements of the blot and combined them in such a way that the rest of the inkblot and the relative position of the parts that are used were ignored. In further contrasting imaginative and confabulating subjects, Rorschach indicated that imaginative subjects gave responses with more complex associations than did confabulators. It is clear that for Rorschach confabulation reflected a kind of stimulus-boundedness, in which the subject simply *perceived* the inkblot, albeit in an idiosyncratic and distorted manner, and then reported what he or she saw, whereas the imaginative subject *interpreted* it. Among his patient samples, Rorschach found confabulated whole responses in the records of "unintelligent normals," "morons," epileptics, organics, and patients with schizophrenia.

Rorschach also discussed several kinds of "combinatory" responses in which the subject interpreted details separately and then combined them into a whole response. He termed one special type of combinatory response the "confabulatory-combined whole answer," which he described as "amalgamations of confabulation and combination in which the forms are vaguely seen and the individual objects interpreted are combined without any real consideration for their relative positions in the picture" (p. 38). Rorschach gave as his initial example of this type of response, the Card VIII response of "Two bears climbing from a rock, over an iceberg, onto a tree trunk" (p. 38). Although he acknowledged that this was an accurately perceived response, he concluded that the "position of the objects in the picture is neglected" (p. 38). Rorschach did not elaborate on this statement and thus left the meaning of what he had in mind somewhat unclear. It appears, however, as if he were introducing a precursor to another type of combinatory response, which Rapaport later termed "fabulized combination"

(Rapaport, Gill, & Schafer, 1946/1968). Rorschach observed that confabuatory-combined responses occurred more often in "confabulating morons, Korsakoff cases, and delirious patients [who] are able to invent whole stories in this way" (p. 38). Patients with schizophrenia and mania, on the other hand, produced fewer of these kinds of deviant whole responses.

Only Rorschach's "contaminated whole response" was found solely in schizophrenia patients, making it the first pathognomonic diagnostic sign of this disorder. Instead of attempting to describe the "contamination" response, Rorschach simply defined the process of contamination by giving his now famous example of a Card IV response: "The liver of a respectable statesman" (p. 38). He said that Card IV is frequently seen as a "degenerated organ" or a man sitting on some sort of a stool. "The schizophrenic interprets the figure twice, once as a liver and once as a man, and then contaminates the two with each other, at the same time tossing in the associated ideas 'respectable' and 'statesman'" (p. 38). Rorschach concluded that patients who have schizophrenia gave many responses in which confabulation, combination, and contamination are intermingled in one response.

Rorschach also noted that patients with schizophrenia may be influenced by factors other than the standard perceptual characteristics of the inkblot or the usual determinants of the response such as form, color, or movement. For example, he observed how such patients may base their responses on absurd features such as the number or position of the elements in the inkblot. Both of these response categories reflected a process in which idiosyncratic meaning was assigned based on concrete aspects of the inkblot. Thus, Rorschach added a fourth category, which he referred to as a "position response," to his rudimentary thought disorder scoring system.

Since Rorschach viewed the inkblots as a test of perception and his three primary "thought disorder" scores as deviations in the perceptual mode of approach to the inkblot, he paid less attention to bizarre verbalizations or the pathological thinking that these verbalizations might represent. Despite his reference to absurd and abstract responses, none of his scoring concepts could adequately capture some very peculiar-sounding responses that he encountered in his patients. His sample Rorschach records from severely psychotic patients contained numerous examples of bizarre ideas and verbalizations that were not captured by his confabulation, confabulatory-combination, or contamination scores. For example, he presented responses from one hebephrenic patient who saw on Card V "[the] Head of an animal which has never existed" and on Card IX "Feces like those made by dwarfs which are sold at fairs" (p. 160). Neither of these peculiar responses received the location score of DW for a confabulation; nor did they merit the scores of confabulatory-combination, contamination, or position. All Rorschach could say about these bizarre responses was that the patient's "associative series were interrupted by typically schizophrenic 'leaps' in his thinking" (p. 161).

Thus, in developing a method of assessing personality based chiefly on perceptual processes and anomalies, Rorschach was unable systematically to track and account for the linguistic, associative-ideational, and representational peculiarities that often occurred in the response processes of his sickest patients. It was then left to Rapaport, some 20 years later, to develop a more comprehensive system that provided a way of coding and understanding these deviant forms of verbalization (Rapaport et al., 1946/1968).

Post-Rorschach developments

In their review of the Rorschach, Klopfer and Kelley (1942) pointed out how after the publication of *Psychodiagnostik* (Rorschach, 1921/1942), Rorschach investigators paid less attention to schizophrenia. And despite Rorschach's introduction of scoring categories for deviant responses, no one built on his thought disorder scoring concepts for the next few decades. When researchers spoke about psychoses or schizophrenia and the Rorschach, they followed an empirical-sign method (Weiner, 1977) that Rorschach had employed. Rorschach's empirical-sign approach set the stage for a generation of researchers to embark on similar attempts to compare single or broad dimensions of Rorschach responses between patients with schizophrenia and other diagnostic groups.

Bohm's special phenomena

Bohm (1958) considered a number of factors that could not be analyzed quantitatively but were of great importance in understanding test responses. Referring to these as "imponderables" (p. 86), Bohm listed these 67 special response phenomena, which he argued had diagnostic significance. Of this broad range of response variables, he identified a number as possibly having diagnostic significance for schizophrenia.

The first of these was what Bohm called "interpretation awareness." Originally taken from Rorschach's description (1921/1942), it reflects the subject's awareness of the nonliteral, interpretative nature of the task. Whereas normal subjects inherently accept that the Rorschach is a task of interpretation (i.e. "What might this be?"), Bohm found that "in most organic psychoses, epilepsy, manic cases ... and also in many schizophrenics," the subject remains uncertain whether the task is one of interpretation or recognition (Bohm, 1958, p. 90).

Bohm also listed confabulations (or confabulatory combinations), contaminations, perseverations, self-reference responses, number and position responses, and color naming as having possible diagnostic significance for schizophrenia, and in some cases manic-depressive psychosis.

None of these primarily European approaches looked specifically at thinking or isolated thinking as a subject of study. However, although their work predated the more direct study of thought disorder per se, Klopfer and Kelley began to shift away from focusing only on perceptual aspects of the response process and started to look more closely at the specific nature of the schizophrenic patient's disturbed thinking and language.

References

Akavia, N. (2013). *Subjectivity in Motion*. New York: Routledge.

Bohm, E. (1958). *Rorschach Test Diagnosis*. New York: Grune & Stratton.

Klopfer, B., & Kelley, D. M. (1942). *The Rorschach Technique: A Manual for a Projective Method of Personality Diagnosis*. Yonkers-on-Hudson, NY: World Book Company.

Rapaport, D., Gill, M., & Schafer, R. (1968). *Diagnostic Psychological Testing* (Rev. ed.). R. R. Holt, Ed. New York: International Universities Press. (Original work published in 1946.)

Rorschach, H. (1942). *Psychodiagnostics* (5th ed.). Bern, Switzerland: Hans Huber. (Original work published in 1921.)

Weiner, I. B. (1977). Approaches to Rorschach validation. In A. Rickers-Ovsiankina (Ed.), *Rorschach Psychology* (pp. 575–608). New York: Krieger.

Chapter 4

Contributions of Rapaport and Holt

This chapter examines the enduring Rorschach contributions of intellectual giants David Rapaport and Robert Holt. Both left indelible marks on the fields of psychological assessment and psychoanalysis, wrote prolifically in and outside of the field of diagnostic testing, and occupy critical places in the evolution of understanding and assessing disordered thinking with the Rorschach. We begin with the intellectual father of thought disorder scoring on the Rorschach, David Rapaport.

Rapaport's analysis of Deviant Verbalization (DV)

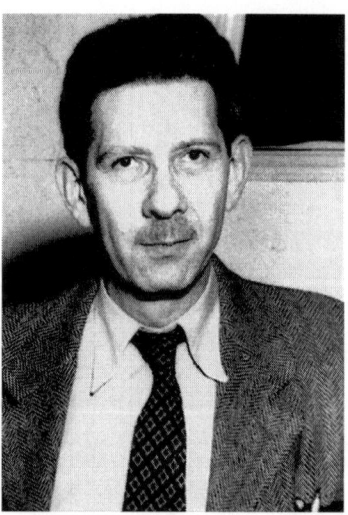

Figure 4.1 David Rapaport.

Unlike Beck and Klopfer, Rapaport's interest in the Rorschach occurred comparatively late in his illustrious career and seemed to wane in the years following his seminal Rorschach contributions (Rapaport, Gill, & Schafer, 1946/1968).

A leading figure in American Ego Psychology, Rapaport drifted away from psychodiagnostic research and clinical use of the Rorschach and instead immersed himself in the more abstract realm of interpreting and systematizing psychoanalytic metapsychology. However, the legacy of his brief years of active involvement in the Rorschach and other psychodiagnostic instruments left an indelible mark on the field of psychological testing in general and the assessment of disordered thinking in particular. Holt, who edited work by Rapaport and colleagues in 1968, in a footnote described Rapaport's work in the area of conceptualizing and measuring forms of disturbed thought processes on the Rorschach as his "most distinctive and original contribution to Rorschach testing" (Rapaport, Gill, & Schafer, 1946/1968, p. 424). Many would agree that Rapaport's contributions in this area are second only to those of Rorschach himself. In fact, most workers in this area value Rapaport's contributions far more than Hermann Rorschach's brief trail-blazing efforts in his final years (R. R. Holt, personal communication, June 21, 2016).

Deciphering the nature of thought pathology

Rapaport had a passionate interest in deciphering the structure and functioning of thought and understanding how thinking progresses from drive-dominated ideation to socialized and logical thought processes (Kleiger, 1993). In particular, he was concerned with how pathology gains expression in formal aspects of thought processes. Rapaport's interest in understanding the organization and pathological expressions of thought led to a shift away from a strict focus on the perceptual characteristics or the content of Rorschach responses and paved the way for the analysis of verbalization. Verbalization, for Rapaport, revealed the organizing principles of thinking and held the key to understanding thought pathology. He stated that the comprehensive and systematic examination of the various types of deviant verbalizations on the Rorschach was "the highway for investigating disorders of thinking" (Rapaport et al., 1946/1968, p. 431).

During his work with Merton Gill and Roy Schafer, Rapaport began to use the term "thought disorder." Prior to its formal introduction in his book *Organization and Pathology of Thought* (1951), this now-familiar phrase had not appeared frequently in Rorschach literature on schizophrenia. Thus, Rapaport's work marked the first time that the Rorschach was used in a sustained way to assess disordered thinking as a separate function of the mental apparatus. In their analysis of Rorschach verbalization, Rapaport and his colleagues introduced a fifth category to Rorschach scoring, which set the standard for almost every subsequent Rorschach system for scoring and conceptualizing thought disorder.

Distance from the blot

Assessing thought disorder through an analysis of deviant verbalizations was based on Rapaport's concept of "distance" from the inkblot. For Rapaport, thinking was always tied to the perceptual reality of the inkblot. Adaptive, reality-based thinking depended on the smooth interdigitation of perceptual and associational processes. In other words, the associations set in motion by the inkblot must not stray too far from the perceptual reality of the inkblot. If associative processes were too far removed from the inkblot, the subject was viewed as showing a disregard for the perceptual reality in front of him or her. On the other hand, rigid attunement to the perceptual features of the inkblot might lead a subject to regard it as too real, hence failing to maintain an appropriate distance or "as if" attitude toward the inkblots.

Schuldberg and Boster (1985) criticized Rapaport for his lack of clarity and conceptual confusion in describing thought disordered responses on the Rorschach. According to these researchers, nowhere was this confusion more prominent than in Rapaport's introduction of his concept of "distance" in the response process. Since the concept of distance formed a pivotal basis for Rapaport's conceptualization of the psychological process underlying pathological responses on the Rorschach, Schuldberg and Boster conducted an empirical analysis of the data on which Rapaport's theoretical construct was originally based. Their analysis included the original thought disorder data from 106 of the 108 Rapaport et al. subjects with schizophrenia and "preschizophrenia." By examining the structure and interrelationships of the original categories of disordered thinking, Schuldberg and Boster sought to specify the psychological processes underlying pathological Rorschach responses.

Considering changes in diagnostic practices over the four decades since the Rapaport group had conducted their seminal study, Schuldberg and Boster concluded that the original subjects were likely individuals suffering from schizophrenia, affective psychoses, and schizotypal and borderline personality disorders. The researchers used a smallest space analysis technique (Guttman, 1968), which enabled them to form a spatial representation of the co-occurrence of 19 of Rapaport's categories across subjects. Based on their statistical analysis, they found that the thought-disordered responses of Rapaport's subjects did not form a unidimensional measure of pathological thinking and verbalization. Instead, they determined that two dimensions provided a reasonably economical representation of the structure of Rapaport's thought disorder scoring categories and his concept of distance. Dimension 1 contained scoring categories having to do with objective versus personalized meaning, while Dimension 2 was found to be related to verbal productivity, reflecting rigid versus fluid sets in approaching the task.

Categories of Deviant Verbalizations

Rapaport and colleagues (1946/1968) labeled all of the categories of disordered thinking on the Rorschach "deviant verbalizations." The names chosen for these variants were based both on the previous Rorschach literature and on their own experience and concepts. Although the group borrowed several of the categories

Table 4.1 Rapaport's Deviant Verbalizations

---

1 Fabulized Responses*
2 Fabulized Combinations*
3 Confabulations*
4 Contaminations
5 Autistic Logic*
6 Peculiar Verbalizations*
7 Queer Verbalizations*
8 Vagueness Responses*
9 Confusion Responses*
10 Incoherent Responses*
11 Symbolic Responses*
12 Absurd Responses*
13 Relationship Verbalizations*
14 Verbalization of Reference Ideas
15 Self-Reference Verbalizations
16 Deterioration Color Response
17 Symmetry Verbalizations
18 Exactness Verbalizations
19 Criticism Verbalizations
20 Verbal Aggression
21 Aggression Responses
22 Self-Depreciation Responses
23 Affective Verbalizations
24 Masturbation & Castration Responses

Note
* The categories with asterisks represent unique conceptual contributions by Rapaport, Gill, & Schafer (1946/1968) in Rorschach thought-disorder scoring.

of pathological verbalization from the extant Rorschach literature, they modified the scoring and extended the meaning of most of these existing categories and identified and labeled several new categories. In all, they proposed 24 different types of pathological verbalizations (Table 4.1). Many of these scores fall outside the realm of thought disorder and represent other kinds of psychological issues that go beyond those considered specific to disordered thinking. However, a number of these categories (marked with an asterisk) represented original thinking about categories of disturbed language and logic expressed in Rorschach responses.

Fabulized Responses

Although fabulized responses generally were said to reflect an increased distance, they were also simultaneously viewed as reflecting a loss of distance, especially when the subject expressed an emotion-laden conviction that the image assigned to the inkblot was not simply a symbolic representation but something vivid and real. For example, the subject who looks at Card I and says "Oh no, it's a dangerous bat!" reveals both an increase in distance (the inkblot does not support the descriptor "dangerous") and a loss of distance (the subject reacts as if the image really is dangerous). Rapaport concluded that the presence of a few mild fabulized responses was not pathological. It was only when there was an abundance of such responses that one should begin to suspect autistic thinking.

Fabulized Combinations

Although Hermann Rorschach (1921/1942) identified a deviant form of combinatory response that he called a "confabulatory combination," it was Rapaport who formalized this scoring concept and introduced the term "fabulized combination" into Rorschach language. The key element in these combinative responses is that the spatial relation between separate areas is taken as a fixed and real relationship. In this sense, Rapaport indicated that fabulized combinations primarily reflect an extreme loss of distance from, or concrete interpretation of, the spatial juxtaposition of aspects of the inkblot.

The unrealistic nature of the relationship or interaction can be based on disproportionate size or an unnatural or bizarre relationship that does not occur in nature. Rapaport allowed that fabulized combinations could occur occasionally in the Rorschachs of more intact subjects; however, they would usually be accompanied by an appreciation of their unrealistic nature.

Confabulations

This represented one of Rapaport's most original contributions to scoring disordered thinking on the Rorschach. Although the term itself was not new, Rapaport extended its meaning beyond its original use by Rorschach and others who followed him. Rorschach used the term "confabulatory whole response" (designated by the symbol DW) to describe those responses in which a subject begins with one detail and generalizes to a whole response. Recall his original example of Card I, which was based on the perceptual generalization from one small detail ("a claw") to an inaccurately perceived whole response ("a crab"). Here the confabulatory, or pathological filling-in, process was based on perceptual and not ideational or associational features. Once again, Rapaport's unique contribution was based on his concept of distance from the inkblot. Confabulation responses were, in essence, fabulized responses taken too far. In other words, the confabulating subject reports seeing images that cannot be justified by realistic aspects of the inkblot. Based on either the unwarranted infusion of affect or fantasy into the response, or an inappropriate degree of specificity, Rapaport believed that confabulations almost always indicated severe thought pathology of at least a preschizophrenic nature.

According to Rapaport, confabulations frequently reflect combinations of pathological loss of and increase in distance from the inkblot. Aspects of the inkblot can be taken too literally and then elaborated in a manner that goes beyond any supporting features of the inkblot. Rapaport (Rapaport et al., 1946/1968) provided such an example with the Card V response: "two people lying down, tired, resting [side figures] ... somebody helping them [central figure], nature might be helping them ... might be God" (p. 433). The infusion of energy or in this case, a lack of energy (i.e. "tiredness" and "resting") reflects an increase in distance that is part of a fabulizing process. Rapaport noted that the literal interpretation of the central figure as a "helper," based on its erect form and spatial relationship to the two side figures that were seen as reclining, is an example of a pathological loss of distance. Finally, there is an extreme leap in fabulizing as the subject takes the concept "helper" and extends it to "nature" or "God," both of which go far beyond what is reasonably suggested by the inkblot.

Rapaport believed that confabulation responses reflected elements of both fabulized responses and fabulized combinations. He was confident that all three types of response, but especially confabulation, signaled the presence of idiosyncratic thinking in everyday situations in which fantasy begins to progressively encroach on one's adherence to reality. Rapaport concluded that confabulations are "the most autistic and most clearly a part of schizophrenic thinking" (p. 435).

Autistic Logic

Rapaport first used the term "autistic logic" to describe the types of fallacious logic that von Domarus (1944) called "paralogical" or "predicate" thinking and that Arieti (1974) referred to as "paleological" reasoning. Rorschach used the symbol "Po," for position-determined response, to depict one common inkblot example of "paralogical thinking." Rapaport and colleagues elaborated on the "Po" category and defined autistic logic responses as those in which the subject's reasoning is explicitly illogical. Typically, the subject's autistic reasoning is heralded by the word "because" as the subject makes his or her reasoning error explicit. For example, the position response to Card IX of "the north pole ... *because* it is at the top" reflects the subject's air of certainty in reaching this illogical conclusion. Although Rapaport noted the rarity of autistic logic responses, he believed that, like contamination responses, they signaled illogical thinking and impaired reality testing and, as such, were almost always pathognomonic of schizophrenia.

Peculiar and queer verbalizations

Whereas several of Rapaport's categories had been previously described by earlier Rorschach investigators, his effort to categorize pathological speech or language independently of the percept involved was pioneering. In these scoring categories, the object of study is not the process of autistic logic, but the verbal end product. Rapaport held that deviant language reflected either pathological loss of or increase in distance from the Rorschach card.

Peculiar verbalizations are the milder of the two types of deviant communication. The criterion for peculiar responses was that the verbalization was only inappropriate or idiosyncratic in the context of the particular Rorschach response.

Outside of that context it was not remarkable. For example, Rorschach verbalizations such as "a cranial skull," "an eagle view of it," "two legs raising each other," and "joined at the hands" strike the listener as odd; however, in a different context, each may have its appropriate usage. Furthermore, in each example, the oddity of expression does not disrupt the intended meaning that the subject tries to convey. Jarring though these peculiar verbalizations may be, the listener can usually follow the subject's ideas.

According to Rapaport, queer verbalizations are expressions that would sound strange in any context. Thus, peculiar and queer verbalizations were seen as different gradients on a continuum of severity. Response verbalizations such as "the echo of a picture," "a split color," and the Rapaport group's example of "an artistic design of a fly's foot" (1946/1968, p. 447) have a bizarre quality, in which the subject tries to convey meaning that is remote and strangely private. Unlike the stilted but discernible peculiar verbalization, queer responses leave the listener feeling confused. Rapaport stated that peculiar verbalizations were more common than queer ones, except in more disorganized patients with schizophrenia. He felt verbal convention could mask pathological thinking and allow many psychotic patients to maintain a good front. Rapaport noted that peculiar verbalizations may occur in neurotic and normal Rorschach records but with far less frequency than in schizophrenic and preschizophrenic ones. Queer verbalizations, however, were felt to be more specific indicators of schizophrenia or, at least, preschizophrenia pathology. Rapaport went so far as to state that peculiar verbalizations in ample frequency were more diagnostic of preschizophrenic conditions, whereas queer verbalizations were indicative of schizophrenia proper.

Vagueness, confusion, and incoherence

The Rapaport group identified three related categories of verbalization that referred to a continuum of "response atrophy" or degradation in which the subject seems to lose hold of the response because of either a perceptual or verbal difficulty. Vagueness of verbalization reflects the subject's difficulty in articulating a response in a clear and sharp manner. In Rapaport's words, the subject has difficulty keeping a percept with a definite form alive. Subjects may reveal their vagueness of verbalization by expressing a degree of perplexity as they attempt unsuccessfully to communicate what they see. Neurotic-level subjects were viewed as better able to communicate their feeling of vagueness, while psychotic individuals typically did not. Rapaport gave examples of vagueness of verbalization that included the Card I response "I can almost get a witch's face but I can't make it" and the Card IV response "a skin tacked on a wall ... I can't quite get it but it is there some place" (p. 449). Rapaport believed that these verbalizations often betrayed a prepsychotic or psychotic condition. In these responses, the first perceptual impression of the inkblot is fleeting and seems to evaporate quickly. Rapaport suggested that the examiner in such cases may have the feeling that he was "digging in quicksand."

Rapaport used the term "confusion" to refer to those responses in which subjects express confusion either in their experience of the inkblot or in their attempt to communicate what they see, or both. According to Rapaport, the subject maintains that she perceives the inkblot a certain way but that this cannot be. In doing so, the subject reveals a distinct confusion about the apparent contradiction between what she sees and what she feels to be the truth. Confusion responses usually reveal some overt or more subtle expression of the subject's perplexity, as in Rapaport's example of a Card II response: "Clowns ... they have three legs ... they can't have three legs!" (p. 450). Rapaport and colleagues viewed the confusion response as a signal of the presence of confusion in everyday life and, at worst, as an inability to maintain conceptual boundaries between contradictory experiences.

Incoherent verbalizations reflect the most severe kind of intrusion into and disruption of the response process. Rapaport reserved this scoring category for those responses that were so laden with extraneous verbiage that they were almost incomprehensible. Rapaport's example of a Card IX response of "limbs and shoulders of men ... always inner ambition that man could make wings and overcome gravity ... that the card reminded me that it can be done," leaves the listener confused, a key criterion for scoring a response as incoherent (pp. 450–451). The listener might well label such a response "disorganized" because it does not follow the rules of conventional orderly thinking, in which the initial link of a thought chain exerts a regulatory effect on the remainder of the chain of ideas and associations. In the above example, the initial percept "limbs and shoulders of men" has no logical, coherent connection with the verbiage that follows, leaving the listener hopelessly confused and wondering if he has misheard or missed something. Rapaport stated that incoherence is always a psychotic indication and usually diagnostic of schizophrenic or organic psychotic conditions.

Symbolic responses

Symbolic responses reflect the subject's attempts to "interpret" abstract levels of meaning into the inkblots. Rapaport suggested that there were two types of symbolic responses, implicit and explicit, and that both types could signal the presence of a psychotic process. However, he also noted that highly imaginative normal or neurotic individuals could produce more toned-down versions of each type of symbolic response. The explicit type of symbolism is clearly present when the subject indicates that something about the inkblot (or the blot as a whole) symbolizes an abstract concept. According to the Rapaport group, psychotic-level symbolism is based on a conviction that the inkblot represents a meaningful idea or truth; however, the interpretation has an autistic and overly private quality that is usually not comprehendible to the listener. Furthermore, the symbolic ideas are not well integrated with the formal qualities of the inkblot and do not enrich the response. The Rapaport example on Card VIII of "the one who drew this must have intended to represent the similarity theory of nature" (p. 452) conveys both the subject's certainty that he has discovered the true meaning of the inkblot and the idiosyncratic nature of his symbolic thought processes, which leaves the listener feeling lost and confused. On the other hand, more intact subjects may attempt to interpret meaning based on symbolism in a way that is both more integrated and conventional. Rapaport mentioned the often-heard Card II response of "Two people fighting and the red might be symbolic of the conflict" as an example of normal/neurotic-level symbolism in which the symbolic interpretation is well integrated and easily comprehended.

Rapaport described implicit symbolism as a process that occurs when a subject makes no direct reference to symbolic meaning but uses images that may symbolize libidinal or aggressive impulses. For example, he suggested that the response to an upper projection on Card IV (where, according to Rapaport, a penis is often seen) of an "erect snake ready to strike" may well represent "latent phallic symbolism." Rapaport indicated that psychotic and nonpsychotic individuals use implicit symbolism when viewing the inkblots. In terms of distinguishing the higher from the lower-level type, Rapaport suggested that elaborate implicit symbolism that does not fit with the blot area might signal the examiner to be alert to other psychotic indicators in the record.

Rapaport also cautioned examiners against making inferences about unconscious contents based on explicit or implicit forms of symbolism. Consistent with his approach to the Rorschach, the formal qualities of symbolic responses were to be interpreted as indications of a particular kind of thought process (e.g. autistic/psychotic) and not as windows into the subject's unconscious conflicts.

Absurd responses

For Rapaport, absurd responses exemplified the concept of pathological distance from the inkblot because there is no justification for what the subject associates with the inkblot. The form is bad by definition in that the response is clearly unrelated to the area of the inkblot chosen. Whereas an adequate response requires that the subject's perceptual and associative processes work in unison—or as Rapaport said, in a "cogwheeling" fashion—absurd responses reflect a marked asynchrony between these two processes. The Rapaport example of the Card V response of "Could it be a hippopotamus spread out like that?" is clearly absurd (p. 458). The examiner is left nonplussed as to the origin of such a response. Rapaport viewed these kinds of patently unjustified responses as suggestive of schizophrenia.

Modifications of the Rapaport system

A number of Rapaport's disciples modified his scoring system and did not carry forward the elaborate list of thought disorder scores that their mentor originally described. Most of the modifications included simplifications of the thought disorder scoring system that attempted to remove ambiguities that some felt plagued his original system.

Following Rapaport, Schafer (1948, 1954) wrote extensively about the psychoanalytic interpretation of the Rorschach. Of all Rapaport's disciples, Schafer remained closest to the letter and spirit of the original list of thought disorder scores that Rapaport, Gill, and he had developed. In each of his books, Schafer presented a number of case studies of thought-disordered patients and listed scores for deviant Rorschach verbalizations under the "Qualitative" heading of the "Summary of Responses" section of the protocol.

Schafer also referred to responses that did not quite reach the scoring threshold of "tendency" responses. For example, a response that approached, but was not quite, a contamination was called a "contamination tendency," while a near confabulation was called a "confabulation tendency." Earlier, Rapaport had hinted that these "tendency" responses should be recognized; however, he did not use this term and never developed the concept of a continuum of severity within each type of deviant verbalization.

In the 1960s, Mayman wrote a Rorschach scoring and interpretation manual, which he copyrighted in 1982 and which was subsequently revised by Appelbaum (1975). Mayman (1982) altered and extended several aspects of the Rapaport–Schafer System. He developed a 5-point scale for identifying degrees of fabulized embellishment of Rorschach responses. The total "fab score" was intended as a measure of the frequency and degree to which the response process became infused with fantasy and departed from object reality. Unlike Rapaport, Mayman used the expression "extreme loss of distance" from the inkblot to refer to those responses embellished with fantasy material that went far beyond what the inkblot could support. Rapaport may have referred to such responses as a product of an extreme "increase of distance" from the blot, as in the case of a confabulation response. Mayman also developed a scale for rating the degree of oral aggressive content in Rorschach responses.

Lerner's texts on psychoanalytic theory and the Rorschach (1991, 1998) were an attempt to represent Rapaport's theoretical/conceptual approach to the Rorschach. Although Lerner supplemented Rapaport's standard ego psychological interpretation of Rorschach determinant and content scores with more contemporary research regarding defenses and self and object relations, he stuck closely to Rapaport's original list of deviant verbalizations. Lerner limited his presentation to ten varieties of pathological responses, including fabulized response, fabulized combinations, confabulation, contamination, autistic logic, peculiar verbalization, queer verbalization, vagueness, confusion, and incoherence.

Holt's primary process scoring system

Robert R. Holt rightly occupies a distinguished position in any list of "Who's Who" in clinical psychology, psychoanalytic research, and personality assessment. He worked tirelessly for more than half a century in studying, critiquing, and reformulating Freudian metapsychology and all of Freud's writings on primary process thinking. Most in our field who reach luminary status for their

Figure 4.2 Robert Holt.

contributions to research and clinical practice retire at some point, and their earlier contributions live on as historical artifacts and footnotes for contemporary investigations and clinical practice. Somehow, Holt never received this notice. Not only did he continue doing research and writing scholarly books long after many of his contemporaries left the field, but he continued developing and refining his original contributions well into his 90s. At the age of 92, he published the two-volume *Primary Process Thinking: Theory, Measurement, and Research* (Holt, 2009), which summarizes a broad body of work on primary process theory and synthesizes his own theoretical position on primary process thinking, which strives for consistency with contemporary neuroscience. Anyone interested in seeing what Holt has been up to in the decades since his *Freud Reappraised: A Fresh Look at Psychoanalytic Theory* (Holt, 1989) will be impressed by the integrative scope of his effort to craft a "new psychoanalytic theory of thinking." After immersing himself in cognitive neuroscience, neuropsychology, and computer models of information processing, Holt presented a detailed outline of "Basic Assumptions" and "Testable Propositions" for a psychoanalytic theory of thinking that incorporates cutting-edge concepts like executive functioning and ToM. For example, he has linked his previous ideas about "control and defense variables," which may mediate primary process material, with more contemporary concepts of linguistic self-monitoring and social cognition.

Those interested in Holt's remarkable career should consult Strack and Kinder's *Pioneers of Personality Science* (2006) for a perspective on Holt's lifelong efforts to conceptualize and assess personality functioning. Most who are familiar with Holt's weighty contributions know that he was a student of Rapaport's at the Menninger Clinic in the 1940s. Like many of Rapaport's early students,

Robert Holt became a prominent psychoanalytic researcher and Rorschach theoretician in his own right. During the course of his research, Holt became interested in the psychoanalytic concept of neutralization or how primary process thinking could be tamed in the service of adaptation. He reasoned that thought processes, as represented by Rorschach responses, could reflect neutralized drive energy to the extent that responses lacked evidence of libidinal or aggressive drive derivatives. Holt developed a "neutralization index" to measure the degree to which primary process material pervaded Rorschach content (Klopfer et al., 1954). The index consisted of the sum of all oral, narcissistic, anal, voyeuristic, exhibitionistic, urethral, phallic, and homosexual content, as well as all manifestations of aggressive or destructive content, and divided this by R.

In examining the Rorschachs of a group of college students, Holt noticed that aspects of primary process thinking could be detected in the Rorschach responses of some students, but that these were frequently balanced by humor and cultural references in those students who were independently judged to have more flexible cognitive styles. Thus, Holt began to pay close attention to the relative effectiveness of a subject's efforts to control or defend against the emergence of primary process material in his Rorschach responses. In doing so, he found that it was possible to distinguish between an unbridled breakthrough of primary process derivatives and the more modulated and socially acceptable expressions of this material.

In addition to conducting a rich and detailed review of theory and research, Holt became interested in establishing a theoretically based Rorschach scoring system that would assess primary process manifestations and, more important, measure aspects of ego control and defense. In collaboration with his colleague Joan Havel (Holt & Havel, 1960), he developed the Pripro Scoring System, as a way of measuring primary process on the Rorschach. The comprehensive Pripro system was envisioned more as a research tool than a clinical instrument (Holt & Havel, 1960).

Holt's complete Pripro scoring manual, along with research done with the system, is presented in a CD that accompanies Volume 2 of his 2009 book. The system and review of research using the Pripro is painstakingly long and detailed (847 pages) but provides some of the most innovative contributions to operationalizing psychoanalytic concepts and applying them to the practice of psychological assessment, particularly using the Rorschach. With close to 100 individual scoring variables grouped together across three broad scoring categories, Holt acknowledged that his scoring system, developed over the last half century, might not be used by clinicians:

> The Pripro system is notoriously laborious. It takes a long time to learn, and any moderately long and complex clinical record takes a long time to score. It has the reputation, therefore, of not being of interest or value to anyone other than researchers. (Holt, 2009, p. 682)

Each of the three scoring categories corresponds to a different aspect of primary process thinking as described by Holt (1956, 1970, 1977, 2009; Holt & Havel, 1960). Originally, these three scoring categories included Content Variables, Formal Variables, and Control and Defense Variables. In his comprehensive 2009 work, Holt laid out seven coding categories: Content Analysis, Formal Aspects, Controls and Defenses, Form Level, Creativity, Demand for Defense, and Defensive Effectiveness.

Content variables

Since primary process thinking is characterized by its wishful quality, Holt constructed a group of *content variables* to reflect the degree of primary process wishfulness present in each response. Holt specified two major content categories reflecting libidinal and aggressive wishes, each of which was then classified as either Level 1 or Level 2 to reflect the extent to which the response was dominated by primary process experience. Level 1 responses were defined as imagery that reflected more blatant, crude, primitive, and unmodulated expressions of libidinal or aggressive impulses. Level 2 responses reflected more socialized, civilized, and modulated expressions of primary process experience.

Formal variables

Holt believed that Rapaport's list of deviant verbalizations was actually a way of categorizing formal manifestations of primary process experience. The scoring manual devised by Holt (1967, 1970, 2009) for assessing formal aspects of primary process thinking was thus an outgrowth and elaboration of Rapaport's work. Holt attempted to correlate primary process manifestations in Rorschach responses with formal characteristics of dreaming—condensation, displacement, and symbolization. However, Holt realized that dreaming and Rorschach thinking differ considerably and could not be considered comparable processes, and that without a subject's associations it is difficult to know when condensation, displacement, or symbolization occurs in Rorschach responses. Nevertheless, he believed that traces of these primary process mechanisms could be detected in disturbed Rorschach responses. In these cases, the subject's failure to cover up the traces of such primary process in his or her thinking resulted in deviations from logical, orderly thinking that is anchored securely in secondary process thinking.

In constructing the formal variables section in his scoring manual, Holt did not restrict himself to the types of formal deviations associated with dream processes but tried to include other deviant processes that were unique to the Rorschach situation. Holt revised this manual a number of times, expanding and refining the operational definitions of the scoring categories, which culminated in his lengthy and exhaustively thorough 2009 manual. Beginning with the concepts of condensation, symbolization, and displacement as broad organizing categories, he derived close to 40 separate scores to measure structural deviations in the perceptual organization and verbalization of the response and the thought processes that underlie them. As with the content variables, each formal scoring category is associated with either a Level 1 or Level 2 designation, indicating the degree to which this aspect of the response represents a more primitive, unmodulated expression of primary process thinking.

As one of the hallmarks of primary process thinking, *condensation* refers to the inability to keep images and ideas stable and separated in a way that is demanded by an accurate view of external reality. Holt identified eight different types of what he termed "image-fusion," scored at either Level 1 or Level 2, or both. Holt indicated that *displacement* often had the effect of making a response more socially acceptable. As a result, some displacements come close to the secondary process end of the continuum. Holt's scoring categories for displacement included both Level 1 and Level 2 responses. Finally, Holt's *symbolism* category pertains to concrete features of the inkblot that are used to represent an abstract idea. In each case, the subject makes explicit his attempt to represent an abstract idea by using the color, shading, spatial arrangement, or form features of the inkblot. Three specific subtypes of explicit symbolism are scored.

Although Freud did not include *contradiction* as a formal characteristic of primary process thinking, Holt extrapolated from Freud's writing and concluded that tolerance of contradictions was a hallmark of primary process experience. Holt scored three types of contradictions: affective contradictions, logical contradictions, and contradictions of reality (formerly called inappropriate activity). Holt at first was not sure how to classify or interpret odd verbalizations. He believed that they were different from deviations in perception and associative elaboration and could not be readily placed under the headings of condensation, displacement, or symbolization. Nonetheless, he included five verbalization scores in his system to capture deviant forms of verbal usage; however, he felt that each should be cautiously interpreted. Holt grouped 11 additional scores under the rubric of this miscellaneous category. These included a number of well-known scores popularized by Rapaport and his predecessors.

Control and defense variables

One of Holt's most original contributions to conceptualizing and scoring examples of disordered thinking on the Rorschach was his effort to operationalize control and defense variables. These categories were to be scored whenever a response included either content or formal variables that warranted separate scores. Holt believed that these scoring categories of defense and control represented both the subject's conscious or latent awareness that the material contained in the response was inappropriate and also his efforts to modulate the way it was expressed and communicated to the examiner. Holt assigned either a minus or plus sign to many of these scores to designate whether the efforts to tone down or control the material were successful (+) or unsuccessful (-). No sign is used if the response is not significantly improved or spoiled by the attempt at control and modulation.

Holt originally identified seven groups of control and defense categories: Remoteness, Context, Reflection, Postponing Strategies, Miscellaneous Defenses, Sequence, and Overtness. He later included Reflection and Sequence under his Miscellaneous category. Holt included a number of heterogeneous scores that reflected familiar defense mechanisms. Some of these were considered maladaptive and as such were assigned minus signs. Others were viewed as more adaptive.

Holt drew upon Schafer's work (1954) to help identify relevant defensive processes that could be inferred from Rorschach responses. In addition to defenses such as negation, denial, rationalization, repudiation, minimization, and undoing, Holt included a number of other variants of defensive activity, including (1) Euphemism, (2) Vulgarity of Verbalization, (3) Adaptive Modification of Response, (4) Rationalization, (5) Negation, (6) Minimization, (7) Counterphobic Defense, (8) Self-Deprecation, (9) Repudiation or Disavowal of a Response, (10) Vagueness of Percept or Communication, (11) Projection, (12) Obsessional Defense, (13) Isolation, (14) Evasiveness and Avoidance, (15) Impotence, and (16) Sequence. Subjects may defend by interspersing primary process responses with more neutral secondary process material. The individual may alternate between either a Level 1 or Level 2 response and an unscorable response or go from a Level 1 to a Level 2 response.

Holt was also interested in rating a response in terms of its level of overt, versus potential, expression of primary process material. Primary process content can be expressed along a continuum of overtness from wishes and thoughts to words and actions. The more a primary process impulse is expressed in the form of action rather than thought, the more it is presumed to be overt and less well defended. For example, the response "This guy is attacking this guy over here" is considered more overt than the response "This guy says to the other guy, 'I'm going to attack you.'" When primary process material is expressed as a wish, feeling, sensation, or fantasy, the level of overtness is further attenuated. For example, responses such as "a hungry wolf" or "angry face" reflect a lessening of immediate primary process drive content, in this case aggression. Finally, primary process material might be expressed only as a potentiality, such as in static or potential movement responses (e.g. "A giant getting ready to get me" or "Snipers about to shoot").

Form level

In the 1970 draft of his scoring manual, Holt presented three rating scales that could be applied to each response. These included rating the form level of the response, the quality of combinations and integrations, and the level of creativity. Holt (1977) later indicated that scoring of creativity and combinations/integrations was optional and not necessary to calculate the overall effectiveness of defensive capacity in containing primary process material. Holt used Mayman's (1964) multi-tiered scale for assessing form level and added quantitative ratings as follows:

F+   Sharp and convincing form that can be seen easily
Fo   Popular and near-popular
Fw+   Reasonably plausible with some stretching
Fw−   Bearing only slight resemblance to the blot
Fs   On the way to an F+ or Fo but the subject spoils the response by introducing something that downgrades the acceptability of the form level
F−   Arbitrary form with little or no resemblance
Fv+   Vague forms that fit the blot well and nondefinite form that is combined with appropriate use of color or shading
Fv   Vague form with no other determinant
Fa   Amorphous responses in which form does not play any role (e.g. pure C, C', or Ch responses).

Demand for Defense

The Demand for Defense (DD) rating represents an elaboration of the Level 1 versus Level 2 distinction. The degree to which the content or formal qualities of the response demand that some defensive or controlling provisions be made to make it more socially acceptable is quantified under the heading of DD. At one extreme, blatant Level 1 content and frankly illogical thinking that is captured by some of the formal scores place significant demands on the subject to explain away the primary process primitivity embedded in the response. At the other extreme are those responses that do not even merit a Level 2 content score and contain no deviations in formal reasoning or logic. Thus, each response is rated quantitatively on the degree of defense demand.

Holt recommended using the following 6-point DD rating scale for each response as a whole: (1) *No apparent need for defense*, including responses that indirectly contain aspects of primary process material that almost go unnoticed; (2) *Slight need for defense*, in which formal or content variables strike the listener as slightly unusual, or any response that contains both Level 2 content and formal scores; (3) *Moderate need for defense*, includes formal or content variables that might cause some tension or embarrassment in a social situation and any response that includes Level 1 or Level 2 formal or content variables; (4) *Considerable need for defense*, e.g. for reference to sexual organs or any response combining Level 1 content and formal aspects; (5) *Great need for defense*, for ideas that are always inappropriate in social conversation (usually suggestive of psychosis because they imply impaired social judgment); (6) *Greatest need for defense*, for responses that depict the most extreme combinations of primitive content and psychotically impaired reasoning.

Defense Effectiveness

Holt also rated the effectiveness of defensive or controlling measures in each response that contained either primary process content or formal qualities. According to Holt (1977), Defense Effectiveness (DE) is rated along a multipoint scale ranging from +2 to -3 by half-point increments. The positive values indicate adaptive regression and effective control, while the negative ratings indicate ineffective defenses and pathologically regressive shifts in functioning. Holt attempted to distinguish successfully defended responses from response creativity, which was rated on a separate scale.

In addition to numerical ratings, some responses are assigned the letter "a" to distinguish undefended responses in which the subject makes no attempt to control or defend against the primary process material. If the response is successful in most respects, the lack of scorable defensive or control measures is not necessarily considered a liability. Mature individuals who are not threatened by primary process thoughts and images may not feel a need to defend against it.

Adaptive Regression Score

The Adaptive Regression Score (ARS) is the product of DD and DE responses summed and divided by the number of primary process responses. Other useful indices include the percentage of responses that contain primary process material (percent total primary process); the percentage of responses containing primary process content (percent content) or the percentage containing formal indications of primary process (percent formal); the percentage of responses at Level 1 or 2 (percent Level 1 or Level 2); and mean form-level rating.

A look back at the contributions of the Rapaport and Holt systems

Assessing the seminal contributions of legendary figures like Rapaport and Holt to the understanding and measurement of disordered thinking on the Rorschach is a task both humbling and daunting. Both rightly take their place in the pantheon of researcher–theoreticians who left enduring marks on the fields of psychoanalysis and psychological assessment. To circumscribe this task, I have chosen to organize my comments about their unique contributions along empirical, conceptual, and clinical lines. Instead of critiquing the Rapaport and Holt systems separately, as I did previously (Kleiger, 1999), I discuss some of the similarities and differences in their study and assessment of disordered thinking on the Rorschach.

Empirical foundations

The underlying methodological problems, glaring statistical errors, and lack of a normative database have been easy, albeit appropriate, targets for critics of the Rapaport System and Rorschach research in general (Goldfried, Stricker, & Weiner

1971; Exner, 1974, 1986, 1993; Wood et al., 2003). Even Rapaport, Gill, and Schafer (1946/1968) recognized the "gross" and preliminary nature of their study, acknowledging that it was not their "claim that the following pages present a complete explanation or systematization of final validity of the material we have excerpted" (p. 425). Holt, in his Editor's Foreword to the revised edition of *Diagnostic Psychological Testing* (Rapaport et al., 1946/1968), discussed the methodological deficiencies of the research design in which the Rapaport group's categories of deviant verbalizations were first used. He maintained that simply discrediting the research on methodological or statistical grounds alone missed the easily overshadowed compensating strengths of some of the methodological procedures, such as careful selection of cases, intra-control group comparisons, the quality of test data, and efforts to check trends in the data against the authors' accumulated clinical and theoretical expertise.

In contrast to the dearth of broad empirical grounding of Rapaport's system for coding deviant verbalizations, the empirical support for Holt's Pripro system has been extensive. Studies over a 50-year period have demonstrated that various aspects of the system are reliable and valid measures for identifying disordered or primary process thinking per se and for understanding the degree to which primary process thinking is controlled and available for adaptive use. Thus, studies using the Pripro scoring scheme have gone far beyond its utility as a single measure of deviant thinking and extend to its relationship with cognitive and affective styles, psychopathology, and creativity. In their 2005 edited volume on empirically valid Rorschach systems, Bornstein and Masling (2005) included a chapter on the Pripro written by Holt.

Holt (2009) devoted his second chapter in Volume 1 to the development of the Pripro scoring scheme and the large body of validation research supporting its use primarily as a research instrument. Holt provided a critical summary of over 100 studies from around the world that had demonstrated its utility in testing psychoanalytic concepts and in aiding diagnostic assessments. Holt concluded his first volume with thoughts regarding future research directions for the Pripro.

A large number of studies have contributed to its construct validity. Holt's system has been used in more than ten specific areas of investigation, establishing a relationship between adaptive regression and the thought processes of people who have undergone religious conversion (Allison, 1962; Maupin, 1965); the capacity for cognitive flexibility and coping with cognitive complexity (von Holt et al., 1960; Blatt, Allison, and Feirstein, 1969; Murray and Russ, 1981); creativity and divergent thinking (Cohen, 1960; Pine and Holt, 1960; Russ, 1988); the capacity to tolerate unrealistic experiences (Feirstein, 1967); emotional sensitivity and nonverbal communication (Weiss, 1971); empathic behavior in therapists (Bachrach, 1968); the ability to tolerate sensory deprivation (Goldberger, 1961; Wright and Abbey, 1965; Myers and Kushner, 1970); and teachers' ratings of coping abilities and achievement scores in second and third graders (Russ, 1980, 1988).

It is interesting that the majority of these diverse studies have demonstrated that the capacity to integrate primary process material in a controlled and adaptive manner is associated with an array of positive findings for males but not for females. Male subjects who have controlled access to primary process thinking, as reflected by their Rorschach responses, seem able to deal more effectively with cognitive complexity, to shift problem-solving strategies flexibly, and to demonstrate divergent thinking, which in turn are positively associated with coping and anxiety management ratings. In contrast, the Rorschachs of females who display similar traits of "adaptive regression" in their nontest behavior are marked by large amounts of *undefended* Pripro material.

Despite its impressive literature and empirical support, not all reviews of the Pripro have been consistently positive. In an unpublished book review, DeFife (n.d.) observed that the research in its support has been spotty. Specifically, he noted the low temporal stability coefficients of some of the measures of foundational cognitive structures and that studies relating the Total Pripro Index to measures of creativity and psychopathology yielded contradictory findings. Holt (2009) has acknowledged some of the weaknesses of the Pripro scoring scheme, noting such inconsistencies as part and parcel of behavioral science research.[1] Nevertheless, DeFife opined that the validation work is weaker and more contradictory than Holt has acknowledged. Other reviewers of Holt's 2009 magnum opus have pointed out that many of the studies supporting the validity of the Pripro scoring scheme were based on unpublished dissertations and studies with small sample sizes (Masling, 2011).

At the same time, DeFife concluded that Level 1 scores, representing blatant and unmodulated expressions of primary process ideation, have been meaningfully related to a range of psychopathology. With large effect sizes, Level 1 Pripro scores have been shown to be correlated with measures of depression, psychopathy, emotional instability, childhood tension, and sexual dysfunction, to name but a few.

Conceptual underpinnings

Perhaps more than any of their successors, the systems pioneered by Rapaport and Holt were extraordinary in their conceptual reach. Both Rapaport and Holt were driven by their passionate interests in critiquing, revising, operationalizing, and measuring psychoanalytic concepts. Whereas Rapaport was more theoretician than researcher, Holt embodied the ideals of the scientist–practitioner. What they might have lacked in unequivocal scientific support, they made up for in their use of testing to elaborate and operationalize theoretical concepts and theory to help explain testing phenomena. Both Rapaport and Holt had broad interests that extended far beyond the field of diagnostic testing or the Rorschach. However, both devoted a sizable portion of their careers to studying normal and pathological thought processes. Each viewed the Rorschach as a method to aid in this study.

Rapaport's description of the rationale of the psychological processes underlying Rorschach responses in general, and deviant verbalizations in particular set the stage for generations of psychologists interested in the conceptual underpinnings of Rorschach responses, scores, and test-taking behavior. His concept of "distance from the inkblot" was both a foundational, yet elusive, lynchpin for understanding the response process, thinking, and verbalization on the Rorschach. Reading Rapaport's explanation of this pivotal concept can be confusing because his language could be difficult to grasp. As Holt noted in his 1968 introduction to his revision of Rapaport et al.'s (1946/1968) book, the concept of "distance from the inkblot" created a great deal of uncertainty and frequently led followers to confuse the pathological concepts of increases and losses of distance. In Holt's opinion, their discussion of whether a particular response reflects loss or increase of distance, or both, could be difficult to follow and tended to obfuscate the more meaningful rationale for each scoring category. As discussed earlier, Schuldberg and Boster (1986) organized their study around Rapaport's opaque concept of distance from the blot.

Holt's contributions during his six decades of prolific teaching and research rival those of his mentor and predecessor, leaving one to wonder how Rapaport might have further developed his ideas about thought disorder and the Rorschach had he lived past the age of 49. In any event, such a comparison is fruitless because both men provided a rich conceptual scaffolding for throngs of students—many of whom became teachers—interested in psychodiagnostic testing and the study of thinking.

Following his study of diagnostic psychological testing, Rapaport turned his attention away from the Rorschach and devoted most of his remaining years to developing and organizing the tenets of psychoanalytic ego psychology. Holt's keen interest in Freud's theory of primary and secondary process thinking (Freud, 1900) and Kris's (1952) concept of regression in the service of the ego never strayed far from his mind. Holt's scoring of such concepts as Defense Demand, DE, and Adaptive Regression is among his most important and distinguished contributions. Equally significant is his designation of levels of severity, the degree to which primary process experience is present in either blatant or attenuated forms. The Rapaport approach could have benefited from considering the severity levels of different forms of deviant verbalization. Rapaport's group may have intended something like this when discussing the psychological rationale underlying disturbed responses, but a discussion of levels of severity, if present, was embedded in Rapaport's recondite text. They never developed a way of designating levels of severity in the way that Holt did.

Clinical considerations

Neither Rapaport's nor Holt's scoring schemes are frequently, if ever, taught to students learning about the Rorschach. The Rapaport system (better termed a "method" because of its loosely systemized nature) was one of five competing approaches to the Rorschach prior to Exner's development of the CS (Exner, 1969, 1974). Even before the advent of the CS, the Rapaport method was taught in small pockets of training programs, like the Menninger Clinic or Austen Riggs, where Rapaport had left his mark. The method suffered from weak or nonexistent norms, an unusual administration style (inquiry conducted after each response), and no real way of quantifying scoring data.

Most of us who learned the Rapaport method at an earlier point in our training respect it for what it was: a preliminary attempt to establish some order to what had been an unsystematically evaluated, and often ignored, component of Rorschach testing. Even with its methodological flaws and occasional conceptual lack of clarity, Rapaport, Gill, and Schafer's contribution to scoring and understanding thought disorder on the Rorschach is fundamental and has formed the backbone of all later efforts to measure pathological thinking with the Rorschach.

Undoubtedly, Holt's Pripro scheme offers one of the most comprehensive methods for assessing the quality of thought organization. However, from a usability standpoint, the instrument is enormously difficult and time consuming to learn, and scoring is burdensome. Furthermore, the introduction of new terminology for describing many of the formal aspects of primary process thinking, though consistent with Freudian concepts, may be intimidating to students of the Rorschach. Holt openly acknowledged that the system was laborious and might not be practical in routine clinical assessments. In fairness, Holt never intended his Pripro scoring to be taught as a clinical scoring method. He viewed it primarily as an investigative tool to conceptualize the essential nature of primary and secondary process thinking and to study the manifestations of adaptive and maladaptive regressive thinking. In this regard, no one has yet developed a Rorschach method for measuring disordered thinking that equals his blending of conceptual elegance with scientific scrutiny.

Note

1 Holt was unfamiliar with Defife's unpublished review and could not comment on his critique (Holt, personal communication, June 21, 2016).

References

Allison, J. (1962). Adaptive regression and intense religious experiences. *Journal of Nervous and Mental Disease, 145*, 452–463.

Appelbaum, S. A. (1975). *A Rorschach Test System for Understanding Personality.* Unpublished manuscript, The Menninger Clinic, Topeka, KS.

Arieti, S. (1974). *Interpretation of Schizophrenia* (2nd ed.). New York: Basic Books.

Bachrach, H. (1968). Adaptive regression, empathy, and psychotherapy. *Psychotherapy: Theory, Practice, and Research, 5*, 203–209.

Blatt, S. J., Allison, J., & Feirstein, A. (1969). The capacity to cope with cognitive complexity. *Journal of Personality, 37*, 269–288.

Bornstein, R. F., & Masling, J. M. (Eds.). (2005). *Scoring the Rorschach: Seven Validated Systems.* Mahwah, NJ: Erlbaum.

Cohen, J. H. (1960). An investigation of the relationship between adaptive regression, dogmatism, and creativity using the Rorschach and dogmatism scale. Unpublished doctoral dissertation, Michigan State University.

DeFife, J. A. (n.d.). [Unpublished review of the book *Primary Process Thinking: Theory, Measurement, and Research* (Vols. 1–2)]. Department of Psychology, Emory University. Manuscript submitted to *Psychoanalytic Psychology*.

Exner, J. E. (1969). *The Rorschach Systems*. New York: Grune & Stratton.

Exner, J. E. (1974). *The Rorschach: A Comprehensive System, Basic Foundations* (Vol. 1). New York: Wiley.

Exner, J. E. (1986). *The Rorschach: A Comprehensive System, Basic Foundations* (Vol. 1, 2nd ed.). New York: Wiley.

Exner, J. E. (1993). *The Rorschach: A Comprehensive System, Basic Foundations* (Vol. 1, 3rd ed.). New York: Wiley.

Feirstein, A. (1967). Personality correlates of tolerance for unrealistic experiences. *Journal of Consulting Psychology, 31*, 387–395.

Freud, S. (1900). The Interpretation of Dreams (Standard Edition, 4 & 5). London, UK: Hogarth Press, 1953.

Goldberger, L. (1961). Reactions to perceptual isolation and Rorschach manifestations of the primary process. *Journal of Projective Techniques, 25*, 287–302.

Goldfried, M. R., Stricker, G., & Weiner, I. B. (1971). *Rorschach Handbook of Clinical and Research Application*. Englewood Cliffs, NJ: Prentice-Hall.

Guttman, L. (1968). A general nonmetric technique for finding the smallest coordinate space for a configuration of points. *Psychometrika, 33*, 469–506.

Holt, R. R. (1956). Gauging primary and secondary process in Rorschach responses. *Journal of Projective Techniques, 20*, 14–25.

Holt, R. R. (1967). The development of primary process: A structural view. In R. R. Holt (Ed.), *Motives and Thought: Psychoanalytic Essays in Honor of David Rapaport* (pp. 345–383). New York: International Universities Press.

Holt, R. R. (1970). *Manual for the Scoring of Primary Process Manifestations and Their Controls in Rorschach Responses*. New York: Research Center for Mental Health.

Holt, R. R. (1977). A method for assessing primary process manifestations and their control in Rorschach responses. In M. A. Rickers-Ovsiankina (Ed.), *Rorschach Psychology* (2nd ed., pp. 375–420). New York: Krieger.

Holt, R. R. (1989). *Freud Reappraised: A Fresh Look at Psychoanalytic Theory*. New York: Guilford Press.

Holt, R. R. (2009). *Primary Process Thinking: Theory, Measurement, and Research* (Vols. 1 & 2). Lanham, MD: Aronson.

Holt, R. R., & Havel, J. (1960). A method for assessing primary and secondary process in the Rorschach. In M. A. Rickers-Ovsiankina (Ed.), *Rorschach Psychology*, (pp. 263–318). New York: Wiley.

Kleiger, J. H. (1993). The Enduring Rorschach Contributions of David Rapaport. *Journal of Personality Assessment, 61*, 198–205.

Kleiger, J. H. (1999). *Disordered Thinking and the Rorschach*. Hillsdale, NJ: The Analytic Press.

Klopfer, B. Ainsworth, M., Klopfer, W., & Holt, R. (1954). *Developments in the Rorschach Technique* (Vol. 1). New York: Harcourt, Brace & World.

Kris, E. (1952). *Psychoanalytic Explorations in Art*. New York: International Universities Press.

Lerner, P. (1991). *Psychoanalytic Theory and the Rorschach*. Hillsdale, NJ: The Analytic Press.

Lerner, P. (1998). *Psychoanalytic Perspectives on the Rorschach*. Hillsdale, NJ: The Analytic Press.

Masling, J. (2011). Measuring primary process thinking [Review of *Primary Process Thinking: Theory, Measurement, and Research* (Vols. 1–2)]. Division 39, American Psychological Association. http://www.apadivisions.org/division-39/publications/reviews/primary-process-thinking.aspx.

Maupin, E. W. (1965). Individual differences in response to a Zen meditation exercise. *Journal of Consulting Psychology, 29*, 139–145.

Mayman, M. (1982). *Rorschach Training Manual*. Unpublished manuscript, The Menninger Clinic, Topeka, KS.

Murray, J., & Russ, S. W. (1981). Adaptive regression and types of cognitive flexibility. *Journal of Personality Assessment, 45*, 59–65.

Myers, T., & Kushner, E. N. (1970). Sensory tolerance as a function of primary process defense demand and defense effectiveness. Unpublished manuscript, Naval Research Institute, Bethesda, MD.

Pine, F., & Holt, R. R. (1960). Creativity and primary process: A study of adaptive aggression. *Journal of Abnormal and Social Psychology, 61*, 370–379.

Rapaport, D. (1951). *Organization and Pathology of Thought*. New York: Columbia University Press.

Rapaport, D., Gill, M., & Schafer, R. (1968). *Diagnostic Psychological Testing* (Rev. ed.). R. R. Holt, Ed. New York: International Universities Press. (Original work published in 1946.)

Rorschach, H. (1942). *Psychodiagnostics* (5th ed.). Bern, Switzerland: Hans Huber. (Original work published in 1921.)

Russ, S. W. (1980). Primary process integration on the Rorschach and achievement in children. *Journal of Personality Assessment, 44*, 338–344.

Russ, S. W. (1988). Primary process thinking, divergent thinking, and coping in children. *Journal of Personality Assessment, 52*, 539–549.

Schafer, R. (1948). *The Clinical Application of Psychological Tests*. New York: International Universities Press.

Schafer, R. (1954). *Psychoanalytic Interpretation in Rorschach Testing*. New York: Grune & Stratton.

Schuldberg, D., & Boster, J. S. (1985). Back to Topeka: Two types of distance in Rapaport's original Rorschach thought disorder categories. *Journal of Abnormal Psychology, 94*, 205–215.

Strack, S., & Kinder, B. N. (Eds.) (2006). *Pioneers of Personality Science: Autobiographical Perspectives*. New York: Springer.

von Domarus, E. (1944). The specific laws of logic in schizophrenia. In J. S. Kasnin (Ed.), *Language and Thought in Schizophrenia* (pp. 104–114). New York: Norton.

von Holt, H. W., Sengstake, C. B., Sonoda, B., & Draper, W. A. (1960). Orality, image fusion and concept formation. *Journal of Projective Techniques, 24*, 194–198.

Weiss, R. (1971). A study of some personality correlates of sensitivity to affective meaning. Unpublished doctoral dissertation, New York University.

Wood, J. M., Nezworski, M. T., Lilienfeld, S. O., & Garb, H. N. (2003). *What Is Wrong with the Rorschach? Science Confronts the Controversial Inkblot Test*. New York: Wiley & Sons.

Wright, N., & Abbey, D. (1965). Perceptual deprivation tolerance and adequacy of defenses. *Perceptual & Motor Skills, 20*, 35–38.

Chapter 5

The Thought Disorder Index

Figure 5.1 Philip Holzman.

Recognizing the complexity and continuum nature of thought disorder phenomena, Johnston and Holzman developed the Thought Disorder Index (TDI) as a summary measure of pathological thinking. First introduced in 1975 as part of an unpublished doctoral dissertation (Johnston, 1975), the TDI later formed the basis of a book entitled *Assessing Schizophrenic Thinking* (Johnston & Holzman, 1979), which presented empirical support for the reliability and validity of the TDI. Although the TDI was the product of a great many collaborators, it has chiefly been associated with the name of Philip Holzman, pictured above. Since Holzman's death, research on the TDI has continued under the direction of Dr. Deborah Levy at McLean Hospital in Massachusetts. The most current and comprehensive summary of the impressive body of work associated with the TDI can be found in a chapter by Holzman, Levy, and Johnston (2005) in Bornstein and Masling's *Scoring the Rorschach: Seven Validated Systems.* Their chapter provides a succinct overview of the historical backdrop for understanding and measuring thought disorder, including the need to approach thought disorder as a continuous, versus discrete, binary variable. There is also a convincing restatement of Johnston and Holzman's original response to psycholinguist critics, who have held that language, not thought, is the key variable under consideration when conceptualizing thought disorder (Johnston & Holzman, 1979). Holzman and colleagues (2005) avoided equivocation on this issue, stating clearly, "We adopt the position that language is the medium through which thought is communicated" (p. 61).

Following their review of conceptual issues, Holzman, Johnston, and Levy provided detailed information about the 23 scoring categories, elaborating on the levels of severity and including examples of each scoring category. The authors also presented broad empirical support for the instrument, including summaries of reliability and clinical validity studies. The psychometrics and extensive validity studies of the TDI stand atop the list of recognized Rorschach systems for measuring disordered thinking.

Background of the Thought Disorder Index (TDI)

Taking Rapaport's deviant verbalization categories on the Rorschach as a starting point, Johnston and Holzman looked for a way to quantify the assessment of schizophrenic thought disorder. They found a suitable precedent for quantifying Rapaport's thought disorder categories in the Delta Index, developed almost 25 years earlier by Watkins and Stauffacher (1952). The Delta Index was the first effort to quantify the Rapaport thought disorder categories. Johnston and Holzman applauded the innovative work of their predecessors but felt that the Delta Index was overly narrow in its scope and stated purpose of differentiating schizophrenia from nonschizophrenia subjects.

The Delta Index consisted of 15 scoring categories, three of which were dropped by Johnston and Holzman because they were considered too rare, too difficult to identify reliably, or because the scoring category was not actually an indication of thought disorder (for example, Johnston & Holzman did not consider fabulized responses, deterioration color responses, and mangled or distorted percepts to reflect thought disorder). To the 12 remaining scores of the Delta Index, Johnston and Holzman added eight other categories to capture a wider range of thought disorder phenomena encountered in verbal interactions with psychotic patients: inappropriate distance, word-finding difficulty, clang, perseveration, incongruous combination, looseness, fluidity, and neologisms. Unlike Watkins and Stauffacher, Johnston and Holzman used four, instead of three, weighted levels of severity (.25, .50, .75, and 1.0 as compared with .25, .50, and 1.0 used in the Delta Index). In 1986, Holzman and a group of colleagues at McLean Hospital (Solovay et al., 1986) further refined the scoring categories of the TDI, renaming some categories and adding three additional ones (flippant responses, playful confabulation, and fragmentation), bringing the total number of scoring categories to 23.

Initially, Johnston and Holzman used the TDI to assess thought disorder on verbal subtests of the WAIS in addition to the Rorschach, believing that the less structured subtests of the WAIS and the Rorschach would be equally likely to provide a context for eliciting disordered thinking. Eventually, Holzman and his colleagues (Holzman, Shenton, & Solovay, 1986) concluded that the WAIS was not as rich a context for eliciting thought disorder as the Rorschach. Although most contemporary studies involving the TDI use the Rorschach only, some researchers have scored deviant thinking using the WAIS-R and WISC-R (Armstrong, Silberg, & Parente, 1986; Harris, 1993; Skelton, Boik, & Madero, 1995).

Thought Disorder Index (TDI) scoring

Johnston and Holzman (1979) established reliability and validity for the TDI based on the Rapaport method of Rorschach administration, which requires the Inquiry to be conducted after each card. This is a key issue, which, as described later, has limited the clinical utility of the TDI. Johnston and Holzman also restricted the number of responses to five or six per card after Card I, for which the subject was allowed to give as many responses as desired, and inquired extensively about each deviant Rorschach response. The Rorschach administration was tape recorded in order to provide a complete verbatim record of the subjects' verbalizations. The transcript was scored using the TDI by trained raters who were blind to group membership.

Johnston and Holzman (1979) recommended that multiple scores could be assigned to a single response. This recommendation was further clarified in the 1986 revision of the scoring manual (Solovay et al., 1986), which specified that scorers should "tag" the category that best captures the pathological process most characteristic of the response. More than one category of thought disorder should be scored only when there are distinct and qualitatively discrete kinds of thought slippage within the same response. For example, a response may contain an incongruous or fabulized combination, but if this is part of a confabulation only the confabulation is scored. If the subject also produces other types of thought disorder that are not part of the combinatory process, such as a peculiar verbalization, then the other processes are scored as well.

Because many of the scoring categories seemed to exist along a continuum of severity, Johnston and Holzman used Schafer's (1948, 1954) "tendency" designation for responses that did not quite reach scoring threshold. These "tendency" scores are weighted at a level just below the standard score. For example, a full confabulation is weighted at the .75 severity level, whereas a confabulation tendency would be given a .50 weighting. TDI categories at the mildest severity level (.25) are not scored at the tendency level.

Like the Delta Index, the mildest instances of thought disorder are given the lowest weight (.25); moderate to severe instances receive intermediate weights

(.50 or .75); and the most severe instances are given the highest weight (1.0). The Total TDI score is derived by summing the product of each severity level and the number of thought-disordered responses at that level, dividing by the number of Rorschach responses and multiplying by 100.

Many of the 23 scoring categories include subcategories that further refine the principal category. The authors emphasized the heuristic value of these subcategories, which were not meant to be scored separately. In fact, Johnston and Holzman indicated that a number of these subcategories could not be reliably distinguished from one another. The 23 scoring categories, at four levels of severity, are briefly summarized below.

.25 level

The mildest severity level is reserved for minor instances of thought slippage that may go unnoticed in conversation. There is little interpretative significance attached to scores at this level unless such instances are unusually frequent or malignant. Categories included at the .25 level are the most frequently scored examples of thought deviance in all subjects, including acutely psychotic individuals, and, as such, the most reliably scored categories.

1 Inappropriate Distance. Based on Rapaport's concept of "distance" (Rapaport, Gill, & Schafer, 1946/1968), this category includes five subscores that refer to the perceptual and ideational "distance" that separates a subject and the inkblots. (a) "Loss or increase of distance." A subject may lose distance from Card I and say, "Oh God! That looks like a werewolf; I don't want to look at it because it scares the hell out of me!" Here, the inkblot loses its symbolic property and is taken as a literal depiction of something so threatening that it evokes an emotional response. Conversely, another subject may demonstrate an increase of distance on the same card and respond, "That looks like a werewolf. Wow! Werewolves make me think of that creepy movie with all those people changing into creatures and going after people; it just gave me the creeps!" In this case, the subject's emotional reaction is triggered by increasingly distant and personalized associations to the original response. (b) "Excessive qualification," based on Rapaport's "exactness verbalization" score, refers to those occasions in which the subject's rigid perfectionism intrudes into the response. The subject may appear troubled that the inkblot does not perfectly resemble the image he or she had in mind. (c) "Concreteness." Here again the inkblot is taken as a literal depiction of reality as the subject fails to take the distance necessary to represent the inkblot symbolically. (d) "Overspecificity." Although similar to excessive qualification responses, the overspecificity response involves an arbitrary and irrelevant specification of details that ruins the response. According to the Holzman research group (Coleman, personal communication, June 1992), these responses are rare and may approach the level of absurdity because the

subject's attempt to be overly precise gives the response a bizarre quality. (e) "Syncretistic response." Whereas overspecificity involves the inclusion of inappropriate detail, syncretistic responses tend to be inappropriately abstract and overinclusive.

2 Flippant Responses. Flippant responses were added to the scoring system in the 1986 revision to capture those instances in which the subject interjects inappropriately humorous, sexually tinged, or sarcastic remarks that reflect a lack of seriousness regarding the task.

3 Vagueness. According to the Holzman group (Coleman and Levy, personal communication, June 1992), vague responses tend to be relatively rare. They are characterized by a poverty of expressed meaning in the response. Subjects who deliver vague responses have trouble elaborating any clear percept or may give a response without stating clearly what they are seeing.

4 Peculiar Verbalizations and Responses. The revised TDI scoring manual describes three subtypes of peculiar responses/verbalizations: (a) "Peculiar expressions," characterized by odd combinations of words within a phrase, resulting in redundant, contradictory, incongruous, or inappropriate verbal expression. Most listeners will hear the odd quality of these expressions, but will be able to comprehend what the subject is trying to convey. (b) "Stilted and inappropriate expression," including awkward, overly intellectualized, or pseudo-scientific terms or expressions that have a stilted and wooden quality. Again, the meaning may not be lost, but the phrasing is distracting. (c) "Inappropriate word usage" includes odd word substitutions or inappropriate metonymy.

5 Word-Finding Difficulty. Subjects merit this score if they give two wrong words before producing the correct word or clearly state that they know the word but are not able to think of it. To give this score, the examiner must be clear that the difficulty is not just due to simple lack of knowledge.

6 Clangs. This comparatively rare scoring category, described also in the Pripro, applies to responses in which the subject's verbalization is based on the sound rather than the meaning of the word.

7 Perseveration. Overvalent ideas that linger across cards and compulsively intrude into consecutive responses reflect a perseverative process. To be scored, the same poor Form Quality response must be given on at least three cards.

8 Incongruous Combinations. Johnston and Holzman incorporated four subtypes into the TDI. (a) "Composite response" (also taken from the Pripro) in which parts from two or more percepts are unrealistically combined to make a hybrid creature or object. (b) "Arbitrary form–color response," scored when the subject does not seem to be aware of or concerned by the inappropriate combination of form and color. (c) "Inappropriate activity response," in which the condensation occurs between an object and an activity that is incongruously ascribed to it. (d) "External–internal responses," which were given a severity rating of .50 because they reflect a more extreme manifestation of strained reasoning.

.50 level of severity

Whereas responses scored at the .25 level may occur in the records of normal individuals (especially under conditions of stress, anxiety, or fatigue), responses at the .50 level convey increasingly odd thinking not typically found in nonpsychotic individuals. Eight scores are represented at this level of severity.

9. Relationship Verbalization. Relationship verbalizations occur rarely on the Rorschach (Coleman, personal communication, June 1992). In order to be scored, the subject must make it clear that the new response is connected with a response given earlier.
10. Idiosyncratic Symbolism. In the revised scoring manual, the criterion for scoring this category requires only that the subject deliver the idiosyncratic symbolization response with conviction and without awareness of its inappropriateness. Two subtypes are specified: (a) "Color symbolism," scored only when color is interpreted symbolically in an odd or bizarre manner, and (b) "Image symbolism," scored when concrete images or spatial details are treated as symbolic representations of abstract ideas in a strained and bizarre-sounding manner.
11. Queer Responses. Whereas peculiar verbalizations may be overlooked or go unnoticed in everyday speech, queer responses strike the listener as odd and difficult to comprehend. A useful rule of thumb for distinguishing between these two is that peculiar responses include real words that are used inappropriately or awkwardly but convey meaning that the listener can grasp, whereas queer responses include real words whose meaning is unclear or made-up words whose meaning is clear. There are three subtypes of queer responses in the TDI: (a) "Queer expressions" are those in which the subject uses an extremely odd expression with a sense of certainty and conviction, but the listener does not know what the subject means. (b) "Queer imagery" is scored when the image, as opposed to the verbal expression, is bizarre and hard to understand. Examples might include images such as "glorified rain," "the intestines of the tunnel," or "colorful numbers." The words are unremarkable by themselves; however, the image depicted makes little sense. (c) "Queer word misusage" involves more extreme versions of idiosyncratic word usage that leave the listener uncertain what the respondent means.
12. Confusion. Unlike other pathological forms of verbalization, the listener/scorer's confusion is not relevant for scoring Confusion responses. Instead, it is the subject who conveys confusion in his or her experience of the inkblot and/or what is seen.
13. Looseness. Holt's formal category of displacement included scores that pertained to degrees of associative looseness. Johnston and Holzman refined Holt's ideas and introduced the looseness category to describe a loss of cognitive focus, in which the subject's associations depart from the task at hand and become tangential or irrelevant.

14. Fabulized Combinations. This well-known score represents unrealistic relationships that are attributed to two or more separate objects on the basis of spatial contiguity.
15. Playful Confabulation. A less severe variant of confabulation responses, playful confabulations have a whimsical or fanciful quality. The percepts show good form level, but they are embellished in a playful and humorous way that reflects greater control over the ideational process than occurs in a confabulation.
16. Fragmentation. Organizational and integrative failures occur rarely but may be found in the records of patients with right cortical damage (Kestenbaum-Daniels et al., 1988). Fragmentation may occur when a subject is unable to verbalize spontaneously an integration of several details into a coherent perceptual whole. For example, a subject might say about Card III, "I see legs here, and these could be arms, I guess, maybe feet or shoes at the bottom" without being able to integrate these disparate parts into a whole object, in this case a human figure.

.75 level of severity

The Holzman group viewed scores at the .75 level as clear indications of disturbances in thinking that usually reflect a psychotic experience. Wild combinatory thinking, unstable and absurd ideas, and severely strained logic are characteristic of the four response categories at the .75 level.

17. Fluidity. Fluid responses are rare scores that may be viewed as the perceptual counterpart of associative looseness. Fluidity is scored when the subject indicates that one percept is changing into something else. Additionally, an inability to remember or locate a previously described percept may be scored as fluid because it appears that the percept has disappeared and cannot be found again.
18. Absurd Responses. By definition, absurd responses are necessarily scored at a minus-form-level and reflect psychotic experience. The absurd response may not sound bizarre in content or syntax, but essentially it has no discernible objective support in the inkblot, even though it is quite specific.
19. Confabulation. Johnston and Holzman retained this Rapaport term to depict responses that demonstrated excessive distance from the task primarily through extravagant embellishment. Both the DW response and the overembellished response are included in the TDI. Johnston and Holzman distinguish a full confabulation (.75) from a confabulation-tendency (.50) response on the basis of how extreme the associative elaboration is and the extent to which the response has any grounding in the inkblot.
20. Autistic Logic. This requires an explicit statement of illogical reasoning, often signaled by expressions such as "because" or "it must be."

1.0 level of severity

Some researchers have found 1.0-level responses, rarest of all responses, to occur in less than three percent of Rorschach records (Koistinen, 1995). Although there are only three scores at this level, each has been considered as almost pathognomonic of a psychotically severe disturbance in thinking and appreciation of the tenets of reality.

21 Contamination. Found in all scoring systems since Rorschach (1921/1942), contamination is scored when at least two distinct percepts are merged into a single, bizarre-sounding response.
22 Incoherence. Taken from Rapaport's original list, the incoherent response is impossible for the listener to comprehend and may even be considered unrelated to the task. These responses have a "word salad" quality.
23 Neologisms are newly coined words that may be the result of verbal condensation. To be scored, it must be clear that the subject lacks the critical capacity to observe the inappropriateness of the invented word. These scorable neologisms contrast with the kind of creative word-play that one finds in the "night language" of James Joyce, where purposefulness, control, and clever, subtle meaning distinguish such efforts from those reflecting a psychotic process. The subject of creative word-play harkens back to Holt's concept of adaptive regression.

Psychometric properties: Reliability, normative, and validity studies

Reliability

Holzman and colleagues (2005) summarized challenges related to establishing reliability with the TDI. They used the term "dialipsis" to denote the variable nature of thought disorder, especially as it occurs in subjects with schizophrenia. Dialipsis, which the researchers referred to as "our own intentional neologism" (p. 72), denotes the intermittent disruptions in performance from what is regularly expected. Because thought disorder will not emerge on each card of the Rorschach, split-half reliabilities of internal consistency may not always reflect adequate reliability of the TDI. However, despite this caveat, Johnston and Holzman (1979) found a statistically significant split-half correlation of .78 with a group of 49 subjects diagnosed with schizophrenia.

In the original reliability studies, Johnston and Holzman (1979) based their inter-rater reliability data on the ratings of two independent scorers who achieved agreement on Total TDI scores based on the Rorschach Pearson product-moment correlations ranging from .82 (controls) to .90 (schizophrenia patients) and .93 (nonpsychotic patients). Inter-rater reliability was slightly lower for TDI scores based on data from the WAIS.

Using only TDI scores based on the Rorschach, Solovay, Shenton, and Holzman (1987) conducted a comparative study of thought disorder using the

TDI and reported two-scorer inter-rater reliabilities of .89 for Total TDI score (with a Spearman-Brown correction), .81 for individual scoring categories, .79 for levels of severity, and coefficients ranging from .84 to .89 for factor structure scores (for four factor groupings).

Four teams of raters from the McLean Psychology Research Laboratory and Hillside Hospital (Coleman et al., 1993) conducted a comprehensive inter-rater reliability study on a variety of features of TDI scoring, including Total TDI score, severity levels, and qualitative factors. The intra-class correlation among the four teams was .74 for Total TDI scores, and the Spearman rank correlations between the different rating teams ranged from .81 to .90 ($p < .01$). In comparing ratings across different severity levels, intra-class correlations ranged from .72 (.25 level) to .77 (.50 and .75 levels). Scores at the 1.0 level of severity were too rare to be assessed.

Using factor groupings of TDI categories, Coleman et al. (1993) reported that rating teams achieved average intra-class correlations of .86 on the irrelevant intrusions factor, .76 on the combinatory thinking factor, and .58 on the idiosyncratic verbalizations factor. All comparisons of the rating teams yielded correlations at the .02 or .01 level of significance.

In comparing the mean Total TDI derived by each team, Coleman's group found different thresholds between teams in "tagging" thought disorder. Teams generally agreed about whether a record was thought disordered and about the ranking of the amount of thought disorder in a record relative to other records, but absolute scores for the total amount of thought disorder often differed.

Other reliability findings are worth noting. Arboleda and Holzman (1985) demonstrated adequate inter-rater reliabilities between two teams' Total TDI scores of severity levels in a sample of children and adolescents. Carpenter, Strauss and Muleh (1993) studied inter-rater reliabilities between 4- and 10-card Rorschach protocols and found highly significant correlations, suggesting that the 4-card forms yield highly adequate composite indexes of Total TDI, severity levels, and serve to identify more frequently occurring qualitative scores. Finally, in a large Finnish study ($N = 583$), Koistinen (1995) found statistically significant inter-rater reliabilities between two teams of raters, each scoring 59 Rorschachs, quite similar to those found in previous studies by the McLean research group.

Normative base

Johnston and Holzman found that Total TDI scores were not related to the sex, ethnicity, or socioeconomic status of the subjects. It is not surprising, however, that they found that TDI scores based on responses to verbal subtests of the WAIS were negatively correlated with IQ. In a separate study, Haimo and Holzman (1979) found that the TDI was a valid measure for assessing disordered thinking, distinguishing it from subcultural language patterns in nonwhites from lower socioeconomic groups. Total TDI scores accurately differentiated schizophrenia patients and parents of schizophrenia patients from normal controls in both Black and Caucasian subjects.

A number of researchers have attempted to establish cutoff scores on the TDI that would correctly identify psychotic individuals. Edell (1987) found that a cutoff of 9.0 discriminated between normal controls and psychiatric patients, but that this cutoff incorrectly identified 25 percent of the normals as psychiatric patients. Koistinen (1995) set out to establish a cutoff point that would distinguish healthy subjects from psychiatric patients; however, he also was unable to achieve such a cutoff. Thus far, efforts to establish cutoff points have not been terribly useful because the sensitivity and specificity of these cutoffs have yielded unacceptably high false negatives and false positives.

Johnston and Holzman (1979) reported that their normal control group had a mean Total TDI score of 4.46. A later sample of normal controls had a mean TDI total of 5.9 (Holzman, Shenton, & Solovay, 1986). Among Edell's (1987) normal controls, the average TDI score was 6.1. In a large sample of Finnish subjects, Koistinen (1995) found a higher mean TDI of 11.7 in healthy subjects but concluded that his group of normal controls was more heterogeneous and did not screen out subjects with minor cognitive deficits or psychopathology.

Arboleda and Holzman (1985) established norms for a sample of 79 normal children and found that the mean TDI scores decreased with age. They found that children aged 5 to 6 (n = 16) had a Total TDI mean of 9.30, children 8 to 10 (n = 23) had a mean of 9.42, 11- to 13-year-olds (n = 22) had a mean of 7.78, and 14- to 16-year-olds (n = 18) had mean TDI scores of 5.34.

Several of the Holzman research group have established a rough hierarchy of severity for different TDI totals (Coleman and Levy, personal communication, June 1992). Scores of 0 to 10 suggest low thought disorder, 11 to 16 suggest mild thought disorder, 17 to 22 suggest moderate thought disorder, and 22+ reflect severe levels of thought disorder.

Factor-analytic studies

In order to study the qualitative features of various forms of thought disorder, Holzman and colleagues looked at four sets of TDI factors that were derived by different statistical methods (Johnston & Holzman, 1979; Holzman, Shenton, & Solovay, 1986; Shenton, Solovay, & Holzman, 1987; Solovay, Shenton, & Holzman, 1987). Johnston and Holzman originally arranged scoring categories into four factors on an a priori basis, according to what made sense conceptually. Then, using a principal-components analysis with a variance maximization rotation, the researchers derived a second set of factors using 97 psychotic patients. Six conceptually meaningful factors emerged from this analysis, each with eigenvalues greater than 1.0. These factors were named Combinatory Thinking, Idiosyncratic Verbalization, Autistic Thinking, Fluid Thinking, Absurdity, and Confusion. Holzman and his colleagues referred to this classification as the "empiric factors," which are presented in Table 5.1.

Table 5.1 Principal component (empiric) classification of TDI categories

Factor	Categories (Loading)	Eigenvalue
Combinatory Thinking	Playful Confabulation (.83) Incongruous Combination (.60) Flippant Responses (.58) Fabulized Combination (.53)	2.11
Idiosyncratic Verbalization	Peculiar Responses (.83) Queer Responses (.69)	4.06
Autistic Verbalization	Autistic Logic (.79) Incoherence (.72)	2.04
Fluid Thinking	Fluidity (.71) Contamination (.69)	1.53
Absurdity	Neologism (.86) Absurd (.49)	1.24
Confusion	Vagueness (.76) Confusion (.76)	1.18

Source: Holzman, P. S., Shenton, M. E., & Solovay, M. R. (1986), Quality of thought disorder in differential diagnosis. *Schizophrenia Bulletin*, 12, 360–371. Reprinted by permission of Oxford University Press.

A third classification, referred to as post hoc factors, was derived from the TDI categories that best differentiated manic from schizophrenic patients. The post hoc factors were called Irrelevant Intrusions, Combinatory Thinking, Fluid Thinking, Confusion, and Idiosyncratic Verbalizations.

Validation studies

Readers are directed to Holzman, Levy, and Johnston (2005) for a concise summary of the scope of clinical validation studies of the TDI. Studies have included (1) differential diagnosis of psychotic disorders, including schizophrenia-spectrum disorders, mania, and schizoaffective disorder; (2) thought disorder in nonpsychotic relatives of psychotic individuals; (3) TDI in children with psychosis risk and adolescent-onset psychosis; (4) thought disorder associated with right hemispheric brain impairment; and (5) effects of medication on TDI scores. Findings from the corpus of these investigations appear in later chapters that focus on negative signs of thought disorder, differential diagnosis of psychotic thought disorder, and assessment of disordered thinking in children and adolescents.

Final thoughts about the Thought Disorder Index (TDI)

As with other instruments, I focus my review on the empirical, conceptual, and clinical contributions and shortcomings of the TDI.

Empirical foundations

Developed over 35 years ago, the TDI is recognized as a robust research tool for studying and assessing varieties of disordered thinking. From a scientific perspective, the TDI occupies a unique position atop the hierarchy of Rorschach methods for studying and measuring disordered thinking. The breadth of solid psychometric support and the clinical validity of the TDI as a research tool is truly impressive. However, what distinguishes the TDI from other instruments is the orientation of those researchers who pioneered its use and application. Although Holzman was a student of Rapaport's at Menninger and a trained psychoanalyst, he was an avid and prolific psychopathology researcher. His team of collaborators, though clinically trained, are known chiefly for their contributions as psychopathology researchers, not as clinical practitioners. In this respect, they followed in the empiricist footsteps of Hermann Rorschach. It is interesting that Holzman, Levy, and Johnston (2005) tipped their hats to Rorschach's "psychological experiment" when summarizing the scope of research contributions of the TDI (p. 89).

Another indication of the scientific DNA of the TDI is to see where the bulk of the studies were published. The major studies can be found in journals like *Schizophrenia Bulletin*, *Archives of General Psychiatry*, *Biological Psychiatry*, and *Schizophrenia Research*. In addition, a smaller number of seminal studies by Holzman group members can be found in psychology journals like *Journal of Abnormal Psychology* (Coleman, Levy, & Lenzenweger, 1996) and *Psychological Assessment* (Coleman et al., 1993), both known for their empirical versus clinical orientation. Thus, it is safe to conclude that the TDI was intended to be a research instrument first and a clinical method second.

A final sign that the TDI is fundamentally a research tool is how it has been used as a metric in an array of investigations into brain morphology, neurophysiology, and genetic linkage of schizophrenia and other psychotic conditions (Gooding et al., 2012). Holzman, Levy, and Johnston (2005) summarized the international scope of these research probes. However, despite TDI's preeminence from a research perspective, studies using the TDI have decreased as psychosis researchers have shifted their attention away from thought disorder to other phenomena such as social and cognitive impairment in schizophrenia and other psychoses.

Conceptual underpinnings

One potential conceptual shortcoming of the TDI concerns the manner in which scores are assigned to different levels of severity. The basis of assignment was not empirically founded and is not always conceptually clear. Wahlberg (1994) agreed with Holzman's (1978) earlier comment that the TDI may construct an artificial continuum of thought disorder by assuming a linear relationship between certain scores at different levels of severity. Athey, Colson, and Kleiger (1993) suggested that the distinctions between the levels of severity themselves are not always consistent with the nature of the scores contained within each level. Each level assumes a measure of homogeneity of severity for all scores within that level, which may not always be the case. For example, a severe incongruous combination such as "a bat with landing gears" would be weighted the same as a mild peculiar verbalization such as "that looks like a hornlike construction on its head." Because the TDI does not recognize varying levels of severity within a particular scoring category (with the exception of noting when there is a tendency to a certain score), both responses would receive a score of .25. However, most people would agree that the first sounds qualitatively more bizarre.

Other researchers have questioned whether each of the individual categories of thought disorder scores exists as a unitary entity or should include a severity continuum. As indicated above, by placing all examples of a particular scoring category within the same severity level, an assumption is made as to the unitary nature of these responses. In other words, the TDI assumes that all incongruous combinations are of equal severity, that all fabulized combinations are .50, and that all contaminations are at the 1.0 level of severity. It is reasonable to consider the possibility that some types of incongruous combinations are more common in normal records (i.e. those that are playful and popular), while others have a more malignant quality and are found primarily in the records of psychotic patients.

Other researchers have argued for a different weighting of several items on the scale (Wahlberg, 1994; Koistinen, 1995). Wahlberg suggested that a more suitable weighting for incongruous combinations would be .50 because of their basic similarity with fabulized combinations. In contrast, Blatt, Tuber, and Auerbach (1990) argued that an incongruous combination marks a more severe disturbance and fabulized combination should be considered more like a contamination tendency. However, it seems that this is more of an empirical question that may be answered in part by examining the frequency with which these responses occur in nonpsychotic and normal records. We know from Johnston and Holzman's original study that incongruous combinations occur more frequently in the records of normal and nonpsychotic subjects than do either fabulized combinations or contaminations. Likewise, Exner (1991) found that incongruous combinations occurred more frequently in the records of 700 nonpatient adults than did fabulized combinations. These findings suggest that most incongruous combinations are the less serious manifestation of disordered thinking and that the lower severity level assigned to them may indeed be appropriate.

Koistinen (1995) also raised questions about the weighting of individual items on the TDI. He presented empirical data to support his contention that perseveration responses should receive a higher weighting by showing that subjects with schizophrenia-spectrum disorders had the highest scores on the perseveration item. In concluding that perseveration is a typical score of subjects with schizophrenia (and of high-risk adoptees with schizophrenic mothers), Koistinen suggested that perseveration scores should be given a weighting of .75. However, Levy (personal communication, December 1997) refuted this contention (see Kleiger, 1999).

The TDI (and nearly all Rorschach thought disorder scoring systems, for that matter) lacks anything like Holt's detailed effort to operationalize control and defense variables. Thus, the TDI offers no method of systematically evaluating either the subject's conscious or latent awareness that the material contained in the response is inappropriate or his or her efforts to modulate the way it is expressed and communicated to the examiner. By not doing so, the scope of the TDI is limited to measuring a single component of ego impairment—the absolute presence, quantity, and type of thought disorder—while giving little systematic consideration to concomitant ego resources and controls that may modulate the negative impact of the absolute elevation of a given TDI score. In fairness to the developers, however, their task was by design more limited in scope than that of Holt. Their intention was not to devise a comprehensive system for studying the conceptual nature of primary and secondary process thinking but to develop a reliable and valid measure of thought disorder. Nonetheless, it is possible that applying something like Holt's DE rating scale to TDI protocols would help identify important differences in adaptive and pathological regression in subjects with similarly high TDI scores.

If by conceptual underpinnings one is referring only to how scoring systems or thought disorder categories link up with theoretical constructs, specifically those that are psychological or psychoanalytic in nature, then the TDI has little to offer. Although he received psychoanalytic training, Holzman, like Rorschach, did not imbue his research findings with psychoanalytic concepts. In this respect, he differed with his predecessors Rapaport and Holt. Holzman's interest lay in developing an empirically sound metric for identifying and quantifying different forms of thought disorder. Unlike Rapaport and Holt, he was not interested in developing an overarching theory or forming linkages to existing theories of thought organization. However, when Holzman addressed underlying conceptual issues having to do with the nature of thought versus language disorders he did so with clarity and simplicity.

Lest we slight the TDI for its relative lack of conceptual underpinning, we need to consider the audience that the developers of the TDI were addressing: neuroscientists rather than clinicians or psychoanalysts. What the TDI might lack in underlying psychological explication of its different scores, it more than makes up for by its probative research into concepts regarding the neurobiological and genetic foundations of schizophrenia and other psychoses.

Clinical considerations

Despite its empirical sturdiness and scientific contributions, the TDI has never gained ascendancy as a clinical diagnostic instrument. Although its developers used the TDI in clinical hospital consultations to aid in differential diagnostic decisions, it has never been a mainstay instrument widely available to clinicians. This cannot be leveled as a criticism, because, in all fairness and accuracy, it was never intended to be such. Researchers learned about the TDI by attending specialized training sessions provided by members of the Holzman team, most notably Deborah Levy and Michael Coleman. In these multi-day sessions, participants learned the basis of the scoring system and practiced coding stacks of Rorschach responses until they achieved an acceptable level of inter-rater reliability with the Holzman team. To my knowledge, the TDI was never offered as a workshop for assessment psychologists interested in learning a new method for scoring thought disorder on the Rorschach. Likewise, one will not gain access to the TDI through conventional publishers of psychological tests. Information about the TDI is available only in scientific publications and journals.

Another difficulty in using the TDI in routine clinical assessments has to do with the basis of Rorschach administration on which the TDI is scored. As mentioned earlier, Holzman and his group followed the Rapaport–Menninger tradition, conducting the Inquiry following each card. In doing so, they departed from contemporary conventions in Rorschach methodology. Their administrative purity in following the Rapaport method further eliminated the TDI from the clinical mainstream, as the majority of Rorshachers follow the Contemporary System or the more recent R-PAS approach.

Finally, like Holt's Pripro, the TDI is not easily accessible to those interested in learning the system. Although less intricate and easier to learn than the Holt system, potential TDI users must invest significant time in mastering the scoring, which can be difficult and time consuming. While inter-rater reliability has been shown to be high, raters may be discouraged to find that their reliability for rating individual responses tends to be much lower than their rating for levels of severity or the Total TDI score. Many contemporary psychosis researchers find the scoring system cumbersome and time consuming and have opted for interview techniques or global clinical rating scales like the BPRS to assess thought disorder (Andreasen, 1979a, 1979b; Harrow & Quinlan, 1985; Marengo et al., 1986).

In summary, the TDI is an empirically sound instrument that recognizes the complexity of thought disorder. Even the most ardent critics of the Rorschach (Wood et al., 2003) have recognized the validity of the TDI in measuring psychotic symptoms like thought disorder. Many regard the TDI as the touchstone of Rorschach-based thought disorder scoring systems. Regardless of where one places it in the ranks of specialized Rorschach scoring methods, the TDI has clearly advanced our understanding and contributed mightily to the scientific study and clinical assessment of disordered thinking.

References

Andreasen, D. B. (1979a). Thought, language, and communication disorders: I. Clinical assessment, definition of terms, and evaluation of their reliability. *Archives of General Psychiatry*, *36*, 1315–1321.

Andreasen, D. B. (1979b). Thought, language, and communication disorders: II. Diagnostic significance. *Archives of General Psychiatry*, *36*, 1325–1330.

Arboleda, C., & Holzman, P. S. (1985). Thought disorder in children at risk for psychosis. *Archives of General Psychiatry, 42*, 1004–1013.

Armstrong, J., Silberg, J. L., & Parente, F. J. (1986). Patterns of thought disorder on psychological testing: Implications for adolescent psychopathology. *Journal of Nervous and Mental Diseases, 174*, 448–454.

Athey, G. I., Colson, D., & Kleiger, J. H. (1993). *Manual for Scoring Thought Disorder on the Rorschach*. Unpublished manuscript, The Menninger Clinic, Topeka, KS.

Blatt, S. J., Tuber, S. B., & Auerbach, J. S. (1990). Representation of interpersonal interactions on the Rorschach and level of psychopathology. *Journal of Personality Assessment, 54*, 711–728.

Carpenter, W. T., Strauss, J. S., & Muleh, S. (1993). Are there pathognomonic symptoms in schizophrenia: An empiric investigation of Schneider's first-rank symptoms. *Archives of General Psychiatry, 28*, 847–852.

Coleman, M. J., Carpenter, J. T., Waternaux, C., Levy, D. L., Shenton, M. E., Perry, J., Medoff, D., Wong, H., Monoach, D., Meyer, P., O'Brian, C., Valentino, C., Robinson, D., Smith, M., Makowski, D., & Holzman, P. S. (1993). The thought disorder index: A reliability study. *Psychological Assessment, 5*, 336–342.

Coleman, M. J., Levy, D. L., & Lenzenweger, M. F. (1996). Thought disorder, perceptual aberrations, and schizotypy. *Journal of Abnormal Psychology, 105*, 501–511.

Edell, W. (1987). Role of structure in disordered therapy in borderline and schizophrenia disorders. *Journal of Personality Assessment, 51*, 23–41.

Exner, J. E. (1991). *The Rorschach: A Comprehensive System, Advanced Interpretation* (Vol. 2, 2nd ed.). New York: Wiley.

Gooding, D. C., Coleman, M. J., Roberts, S. A., Shenton, M. E., Levy, D. L., & Erlenmeyer-Kimling, L. (2012) Thought disorder in offspring of schizophrenic parents: Findings from the New York high-risk project. *Schizophrenia Bulletin, 38*, 263–271.

Haimo, S. F., & Holzman, P. S. (1979). Thought disorder in schizophrenics and normal controls: Social class and race differences. *Journal of Consulting and Clinical Psychology, 47*, 963–967.

Harris, O. (1993). The prevalence of thought disorder in personality-disordered outpatients. *Journal of Personality Assessment, 61*, 112–120.

Harrow, M., & Quinlan, D. (1985). *Disordered Thinking and Schizophrenic Psychopathology.* New York: Garden Press.

Holzman, P. S. (1978). Cognitive impairment and cognitive stability: Towards a theory of thought disorder. In G. Serban (Ed.), *Cognitive Defects in the Development of Mental Illness*, (pp. 361–376). New York: Brunner/Mazel.

Holzman, P.S., Levy, D.L., & Johnston, M. H. (2005). The use of the Rorschach technique for assessing formal thought disorder. In R. F. Bornstein and J. M. Masling (Eds.), *Scoring the Rorschach: Seven Validated Systems*. Mahwah, NJ: Erlbaum.

Holzman, P. S., Shenton, M. E., & Solovay, M. R. (1986), Quality of thought disorder in differential diagnosis. *Schizophrenia Bulletin, 12*, 360–371.

Johnston, M. H. (1975). Thought disorder in schizophrenics and their relatives. Unpublished doctoral dissertation, University of Chicago, IL.

Johnston, M. H., & Holzman, P. S. (1979). *Assessing Schizophrenic Thinking*. San Francisco, CA: Jossey-Bass.

Kestenbaum-Daniels, E., Shenton, M. E., Holzman, P. S., Benowitz, L. I., Coleman, M., Levin, S., & Levine, D. (1988). Patterns of thought disorder associated with right cortical damage, schizophrenia, and mania. *American Journal of Psychiatry, 145*, 944–949.

Kleiger, J. H. (1999). *Disordered Thinking and the Rorschach.* Hillsdale, NJ: The Analytic Press.

Koistinen, P. (1995). *Thought Disorder and the Rorschach.* Oulu, Finland: Oulun Yliopistd.

Marengo, J. T., Harrow, M., Lanin-Lettering, I., & Wilson, A. (1986). Evaluating bizarre-idiosyncratic thinking: A comprehensive index of positive thought disorder. *Schizophrenia Bulletin, 12,* 497–509.

Rapaport, D., Gill, M., & Schafer, R. (1968). *Diagnostic Psychological Testing* (Rev. ed.). R. R. Holt, Ed. New York: International Universities Press. (Original work published in 1946.)

Rorschach, H. (1942). *Psychodiagnostics* (5th ed.). Bern, Switzerland: Hans Huber. (Original work published in 1921.)

Schafer, R. (1948). *The Clinical Application of Psychological Tests.* New York: International Universities Press.

Schafer, R. (1954). *Psychoanalytic Interpretation in Rorschach Testing.* New York: Grune & Stratton.

Shenton, M. E., Solovay, M. R., & Holzman, P. (1987). Comparative studies of thought disorders: II. Schizoaffective disorder. *Archives of General Psychiatry, 44,* 21–30.

Skelton, M. O., Boik, R. J., & Madero, J. N. (1995). Thought disorder on the WAIS-R relative to the Rorschach: Assessing identity-disordered adolescents. *Journal of Personality Assessment, 65,* 533–549.

Solovay, M. R., Shenton, M. E., Gasperetti, C., Coleman, M., Kestenbaum, E., Carpenter, T., & Holzman, P. S. (1986). Scoring Manual for the Thought Disorder Index. *Schizophrenia Bulletin, 12,* 485–492.

Solovay, M. R., Shenton, M. E., & Holzman, P. S. (1987). Comparative studies of thought disorders: I. Mania and schizophrenia. *Archives of General Psychiatry, 44,* 13–20.

Wahlberg, K. E. (1994). Vanhempian kommunidaation merkitys lapsen ajatvshairioissa. *Acta Universitatis Ouluensis,* Series D, Medica, 305.

Watkins, J. G., & Stauffacher, J. C. (1952). An index of pathological thinking in the Rorschach. *Journal of Projective Techniques, 16,* 276–286.

Wood, J. M., Nezworski, M. T., Lilienfeld, S. O., & Garb, H. N. (2003). *What Is Wrong with the Rorschach? Science Confronts the Controversial Inkblot Test.* New York: Wiley.

Chapter 6

The Comprehensive System and Rorschach Performance Assessment System

Because of their overlapping history and shared intellectual and empirical DNA, a review of thought disorder scoring concepts in the Comprehensive System (CS) and Rorschach Performance Assessment System (R-PAS) merit examination together despite the controversies that continue to divide them. I focus narrowly on each system's approach to describing and coding categories of thought disorder and related phenomena. The story of both systems begins with the work of John Exner, together with the contributions of Irv Weiner.

Figure 6.1 John Exner.

Figure 6.2 Irving Weiner.

Comprehensive System (CS): Special Scores, WSUM6, and Perceptual-Thinking Index (PTI)

From the 1970s through the first decade of the new millennium, John Exner's CS was synonymous with Rorschach's. By synthesizing the most reliable and valid variables from existing Rorschach systems, Exner (1969, 1974, 1978, 1986a, 1990, 1991, 1993, 2003; Exner & Weiner, 1982, 1995) successfully addressed previous criticism that questioned whether the Rorschach was a psychometrically sound and clinically valid instrument (Buros, 1965). No higher praise for Exner's contributions to the survivability of the Rorschach could have been given than that offered by Margarite Hertz, the grand dame of Rorschach testing herself, who stated that Exner and his colleagues had "brought discipline into our ranks and a sense of optimism to our field" (Hertz, 1986, p. 405).

It may seem surprising that Exner's initial effort to construct a comprehensive Rorschach system (1974) omitted any formal scoring for thought-disordered responses. Although he referenced the scoring systems of Rapaport and Holt, Exner questioned whether many of these scores could be reliably coded and supported by the empirical literature. Reliability of scoring was, after all, one of Exner's most significant concerns about the Rorschach. Thus, when he published his first text on the CS, Exner concluded that thought disorder scores generally lacked definitional clarity and were too unreliable to score in a system that prized itself on psychometric precision. At the same time, however, he maintained that unusual verbalizations could be interpretively significant. Despite his decision to exclude formal thought disorder categories from his original CS, he included several incongruous combination scores in one of the sample protocols in his case examples.

It was not long before Exner began a serious study of thought disorder scoring, seeking ways to incorporate reliable and valid Special Scores into his CS. Shortly after the publication of his introductory text, Exner, Weiner, and Schuyler (1976) began to develop scoring criteria for thought disorder scores that would allow for acceptable levels of inter-rater reliability and empirical validity. Exner's collaboration with Weiner clearly enriched the CS. Ten years earlier, Weiner (1966) had written extensively about the Rorschach characteristics of disordered thinking. Exner and his colleagues eventually developed two broad categories of special scoring in the CS: Perseverations and Unusual Verbalizations, which Exner (1986a) later labeled Unusual Verbalizations and Perseveration and Integration Failure.

Unusual verbalizations

Exner and colleagues (1976) initially described three categories of Unusual Verbalizations: Deviant Verbalizations, Inappropriate Combinations, and Inappropriate Logic. They felt that these scores were not specific to any particular diagnosis, and while often found in the records of patients with schizophrenia, they could occur in the records of nonschizophrenic and normal subjects as well. Exner and his colleagues also noted that these scores might be more common in younger children and that they should not necessarily be taken as indications of psychopathology across the developmental spectrum. Eventually Exner elaborated these three categories of Unusual Verbalizations into six critical Special Scores, which are described below. The Special Scores include Deviant Verbalizations, Deviant Responses, Incongruous Combinations, Fabulized Combinations, Autistic Logic, and Contaminations.

Deviant Verbalization (DV)

DVs were characterized by "distorted language usage or idiosyncratic modes of expression that impede the subject's ability to communicate clearly" (Exner, Weiner, and Schuyler, 1976, p. 47). The group included two fairly broad and nonspecific subtypes of DV responses that subsumed Rapaport's categories of peculiar and queer verbalizations and the neologisms of the TDI. Although Exner and colleagues initially used the terms "queer" and "peculiar" in describing these two subtypes, they defined these terms somewhat differently than did Rapaport and seemed to obscure the distinction.

In defining their first DV subtype, which they loosely referred to as the "queer response," both Exner et al. (1976) and Weiner (1966) relied on Holt's statement that queer verbalizations result from a failure to maintain an appropriate set in talking about the subject matter at hand. Their example of such a response, "A crab *but I was hoping for an octopus*," depicts this odd loss of focus, in which the patient interjects an irrelevant phrase that clearly detracts from the original subject.

Their second form of DV was characterized by odd use of language that is not explained on the basis of subcultural idioms. Exner and colleagues referred to these as "peculiar" responses, which are distinguished by their stilted or redundant quality. Although some of these words or expressions may be appropriate in the context of the Rorschach test, they almost always strike the listener as odd. Exner and colleagues went on to list neologisms as a common manifestation of the peculiar DV.

In his 1978 text, Exner attempted to refine and elaborate on his distinctions between the subtypes of DVs. He dropped the somewhat confusing use of the terms "peculiar" and "queer" and presented the following four overlapping DV subtypes:

1 Inappropriate Commentary. The subject interjects a highly personalized association as an afterthought. An example of this would be the response "A crab, *but I was hoping to see an octopus*."
2 Loss of Appropriate Set. The subject loses focus in describing the object that he/she perceives. Exner's example was "A monster *that no one has ever seen*" (Exner, 1978, p. 22).
3 Odd Use of Language. The subject responds in a stilted or redundant manner, as in "A slide of microscopic aspects of some organism" (stilted response) or "A male penis" (redundant response).
4 Neologisms. The subject uses an incorrect word in place of a correct word.

Exner (1986) eventually streamlined the DV category to eliminate the overlap and clarify his earlier attempts to delineate subtypes. He did away with the "inappropriate commentary" and "loss of appropriate set" DVs and placed them in a new Deviant Response (DR) category, ending up with two clear-cut, albeit comparatively narrow subtypes of DVs: neologisms and redundancy responses, which describe answers that have "a strange and peculiar quality" manifested in one of two ways:

1 Inappropriate Phrases. These responses were originally subsumed under the DV category as "queer" responses and later as "inappropriate commentary." They include irrelevant or personalized interjections. This subtype also includes what Exner had previously referred to as "loss of appropriate set" DVs.

2 Circumstantial Responses. Exner added this new subtype of DV to capture responses that were fluid, rambling, vague, or inappropriately elaborative. Exner gave numerous examples of Circumstantial DRs that were characterized by the subject's tendency to wander off target into some overly personalized, excessively detailed, or inappropriately elaborative verbalization that had little to do with the inkblot or initial response. The subject may deviate from his or her original focus without ever returning to the point. Although the language that the subject uses may not be bizarre in itself, it is the process of wandering off track that distinguishes this DR subtype.

Exner and Weiner (1995) subsequently elaborated on the definition of the DR. They invoked Rapaport's concept of "increased distance" by emphasizing the rambling and disjointed nature of DRs in which the subject loosely associates to her or his initial response and ends up taking excessive distance from the inkblot. They also referred to inappropriate phrase DRs as "queer responses," again attempting to link this category to Rapaport's concept of queer verbalizations.

Exner and Weiner added a third subtype of DR to include those responses characterized by the subject's vagueness in responding to the examiner's questions. They noted that this type of DR results in a discontinuity or communication breakdown between the examiner's questions and the subject's answers.

Inappropriate Combinations

Exner and colleagues (1976) introduced the term Inappropriate Combinations to depict a category of cognitive slippage that Weiner (1966) referred to as "combinative thinking." Following Weiner's lead, Exner and his colleagues listed three types of Inappropriate Combinations: Incongruous Combinations, Fabulized Combinations, and Contaminations.

Incongruous Combination (INCOM)

The INCOM response in the CS includes some scores from Holt's Condensation category and overlaps considerably with Incongruous Combinations in the TDI. Exner remained consistent with these other systems by defining INCOMs as the inappropriate condensation of blot details or images into a single incongruous and unrealistic object.

However, Exner's definition of INCOM was somewhat narrower in scope than this category in the TDI. This more precise definition of INCOM may have been an effort to increase the reliability of the scoring. For example, the TDI includes two Incongruous Combination subtypes, the external–internal and inappropriate activity responses, which are not clearly specified as examples of INCOMs in the CS. Unlike the TDI, Exner included external–internal responses under the FABCOM category, which he considered to be a more serious sign of disturbed thinking.

Furthermore, Exner was explicit regarding whether the combination of objects and inappropriate actions (e.g. "A laughing insect") should be scored as an INCOM. In his original description of the larger category of inappropriate combinations (Exner, Weiner, & Schuyle, 1976), Exner indicated that these responses occurred when subjects inferred unrealistic relationships "between images, blot qualities, objects, or *activities attributed to objects*" (p. 48, emphasis added). However, in his subsequent texts (Exner, 1978, 1986a, 1993), he does not specifically refer to inappropriate activity responses while discussing INCOMs. Although he consistently mentioned the inappropriate combination of color and form as a special example of the INCOM, he did not clearly include the incongruity between an object and its action as a subtype of the INCOM response.

Fabulized Combination (FABCOM)

Like Johnston and Holzman, Exner and Weiner followed Holt's lead in delineating three different kinds of impossible relationships that subjects may infer between different blot elements: those based on size discrepancy, those that do not occur together in nature or reality, and those that mix natural and supernatural frames of reference. One noteworthy difference, however, was that Exner's FABCOM category included implausible transparencies, scored as severe variants (.50 vs. the .25 level) of the TDI's Incongruous Combination category (i.e. the external–internal response). Because such responses unrealistically condense different blot elements into a single incongruous object, Weiner (1966) also originally designated such transparency responses as INCOMs.

Given that Exner's definition of an INCOM indicated that blot elements were merged into a single object, it would appear more consistent to score the transparency response as an INCOM instead of a FABCOM. It is reasonable to assume that Exner allowed for this apparent inconsistency and designated these responses as FABCOMs in order to capture what he and others (Johnston & Holzman, 1979) believed was a more severe manifestation of disturbed thinking.

Contamination (CONTAM)

In describing the fusion of two or more impressions or blot elements into a single bizarre response, Exner presented the metaphor of a photographic double exposure in which one response has been psychologically superimposed on the other. In his earlier work (Exner, Weiner, & Schuyler, 1976), Exner maintained that all CONTAM responses were assigned a minus FQ; however, Exner (1986a) subsequently changed this rule by distinguishing perceptual processes, depicted by Form Quality (FQ), from ideational activity, depicted by the merging of two ideas or percepts into one. This distinction is consistent with Rapaport's ego psychology-based dialectic between perceptual and associational processes, and implicitly recognizes a range of severity in the types of contaminated responses.

Inappropriate logic

In establishing a separate category for explicit statements of disturbed logic, Exner was consistent with other systems that scored examples of what was referred to as Autistic Logic (ALOG). However, whereas Weiner's earlier description of ALOG and the TDI definition of this category both suggested that milder forms of ALOG responses may also be scored, Exner was closer to Holt in excluding the scoring of milder tendencies toward ALOG. In both the Holt and Exner systems, there is no Level 1 versus Level 2 severity distinction given for ALOG responses.

Perseveration and integration failures

Exner originally described two lesser categories of Special Scores indicative of cognitive dysfunction: Perseveration (PSV) and Confabulation (CONFAB). Both scores were subsequently removed from the CS because of their infrequency.

Perseveration (PSV)

Exner and colleagues (1976) described only two types of perseveration: "within card" and "content" perseveration. He later added a third type, which he called "mechanical perseveration." No distinction between these three varieties was made in the scoring system as each incidence of perseveration receives a score of PSV.

Within Card Perseveration was scored when a subject used the same location, determinant(s), content, Developmental Quality (DQ), Form Quality (FQ), and Z score as had been used in the preceding response. Even though the content may vary slightly, the general content category is the same. For example, seeing Card V first as a "bat" and then as a "butterfly" warranted the score of PSV when all the features mentioned above are the same.

Content Perseveration was scored when a subject indicated that a response was the same as an earlier one. The two responses are often not consecutive or even given within the same card and do not have to share any scores in common. This kind of perseverative activity was scored as a Relationship Verbalization in the Rapaport System and TDI, which is given a higher severity weighting (.50) than a Perseveration score (.25).

Mechanical Perseveration, Exner noted, reflected either neurological or intellectual impairment or a defensive avoidance of the task. In such cases, subjects may give the same simple response on several cards without consideration of the goodness of fit.

Confabulation (CONFAB)

Exner introduced the CONFAB into his CS in 1986 to describe the kind of perceptual overgeneralization originally referred to by Rorschach (1921/1942) as the Confabulated DW response. Unlike those of Rapaport and the developers of the TDI, Exner's CONFAB did not refer to ideationally embellished responses but only to the traditional DW process in which the subject generalizes inappropriately from one blot detail to a larger area or the entire inkblot. The form level of these responses is almost always poor because of the arbitrary nature of the generalization.

In their effort to link Special Scores with psychoanalytic theory, Meloy and Singer (1991) recommended that the CONFAB category be scrapped because of its rarity and lack of sensitivity and specificity to psychopathology, and that the DR category be renamed CONFAB because they felt that DR was essentially synonymous with Rapaport's confabulation concept. Kleiger and Peebles-Kleiger (1993) disagreed and provided a detailed critique of the DR score. In particular, they pointed out that Exner's category of DR addressed only the "wandering away" phenomenon (i.e. increased distance or, in his terms, "circumstantiality") but did not fully develop the concept of "fantasy immersion" or inappropriately embellished responses.

As noted above, the contemporary CS no longer includes PSV or CONFAB among its cadre of Special Scores. Like the former planet Pluto, these coding categories lost their preferred status in official scientific registries because of problems with frequency and reliable scoring. Nonetheless, as Exner (1974) originally noted about thought disorder scoring in general, problems in reliable scoring or infrequency do not preclude the existence of these response variables or diminish their interpretive meaning when they do occur.

Special content scores

Exner added six special content scores to the CS to identify response features that may reflect specific psychological characteristics. Of the six, his Abstraction (AB) score may be most indicative of pathological thought processes.

Abstraction (AB)

Initially referred to as Abstract Content, the Special Score AB is used for responses that either describe human emotion, sensory experience (coded under content as Hx), or clearly specify symbolic representation. The latter class of responses may reflect the kind of idiosyncratic symbolizing that Rapaport, Holt, and Johnston as well as Holzman tried to capture in their thought disorder scoring systems. Exner and Weiner (1982, 1995) indicated that intellectually oriented normal subjects often attribute symbolic meaning to Rorschach cards. Roughly 14 percent of nonpatient adults give symbolic responses. When they occur in the records of nonpatients, Exner and Weiner pointed out that they are second or third responses or given as whimsical elaborations of completed responses. According to Exner and Weiner, when AB scores become more prevalent and occur as first or primary responses that are delivered with an air of certainty, the subject has demonstrated a pathological preoccupation with inappropriate levels of abstraction.

Although there are no specifically designated subtypes of AB or pathological symbolism in the CS, Exner and Weiner described two classes of deviant symbolism, which they referred to as "idiosyncratic symbolism" and "overly abstract elaborations." Idiosyncratic symbolism is based on referents that are peculiar to the subject and quite distant from consensually validated experience. This class of responses includes both the unconventional color and image symbolism responses scored at the .50 level of severity in the TDI.

Overly abstract elaborations include highly elaborated responses in which abstract ideas take on a life and reality of their own. The authors give several examples of this type of response, including the Card IX response: "It gives me a feeling of nature up here and of Hell down here, one against the other, beauty against evil, with a sense of really high ideals coming out of the whole thing" (Exner & Weiner, 1995, p. 140). Clearly Rapaport and the TDI would score such a response as a severe confabulation. Exner and Weiner also agreed that in addition to giving it the Special Score AB, such a response would merit a DR score as well.

Inadequate M responses

Exner pointed out that Human Movement responses are sensitive indicators of the quality of an individual's thinking. He recognized two types of Inadequate M responses as possible signifiers of deviant thought processes. The first of these is the M- response. According to 1993 CS norms (Exner, 1993), M- responses were rare in adult nonpatients (roughly 3 percent) although quite common in the records of different patient groups such as character disorders (32 percent), depression (40 percent), and schizophrenia (80 percent). Following Rorschach tradition, Exner maintained that even one M- may be suggestive of peculiarities in thinking, and more than one M- response raises the likelihood of "disoriented, very strange thinking" (Exner, 1993, p. 482). Paying attention to whether the M- is of a passive or active sort may also be important in evaluating the quality of the disordered thought process. According to Exner, passive M- responses may reflect the potential for "delusional operations." Exner recommended studying the content of M- responses to find possible clues about the nature of the delusional material. He added that patients suffering from reactive psychoses often give homogeneous content in such passive M- responses, reflecting "well-fixed delusional systems."

The second type of Inadequate M indicative of disordered thought is what Exner termed the Formless M response. These are usually highly symbolic responses that focus on some aspect of emotion or sensation. For example, responding to an inkblot as "It looks like depression" or "It reminds me of the joyful feeling of togetherness" all but ignores the critical features of the blot. Formless M responses will also receive the Special Scores of AB and possibly DR (given the confabulatory embellishment that cannot be supported by stimulus aspects of the inkblot). Exner mentioned that Formless Ms may "have features that are quite similar to a hallucinatory-like operation" (Exner, 1993, p. 482).

Levels of variable severity and WSUM6

After the Rorschach Schizophrenia Index (SCZI) was developed, Exner concluded that the weights assigned to the six critical Special Scores did not reflect the appropriate degree of severity of each score. For example, some INCOMs were quite severe in nature, whereas others were more benign, developmentally not unusual, and often found in the records of children. Exner recognized that these two expressions of the same Special Score needed to be differentially weighted. The simplest and best way to address the variability within each scoring category was to assign a value of 1 or 2 to the following four Special Scoring categories: DV, DR, INCOM, and FABCOM. Level 1 ratings reflect mild or modest instances of illogical, peculiar, or fluid slippage in thinking. Most of these responses would merit similar TDI scores from the .25 level of severity.

Level 2 ratings refer to moderate to severe impairment of fluidity in thinking, lapses in logic, or more bizarre examples of reasoning or judgment. These responses would receive comparable TDI scores from the .50, .75, and, potentially, 1.0 levels of severity. Because ALOGs and CONTAMs fall at the more severe end of the Rorschach thought disorder scoring continuum, Exner considered them, by definition, to be Level 2 Special Scores.

Since nearly 81 percent of nonpatient adults gave at least one Level 1 Special Score and nonpatient children gave an even greater number, Exner (1993) viewed the presence of Level 2 scores as cause for greater concern. However, he found that at least one Level 2 score was also often seen in the records of normal children (e.g. in almost 25 percent of the records of 13-year-olds) and even more frequently in the records of nonschizophrenia patient groups (71 percent of inpatient depressives and 38 percent of a mixed sample of outpatients). Based on these normative findings, Exner concluded that Level 2 scores may have no specific diagnostic significance other than as general indicators of more severe cognitive slippage, and that the presence of a single Level 2 score should not be viewed as a pathognomonic sign of thought disorder.

Using frequencies and means from patient and nonpatient adult and developmental age groups, Exner was able to construct a rough hierarchy of severity for the Special Scores according to their relative frequency in his large nonpatient and patient samples. In essence, his normative data provided some basis for an empirically derived continuum of severity for the critical Special Scores. For example, over half of his 700 nonpatient adults (53 percent) had at least one DV1, 46 percent had an INCOM1, 15 percent a DR1, 16 percent a FABCOM1, 1 percent a DV2, .5 percent an INCOM2, 4 percent an ALOG, 2 percent a DR2 or FABCOM2, while none had a CONTAM in their records. Of the 320 schizophrenia subjects, 227 had at least one Level 2 score, 63 percent gave at least one FABCOM2, and 5 percent gave at least one CONTAM, a rare score under any circumstances. In this schizophrenic patient sample, the mean number of Special Scores per record was 9. Extensive normative data for patient and age groups can be found in Volume 1 of Exner's text (1986a, 1993). Additional norms are available for samples of borderline and schizotypal subjects that Exner collected prior to the differentiation between Level 1 and 2 Special Scores (Exner, 1986b).

Since almost 81 percent of the nonpatient adults (and the majority of normal children) in his sample had at least one Special Score in their records, Exner cautioned that low frequencies of Special Scores in patients' records should not necessarily be interpreted as evidence of disturbances in thinking, unless the scores in question were DR2s, FABCOM2s, or CONTAMs. Based on existing normative data, Exner offered a continuum of Special Scores, ranging in severity from DV1, to INCOM1, DR1, DV2, and FABCOM1. At the most severe end, the scores ranged from INCOM2, to ALOG, FABCOM2, and CONTAM.

Exner felt that as many as three DV1s may mean little in a record but that the presence of a single DV2 might be cause for concern. He also indicated that a few INCOM1s in a record are not highly interpretable unless the subject begins to give more bizarre condensations (INCOM2). As for FABCOMs, Exner pointed out that they are common in the records of children and patients with schizophrenia and personality disorders and should only be regarded as a negative sign in adults and adolescents if there are more than two FABCOM1s or if there is a single FABCOM2. The presence of DR2s, ALOGs and CONTAMs, of course, suggest more serious disturbances in thinking.

In summary, Exner concluded that the presence of greater than five Special Scores in the records of adults and greater than one standard deviation above the age mean for younger children suggested that a thought disorder might exist. He offered a rough cutoff for a WSUM6 of 9 to demarcate the normal range of cognitive slippage from clinically meaningful pathology of thinking. However, he also cautioned against a strictly quantitative approach and recommended that clinicians examine each incidence of special scoring separately.

Rorschach Schizophrenia Index (SCZI) and Perceptual-Thinking Index (PTI)

Exner's first attempt to develop a composite index to detect schizophrenia (SCZI) occurred shortly after he and his colleagues introduced Special Scores into the CS in 1976. Exner based his experimental index on Weiner's conceptually-based criteria for characterizing schizophrenia. Following Weiner's lead, Exner identified the four Rorschach indicators of schizophrenia: (1) disturbed thinking (poor human movement responses [M-] and/or examples of the five Special Scores—DV, INCOM, FABCOM, ALOG, or CONTAM); (2) impaired reality testing (poor form level or low X+ and F+%); (3) poor emotional controls (CF+C > FC); and (4) interpersonal ineptness, absence of pure H responses or (H) > H.

The six critical Special Scores were each weighted according to relative severity as follows: DV = 1, INCOM = 2, DR = 3, FABCOM = 4, ALOG = 5, and CONTAM = 7. Along with a low X+% and the presence of at least one M-, the weighted sum of these six scores (WSUM6) was one of the key components of the SCZI. Exner's (1986a) SCZI was made up of the following five variables related to disturbed perception and thinking: (1) X+% < 70 (the sum of good form level responses is less than 70 percent); (2) Sum X- > sum Xu or X-% > 20% (the sum of poor form-level responses is greater than the sum of unusual form-level responses, or poor form-level responses are greater than 20 percent); (3) M- > 0 or WSUM6 > 11 (poor human movement responses are greater than zero or the weighted sum of critical Special Scores is greater than 11); (4) DV + DR + INCOM + FABCOM + ALOG + CONTAM > 4 (the unweighted sum of critical Special Scores is greater than four); and (5) Sum DR + FABCOM + ALOG + CONTAM > Sum DV + INCOM or M- > 1 (the sum of Deviant Responses, FABCOMs, ALOGs, and CONTAMs is greater than the sum of DVs and INCOMs, or poor human movement responses total more than one).

A score of 5 on the SCZI was considered quite diagnostic of schizophrenia, whereas a score of 4 produced many false positives. Investigations designed to make the SCZI a more sensitive and specific index of schizophrenia continued over the next six years. The SCZI was revised again in 1990 (Exner, 1990) in order to improve the false-positive and false-negative rates. The improvement was greatly advanced by the addition of Level 1 and 2 scores (described below) and S- % (minus-form white space responses) variables to the index. Based on correlational and discriminant function analyses, Exner settled on six items consisting of a total of 10 variables for his revised SCZI.

Because they chose to call it the Schizophrenia Index, Exner and his colleagues implied that the SCZI should be sufficiently sensitive and specific to schizophrenic conditions. Extensive research went into refining the SCZI to maximize accurate identification of schizophrenic patients and minimize false-positive and negative rates. Exner's studies suggested that a SCZI of 4 should be interpreted with great caution, while a SCZI of 6 indicated a much greater likelihood that schizophrenia is present.

Hilsenroth, Fowler, and Padawer (1998) investigated the reliability, internal consistency, and diagnostic efficiency of the SCZI in classifying schizophrenic and other psychotic subjects in comparison with other groups. Although they demonstrated that the total value of SCZI was significantly positively correlated with the presence of a DSM-IV psychotic disorder, Hilsenroth and his team indicated that the SCZI assessed a continuum of disordered thinking, with lower relative values among borderline and Cluster A personality disorders (a mean SCZI of roughly 3.0). They suggested that a value of 4 seemed adequate for the purposes of distinguishing psychotic disorders from milder personality disorders, whereas a value of 5 improved the diagnostic efficiency with more disturbed borderline and Cluster A personality disorders.

More importantly, Hilsenroth and colleagues concluded that the SCZI was probably not as diagnostically specific to schizophrenia as the name of the index suggested. They stated that as a measure of perceptual inaccuracy, impaired reality testing, and deviant thought processes, the SCZI would be elevated in bipolar, delusional, and schizoaffective psychoses as well. Thus, they concluded that the SCZI should be employed as a dimensional measure of psychosis and renamed Psychosis Index to assess the extent of impaired reality testing and thought disorder among a wider variety of patients. Around this same time, Holaday (2000), in her Rorschach studies of children with PTSD, also recommended that the SCZI be renamed the Perception and Thinking Index (PATI) to avoid the issue of false-positive diagnoses of schizophrenia associated with it.

Exner (2000a, 2000b) replaced SCZI with the Perceptual-Thinking Index (PTI) for both conceptual and psychometric reasons. From a conceptual perspective, Exner recognized that the SCZI was a misnomer. The name "Schizophrenia Index" proved misleading and shifted focus away from assessing personality functions such as reality testing and ideational clarity, and impaired establishing a formal diagnosis. The PTI consists of nine variables with five criterion tests: (1) XA% < .70 and WDA < .75; (2) X-% > .29; (3) Level 2 > 2 and FAB2 > 0; (4) R < 17 and WSUM6 > 12, or R > 16 and WSUM6 > 17 (with adjustments for age 13 and younger); and (5) M- > 1 OR X-% > .40. Unlike the SCZI, the PTI substituted XA% and WDA% for X+% and FQ- variables in the SCZI. Adjustments were also made for protocol length and age for Special Scores containing WSUM6.

Although the PTI is viewed as a continuous variable without prescribed cutoff points, as opposed to a diagnostic index, researchers have found that cutoff scores of >2 (Smith et al., 2001) and ≥3 (Dao & Prevatt, 2006) provided the best classification and tradeoff between false positives and false negatives. Studies have supported the validity of the PTI in identifying children and adolescents with elevated scores on measures of thought disorder and other psychotic symptoms (Smith et al., 2001), in distinguishing patients on the schizoprhenia spectrum from those diagnosed with major depression (Dao & Prevatt, 2006), in differentiating psychotic and nonpsychotic patients (Benedik et al., 2013; Biagiarelli et al., 2015), and in distinguishing patients with chronic and acutely aggravated schizophrenia (Gomilla, 2011).

There have been no further developments in thought disorder scoring in the CS since Exner's death in 2006. The most significant Rorschach-related development over the last ten years has been the advent of R-PAS.

R-PAS: Cognitive Codes and Perception and Thinking Domain

It is with poetic resonance that Greg Meyer, Don Viglione, Joni Mihura, Bob Erard, and Phil Erdberg developed the R-PAS. Consider how 40 years ago "student" John Exner took the most reliable and well-validated scores from the systems of five preeminent Rorschach figures and integrated them into his CS. With R-PAS, we have five distinguished students of Exner (most of whom had formerly served on Exner's Rorschach Research Council), taking the most empirically robust variables from the CS and incorporating them into their revised method, the R-PAS (Meyer et al., 2011). To paraphrase Hertz (1986, p. 405), the R-PAS, like the CS before it, has brought a renewed "discipline into our ranks and a sense of optimism to our field."

Figure 6.3 Greg Meyer.   *Figure 6.4* Don Viglione.   *Figure 6.5* Joni Mihura.

Figure 6.6 Robert Erard.   *Figure 6.7* Phil Erdberg.

Some Rorschach traditionalists might have been disappointed and displeased that a number of favored scoring variables did not pass psychometric and empirical muster and were excluded from both the CS and R-PAS. Change in practice methods and prized beliefs are always difficult and evoke resistance. Such was the case when the CS became the standard of practice in Rorschach testing. Now we find similar growing pains facing the Rorschach community as R-PAS gains ascendancy.

Strength of Evidence for Detecting Psychosis

Although R-PAS and CS share a similar evidence-based heritage, what distinguishes R-PAS for our purposes is the strength of empirical support for variables targeting cognitive and perceptual processes. Recall that when Exner (1974) published his first CS text, he did not include Special Scores because he did not believe they could be reliably scored. In contrast, variables for assessing thought disorder and poor reality testing are showcased in R-PAS. In fact, in Mihura's landmark meta-analytic study of CS variables (Mihura et al., 2013), the PTI, Critical Special Scores, and Distorted Form (FQ-) received the strongest validity support. Long-time Rorschach critics agreed that there is compelling evidence for scores related to cognitive impairment and thought disorder (Wood et al., 2015).

Cognitive Codes

The R-PAS developers extended and renamed some familiar variables for assessing problems in thinking, judgment, and perception. Special Scores from the CS are referred to as Cognitive Codes and include the same scores as in the CS, with the exception of ALOG, which was renamed PEC (Peculiar Logic). As with the CS, there are six coding subtypes, four of which are scored according to level of severity (Level 1 or Level 2). Three codes are described as Language and Reasoning scores (DV, DR, and PEC) because they involve idiosyncratic verbalization or justification of the response. In contrast, Perceptually Based codes (INC, FAB, and CON) reflect oddities in how images are condensed and combined. Each code is weighted from 1 to 7, reflecting the severity of disruptions in thinking. Definitions and weights for Cognitive Codes were derived from the CS (Exner, 2003).

Perception and Thinking Domain

The set of variables collectively grouped under the "Perception and Thinking Domain" is related to severity of psychopathology as it pertains to disturbances in thought organization, reasoning, and reality testing. According to Meyer and colleagues (2011), the combination of low engagement, low productivity, and lack of cognitive complexity, together with elevated scores within this domain, are associated with the most pathological conditions.

1. Ego Impairment Index-3 (EII-3). Based on the well-researched Ego Impairment Index (EII; Perry & Viglione, 1991; Perry, Viglione, & Braff, 1992), EII-3, the most current version of the Index (Viglione et al., 2011), is a key variable within the Perception and Thinking Domain. Derived from a combination of FQ- (a measure of reality distortion), WSUMCog (a composite of disordered thinking), M-, PHR, GHR (measures of social misperception), Critical Contents (blatant and primitive thought content), and R, the EII-3 is an aggregate measure of the severity of psychopathology and, more specifically, disturbances in thinking and reality testing.
2. Thought and Perception Composite (TP-Comp). Similar to EII-3, TP-Comp assesses both reality testing and disturbance in thinking. However, unlike EII-3, it does not include Critical Contents. TP-Comp is derived from FQ-%, WD-%, M-, WSUMCog, FAB2, and R. Raw scores greater than 3.5 are considered extremely high and are reportedly found in schizophrenia-spectrum disorders, bipolar psychoses, and drug-induced psychoses. The authors further indicate that extreme elevations are less likely to be the products of malingering or trauma. Mid-range elevations (raw scores > 2) reportedly suggest a vulnerability to psychotic-like experiences and may be associated with borderline-level functioning, as well as trauma and malingering.
3. Weighted Sum of Six Cognitive Codes (WSUMCog). A measure of disturbed thinking, WSUMCog reflects the weighted sum of all Cognitive Codes in the

record. Assessors can make distinctions between Level 1 and Level 2 codes in order to determine whether problems in thinking are mild departures or examples of cognitive immaturity (Level 1) or more deviant kinds of verbalizations, perceptual condensations, or severe strains in reasoning (Level 2).
4 Severe Cognitive Codes (SevCog). SevCog is a narrower variable that captures the most severe examples of disordered thinking (DV2 + DR2 + INC2 + FAB2 + PEC + CON). Although the authors indicate that SevCog reflects psychotic-level disturbances in thinking, reasoning, conceptualization, and verbalization, they also caution that elevations might also reflect deliberate attempts to dramatize, shock the examiner, or flout convention.
5 FQ Percentages. WD-% and FQ-% both represent reality testing. Minus-form-level coding on all responses (FQ-%) is contrasted with minus-form-level scoring when more common, more easily seen blot locations are used (WD-%).

One casualty of Mihura's meta-analysis was that M- no longer proved to be a valid measure of thought disorder. Recall that in the CS, M- was considered to be an indicator of disturbed thinking. Research has not supported this claim. Still, M- is recognized as a measure of misperception and misunderstanding of social stimuli.

Thoughts about CS and R-PAS assessment of disordered thinking

Both the CS and R-PAS are complete interpretative systems that go well beyond the scoring of disordered thinking. As such, I restrict my summary comments regarding empirical, conceptual, and clinical issues to the CS and R-PAS assessment and interpretation of disordered thinking.

Empirical foundations

Exner established the CS as an empirically robust system that became the coin of the realm for Rorschach psychologists around the world. Initially hesitant to make thought disorder scoring a formal part of the system, Exner and Weiner eventually incorporated a lean and efficient set of Special Scores to capture deviant language and logic. Meyer, Viglione, Mihura, Erdberg, and Erard have succeeded in making R-PAS the next generation of a scientifically robust Rorschach system. With minor variations, the Cognitive Codes and perception and thinking variables are the offspring of the Special Scores, WSUM6, and PTI.

Thought disorder scoring in the CS and R-PAS, like other coding variables, has been subjected to rigorous reliability, validity, and normative studies. Examples of disordered thinking could be tagged and scored with acceptable levels of inter-reliability in both systems. Validity studies of CS Special Scores, SCZI, and PTI have focused primarily on differential diagnosis, psychosis risk, and identifying thought disorder in children (Exner, 1986a; Singer & Brabender, 1993; Hilsenroth, Fowler, & Pawader, 1998, Smith et al., 2001; Viglione & Hilsenroth, 2001; Dao & Prevatt, 2006; Kimhy et al., 2007; Ilonen et al., 2010; Inoue, Yorozuya, & Mizuno, 2014; Rothschild-Yakar et al., 2015). Perhaps more than anyone, Mihura and colleagues' (2013) meta-analysis of CS scores consolidated the robust empirical support for using these variables to detect and differentiate patients with psychotic disorders. Again, it is worth noting that even the most ardent critics of the CS, who once called for a moratorium on the usage of the Rorschach in the belief that it lacked sufficient merit, reiterated that there was abundant scientific basis for using Special Scores and FQ in clinical practice (Wood et al., 2015).

Despite its solid research base, the breadth of validity studies of thought disorder variables in the CS and R-PAS is less extensive relative to the collective body of clinical validity investigations with the TDI. However, R-PAS is relatively new, and with the strength of the findings from Mihura's meta-analysis (which, in some respects, helped launch R-PAS), it is likely that there will be increasing numbers of R-PAS studies of disordered thinking and psychosis in years to come.

The normative base of the CS was light years ahead of any of its predecessor systems. Special Scores, like all CS variables, could be compared to empirically derived norms based on respectable sample sizes of age groups ranging from young children to adults. However, the norms for the CS came under some fire when investigators found significant variability in international samples, particularly with respect to child and adolescent norms (Meyer, Erdberg, & Schaffer, 2007). Questions about norms for variables like FQ-% and among different age groups served as another impetus for developing R-PAS. One of the strengths of R-PAS is its use of international norms and the ongoing revision of norms for children and adolescents.

Conceptual underpinnings

It is clear that the CS and R-PAS are driven primarily by empirical data. Both systems selected the variables with the strongest empirical support. Descriptions of the psychological rationale and conceptual basis for the score categories and indices, though not neglected, are of secondary importance. Both systems describe how the scoring categories broadly reflect qualities of language, thinking, and reality testing.

In addition, both systems provide useful distinctions between levels of severity, attempting to differentiate scores that reflect minor slippage, immature thinking, and capricious thinking (Level 1) from that which is more confusing and bizarre (Level 2). R-PAS includes a crisp way of capturing the most severely disturbed clustering of thought-disordered responses with the SevCog variable, which is narrower in scope than the WSUMCog. In principle, SevCog represents a composite of the most extreme psychotic-level disruptions in thinking.

The CS made distinctions between Deviant Verbalizations (DV and DR), Inappropriate Combinations (INCOM, FABCOM, and CONTAM), and Autistic Logic (ALOG). These broad categories purported to group together scores that reflected similar processes (verbalizations, combinations, and logic); however, there was little explanation about the nature of the underlying psychological or cognitive processes involved in each. In R-PAS, conceptual distinctions are organized into language and reasoning Cognitive Codes (DV, DR, and PEC), which reflect idiosyncratic ways of justifying responses, and perceptually based Cognitive Codes (INC, FAB, and CON), which involve illogical combinations of visual images. Despite efforts to provide psychological rationale for the Cognitive Codes and variables within the Perception and Thinking Domain, the distinction that R-PAS makes between language and reasoning versus perceptually based Cognitive Codes needs further clarification. The idea seems to be that the former categories are based more on what a patient *says*, while the later set of scores reflect more of what the patient *sees*. While this distinction makes some sense, combining language and reasoning in the first group is confusing.

Special Scores and Cognitive Codes are also placed along a 7-point continuum of severity on which each is a weighted variable in the WSUMCog (R-PAS) or WSUM6 (CS). Although these indices are empirically derived, there remains confusion and inconsistency between this continuum of severity and what is known about the nature of thought disorder from clinical investigations. For example a DV2 only receives a weighting of (2) compared to other Level 2 scores, which receive much higher weightings: INC2 (4), DR2 (6), and FAB2 (7). According to this empirically based weighting of severity, a benign and relatively common Card II response of "Two bears giving each other high fives" would be scored FAB1 and receive a weighting of (4). Contrast this with the Card I response, "These spiders are dracnoids that exist for folly." Not only is dracnoids a neologism but the response as a whole makes no sense. This response would receive a score of DV2 with a weighting of (2). Neologisms that in the TDI receive the highest severity weighting (1.0) are scored DV2 in the CS and R-PAS. The research of the Holzman group (Shenton, Solovay, & Holzman, 1987) on qualitative distinctions in thought disorder among different psychotic groups demonstrated that thought disorder in schizophrenia-spectrum patients, characterized primarily by confusion and severely idiosyncratic verbalizations, most likely scored a DV2 in the CS and R-PAS. Thus, it is difficult to understand why CS and R-PAS coding would not view DV2 as a more serious indication of deviant language or thinking. Similarly, the benign FAB1 of "Two bears giving each other high fives" would receive the same weighting (4) as a more bizarre Card V response (INC2) of "A bat with landing gears."

Despite the many strengths and appeal of the Special Scores and Cognitive Codes, efforts to establish a set of reliably scored categories may have limited the scope of scorable DRs. In their attempt to be parsimonious, CS and R-PAS developers condensed or overlooked discrete types of pathological verbalizations that may have particular diagnostic significance. Several examples of this possible tendency to condense or oversimplify categories exist among the Special

Scores. For example, the DV category appears to be rather narrowly defined. By limiting DV scores to either redundancies or neologisms, a broader array of idiosyncratic verbalizations may be overlooked. Technically, many of the examples of odd and stilted expressions and idiosyncratic word usage and images, scored as peculiar and queer verbalizations in the TDI, may not be scorable as DVs in the CS because they are neither redundancies nor neologisms. Furthermore, responses such as "two legs raising each other," "potential ears," "a perverted jack-o'-lantern," "a foxed comic dog," or "an echo of a picture" include neither redundancies nor neologisms per se, and as such, may not merit a Special Score of DV.

The DR scoring category is even more problematic in terms of its lack of specificity and crispness of conceptual boundaries. Meloy and Singer (1991) equated the DR score with the concept of confabulation in Rapaport's original scoring schema but acknowledged that DR was a slightly more expansive category. Although intended to capture responses in which the subject "wanders off target," I believe that DR is more than "slightly expansive" and has become so broad in scope that it risks becoming a "wastebasket" category for a variety of different responses. A crude comparison between Special Scores and scoring categories in the TDI suggests that the breadth of the DR category may subsume a number of separate scoring categories in the TDI. For example, TDI categories roughly equivalent to DR1 and DR2 may include such disparate scores as inappropriate distance, flippant responses, vagueness and confusion, looseness, playful confabulations and confabulations, fluid, and incoherent responses. The TDI separate factors of Irrelevant Intrusions, Combinative Thinking, Confusion, and Fluid Thinking all contain scores that would likely be scored DR1 or 2 in the CS.

Besides the overly broad quality of the DR category, there is a paradoxically narrow aspect to the definition of DR. By defining DR as a "wandering off target," in which the subject either produces an "inappropriate phrase" (e.g. "It's a bat but I was hoping for a butterfly") or a "circumstantial response," the meaning of DR is restricted to those responses in which the subject essentially departs from the task and becomes inappropriately discursive or loose. However, some subjects do not "wander away" from the blot but become inappropriately immersed in it. These subjects are not circumstantial according to the definition of DR, but they become lost in an elaborate description of the blot itself. For example, consider the response "Looks like a beetle that's been injured. It looks frightened, angry, and aggressive. And uh … very intent on … attacking in um … in retaliation for something that's bothering it." This response is clearly not an inappropriate phrase DR and also is not circumstantial. The subject does not wander from the response but becomes immersed in the fantasy of the response. Most would agree that such a response should receive a DR score. However, this type of "fantasy immersion" response is not clearly described under the realm of DR in the CS. It would have been clinically useful had the CS and R-PAS adhered to Rapaport's distinction between "increased distance" and "loss of distance." Highly elaborated and embellished DRs can reflect either one or both kinds of problems in maintaining appropriate distance from the blot. Exner's DR category seems to address only the "wandering away" phenomenon (i.e. increased distance or, in his terms, "circumstantiality") but does not fully develop the concept of "fantasy immersion." Kleiger and Peebles-Kleiger (1993) addressed this conceptual difficulty with the DR response, noting absence of an adequate description of this latter type of DR process.

Exner further confused an already confusing issue by retaining, then subsequently dropping, the score CONFAB, which had been applied only to the DW score that appeared in earlier Rorschach systems. In their effort to link Special Scores with psychoanalytic theory, Meloy and Singer (1991) recommended that the CONFAB category be scrapped because of its rarity and lack of sensitivity and specificity to psychopathology and that the DR category be renamed CONFAB because they felt that DR was essentially synonymous with Rapaport's confabulation concept. Kleiger and Peebles-Kleiger (1993) disagreed with Meloy and Singer's equating DR with confabulation and felt that Meloy and Singer did not sufficiently recognize the heterogeneity in the DR category. In their detailed critique of the DR score, Kleiger and Peebles-Kleiger proposed a modification of DR scoring to make it more precise and to capture the different nuances of the process of confabulation.

Clinical utility

Criticisms notwithstanding, both the CS and R-PAS are credited with developing an empirically valid, easily scored, and reliably coded set of scoring variables that capture most of the major categories of deviant thought and language on the Rorschach. The ease with which the Special Scores and Cognitive Codes can be learned and scored makes them attractive alternatives to more intricate and cumbersome methods like the TDI and Holt's Pripro. Limiting the number of scoring categories might improve reliability but also might come at the risk of short-changing conceptual understanding of what it is that we are scoring. When faced with more difficult questions of differential diagnoses in patients already suspected of being psychotic, however, clinicians may have more confidence using a scoring system like the TDI. Furthermore, if it is important diagnostically to describe the specific nature of the psychotic process in a given patient, the TDI may offer clinicians a wider variety of categories from which to choose in attempting to score different nuances of disordered thinking.

References

Benedik, E., Coderl, S., Bon, J., & Smith, B. L. (2013). Differentiation of psychotic from nonpsychotic inpatients: The Rorschach Perceptual Thinking Index. *Journal of Personality Assessment, 95*, 141–148.

Biagiarelli, M., Roma, P., Comparelli, A., Andrados, P., Di Pomponio, I., Corigliano, V., Curto, M., & Ferracuti, S. (2015). Relationship between the Rorschach Perceptual Thinking Index (PTI) and the Positive and Negative Syndrome Scale (PANSS) in psychotic patients: A validity study. *Psychiatry Research, 225*, 315–321.

Buros, O. K. (1965). *The Sixth Mental Measurements Yearbook*. New York: Gryphon Press.

Dao, T. K., & Prevatt, F. (2006). A psychometric evaluation of the Rorschach Comprehensive System's Perceptual Thinking Index. *Journal of Personality Assessment, 86*, 180–189.

Exner, J. E. (1969). *The Rorschach Systems*. New York: Grune & Stratton.

Exner, J. E. (1974). *The Rorschach: A Comprehensive System, Basic Foundations* (Vol. 1). New York: Wiley.

Exner, J. E. (1978), *The Rorschach: A Comprehensive System, Advanced Interpretation* (Vol. 2). New York: Wiley.

Exner, J. E. (1986a). *The Rorschach: A Comprehensive System, Basic Foundations* (Vol. 1, 2nd ed.). New York: Wiley.

Exner, J. E. (1986b). Some Rorschach data comparing schizophrenics with borderline and schizotypal personality disorders. *Journal of Personality Assessment, 50*, 455–471.

Exner, J. E. (1990). *Rorschach Workbook for the Comprehensive System* (3rd ed.). Asheville, NC: Rorschach Workshops.

Exner, J. E. (1991). *The Rorschach: A Comprehensive System, Advanced Interpretation* (Vol. 2, 2nd ed.). New York: Wiley.

Exner, J. E. (1993). *The Rorschach: A Comprehensive System, Basic Foundations* (Vol. 1, 3rd ed.). New York: Wiley.

Exner, J. E. (2000a). *A Primer for Rorschach Interpretation*. Asheville, NC: Rorschach Workshops.

Exner, J.E. (2000b). *2000 Alumni Newsletter*. Asheville, NC: Rorschach Workshops.

Exner, J. E. (2003). *The Rorschach: A Comprehensive System, Basic Foundations* (Vol. 1, 4th ed.). New York: Wiley.

Exner, J. E., & Weiner, I. B. (1982). *The Rorschach: A Comprehensive System,. Assessment of Children and Adolescents* (Vol. 3). New York: Wiley.

Exner, J. E., & Weiner, I. B. (1995). *The Rorschach: A Comprehensive System, Assessment of Children and Adolescents* (Vol. 3, 2nd ed.). New York: Wiley.

Exner, J. E., Weiner, I. B., & Schuyler, S. (1976), *A Rorschach Workbook for the Comprehensive System*. Bayville, NY: Rorschach Workshops.

Gomilla, M. V. (2011). The Rorschach Test in the differential diagnosis of 245 schizophrenic inpatients. *Annuary of Clinical and Health Psychology, 7*, 79–93.

Hertz, M. R. (1986). Rorschachbound: A 50-year memoir. *Journal of Personality Assessment, 50*, 396–416.

Hilsenroth, M., Fowler, J. C., & Pawader, J. R. (1998). The Rorschach Schizophrenia Index (SCZI): An examination of reliability, validity, and diagnostic efficiency. *Journal of Personality Assessment, 70*, 514–534.

Holaday, M. (2000). Rorschach protocols from children and adolescents diagnosed with posttraumatic stress disorder. *Journal of Personality Assessment, 75*, 143–157.

Ilonen, T., Heinimaa, M., Korkeila, J., Svirskis, T., & Salokangas, R. K. R. (2010). Differentiating adolescents at clinical high risk for psychosis from psychotic and non-psychotic patients with the Rorschach. *Psychiatry Research, 179*, 151–156.

Inoue, N., Yorozuya, Y., & Mizuno, M. (2014). Identifying comorbidities of patients at ultra-high risk for psychosis using the Rorschach Comprehensive System. Paper presented at the XXI International Congress of Rorschach and Projective Methods, Istanbul, Turkey.

Johnston, M. H., & Holzman, P. S. (1979). *Assessing Schizophrenic Thinking*. San Francisco, CA: Jossey-Bass.

Kimhy, D., Corcoran, C., Harkavy-Friedman, J. M., Ritzler, B., Javitt, D. C., & Malaspina, D. (2007). Visual form perception: A comparison of individuals at high risk for psychosis, recent onset schizophrenia and chronic schizophrenia, *Schizophrenia Research, 97*, 25–34.

Kleiger, J. H., & Peebles-Kleiger, M. J. (1993). Toward a conceptual understanding of the deviant response in the Comprehensive Rorschach System. *Journal of Personality Assessment, 60*, 74–90.

Meloy, J. R., & Singer, J. (1991). A psychoanalytic view of the Rorschach Comprehensive System "special scores." *Journal of Personality Assessment, 56*, 202–217.

Meyer, G. J., Erdberg, P., & Shaffer, T. W. (2007). Toward international normative reference data for the Comprehensive System. *Journal of Personality Assessment, 89*, S201–S216.

Meyer, G. J., Viglione, D. J., Mihura, J. L., Erard, R. E., & Erdberg, P. (2011). *Rorschach Performance Assessment System: Administration, Coding, Interpretation, and Technical Manual*. Toledo, OH: Rorschach Performance Assessment System.

Mihura, J. L., Meyer, G. J., Dumitrascu, N., & Bombel, G. (2013). The validity of individual Rorschach variables: Systematic reviews and meta-analyses of the Comprehensive System. *Psychological Bulletin, 139*, 548–605.

Perry, W., & Viglione, D (1991). The Ego Impairment Index as a predictor of outcome in melancholic depressed patients treated with tricyclic antidepressants. *Journal of Personality Assessment, 56*, 487–501.

Perry, W., Viglione, D., & Braff, D. (1992). The Ego Impairment Index and schizophrenia: A validation study. *Journal of Personality Assessment, 59*, 165–175.

Rorschach, H. (1942). *Psychodiagnostics* (5th ed.). Bern, Switzerland: Hans Huber. (Original work published in 1921.)

Rothschild-Yakar, L., Lacoua, L., Brener, A., & Koren, D. (2015). Impairments in interpersonal representations and deficits in social cognition as predictors of risk for schizophrenia in non-patient adolescents. Paper presented at the annual meeting of the Society for Personality Assessment, Brooklyn, NY.

Shenton, M. E., Solovay, M. R., & Holzman, P. (1987). Comparative studies of thought disorders: II. Schizoaffective disorder. *Archives of General Psychiatry, 44*, 21–30.

Singer, H. K., & Brabender, V. (1993). The use of the Rorschach to differentiate unipolar and bipolar disorders. *Journal of Personality Assessment, 60*, 333–345.

Smith, S. R., Baity, M. R., Knowles, E. S., & Hilsenroth, M. J. (2001). Assessment of disordered thinking in children and adolescents: The Rorschach Perceptual-Thinking Index. *Journal of Personality Assessment, 77*, 447–463.

Viglione, D. J., & Hilsenroth, M. J. (2001). The Rorschach: Facts, fictions, and future. *Psychological Assessment, 13*, 452–471.

Viglione, D. J., Perry, W., Giromini, L., & Meyer, G. J. (2011). Revising the Rorschach Ego Impairment Index to accommodate recent recommendations about improving Rorschach validity. *International Journal of Testing, 11*, 349–364.

Weiner, I. B. (1966). *Psychodiagnosis in Schizophrenia*. New York: Wiley.

Wood, J. M., Nezworski, M. T., Garb, H. N., & Lilenfeld, S. O. (2015). A second look at the validity of widely used Rorschach indices: Comment on Mihura, Meyer, Dumitrascu, and Bombel (2013). *Psychological Bulletin, 141*, 236–249.

Chapter 7

Alternative Rorschach approaches for assessing disordered thinking

In addition to the major research and clinical thought disorder scoring systems, there are a number of relatively obscure and novel approaches for scoring thought disorder on the Rorschach. Whether developed specifically for research purposes or proposed for use in clinical practice, these "secondary" systems employ a mixture of generally accepted scoring concepts along with novel additions and modifications.

Some like Singer and Wynne's (1966) scoring of "communication deviance" on the Rorschach are of more historic interest. Others like the research-based scoring system of Harrow and Quinlan (Quinlan et al., 1972; Harrow & Quinlan, 1977, 1985) or the Menninger Thought Disturbance Scales (Athey, Colson, & Kleiger, 1993) offered novel ways of capturing critical aspects of thought disorder on the Rorschach. Clinical approaches like the one proposed by Aronow, Reznikoff, and Moreland (1994) based on Schuldberg and Boster's two-dimensional model (1985), and the even more obscure psychoanalytically rooted system of Burstein and Loucks (1989) are far outside the mainstream but offer interesting ideas for contemplating disordered thinking on the Rorschach. Included among these secondary systems is Wagner's TRAUT System, which he developed as an empirical and theory-free method to detect "autisms" on the Rorschach (Wagner & Rinn, 1994; Wagner, 1998). Finally, novel "off-book" approaches to scoring thought disorder include two methods for assessing disordered thinking employing abbreviated card sets: those of Carpenter and colleagues (1993) and Eblin et al. (2014).

TRAUT System

Wagner (Wagner & Rinn, 1994; Wagner, 1998) developed his Tripartite Classification of Autisms, or TRAUT System, as an empirical and theory-free method to detect "autisms" on the Rorschach. By "autisms" he meant the kinds of perceptual aberrations and absurd responses indicative of thought disorder. Wagner was critical of current trends in thought disorder scoring. He found Rapaport's distance rationale unwieldy and criticized the CS for the absence of any logical rationale for viewing a response as thought disordered.

Furthermore, he believed that the WSUM6 in the CS lacked sufficient temporal stability and sensitivity to identify subtle and transient manifestations of disordered thought. To remedy these perceived conceptual and psychometric difficulties, he developed the TRAUT as an empirical method that viewed autisms in the context of Rorschach task demands. Responses are considered autisms when the subject deviates from the explicit or implicit requirements. Viewing the Rorschach strictly as a test of perception, Wagner concluded that any violations of the standard instruction "Look at this and tell me what it might be" would signal autistic thinking. Thus, he limited his study to perceptual anomalies while excluding linguistic oddities.

Wagner proposed three major categories of TRAUT that included what he termed HYPOs, HYPERs, and RELERs. Each category subsumed four to six subdivisions, making for a total of 16 subscores in the TRAUT. HYPOs (hypo-attentional errors) are scored when the subject ignores to varying degrees the shapes and contours of the blot and instead uses the stimuli as a springboard to private fantasies, images, or sensations. HYPERs (hyper-attentional errors) reflect the subject's tendency to ignore differentially recognizable shapes and search for tiny, hidden, or impossible to find percepts to confirm private interpretations without regard for consensual validation. Whereas HYPOs ignore the reality of the inkblot, HYPERs overinterpret tiny or insignificant aspects of the blot. RELERs (relationship errors) involve questionable relationships between and among inkblot areas based on spatial proximity instead of logically based events and objects. RELERs include inappropriate combinations (INCOM, FABCOM, CONTAM), as well as ALOG, and CONFAB responses.

Wagner has constructed a simple and practical method for screening disordered thinking on the Rorschach. His TRAUT System appears to offer a reliable alternative to traditional mainstream approaches. As with the other systems presented in this chapter, however, one should consider whether the advantages of adopting a new system outweigh the disadvantages of abandoning traditional and more broadly studied approaches. To justify adopting a new language, a system must offer a conceptual structure or some other unique feature that cannot be found in existing systems. Therefore, the reader should ask whether Wagner's categories and rationale are sufficiently unique and not already addressed adequately in other scoring systems. I believe that much of what Wagner describes can be accounted for with concepts and scoring categories that already exist. For example, many of his HYPOs could be conceptualized as variants of confabulatory thinking. Additionally, Wagner asserted that the TRAUT can account for unusual responses that other systems cannot. He gave the example of a patient who saw Card III as "These are two people beating on drums [usual side and middle Ds], and these are the drums that they threw in the air [top side red Ds]" (Wagner, 1998, p. 740). When asked, the subject indicated that he saw the drums both as stationary and simultaneously as being in the air. Wagner described this response as a "heretofore unknown subspecies of RELERs" (Wagner, 1998, p. 740). However, such a response can already be understood as a contamination response, in which two distinct conceptual and spatial frames of reference (here and there) are merged.

Finally, the exclusion of all DVs seems to be an important omission. Wagner indicated that verbalizations may be "interesting in their own right" but that perception, and not secondary verbalization, is what constitutes thought-disordered responses. This assertion flies in the face of much of what is understood about thought disorder. Wagner's strict adherence to a perceptual model of the Rorschach limits the TRAUT's ability to account for distinctly thought-disordered responses such as peculiar and queer verbalizations, or DVs, incoherent responses, and neologisms. These linguistic anomalies have not only been widely associated with the presence of disordered thinking, but, as we shall see in later chapters, they may have differential diagnostic implications as well.

Abbreviated card set methods

Two groups of researchers have studied the utility in employing abbreviated card sets to assess disordered thinking. Part of their rationale has to do with the obvious promise of allowing busy clinicians to save the time it takes to administer a full 10-card Rorschach.

TDI 4-card sets

The extensive body of TDI research included a study that compared TDI scores on different combinations of 4-card Rorschach sets with TDI scores on the standard 10-card set (Carpenter et al., 1993). The inter-set correlations and the correlations with the 10-card set were high, ranging from 0.79 to 0.97. In summarizing this research, Holzman, Levy, and Johnston (2005) noted that the different card combinations did not correlate well in terms of individual TDI categories.

The authors concluded that the 4-card sets may have a place in clinical settings in which only the global amount of thought disorder is needed. However, they cautioned that their abbreviated card-set approach was not useful in situations where an in-depth understanding of both the amount, severity, and quality of disordered thinking was necessary. In such cases, they advocated using the standard set of ten cards.

TPAS

Leading developers of R-PAS recently investigated the utility of using the standard 10-card set and alternative 3-, 4-, and 5-card sets (Eblin et al., 2014), which they referred to as TPAS. They analyzed data from various archival clinical and nonclinical samples and found that the mean scores across abbreviated card sets were equivalent and demonstrated acceptable inter-rater reliability and validity for the standard 10-card set and the short forms. The researchers found that the 5-card sets had the highest part–whole reliability coefficients and the strongest validity. Using the 3-card series shaved off more time at only a small cost in terms of validity. The investigators also concluded that the 3-card series provided the advantage of offering an additional unique set of cards that can be used for test–retest administrations. Their bottom line was that the use of the 4-card series was least optimal and that only the 5- and 3-card sets should be used for future research.

Eblin and colleagues (2014) were surprised to find that the validity of the FQ variables was lower and that of the Thinking variables was higher than had been anticipated. Although the results were preliminary, the researchers believed that the use of abbreviated 3- and 5-card series could contribute to the science and practice of psychosis assessment.

Finally, Choca, Rossini, and Garside (2016) devised an abbreviated 4-card set they referred to as "Herm." Their practical Rorschach approach is based on the belief that busy clinicians do not have enough time to administer all 10 cards. The group found significant correlations (.94–.97) between variables on their 4-card set and similar variables from a standard 10-card administration. Special scores yielded significant correlations, reinforcing the authors' view that their abbreviated Herm method saves time and accurately identifies thought disorder as well as the standard 10-card approach does. Choca and colleagues are enthusiastic about their Practical Rorschach method; however, they suggested that there are situations, like forensic assessments or when confronted with special referral questions, in which the 10-card administration is preferable. As the TDI and TPAS groups have shown, if the main interest is binary in nature—that is, determining the presence or absence of disordered thinking—then abbreviated card sets might be useful. However, in my opinion, they are less suited to a fine-grained assessment of the individual's ego functioning and internal aspects of self and other experiences.

References

Aronow, E., Reznikoff, M., & Moreland, K. (1994). *The Rorschach Technique: Perceptual Basics, Content Interpretations, and Applications.* Boston, MA: Allyn and Bacon.

Athey, G. I., Colson, D., & Kleiger, J. H. (1993). Manual for Scoring Thought Disorder on the Rorschach. Unpublished manuscript, The Menninger Clinic, Topeka, KS.

Burstein, A. G., & Loucks, S. (1989). *Rorschach Test: Scoring and Interpretation.* New York: Hemisphere Publishing.

Carpenter, J. T., Coleman, M. J., Waternaux, C., Perry, J., Wong, H., O'Brian, C., & Holzman, P. S. (1993). The Thought Disorder Index: Short for assessments. *Psychological Assessment, 5,* 75–80.

Choca, J., Rossini, E., & Garside, D. (2016). The Practical Rorschach: Adjusting the Rorschach for the 21st Century. Symposium presented at the annual meeting of the Society for Personality Assessment, Chicago, IL.

Eblin, J. J., Meyer, G. J., Mihura, J. L., & Viglione, D. J. (2014). Development and Preliminary Validation of a Brief Behavioral Measure of Psychotic Propensity. Unpublished Manuscript.

Harrow, M., & Quinlan, D. (1977). Is disordered thinking unique to schizophrenia? *Archives of General Psychiatry, 34*, 15–21.

Harrow, M., & Quinlan, D. (1985). *Disordered Thinking and Schizophrenic Psychopathology.* New York: Garden Press.

Holzman, P. S., Levy, D. L., & Johnston, N.H. (2005). The use of the Rorschach technique for assessing formal thought disorder. In R. F. Bornstein and J. M. Masling (Eds.), *Scoring the Rorschach: Seven Validated Systems.* New York: Routledge.

Quinlan, D., Harrow, M., Tucker. G., & Carlson, K. (1972). Varieties of "disordered" thinking on the Rorschach findings in schizophrenic and nonschizophrenic patients. *Journal of Abnormal Psychology, 79*, 49–53.

Schuldberg, D., & Boster, J. S. (1985). Back to Topeka: Two types of distance in Rapaport's original Rorschach thought disorder categories. *Journal of Abnormal Psychology, 94*, 205–215.

Singer, M. T., & Wynne, L. C. (1966). Principles for scoring communication defects and deviances in parents of schizophrenics: Rorschach and TAT scoring manuals. *Psychiatry, 29*, 260–288.

Wagner, E. (1998). TRAUT: A Rorschach index for screening thought disorder. *Journal of Clinical Psychology, 54*, 719–762.

Wagner, E., & Rinn, R. C. (1994). A proposed classification scheme for Rorschach autisms. *Perceptual and Motor Skills, 77*, 1–2.

Chapter 8

Integrated model of Rorschach signs of disordered thinking

The extant major Rorschach systems for identifying, coding, and scoring individual examples and composites of disordered language and thinking capture a wide array of forms of disordered verbalization and thought that, with proper training, can be reliably scored. Thought disorder factors from the TDI and composite indices from the CS and R-PAS have been shown to be valid measures of disordered thinking associated with various kinds of diagnostic, demographic, and developmental groups. However, despite some effort to group scores into broad categories according to levels of severity or pertinence to language, reasoning, and/or visual image, to date there has been little attempt to organize existing scores in a manner that is both conceptually coherent and consistent with what is known clinically about thought disorder.

From a conceptual perspective, these systems lack a deeper understanding of what different categories of thought disorder might represent in terms of typical modes of thinking and perceiving, neurocognitive difficulties, developmental theory, or aspects of self and other experiences. The scores have become reified to the point that we often stop with the knowledge that a patient has a DR or gives FABCOMs. These labels too often are endpoints in our psychodiagnostic thinking instead of serving as starting points for trying to understand the psychological, developmental, and even psychodynamic concepts underlying the labels. Additionally, current ways of arranging or grouping thought disorder scores do not link up with what is currently understood about the clinical phenomena of thought disorder or with broader perspectives regarding psychological functioning. Thus, in the end we stop with the language of the test and become content with our assembly of scores without attempting to understand more about what they mean psychologically and how they connect with broader clinical psychopathological constructs concerning thought disorder. In this sense, typical approaches become narrow and circular. Assigning different thought disorder codes to Rorschach responses often leads to the conclusion that the respondent has a thought disorder. This leaves unexplored useful diagnostic questions such as: What might this score suggest about the way that the patient views the world, organizes information, or is likely to behave? What kind of clinical thought disorder is represented by the patient's Special Scores or Cognitive Codes? The essential point is that we can explore further and explain more.

The aim of this chapter is to propose a way of organizing what we currently know about categories of thought disorder scores on the Rorschach. My intention is to arrange existing scores into conceptually meaningful domains.

Conceptual models for organizing dimensions of thought disorder

Much has been written about the role that conceptualization and theory can play in making inferences and integrating data from psychodiagnostic testing (Schafer, 1954; Jaffee, 1990; Lerner, 1990, 1991; Sugarman, 1991; Kleiger, 1992a, 1992b, 1999; Holt, 2009). Weiner (1986) indicated that conceptual approaches to the Rorschach not only offer clinicians the pleasure of understanding what lies behind test scores, but they also broaden the horizons of our knowledge of Rorschach psychology by encouraging clinicians to explore linkages between test variables and nontest behavior. Several existing factor-based models of thought disorder can serve as a conceptual basis for organizing what is known about Rorschach thought disorder categories.

The DSM-III (American Psychiatric Association, 1980) listed four signs of thought disorder that included (1) loose associations, (2) incoherence, (3) illogical thinking, and (4) poverty of content of speech. Caplan et al. (1989) operationalized these signs in their K-FTDS instrument for assessing thought disorder in children. The first two signs can be combined because they both involve the sequencing and organization of verbalizations.

Other factor-analytic models of schizophrenia symptomatology shed light on different dimensions of psychopathology and specific characteristics of disordered thinking. Liddle (1987) proposed a three-factor model that included: (1) disorganization (formal thought disorder, inappropriate affect, and bizarre behavior; (2) symptoms of reality distortion (i.e. positive symptoms such as delusions and hallucinations); and (3) psychomotor poverty (poverty of speech, flat affect, and decreased voluntary movement). Using Rorschach and TAT data, Liddle and colleagues (2002) developed the TLI as an alternative instrument to assess thought disorder. They factor analyzed thought disorder responses in patients with acute and chronic forms of schizophrenia and found three nearly independent factors that captured characteristics of positive and negative thought disorder: (1) impoverished thought and language (poverty of speech and speech content); (2) disorganized thought and language (looseness, peculiar word usage, poor syntax and logic); and (3) nonspecific dysregulation of thought (perseveration and distractibility).

Findings from these studies suggest three dimensions of thought disorder, which can be conceptualized as disorganization, illogicality, and impoverishment. As noted in Chapter 1, Kleiger and Khadivi (2015) approached thought disorder more broadly from four points of view, including (1) *How* things are said;

(2) *What* is said; (3) *Where* the conclusions and inferences come from or how they are formulated; and (4) *Who* one's thoughts and words are shared with and *When* they are communicated. To stay focused on the process of thinking and verbalizing, and not on the content of one's thoughts or perceptions (i.e. *What* is said, such as delusions and hallucinations), we can modify the four points of view as follows: (1) *How* things are said; (2) *Where* the conclusions and inferences come from and *How* they are formulated; (3) *Whether* one can perceive, think, and verbalize with sufficient adequacy and detail; and (4) *With Whom and When* one's thoughts and words are shared. The first three perspectives conform to the dimensions of (1) disorganization (*How* things are said or what is typically known as "formal thought disorder"); (2) illogicality (*Where* one's conclusions and inferences come from or *How* one reasons); and (3) impoverishment (*Whether* one can think and verbalize adequately and with sufficient detail and elaboration). The fourth aspect addresses the social appropriateness of what one says. By adding this element to our understanding of thought disorder, we can include issues related to whether the individual is aware of the social implications of what he or she has said.

An integrated Rorschach model for conceptualizing thought disorder

The proposed model conceptualizes disordered thought processes in terms of (1) Disorganization; (2) Illogicality; (3) Impoverished Speech and Thinking; and (4) Awareness of Disturbance. The model does not introduce new scores or rename existing scores to capture novel examples of disordered thinking. Instead, the model utilizes widely accepted scoring categories from the CS and R-PAS with acceptable reliability and validity. Although many categories from the Rapaport and Holt systems and the TDI (as well as some from other, nontraditional systems) contribute to understanding the nuances of disordered thinking as it comes to life on the Rorschach, the effort here is to incorporate them into existing categories in the CS and R-PAS. The purpose of introducing this model is to help diagnosticians conceptualize beyond the scores themselves and organize Rorschach TD scores in a manner that comports with what is understood about thought disorder in clinical settings.

Disorganized or idiosyncratic speech: Language, focusing, and filtering problems

Deviant Verbalizations (DVs)

DVs involve problems in language production and semantics; retrieval may also be present. When giving a DV, the respondent selects an inappropriate or inaccurate word or phrase to express his ideas. Milder DVs are common in speech samples and may reflect situational anxiety, educational, cultural, or regional factors. Word misusage with meaning preserved typically merits Level 1 scoring. As words and phrases become increasingly private or invented language becomes difficult to understand, the response should be scored DV2. In some cases, the words used are unremarkable; however, meaning is obscured. Absurd DVs contain entire phrases that are nonsensical and unrelated to anything in the inkblot.

- "These look like the *antlers* of the bug." (Common word substitution; DV1)
- "The ways these here flare out. It's just the *flarage* of this part here that I'm talking about." (Mild neologism. Meaning is not obscured; DV1)
- "An *ancillarian vestige* pig." (Nonsensical neologism; DV2; Meyer et al., 2011, p. 114)
- The *echo of a picture*." (Real words used in an overly private, obscure manner; DV2; Holzman, Levy, & Johnston, 2005, p. 68)
- "Bits and pieces of Brazil." (Absurd DV2)
- "The dead mouth of a cat." (Absurd DV2)

Deviant Responses (DRs)

DRs are a broad class of response types that reflect disturbances in focusing (either loss of focus or hyper-focus), filtering (inhibition), and self-monitoring. As such, they may represent isolated deficiencies in executive functions. In responding, subjects may either abruptly depart or progressively wander away from the blot, or they may attribute inappropriate detail and meaning to the inkblot. In some cases, the respondent may lose focus and associate *away* from the blot. In other cases, the respondent may become hyper-focused and overassociate *into* the blot. In either case, there is a failure to maintain a rule set (i.e. "What might this be?") and filter associations and verbalizations that are inappropriate to task instructions of the stimulus features of the inkblot.

Another way to think about DRs is to consider Rapaport's concept of distance from the inkblot. Here, we can distinguish between two types of distance, *associative distance* and *interpretive distance*. By associative distance, we mean that the subject begins with a response to the card and then moves away from this response with subsequent associations. Hence, his associations become progressively distant from the inkblot and initial response. In interpretive distance, the respondent moves further away from the card and the initial response; but this time, it is the interpretation of the blot, and not the verbal associations to the blot, that becomes increasingly distant or removed.

With DRs, there is a loss of focus or loss of set, leading to either brief irrelevant intrusions or rambling, sometimes incoherent, departures from or overinterpretations of the Rorschach task. As Rorschach representations of disordered thinking, DRs typically reflect distractible speech, derailment, looseness, tangentiality, or circumstantiality. However, in some cases the process involves failure to modulate the amount of detail or attributing an inappropriate level of specificity to the inkblot. Here, the problem becomes one of overinterpretation, or perhaps projection, where one superimposes internal ideas onto external reality.

The DR category contains heterogeneous response types, each of which reflects a unique kind of derailment from or embellishment of the initial response. Six subtypes include:

1. Inappropriate Phrase DRs. Brief, sidebar comments that are intrusive and irrelevant to the task and response.
   - "A bat *but I was hoping to see a butterfly.*" (DR1)
   - "Looks like two children playing. *You have boys right? They don't play these games.*" (DR1)
   - "Two circus animals, back to back. *I really detest circuses with how they treat animals.*" (DR1)
2. Circumstantial Response DRs. These responses are essentially Rorschach examples of "loose associations." The associations and verbalization ramble away from the initial response. These responses typify difficulties with associative distance. Each consecutive association may prompt additional derailment as in the example below. However, the narrative quality of the response, though rambling and distant, is not incoherent.
   - "This looks like a bat … My uncle shot one in his backyard. I really hate bats, but I'm told they are good for the environment, which has all sorts of problems with air pollution. The government really needs to do something about all of this stuff. The leaking of classified documents is what happens when the government loses control over what is put over the air." (DR2; Kleiger & Khadivi, 2015, p. 105)
3. Fluid Verbalization DRs. Similar to Circumstantial DRs, except that the response loses coherence. In a Circumstantial DR, the respondent associates loosely, but each association, taken as a unit, is reasonably comprehensible. In Fluid Verbalization DRs, the verbal associations are so unstable and disorganized that the response is incoherent, making the default score a DR2.
   - "Two animals with their pillows right here, they got a rat-snake ears and their shame here, I see them down home, down here. They had a house in the woods with a rat and snake. I took the broom…" (DR2; Meyer et al., 2011, p. 116)
4. Flippant Response DRs. The subject departs from the usual social/professional context of the testing situation and makes an inappropriate sidebar comment. Flippant responses are highlighted because of their potential as diagnostic features of manic thought disorder (Solovay, Shenton, & Holzman, 1987; Khadivi, Wetzler, & Wilson, 1997). In some cases, Flippant DRs also reflect a breach in the social context of the Rorschach. In other words, either with intention or not, the subject says something that he should not.
   - A vagina. *Hey, you must think I'm a sex addict. Don't write that one down; they'll take me away!* (DR1)

- Is this helping you? Good, 'cause I wouldn't do it if it wasn't helping you. Being my generous personality. (Holzman, Levy, & Johnston, 2005)
5 Confabulatory DRs. Responses are characterized by inappropriate degrees of elaboration, embellishment, and attributing meaning beyond what is justified by the stimulus properties of the inkblot. These responses reflect a problem of interpretive distance. Confabulation DRs are distinguished from typical DRs, which reflect a loss of focus, wandering away, or digression from the task. Here, the filtering problem pertains to being unable to contain, rein in, and limit one's ideational elaboration of the response. Confabulation DRs are characterized not by a loss of focus but by a hyper-focus on the significance of certain details, an inappropriate attribution of meaning, or a narrative elaboration of the response (Kleiger & Peebles-Kleiger, 1993; Kleiger, 1999). As such, Confabulation DRs are understood as interpretive or reasoning errors as opposed to products of loss of focus and derailment. Four criteria for judging overinterpretation (Saunders, 1991) and inappropriate specificity include: (1) Adding unseen characters not represented in the blot; (2) Adding a time sequence. Look for mention of what "was before" or "will come after" the image; (3) Attributing internal states (thoughts, complex or elaborated affects, motivation) to percept. Simple, singular affect attribution such as "angry, sad, or happy faces" are considered to fall below the threshold for DR Confabulation because there may be form features (e.g. shape of eyes or mouth) that may justify attribution of these simpler affects; and (4) Attribution of characteristics (age, species, origin, type) that are not justified.
- "Two bloody rabbits that were killed by a hunter." (Introduction of unseen characters; DR1)
- "Baby birds. They look hungry and scared." (Attributing internal states; DR1)
- "Two women who were out shopping and later stopped for lunch and a chat." (Introduction of time sequence; DR1)

Level of severity is based on loss of coherence and degree of inappropriate (and in some cases absurd) attribution of qualities that cannot be justified by inkblot features.

- "It looks like two women from different cultures. They are the same but different. You can tell that they come from the same background but have gone their separate ways. Their looks and postures indicate that they have hostile intentions, plotting revenge against each other. Or maybe both are trying to get the same man who they fell in love with. But he probably chose one or the other, and now they are trying to settle the score." (DR2: Kleiger & Khadivi, 2015, p. 106)
- "Two schnauzers. Look like females, probably three to four years old." (Overly specific qualification; DR2)

6 Overly Symbolic DRs. Confabulatory DRs may reflect the infusion of an inappropriate level of symbolism into the response. Symbolism is part of the representational process; however, symbolism gone awry is typically a result of an overattribution of meaning based on concrete features of the blot (color, form, or position). In each case, there may be a movement away or a reading in of meaning.
- "The hearts indicate that they are in love and the things at the side show the music they are listening to." (DR1)
- "Here is heaven and earth. The red symbolizes how all life began in the fire. The blue represents the cooling of life as we evolved throughout the ages, as is true for all life forms reaching for the ultimate place in the universe, which is at the top there." (DR2)

Experts in both CS and R-PAS scoring (Viglione, 2010; Meyer et al., 2011) have provided an operational two-step guideline for determining when a DR reaches the threshold for a Level 2 designation.

Illogicality: Errors in reasoning and problems in conceptual thinking and inference making

Combinatory reasoning

Inappropriate—incompatible, implausible, illogical, or impossible—links are formed between discrete, often contiguous, parts of the inkblot. The boundaries of each part of the blot remain separate and intact.

Perceptual and thought processes: In combinatory reasoning, perceptual reality trumps conceptual reality. Inkblot details are combined in a manner that defies logic. The deviant reasoning process is based on spatial or temporal contiguity, with things that occur close together believed to have a meaningful connection.

There are two separate categories, both of which can be scored as either Level 1 or Level 2. Score INC1 or FAB1 for cartoon-like combinations or those that are whimsical. Score INC2 or FAB2 when the combination is more illogical and bizarre. The reader is directed to the R-PAS manual for examples of INC and FAB responses (Meyer et al., 2011, pp. 120–124). Playful combinations can be either INCs or FABs, which are fanciful and involve inappropriate combinations and overelaboration.

1 Incongruous Combinations (INC). The inappropriate combination is *within* a single object and can be viewed in terms of:
- Inappropriate detail combination: "*A man with a beak.*" (INC1)
- Inappropriate color combination: "*Red* bears." (INC1)
- Inappropriate image-action combination, benign: "*Dancing* insects." (INC1)
- Inappropriate image-action combination, bizarre: "A man *shedding his skin.*" (INC2)

- Inappropriate image-substance combination: "Bushes *made of smoke*." (INC2)
- Inappropriate spatial relationships: transparencies: "Torso, see the shoulders and biceps. *You can see the heart and stomach too.*" (INC2)

2 Fabulized Combinations (FABs). The inappropriate combination is *between* two or more objects, each of which remains intact. The inappropriate combination can be viewed in terms of:
  - Inappropriate relationship combination, benign: "Two bears *playing patty cake*." (FAB1)
  - Inappropriate relationship, bizarre: "Two girls with *worms coming out of their heads*." (FAB2)
  - Inappropriate relationship combination based on size: "Lions climbing up a *Xmas tree*." (FAB1)

3 Playful Combinations. Some INC or FAB responses can be characterized as "Playful Combinations" (elsewhere referred to as "playful confabulations") (Solovay et al., 1986), which have been found to have diagnostic significance in manic conditions (Solovay et. al., 1987; Khadivi, Wetzler, & Wilson, 1997). Playful Combinations are fanciful and playful images that have a humorous quality. Form level may be preserved.
  - "Ants in tuxedos at a disco." (FAB1)
  - "A butterfly on steroids." (INC1)
  - "Insects celebrating at the Mardi Gras." (FAB1)

Confabulatory reasoning

Although we have retained the score of DR for conceptual purposes, we include Confabulatory Reasoning among the errors of reasoning and logic because it fundamentally involves a faulty thinking process characterized by inappropriate attribution of meaning.

Peculiar reasoning

Referred to as ALOG in other Rorschach systems, PEC in R-PAS is coded for spontaneous and explicit expressions reflecting "strained, confused, or overly concrete reasoning" (Meyer et al., 2011, p. 118). As indicated in the R-PAS manual, the illogicality in a PEC response can either be given as a brief, explicit rationale or imbedded in a wordy response with bizarre content and repetitive casual explanations. In the R-PAS, PEC can only be scored if it occurs spontaneously (in either the response process (RP) or clarification process (CP)). It cannot be scored if prompted by the examiner. Readers should note that this is not the case with scoring ALOG in the TDI.

Thought process: Peculiar reasoning often reflects what Arieti (1974) referred to as "paleologic thinking," in which a conclusion is based simply on two entities sharing a similar quality, or two subjects sharing the same predicate. Some PECs reflect illogical conclusions based on concrete elements such as position, color, or number. Other PECs reflect bizarre and convoluted reasoning that is wordy and long-winded.

- "It's on top, *so it must be* a crown." (Concrete Positional PEC; Meyer et al., 2011, p. 118)
- "It's green, *so it's gotta be* a maple leaf." (Concrete Color PEC; Meyer et al., 2011, p. 118)
- "*It must be* a man and woman *because* they are two." (Concrete Number PEC; Meyer et al., 2011, p. 118)
- "*It has to be* kidneys because it is next to the horse." (Bizarre PEC; Meyer et al., 2011, p. 118)
- "An animal or a bug. (What made it look like that?) The colors, the way they were in order ... I associate color with moving around and animals aren't very stationary usually; anything that is colorful is movable ... like a wall would be of one color and that was a series of colors and therefore movable and animals are usually very active." (Bizarre ALOG; Rapaport, Gill, & Schafer, 1946/1968, p. 440).

Although PECs or ALOGs are not assigned Level 1 and 2 severity designations, one can listen for the pregnant quality of strained reasoning even in responses that do not meet strict criteria for receiving such scores. For example, clinicians should pay attention to a PEC/ALOG even when it occurs late in the Inquiry (CP in R-PAS parlance). Even though one would not assign this score, the subject might be revealing a strain in logic when questioned closely and pressed to justify her conclusions.

Condensed Reasoning

Condensation, symbolism, and displacement are three forms of primary process ideation. In Condensed Reasoning, two or more percepts or ideas lose their separate identities and become comingled. The condensation of blot images may reflect partial interpenetration of one image into another or a complete merging and fusion of separate images into a single bizarre image.

Thought process: Condensation reflects boundary porousness, penetration, and collapse. The subject demonstrates difficulty maintaining perceptual and ideational boundaries between self and non-self (Blatt & Ritzler, 1974) or maintaining separate and distinct frames of reference.

Fluid shifting between separate alternative images in which there is a lesser degree of infiltration or interpenetration of one image into the other falls short of a complete merging of images. For example, the following responses demonstrate how separate concepts begin to lose their separate identity.

- "Clouds or dogs ... dogs on clouds, or clouds covering dogs ... kind of cloudy colored dogs but really just clouds, I guess."

- "A rug or a bear ... rug. Like a bear or a rug. A bearskin rug. Some kind of furry rug or animal like a bear with four legs."

I refer to such responses as "image fluidity." Unfortunately, these responses cannot be scored as mild Contaminations because CONTAM does not include levels of severity. The appropriate score from R-PAS and the CS would be a DR2. However, it is important for clinicians to ascertain the underlying process of condensation in the subject's thinking as he gives such as response. There are two subtypes of contamination responses: Fusion and Simultaneous.

1 Fusion Contamination. These are bizarre-sounding condensations in which two different images are merged into a single percept, often producing a verbal condensation (neologism):
    - "Looks like a bat and pumpkin. Like a bat-o-lantern." (CONTAM)
    - "Looks like bigfoot Tutankhamen." (CONTAM)
2 Simultaneous Contamination. These are more benign-sounding responses when they are first given. However, we later find that the subject is using the same location to represent both a part and the whole:
    - "Looks like a bat. The whole thing." (Card I. The subject explains that the Popular W is both the whole bat and the bat's face.)
    - "Two women eating shrimp." (Card VII. The W is both the two women and the shrimp.)

Impoverished speech and thinking: Fragmentation, constriction, and poverty of speech and ideas

This category of Rorschach response phenomena lacks specific scoring categories in the CS and R-PAS. The TDI has a few scores that can be associated with negative thought disorder and cognitive impairment, such as Fragmentation, Vagueness, and Confusion responses. However, these scores occur infrequently, and it may be difficult to establish suitable anchor points for reliable scoring. Nonetheless, clinicians can be alert to the possible significance of these "soft" categories for diagnostic purposes,

Thought process: These responses reflect impoverishment or impairment in perceptual, ideational, and linguistic processes. In cases of cognitive impairment, the respondent may lack the interpretive resources to manage the Rorschach. This lack of "interpretive awareness" may lead the respondent to try to recognize, as oppose to interpret, the blots. This challenge may be too much for the subject, who either responds with a scarcity of words, ideas, and associations or with perplexity and confusion. The complexity of the Rorschach may give way to perseverative responding, wherein the respondent gives the same or variations of the same simple response to many, if not all, of the cards. Perseveration on the Rorschach may reflect defensiveness and resistance to task engagement, developmental immaturity, avolitionality, amotivation, or cognitive impairment.

Perceptually, subjects may either focus on single details, avoiding the more cognitively complex task of synthesizing blot elements or fragmenting the blot into unusual details. Rorschach called these responses "oligophrenic details" or "Do" responses, in which the respondent focuses only on a part of a blot area for his response, instead of the typical D or W usually associated with that response (Rorschach, 1921/1942). Rapaport gives the example of a subject who sees "Heads of two men" on Card III but does not see their trunks or arms (Rapaport, Gill, & Schafer, 1946/1968).

Two of Rapaport's scores, codified in the TDI, were Vagueness and Confusion responses. Rapaport regarded them in terms of a "withering of the response itself, whether due to perceptual or verbal difficulty" (Rapaport, Gill, & Schafer, 1946/1968, p. 448). Both can be diagnostically useful; however, their rarity offsets their diagnostic utility. Vagueness responses are characterized by a poverty of expressed meaning in the response. The vague response contains too little information to score. It may be a short, cryptic phrase or a long, meandering, circumstantial paragraph. Vague responses might reflect the subject's unwillingness to engage, a masked attempt to avoid giving a response. If this sort of defensive set can be ruled out, a vague response may reflect the individual's inability to hold onto the percept and elaborate a response. According to Rapaport, "vagueness of verbalization refers to the subject's weak hold on a definite form percept; confusion refers to a confusion within the response itself or in the subject's experiencing and communication of the response" (p. 448). As with many atypical responses, we would assign DR to such impotent verbalizations.

- "A picture of … like depth and stuff, like distance." (Vague DR1)
- "This just has a … sorta feeling of … of openness about it, that … it's sort of like … open through here, with all the white space…" (Vague DR1)

When the subject, not the examiner, becomes confused by what he or she is seeing and trying to recognize or interpret, then his/her expression of perplexity or impotence (Piotrowski, 1937) suggests an ideational or more general cognitive impoverishment.

- "These things could be doing something together but I don't know what. Looks like maybe people but I can't be sure because they don't look like anything I've ever seen before and none of it makes sense. It seems out of place with the rest of it. It doesn't fit in any way. I just said some things together because that's the way I said it. But I'm really not sure." (Confusion DR2)
- "A crab, maybe have red legs … I don't know … it's, it's … I haven't seen a crab in the ocean for a long time. Not ocean, but … you know what I mean … you know when the … when … when there is … is … a way … to know … that … there is something … to do … with … the water an' the crab, but … uh, I would say … uh … I don't know, I mean the crab … usually isn't that far in the ocean, it's only about this much water, in … a … uh…" (Confusion DR2)

Awareness of disturbance: Social cognitive aspects of thought disorder

This is the newest and most novel aspect of thought disorder. Only recently have researchers begun to explore ways to determine subjects' awareness of the disturbance in their thinking and perception. Methods to assess awareness address the *When and With Whom* aspect of thought disorder (Rothschild-Yakar et al., 2015). Typically addressed by post-inquiry testing of limits, techniques for assessing the patient's awareness of the social inappropriateness of what she or he saw and said will prove to be an increasingly important component of assessing disordered thinking on the Rorschach.

The proposed model is not intended to supplant existing scoring systems that have gained prominence through empirical support and convention. The purpose of presenting an integrated model is twofold. First, the intention is to move beyond the scores themselves toward a fuller conceptual understanding of the psychological processes that they represent. As stated at the beginning of this chapter, Rorschach thought disorder scores suffer from reification. In other words, incidents of disorganization, illogicality or impoverishment are tagged, coded, and simply referred to as indices of loose, scattered, or disordered thinking. Second, the proposed model serves to organize the panoply of scores in a coherent manner, which conforms to how thought disorder is regarded clinically. The ultimate aim is to enrich current scoring systems like the CS and R-PAS informally rather than by introducing formal changes into the scores themselves. As clinicians come to understand the processes underlying the scores they use and form linkages with the existing clinical concepts, they can fulfill their roles as expert diagnostic consultants.

References

American Psychiatric Association. (1980). *Diagnostic and Statistical Manual of Mental Disorders* (3rd ed.). Washington, DC: Author.

Arieti, S. (1974). *Interpretation of Schizophrenia* (2nd ed.). New York: Basic Books.

Blatt, S. J., & Ritzler, B. A. (1974). Thought disorder and boundary disturbances in psychosis. *Journal of Consulting and Clinical Psychology, 42*, 370–381.

Caplan, R., Guthrie, D., Fish, B., Tanguay, P. E., & David-Lando, G. (1989). The kiddie formal thought disorder rating scale: Clinical assessment, reliability, and validity. *Journal of the American Academy of Child & Adolescent Psychiatry, 28*, 408–416.

Holt, R. R. (2009). *Primary Process Thinking: Theory, Measurement, and Research* (Vols. 1 & 2). Lanham, MD: Aronson.

Holzman, P. S., Levy, D.L., & Johnston, M. H. (2005). The use of the Rorschach technique for assessing formal thought disorder. In R. F. Bornstein & J. M. Masling (Eds.), *Scoring the Rorschach: Seven Validated Systems*. New York: Routledge.

Jaffee, L. S. (1990). The empirical foundations of psychoanalytic approaches to psychological testing. *Journal of Personality Assessment, 55*, 746–755.

Khadivi, A., Wetzler, S., & Wilson, A. (1997). Manic indices on the Rorschach. *Journal of Personality Assessment, 69*, 365–375.

Kleiger, J. H. (1992a). A conceptual critique of the EA: es comparison in the Comprehensive Rorschach System. *Psychological Assessment, 4*, 288–296.

Kleiger, J. H. (1992b). A response to Exner's comments on "A conceptual critique of the EA: es comparison in the Comprehensive Rorschach System." *Psychological Assessment, 4*, 301–302.

Kleiger, J. H. (1999). *Disordered Thinking and The Rorschach*. Hillsdale, NJ: The Analytic Press.

Kleiger, J. H., & Khadivi, A. (2015). *Assessing Psychosis. A Clinician's Guide*. New York: Routledge.

Kleiger, J. H., & Peebles-Kleiger, M. J. (1993). Toward a conceptual understanding of the deviant response in the Comprehensive Rorschach System. *Journal of Personality Assessment, 60*, 74–90.

Lerner, P. (1990). The clinical inference process and the role of theory. *Journal of Personality Assessment, 55*, 426–431.

Lerner, P. (1991). *Psychoanalytic Theory and the Rorschach*. Hillsdale, NJ: The Analytic Press.

Liddle, P. F. (1987). The symptoms of chronic schizophrenia: A re-examination of the positive-negative dichotomy. *The British Journal of Psychiatry, 151*, 145–151.

Liddle, P. F., Ngan, E. T. C., Caissie, S. L., Anderson, C. M., Bates, A. T., Quested, D. J., White, R., & Weg, R. (2002). Thought and Language Index: An instrument for assessing thought and language in schizophrenia. *The British Journal of Psychiatry, 181*, 326–330.

Meyer, G. J., Viglione, D. J., Mihura, J. L., Erard, R. E., & Erdberg, P. (2011). *Rorschach Performance Assessment System: Administration, Coding, Interpretation, and Technical Manual*. Toledo, OH: Rorschach Performance Assessment System.

Piotrowski, Z. A. (1937). The Rorschach ink-blot method in organic disturbances of the central nervous system. *Journal of Nervous and Mental Disease, 86*, 525–537.

Rapaport, D., Gill, M., & Schafer, R. (1968). *Diagnostic Psychological Testing* (Rev. ed.). R. R. Holt, Ed. New York: International Universities Press. (Original work published in 1946.)

Rorschach, H. (1942). *Psychodiagnostics* (5th ed.). Bern, Switzerland: Hans Huber. (Original work published in 1921.)

Rothschild-Yakar, L., Lacoua, L., Brener, A., & Koren, D. (2015). Impairments in interpersonal representations and deficits in social cognition as predictors of risk for schizophrenia in non-patient adolescents. Paper presented at the annual meeting of the Society for Personality Assessment, Brooklyn, NY.

Saunders, E. A. (1991). Rorschach indicators of sexual abuse. *Bulletin of the Menninger Clinic, 55*, 48–71.

Schafer, R. (1954). *Psychoanalytic Interpretation in Rorschach Testing*. New York: Grune & Stratton.

Solovay, M. R., Shenton, M. E, Gasperetti, C., Coleman, M., Kestenbaum, E., Carpenter, T., & Holzman, P. S. (1986). Scoring Manual for the Thought Disorder Index. *Schizophrenia Bulletin, 1*, 485–492.

Solovay, M. R., Shenton, M. E., & Holzman, P. S. (1987). Comparative studies of thought disorders. *Archives of General Psychiatry, 44*, 13–20.

Sugarman, A. (1991). Where's the beef? Putting personality back into personality assessment. *Journal of Personality Assessment, 56*, 130–144.

Viglione, D. J. (2010). *Rorschach Coding Solutions: A Reference Guide for the Comprehensive System* (2nd ed.). San Diego, CA: Author.

Weiner, I. B. (1986). Conceptual and empirical perspectives on the Rorschach assessment of psychopathology. *Journal of Personality Assessment, 50*, 472–479.

Part III

Dimensions of disordered thinking

Chapter 9

Disorganization
Problems in focusing, filtering, and language usage

When discussing the disorganization dimension of thought disorder, we are thrust back into the dialectics of thought and speech—namely, whether it is more accurate to conceive of thought disorders as problems of speaking or thinking. This question was introduced in Chapter 1 and revisited in Chapter 8, in which I proposed a broad-based model for organizing thought disorder scores on the Rorschach. Although it may be artificial to make a hard distinction between thought disorders that primarily involve verbalizing and those that reflect thinking, I choose to make a softer distinction. This does not imply that the thinking underlying speaking is not also disorganized, but for the sake of clarity I focus primarily on disorganization as a dimension observed through expressive speech. Thus, my interest in this chapter is on what makes speech disorganized, how to capture this on the Rorschach, and how to conceptualize it from multiple perspectives (psychological, psychopathological, linguistic, neuropsychological, psychotherapeutic, and psychoanalytic).

What makes disorganized speech disorganized?

This section heading may strike the reader as obvious and unnecessary. Most people are willing to accept the circular definition that disorganized speech is characterized by disorganization. However, it is useful to peel back the circularity and offer some operational concepts that help explain what makes speech sound disorganized.

From the speaker's perspective, we regard verbalizations that lack order, direction, sequence, structure, and linkage as being less organized. From the listener's perspective, verbal communication that lacks clarity, becomes confusing, and loses coherence can be termed "disorganized." When someone speaks in ways that confuse us, we consider the possibility of thought disorder. When individuals link their words in ways that defy conventional order, disrupt the rules of syntax, fail to filter irrelevant bits of information, and leave us in the dark, we regard their speech as disorganized. When someone uses words idiosyncratically and misuses or invents them so as to obscure meaning and coherence, then it is reasonable to consider the possibility of a thought disorder. Disorganization

126 Dimensions of disordered thinking

is the essence of the historic concept of formal thought disorder. It is what the DSM-5 is now calling "Disorganized Thinking (Speech)" (American Psychiatric Association, 2013, p. 88).

Rorschach indicators of disorganization: Coded and uncoded

In Chapter 8, I delineated Rorschach subcategories of DV and DR as the primary representatives of disorganization and idiosyncratic language. Referred to by different names over the years, these scores capture verbalizations that reflect idiosyncratic language and disorganized verbal expression. However, in addition to noting these familiar codes for deviant and disorganized verbalization, examiners should remain attuned to more subtle forms of disjointed verbal expression that might elude traditional categories of DV and DR. First, though, let us look more closely at DV and DR.

Traditionally coded responses

The R-PAS manual (Meyer et al., 2011, pp. 113–117) devoted great care to defining and delineating DVs and distinguishing between Level 1 and Level 2 severity. However, it is useful to pull apart the Rorschach categories of DV and DR that we have been using and take a fresh look at Holt's rich and bountiful taxonomy of thought disorder scoring categories presented in his most recent book (2009). Several categories from Holt's manual for measuring primary process thinking on the Rorschach and TAT are consistent with what I am referring to as disorganization.

In particular, Holt's categories of Displacement and Verbalization reflect disturbances in verbal associative or linguistic dimensions of the response. For example, Displacement responses, scored DR1 and DR2 in the CS and R-PAS, include fluid associative thinking, clang associations, puns, figures of speech, anachronisms, and verbal slips. In coding DRs, Viglione and the R-PAS team (Viglione, 2010; Meyer, et al., 2011) followed Holt's lead by specifying that the subject needed to make at least two associative departures from the initial response focus in order to score a DR. Examples of Holt's Displacement DRs are presented below.

1   Chain Association (D-chain): Fluid associative thinking, in which the speaker goes from one idea to another without guidance or an organizing set, making at least two associative jumps away from the original topic.
    • "A star (Query). This and this and ... 6-point star, 106th Division, see I was in an ambulatory division, I wasn't a doughboy—I think is the word some KP call them [tells story about KP] ... " (Holt, 2009, p. 98).
2   Distant Association (D-dist): Characterized by nonsense or inappropriate elaboration, which may or may not be possible to follow. Holt recommended scoring when the speaker strays from the focus according to some loose

principle or clang association. Here, the subject is not simply changing the topic but is talking about some aspect of the original idea that is not related to the ongoing verbalization.
- "Blood of a rabbit; here's his paws—the rabbit's name is George; a woman's vagina, what we all try to bow to; I'm not certain if that is a crawfish or shrimp but we do know that they are cold-blooded; it could look like a vagina; I wouldn't say it was. It's hard enough to read a financial statement, let alone that" (Holt, 2009, p. 99).

3 Puns and Malapropisms (D-clang): Substituting one word with another of similar sound, or by a homonym, perhaps with humorous intent. Malapropisms involve an incorrect word substitution.
- *"That looks like a sexy sports car, it's auto-erotic."*
- *"A moth and these are the hands* [legs] *and its feelings* [feelers]."

4 Verbal Slips (DS). Scored when one word is substituted for another. Slips are assumed to reflect a disruption of language under the pressure of a primary process idea, which might be reflected by the intruding word.
- "Bats are supposed to sleep, *standing* upside down" (Holt, 2009, p. 102).
- "This looks like two women blowing up balloons. Just taking *breasts* as they keep doing this."

Verbalization responses include separate scores for peculiarity, queerness, verbal condensation, and incoherence. Some examples from Holt's Verbalization category include the following scores.

5 Peculiar Verbalizations (VP): Peculiar verbalizations catch the listener's ear, like a musical note that is slightly off key. However, unlike Queer verbalizations, the meaning is not lost. Peculiar verbalizations receive a DV1 score in the CS and R-PAS.
- "Looks like a rabbit because it has resembling ears."
- "There's a segregation between the mouth and nose" (Holzman, Levy, & Johnston, 2005, p. 67).

6 Queer Verbalizations (VQ): Queer verbalizations reflect a distortion in language expression. Holt maintained that VQ responses reflect a failure to maintain an appropriate set when talking about what one sees. The language may be stilted, idiosyncratic, or overly private. These are typically scored DV2 in the CS and R-PAS.
- "The adhesive adjunctive extensions" (Holzman et al., 2005, p. 68).
- "A foxed comic dog" (Holzman et al., 2005, p. 68).

Sometimes, the image, as opposed to the verbalization, is queer sounding and difficult to comprehend.

- "A tree head kind of a person" (Holzman et al., 2005, p. 68).
- "Glorified rain; intestines of the tunnel" (Kleiger, 1999, p. 86).

The R-PAS manual makes a clear distinction between Peculiar (DV1) and Queer (DV2) responses by focusing on the clarity or lack of clarity of the intended meaning (Meyer et al., 2011).

7 Verbal Condensations (VC): These are neologisms or portmanteau words that condense separate elements. The levels of severity can be mild (Level 1) or severe (Level 2).
   - "Diaphragram." Condenses diagram and diaphragm. Level 2 severity.
   - "Ambisextrous." Condenses ambidextrous and bisexual. Level 2 severity.
8 Verbal Incoherence or Confusion (VI): Holt scores this when the associations are extremely bizarre, the connections omitted, or connections are made on idiosyncratic, arbitrary grounds. The result is the use of words that "fail to communicate and become unintelligible. VI is unlikely to occur except in schizophrenia, organic psychoses, LSD intoxication, or other gross interferences in thought and speech" (Holt, 2009, p. 134).
   - "Dopey—like a double take of himself. [Examiner question] Uh-huh. For whatever twist at this point (laugh) I can't seem to always feel as if—but of course, I'm speaking about myself and that, well, relationship that (laugh). [Examiner question] Well, that, I mean, not that I can't feel anything, it's just that, I guess, I seem to lose grasp of the situation…" (Holt, 2009, p. 134).

Uncoded verbalizations

Beyond searching for scorable forms of disorganized verbalization in Rorschach responses, it is equally important for examiners to listen to the wording and uses of language that may easily evade detection and not be captured by conventional scoring categories. I refer here to formal linguistic qualities such as the subject's cadence, rate, rhythm, linkage, and the cohesion and coherence of what he is saying. Sensitivity to sentence structure and listening for shifts in cadence and subtle breaks in the patient's speech can reveal underlying fragmentation in the patient's thinking (Hussein, Personal communication, March 11, 2016). Taking a broader view of disorganization frees us from becoming overly bound to scoring categories and more attuned to how an individual is speaking and, by inference, the formal qualities of his or her thinking.

In approaching the TAT, Shentoub (1987) spoke about the "readability" of the narrative as a first "filter" for determining whether the listener can understand the speaker (Hussein, Personal communication, March 11, 2016). Although verbal samples are more restricted in Rorschach responses, it is important to listen to the subject's sentence structure. Hussein pointed out that in conventional verbal communication, sentences typically require a subject, verb, and object. In contrast, sentences in thought-disordered speech may lack at least one of these elements, leading to fragmented verbal communication. As listeners, we may "fill in the gaps"; however, in doing so, we might overlook the fact that the subject's verbal fragmentation might also reflect fragmented thinking. For example, the subject might respond to Card II with *"Animal ... blood there. See. Bloody paws."* We take for granted that the subject is focusing on what looks like an animal and blood. However, careful listening reveals that something is missing. There is a gap between "animal" and "blood." What happened to the animal? How do the two words or concepts (animal and blood) fit together? Clearly, there is nothing that would merit a formal score, like DV or DR; however, this contracted verbalization might reflect a breaking apart of a violent thought, which finds expression in an incomplete sentence.

Other subtle verbal expressions, which would not be coded in the CS and R-PAS, include verbal repetitions or "stereotypies," as noted by Hussein. Not quite reaching the level of a perseveration, these repeated words or phrases should catch the examiner's ear. For example, the subject who repeatedly responds with the phrase, "Maybe it might be" is not revealing thought disorder per se, but there might be something meaningful embedded in this stilted repetition. The subject might be concealing the edge of his confusion or perplexity (perhaps suggestive of an underlying thought disorder), or his defensive intent is not to be pinned down (possibly suggestive of a paranoid guardedness). In any event, it is important to listen to what is said, how it is said, and what is left out in the subject's verbalization.

Continuum of severity

With both coded responses and uncodable examples of verbal looseness and language peculiarities, it is important to bear in mind the existence of a continuum of severity, which ranges from disorderly speech, verbal slips, and malapropisms that occur within the nonclinical population to those more malignant examples of DVs and DRs that might represent a formal thought disorder. To some extent, distinguishing between Level 1 and 2 DRs and DVs addresses this issue; however, if we extend our thinking beyond Rorschach scores, the notion of a continuum of disorganized thinking/speech is consistent with current views regarding the continuous nature of psychotic-like phenomena across the population. For example, among nonclinical groups of so-called "normals," discourse coherence and word selection vary according to social, regional, educational, and intellectual differences, as well as by the presence of anxiety and emotional arousal.

Conceptualizing disorganization

To avoid circularity in our efforts to understand and explain disorganized verbalizations by referring to them as language and thinking that is disorganized, we can turn to a variety of useful perspectives to add some conceptual heft to what we have discovered in our careful listening and scoring of Rorschach responses. None of these perspectives provides a complete understanding, but like the proverbial blind men and the elephant, each might perceive more subtle and nuanced implications of a particular disorganized or peculiar-sounding response.

Psychological perspectives

One of Rapaport's (Rapaport, Gill, & Schafer, 1946/1968) greatest contributions was his effort to provide psychological rationale for Rorschach scoring variables. As noted earlier, he employed his concept of distance from the blot in order to conceptualize different forms of pathological verbalization. Although his concept was criticized for its lack of clarity (Schuldberg & Boster, 1985), Rapaport turned to both a loss and increase of distance in explaining the psychological process underlying Peculiar and Queer Verbalizations. For example, he referenced the Card II response of "two low-built low dogs" as an odd expression, which was "communicating a very subjective and affectively charged attitude toward the card, as though the subject were perceiving a real dog (Rapaport, Gill, & Schafer, 1946/1968, p. 443). He believed that this and other examples of Peculiar and Queer responses reflected the subject's attempt to recognize, as opposed to interpret, the card, or his loss of interpretative awareness. Rapaport also gave examples of Peculiar and Queer responses that reflected an increase of distance from the blot. His examples typically were those in which the subject responded to the inquiry without being able to justify anything in the card that substantiated the response.

Schuldberg and Boster (1985) contributed to the understanding of DV and DR (or Peculiar and Queer) responses by viewing DRs as loading high on both the personal meaning (versus objective meaning) and the fluid (versus rigid) response set dimensions of their factor-analytic study. They viewed the second dimension as a reflection of the subject's attentional set. In overly rigid responses, the subject has difficulty breaking a mental set in order to produce a new response. At the other extreme, subjects respond in a fluid, unstable manner, reflecting their inability to maintain and control their attentional focus.

I believe that no one offered a clearer articulation of the psychological processes underlying disturbed and disorganized verbalizations than Weiner (1966). In conceptualizing thought processes as a product of cognitive focusing, Weiner wrote: "Thinking entails the scanning of stimuli impinging on the perceptual apparatus, reasoning about the relationships between these stimuli, and the formation of concepts that integrate these relationships" (p. 27). He punctuated his rationale by stating that cognitive focusing is characterized by three related capacities: selecting and establishing an attentional focus, maintaining a focus for the duration of the task at hand, and shifting attention or cognitive sets as the situation requires. Elaborating on these key aspects of attention, Weiner added three additional capacities: focusing on relevant aspects and excluding the irrelevant, inhibiting the expression of inappropriate or idiosyncratic associations, and maintaining consistent pacing of the rate and flow of associations.

Weiner indicated that problems in establishing a focus might be reflected in unusual location (Dd%) or blurring of figure and ground (overusage of white space). He also suggested that infrequent examples of clang associations or echolalia reflected an inappropriate focus on the phonetic qualities, or sound of the words, rather than the meaning of the verbalization.

Maintenance of a cognitive or attentional set simultaneously involves controlling the intrusion of irrelevant associations. A key psychological function mediating this variable is the ability to filter what is unnecessary, irrelevant, and distracting to the primary focus. Weiner stated that this inability to filter is represented psychodiagnostically in dissociation and DVs. By dissociation, Weiner referenced Bleuler's (1911/1950) notion of disconnectedness between ideas. Whereas people typically associate ideas on the basis of similarity and contiguity, the individual with schizophrenia may erroneously also assume an identity between different ideas (Arieti, 1974). While a typical association might be between Washington, Grant, and Eisenhower as generals who became president, a thought-disordered response to the question of "Who was the first president?" might be "Grant" or "Eisenhower," assuming an identity on the basis of similarity.

Weiner referred to Cameron's (1938) term "asyndesis" as another example of a lack of causal connection between associations. Cameron described the asyndetic thinker as losing focus while verbalizing loosely connected and irrelevant ideas that intrude into the subject's responses. Weiner indicated that when the intrusion involves a linguistic element, it would receive a score of Peculiar or Queer Verbalization (DV). On the other hand, when the intrusion involves a more substantial departure or irrelevant association, the contemporary scoring would certainly fall within the DR category, as the speaker fails to inhibit or filter the incursion of inappropriate information.

Weiner's discussion of pacing and flow is similar to Hussein's (Personal communication, March 11, 2016) interest in disruptions in tempo, rate, and completeness of verbal expression. Weiner pointed out that the paucity of causal links in the individual's associations might become apparent in more subtle discontinuities between the examiner's questions and the fragmented or oblique nature of the response.

Psychopathological perspectives

Andreasen (1978, 1979a, 1979b), known for her taxonomy of disordered speech, distinguished two types of formal thought disorder, the first of which is positive thought disorder. As described in Chapter 1, positive thought disorder is characterized by derailment, disorganization, and disconnectedness of the thought processes and is represented by circumstantial thinking, tangentiality, derailment, distractible speech, clang associations, and incoherence. Several types of thought disorder on her TLC scale are pertinent to Rorschach's DVs, DRs; in addition, more subtle manifestations of slips and disconnectedness are represented in Table 9.1.

132 Dimensions of disordered thinking

Table 9.1 TLC categories of formal thought disorder reflecting disorganization

Type of Disorder	Definition	Rorschach Example	Rorschach Score
Pressure of Speech	An increase in the amount of spontaneous speech	"These look like two rabbits men playing patty cake lungs and a rocket at night" (verbalized without pause or indication that each is a separate response)	No score
Distractible Speech	The subject changes focus mid-speech while responding to a stimulus	"This looks like two bears climbing a cliff. Hey did you go to Harvard?"	DR1
Tangentiality	Replying to a question in an oblique, irrelevant manner	(What might this be) "Well, these things are made by pressing two sides of a page together, so could be anything or nothing at all."	DR1
Derailment	Ideas slip off track onto another train that is obliquely or unrelated	"This looks like a bat... My uncle shot one in his backyard. I really hate bats, but I'm sure they are good for the environment, which has all sorts of problems with air pollution. The government really needs to do something about all this stuff. The leaking of all these classified documents...." (Kleiger & Khadivi, 2014, p. 105)	DR2
Incoherence (Word Salad)	Speech that is incomprehensible	"Tears go up in the air, blood, and break their neck, you know reject" (Holzman, et al., 2005, p. 71)	DR2
Clanging	Sounds, rather than meaning, govern the words chosen	"Man, a bat for sure, I'm sure it's pure Batman"	DV2
Neologisms	Invented words	"The lungs, tubes, and intesticles down here"	DV2

Type of Disorder	Definition	Rorschach Example	Rorschach Score
Word Approximations	Old words are used in a novel and unconventional manner	"This looks like a bug with his feelers or sense receptacles"	DV1
Stilted Speech	Excessively formal, stiff, or affected words or expressions	"This resembles a rather hominid- like representation of a figure"	DV1
Circumstantiality	Speech that is encumbered by verbosity and indirectness in reaching its goal	"This could be one of those things that you typically find in Delaware or other regions of the Mid-Atlantic or even the northern states that enjoys copious amounts of seafood like these crabs here"	DR1

Factor-analytic studies have attempted to delineate the separate psychopathological dimensions for the diverse clinical symptomatology associated with psychosis. Originally Crow (1980) suggested two subtypes of schizophrenia based on the presence of positive or negative symptoms. Liddle (1987) added a third cluster of symptoms, which he called "Cognitive Disorganization," that included problems in focusing, filtering, and disturbances in language. In their study of symptom dimensions of psychosis, Reininghaus, Priebe, and Bentall (2013) identified five factors in samples of early and chronic psychosis. In addition to symptom clusters that include positive symptoms, negative symptoms, manic excitement, and depression, the group found a separate "Cognitive Disorganization" factor that included difficulties with conceptual thinking, poor attention, disorientation, stereotyped thinking, and odd mannerisms. Finally, the Psychotic Disorder Work Group associated with the development of the DSM-5 proposed an eight-factor model (Barch et al., 2013). They included in their multi-factor model a "Disorganized Speech" dimension that focused narrowly on speech cohesiveness and coherence.

Thus, psychosis researchers have empirically identified a distinct dimension defined primarily by cognitive disorganization and idiosyncratic speech. Rorschach examiners can anchor their scoring of DVs and DRs in psychopathology research, which has identified disorganized and pathological verbalizations as discrete symptom features associated with psychosis.

Linguistic perspectives

In Chapter 1, I introduced a study by Berenbaum and Barch (1995), who used both clinicians and linguists to rate samples of disordered thinking and speech.

They found four categories that accounted for the key dimensions of thought disorder: disturbances in fluency, discourse coherence, content, and social convention. Responses from the TLC and TDI—which reflected tangentiality, derailment, looseness, grammatical lapses, neologisms, incoherence, and loosely connected associations—were emblematic of disturbances in fluency and discourse coherence, leading Berenbaum and Barch to hypothesize that problems in fluency and discourse coherence reflect disturbances in the "language production system." They indicated that language production was mediated by attentional and executive resources responsible for planning, monitoring, editing, as well as ensuring that the phonological and grammatical information was correct. Their "Fluency" category was represented by disturbances in the ability to produce independent, grammatical speech with understandable (real) words. Judges rated Rorschach responses reflecting word approximations, word-finding difficulties, idiosyncratic word usage, strange verbalizations, and neologisms as belonging to the Fluency category.

The Discourse Coherence category included TLC speech samples and TDI Rorschach responses that reflected verbal disorganization or a disturbance in the sequential flow of information. Discourse Coherence included non sequiturs; tangential, loose, and derailed responses; flippant, stilted, vague, and incoherent speech. In contrast to these primarily linguistic elements, disturbances of content and social convention were associated with problems in thinking, reasoning, and impaired social perspective (Harrow, Lanin-Kettering, & Miller, 1989).

From a linguist's perspective, discourse coherence pertains to communication in which the speaker presents the listener with a clear and coherent message. Deficits in discourse coherence in individuals with schizophrenia include impairment of cohesive links that tie together contents of one sentence to those that follow (Rochester & Martin, 1979). During conversation, patients with formal thought disorders have trouble processing and organizing their thoughts from one sentence and paragraph to the next. At the microstructural level (i.e. word or sentence level), normal speakers typically employ a step-by-step construction to achieve discourse continuity, or cohesiveness, through connections between words across sentence boundaries (Halliday & Hasan, 1976). These cohesive devices tie together the ideas, objects, subjects, and events that the speaker expresses both within and across sentences. However, conjunctions and references (demonstrative, definite, or comparative pronouns) can become ambiguous and confusing to the listener, resulting in loss of discourse coherence. As a result, the listener is likely to feel that the speaker is communicating in a disconnected, disorganized, or disorderly manner.

The DR2 response that lacks cohesion from sentence to sentence will disrupt coherence and leave the examiner confused as to what the patient is saying. Lauren, an 18-year-old student referred for testing by her psychiatrist, gave the following confusing response to Card VII:

> Reminds me of a person—lady, female gender. This is so ... this is so ... ok ... the way my mother brought me up, not brought up. This is very

stereotypical and a sexist part of me. She is like this old picture. It's not a modern image but she is. It looks like in the past when she would look out a window and say there were set guidelines for wearing a blouse and dress. The blouse tucked in and waist very small. Reminded me of woman because of society and the media and it looks like they have a big up-do that was she was always very proud of. I guess she's sort of relaxed and she may not be relaxed but is looking out a window (DR2).

One can almost follow along to a point, but Lauren's ambiguous cohesive ties make it unclear who, what, when, and where she is talking about. Is it she, her mother, the female image in the blot? Is she speaking about Card VII or comingling past reverie with present perception? It is simply unclear.

Neuropsychological perspectives

Both Kraepelin and Bleuler paved the way for later efforts to examine the neurocognitive underpinnings of thought disorder psychologically by highlighting the attentional deficits in schizophrenia. Researchers have sought to conceptualize disordered thinking from a cognitive neuroscience perspective (McGhie & Chapman, 1961; Nuechterlein & Dawson, 1984; Elevag & Goldberg, 2000; Goldberg & Weinberger, 2000; Barch, 2005). From this perspective, disorganized thinking or speech is viewed in terms of impairments in neuropsychological functions such as attention, memory, verbal fluency, executive functioning, and processing speed. Nuechterlein & Dawson (1984) concluded from their studies that impairments in attention might be more of a "trait" variable for schizophrenic subjects than for manic ones. In another series of investigations, Braff and his colleagues demonstrated that individuals with schizophrenia exhibit abnormal information processing when compared to nonpatient controls (Braff & Saccuzzo, 1981; Braff & Geyer, 1990; Braff, Saccuzzo, & Geyer, 1991; Braff, Grillon, & Geyer, 1992). When attention and information-processing functions are impaired, people with schizophrenia may experience increased distractibility in response to a flood of excessive and poorly inhibited internal and external stimuli, leading to cognitive fragmentation and markedly disordered thinking.

Deficits in working memory are related to the attentional vulnerabilities found in patients suffering from schizophrenia. The working memory system enables a person to hold relevant information in mind while utilizing it to solve problems at hand. A number of studies have found a link between working memory deficits and thought and communication disturbances (Oltmanns & Neale, 1978; Goldberg & Weinberger, 2000). Moreover, emotional arousal may further disrupt working memory in vulnerable individuals.

Bentall (2003) noted how impairment in the semantic memory may play a role in disrupting associative links between related ideas. The semantic memory system, which stores ideas and knowledge, is an intricate network of concepts tied together by associations. Impairment in semantic memory can disrupt associative linkages between ideas, leading to looseness and disconnection between one idea and the next.

Executive functions like self- and source monitoring may also contribute to disordered thinking. Self-monitoring refers to the subject's ability to monitor and adjust her speech to the communication needs and perspectives of her listeners. The ability to comprehend that others have minds and needs separate from one's own reflects a capacity to have a ToM. It follows that deficits in ToM might prevent a person from recognizing that others might not be able to comprehend what he is trying to say, resulting in an impaired social perspective. Deficits in source monitoring (which is similar to the concept of reality testing) may prevent one from identifying the source of a particular stimulus. Thus, the individual may be uncertain whether he/she actually *said it* or simply *thought it*. As a result, when speaking, deficits in source monitoring may predispose an individual to leave out important segments of information or disregard the essential cohesive ties that make speech coherent to others. Challenging traditional concepts of thought disorder, Bentall (2003) hypothesized that an integrated set of deficits in working and semantic memory, together with impairments in self- and source monitoring, could lead to speech that is loose and incomprehensible to others.

Psychotherapeutic perspectives

As diagnosticians, we are often more comfortable with identifying and classifying pathology than with trying to understand it. In his critique of traditional approaches to understanding psychosis and thought disorder, Bentall (2003) addressed the idea that despite the assessor's trouble in understanding a patient, the patient is attempting to communicate something of importance. Bentall presented a lengthy case example referenced in Laing's *The Divided Self* (1960). In this case, Kraepelin presents a psychotic man to his medical students. After his interview with this man, Kraepelin explained that the individual had given no useful information and had only spoken in disconnected sentences that had no relationship to his situation. Laing reinterpreted Kraepelin's case presentation and conclusions and suggested that the patient's discourse needed to be understood in the context of the examination setting and Kraepelin's imperious manner of conducting an interview, as if the patient were a specimen on display. Laing concluded that Kraepelin's belief that the patient was simply disorganized and incoherent missed a more obvious point: that the patient was objecting to being observed, measured, and tested, and that he wanted to be heard.

Bentall (2003) referred to another study by Harrow and Prosen (1978), who asked patients to explain their bizarre and idiosyncratic responses from a proverb test. When one of the investigators conducted a careful, empathically attuned interview that communicated an interest in learning what the subjects had on their minds, patients were often able to give coherent explanations of their disorganized and incoherent responses. It turned out that their idiosyncratic language and disorganized verbalizations frequently reflected the intrusion of personally meaningful, affect-laden ideas. The investigators and Bentall concluded that when responding to interview or testing questions, the patients were unable to filter out issues that were particularly meaningful to them. Whether we interpret this as a failure in self-monitoring, filtering, or inhibition, there is value in the notion that vulnerable individuals are more likely to speak in disorganized ways when they are emotionally aroused and speaking about personally meaningful issues. A static-sign approach to identifying thought disorder responses from an interview, or on the Rorschach or any other diagnostic test, runs the risk of treating people as pathological specimens, who, as Kraepelin mistakenly assumed, were unintelligible. What this means for those of us using the Rorschach is that we should shift from a strictly evaluative-labeling position to one of attempting to understand our patients and find something that is meaningful to them in those confusing responses that we code as DRs and DVs.

Psychoanalytic perspectives

This is an apt segue to the final section of this chapter on psychoanalytic perspectives, which pays less attention to the scores themselves and more to the experiential, conceptual, and theoretical underpinnings of the response. The aim here is to bring Rorschach manifestations of disorganization and idiosyncratic language in line with pluralistic psychoanalytic models of thinking and thought disorder. After a review of traditional Freudian concepts of primary process thinking, I then touch upon the relevance of psychoanalytic ego psychology and the contributions of Klein and Bion to understanding examples of disorganized speech and language that we might find on the Rorschach.

Primary process: Energy forces and disordered thinking

Although Freud introduced the terms "primary" and "secondary" processes in his *Project for a Scientific Psychology* (1895/1966), he laid out his principal understanding of these processes in *The Interpretation of Dreams* (1900/1953). Freud maintained that primary process thinking involves energies that are uninhibited, free, and not neutralized, while secondary process energy is inhibited, bound, and neutralized. Freud equated primary process with both drive-dominated and wishful thought content. In the *Interpretation of Dreams*, he described condensation, displacement, and symbolization as the formal mechanisms of dream work and primary process mental activity.

Various researchers attempted to conceptualize thought disorder as the intrusion of uninhibited drive energies, or primary process material, into secondary process thinking. As we have seen, the use of the Rorschach to study free versus bound psychic energy is represented primarily in the work of Holt (1956, 1967, 1970, 1977, 2009), and subsequently in the writings of Meloy (1984, 1986).

Mechanisms of primary process thinking

As we know, Holt organized his formal scoring variables around Freud's three mechanisms of primary process—condensation, displacement, and symbolization. Holt noted that Freud said little about the primary process manifestations represented by peculiarities in verbalization. Because these were historically associated with thought disorder, Holt decided to include them under a separate formal scoring category made up of verbalization scores.

Holt believed that displacement was represented by scores reflecting fluid or inappropriate associative thinking, for example, responses reflecting chain, distant, and clang associations or inappropriate figures of speech, puns, or malapropisms. In his 2009 volume, Holt reintroduced from his earlier book (1997) the hypotheses of Rubinstein, who wrote about the fragmentation of concepts and images. In writing about psychoanalytic interpretation and dream formation, Rubinstein proposed that mental representations are broken apart and that the fragments may be recombined or shuffled around. Holt concluded that as a result of this fragmentation, shuffling, and recombination, features of preexisting images and words and the usual connections among them could be either condensed or displaced. Much like Bentall (2003), Holt stated that in people with inherent neurocognitive vulnerabilities, emotional ("high temperature") arousal might neutralize existing monitoring and organizing functions and precipitate the emergence of unusual words and distant associations. Regarding these loose and seemingly disconnected associations between ideas, Holt pointed to the mechanism of displacement, in particular, as the means by which the usual connections between mental representations were disrupted and shifted to distant and unconnected ideas.

Meloy (1986) contributed to an understanding of the relationship between primary process and formal thought disorder. He viewed condensation and displacement as stable and structured dimensions that he believed explained primitive or paleological thought. Like Holt, Meloy viewed displacement as the primary process mechanism underlying tangential, fluid, and rambling associations, flight of ideas, and incoherence. He explained that the three levels of language—connotation, denotation, and verbalization—are disrupted in thought-disordered individuals. Meloy espoused that the fluid and rapid shifting of associations in thought-disordered communication was based solely on verbalizations, without regard to connotation (concepts) or denotation (objects of reference). Thus, according to Meloy, displacement represents "a vertical shift from abstractions (connotations) to objects and functions (denotations) to phonemes (verbalizations)" (p. 54). In other words, in the thought-disordered person, the flow and sequence of speech becomes governed by the sound of words and not by conventional associative laws of contiguity and similarity.

Formal thought disorder as a disturbance in ego functioning

Ego psychology is probably the most widely used model for understanding the conceptual underpinnings of formal thought disorder. Freud (1911/1958) hinted at the links between ego pathology and psychotic disturbances in thinking and reality testing before he developed his tripartite model of the mind. Tausk (1919/1933) subsequently elaborated the links by viewing schizophrenia as a loss of ego boundaries and a deficiency in ego strength. After the advent of his structural model (Freud (1923/1961) stressed that disturbances in the ego play a determining role in symptom formation in schizophrenia. Hartmann (1953) extended the role of ego impairments in the process of schizophrenia but indicated that it was important to specify which ego functions were impaired. Federn (1952) developed a distinct school of ego psychology by attempting to apply psychoanalytic principles to understanding psychotic patients. Although his concept of ego differed significantly from the ego of Freud and Hartmann, Federn used the term "ego boundaries," or loss of ego boundaries, to explain schizophrenic symptomatology.

Early ego psychologists enumerated lists of various ego functions (Freud, 1937; Hartmann, Kris, & Loewenstein, 1946; Bellak, 1949). Beres (1956) included seven functions in his list, which included a separate category for "thought processes"; Arlow and Brenner (1964) also listed "thought" as a central function of the ego. With thought and reality testing being key domains of the ego, it naturally followed that "disturbances in thinking" were considered a constituent of ego functioning as well.

Rapaport (Rapaport, Gill, & Schafer, 1946/1968) viewed psychoanalytic ego psychology as the only theoretical guide with sufficient depth and breadth to illuminate the nature of thought processes. He was an early critic of a theory of psychic energy that did not include structural mechanisms as well. Motivational considerations alone could not adequately explain normal or pathological thought organization. Not only was the concept of ego necessary to understand the vicissitudes of thinking, but Rapaport also insisted that disturbances in thought processes involve all aspects of thinking, including the component ego functions of perception, attention, concentration, concept formation, and reasoning.

Weiner's (1966) psychodiagnostic study of schizophrenia can also be placed under the umbrella of ego psychology because of his premise that thought disorder is essentially an impairment in ego functioning. As noted above, Weiner viewed disorganized and idiosyncratic verbalizations in terms of deficits in cognitive focusing and filtering.

Kleinian concepts

Melanie Klein did not focus on disordered thinking and language per se, but she introduced a number of concepts relevant to the psychoanalytic understanding of psychosis (Klein, 1959). The broad reach of her theoretical and clinical contributions is beyond the scope of the current focus; however, her seminal ideas about internalized splitting, part-object representations, and mental processes characteristic of the paranoid–schizoid position, in particular, are relevant to understanding formal thought disorder. She surmised that psychosis is dominated by part-object representations and paranoid anxieties originating from the paranoid–schizoid position. Klein introduced the concept of projective identification to describe the process by which parts of the self are split off and projected into another person, who then becomes an object of identification. She believed that symptoms of schizophrenia arose from the extreme use of projective identification, leading to confusion between the mental contents of self and other.

Segal (1973) developed Klein's ideas, by linking them to impairment in the capacity for symbolism. Segal introduced the term "symbolic equation" to describe situations in which the symbol is equated with the original object, which gives rise to concrete thinking. Proper use of symbolism helps one differentiate internal from external reality. In psychosis, symbolism is replaced by a more regressed process, by which one assumes an identity between the symbol and object. A relevant Rorschach reference is the absence of interpretative awareness, which occurs when the subject does not distinguish the symbol (inkblot) from that which is symbolized. The result is a form of concreteness, which Rapaport would have called a loss of distance from the card. As noted previously, he viewed some Peculiar and Queer responses as attempts to recognize, as opposed to interpret, the card. Although not a Kleinian, Leichtman (1996), writing about thought disorder on the Rorschach from a developmental perspective, also discussed how the collapse between symbol (inkblot) and object (representative percept) and between self (person taking the Rorschach) and other (examiner) may lead to disturbances in language, in which words lose their connotative and denotative reference and lead to disorganized and peculiar verbalizations.

Bion: Attacks on linking

Although hugely influenced by Melanie Klein, Bion (1959) developed a trove of original ideas about thinking and mental processes in psychosis that went far beyond those of Klein. He believed that from early development there exists a split-off psychotic part of the person that attacks all aspects of mind that link ideas, association, speech, and awareness. He viewed thought disorder in psychotic individuals as a product of an attack on the links that allow them to think reflectively, connect ideas, and form symbols. The result is a breaking apart of sensory impressions, attention, memory, judgment, and thoughts, which exist as fragments to be projected into others. The pathological splintering and projective identification of these unprocessed fragments, which Bion called "beta elements," results in the formation of bizarre objects to be feared and controlled. According to Bion, the psychotic person lacks the capacity for symbolic thinking because the link between object and symbol has been destroyed. Furthermore, in this regressed state the individual cannot think in a reflective manner. Instead, the person can only splinter her or his mental processes and attempt to expel the fragments into others. Thus, from a Bionian perspective, we might view disrupted speech, rambling and fluid verbalizations, and idiosyncratic wording of Rorschach responses as casualties of a psychotic attack on the mental linkages that provide cognitive adhesiveness and give words, sentences, and discourse shared meaning.

Bringing meaning to disorganization

To summarize these diverse conceptual and theoretical viewpoints, cognitive disorganization, which gives rise to DVs and DRs on the Rorschach, reflects impairments in cognitive and language processing. An inability to focus on relevant stimuli and prevent the intrusion of inappropriate words and/or irrelevant associations reflects problems in executive control (inhibition), monitoring (source and self), and ToM (appreciating that others might not comprehend what you are saying). Whether these deficits are strictly the result of underlying neuropsychological impairment, symbol formation, conflict, or a psychotic fragmentation of connective tissue between linguistic and cognitive elements and between integrated representations of self and others is not the main point. Certainly, the same phenomena can be viewed from multiple perspectives.

The essential point for Rorschach clinicians is to move beyond static, test-bound definitions of DVs and DRs and understand what they might represent outside of the Rorschach situation. In addition to forming links between diverse but related disciplines, which all have something to offer in terms of understanding cognitive disorganization, it is important not to lose sight of the person who is ineffectively attempting to communicate something important. Instead of viewing the individual as a set of scores or symptoms, we need to gear our diagnostic efforts to understanding what he or she is trying to say. Being curious and interested enough to discover the embedded meaning in what the person is attempting to communicate through his/her disorganized sentences, disrupted syntax, and odd use of words may help us discover the conditions under which they are able to express their ideas more coherently.

References

American Psychiatric Association. (2013). *Diagnostic and Statistical Manual of Mental Disorders* (5th ed.). Washington, DC: Author.

Andreasen, N. (1978). *The Scale for the Assessment of Thought, Language, and Communication (TLC)*. Iowa City, IA: University of Iowa Press.

Andreasen, N. (1979a). Thought, language, and communication disorders: I. Clinical assessment, definition of terms, and evaluation of their reliability. *Archives of General Psychiatry, 36*, 1315–1321.

Andreasen, N. (1979b). Thought, language, and communication disorders: II. Diagnostic significance. *Archives of General Psychiatry, 36*, 1325–1330.

Arieti, S. (1974). *Interpretation of Schizophrenia* (2nd ed.). New York, Basic Books.

Arlow, J. A., & Brenner, C. (1964). *Psychoanalytic Concepts and the Structural Theory*. New York: International Universities Press.

Barch, D. M. (2005). The cognitive neuroscience of schizophrenia. *Annual Review of Clinical Psychology, 1,* 321–353.

Barch, D. M., Bustillo, J., Gaebel, W., Gur, R., Heckers, S., Malaspina, D., Owen, M. J., Schultz, S., Tandon, R., Tsuang, M., van Os, J., & Carpenter, W. (2013). Logic and justification for dimensional assessment of symptoms and related clinical phenomena in psychosis: Relevance to DSM-5. *Schizophrenia Research, 150,* 15–20.

Bellak, L. (1949). A multiple-factor psychosomatic theory of schizophrenia. *Psychiatric Quarterly, 23,* 730–750.

Bentall, R. P. (2003). *Madness Explained: Psychosis and Human Nature.* New York: Penguin Group.

Berenbaum, H., & Barch, D. (1995). The categorization of thought disorder. *Journal of Psycholinguistic Research, 24,* 349–376.

Beres, D. (1956). Ego deviation and the concept of schizophrenia. *The Psychoanalytic Study of the Child* (pp. 164–235). New York: International Universities Press.

Bion, W. R. (1959). Attacks on linking. *International Journal of Psycho-Analysis, 40,* 308–315.

Bleuler, E. (1950). *Dementia Praecox or the Group of Schizophrenias.* (J. Zinkin, Trans.). New York: International Universities Press. (Original work published in 1911.)

Braff, D. L., & Geyer, M. A. (1990). Sensorimotor gating and schizophrenia: Human and animal model studies. *Archives of General Psychiatry, 47,* 181–188.

Braff, D. L., Grillon, C., & Geyer, M. A. (1992). Gating and habituation of the startle reflex in schizophrenic patients. *Archives of General Psychiatry, 49,* 206–215.

Braff, D. L., & Saccuzzo, D. P. (1981). Information processing dysfunction in paranoid schizophrenia: A two-factor deficit. *American Journal of Psychiatry, 138,* 1051–1056.

Braff, D. L., Saccuzzo, D. P., & Geyer, M. A. (1991). Information processing dysfunctions in schizophrenia: Studies of visual backward masking, sensorimotor gating and habituation. In J. Zubin, S. Steinhauer, & J. H. Gruzelier (Eds.), *Handbook of Schizophrenia: Neuropsychology, Psychophysiology, and Information Processing,* (Vol. 5, pp. 303–334). Amsterdam: Elsevier.

Cameron, N. (1938). Reasoning, regression and communication in schizophrenics. *Psychological Monographs, 50,* 1–340.

Crow, T. J. (1980). Molecular pathology of schizophrenia: More than one dozen procedures. *British Medical Journal, 280,* 66–68.

Elvevag, B., & Goldberg, T. E. (2000). Cognitive impairment in schizophrenia is the core of the disorder. *Current Reviews in Neurobiology, 14,* 1–21.

Federn, P. (1952). *Ego Psychology and the Psychoses.* New York: Basic Books.

Freud, A. (1937). *The Ego and the Mechanisms of Defense.* New York: International Universities Press.

Freud, S. (1953). The interpretation of dreams. In *Standard Edition of the Complete Works of Sigmund Freud* (Vols. 4 & 5). London, UK: Hogarth Press. (Original work published in 1900.)

Freud, S. (1958). Psycho-analytic notes on an autobiographical account of a case of paranoia (dementia paranoides). In *Standard Edition of the Complete Works of Sigmund Freud* (Vol. 12, pp. 1–82). London, UK: Hogarth Press. (Original work published in 1911.)

Freud, S. (1961). The ego and the id. In *Standard Edition of the Complete Works of Sigmund Freud* (Vol. 19, pp. 12–66). London, UK: Hogarth Press. (Original work published in 1923.)

Freud, S. (1966). Project for a scientific psychology. In *Standard Edition of the Complete Works of Sigmund Freud* (Vol. 1, pp. 283–397). London, UK: Hogarth Press. (Original work published in 1895.)

Goldberg, T. E., & Weinberger, D. R. (2000). Thought disorder in schizophrenia: A reappraisal of older formulations and an overview of some recent studies. *Cognitive Neuropsychiatry*, 5, 1–19.

Halliday, M. A. K., & Hasan, R. (1976). *Cohesion in Spoken and Written English*. London, UK: Longmans.

Harrow, M., Lanin-Kettering, I., & Miller, J. G. (1989). Impaired perspective and thought pathology in schizophrenic and psychotic disorders. *Schizophrenia Bulletin*, 15, 605–623.

Harrow, M., & Prosen, M. (1978). Intermingling and disordered logic as influences on schizophrenic thought. *Archives of General Psychiatry*, 35, 1213–1218.

Hartmann, H. (1953). The metapsychology of schizophrenia. *The Psychoanalytic Study of the Child, 8*, 177–198. New York: International Universities Press.

Hartmann, H., Kris, E., & Loewenstein, R. M. (1946). Comments on the formation of psychic structure. In *Psychological Monographs: No. 14. Papers on Psychoanalytic Psychology* (pp. 27–55). New York: International Universities Press.

Holt, R. R. (1956). Gauging primary and secondary process in Rorschach responses. *Journal of Projective Techniques*, 20, 14–25.

Holt, R. R. (1967). The development of primary process: A structural view. In R. R. Holt (Ed.), *Motives and Thought: Psychoanalytic Essays in Honor of David Rapaport* (pp. 345–383). New York: International Universities Press.

Holt, R. R. (1970). *Manual for the Scoring of Primary Process Manifestations and Their Controls in Rorschach Responses*. New York: Research Center for Mental Health.

Holt, R. R. (1977). A method for assessing primary process manifestations and their control in Rorschach responses. In M. A. Rickers-Ovsiankina (Ed.), *Rorschach Psychology* (2nd ed., pp. 375–420). New York: Krieger.

Holt, R. R. (1997). On the clinical psychoanalytic theory and its role in the inference and confirmation of particular clinical hypotheses. In R. R. Holt (Ed.), *Psychoanalysis and the Philosophy of Science: The Collected Papers of Benjamin B. Rubinstein* (pp. 273–324). New York: International Universities Press.

Holt, R. R. (2009). *Primary Process Thinking: Theory, Measurement, and Research* (Vols. 1 & 2). Lanham, MD: Aronson.

Holzman, P. S., Levy, D.L., & Johnston, M. H. (2005). The use of the Rorschach technique for assessing formal thought disorder. In R. F. Bornstein & J. M. Masling (Eds.), *Scoring the Rorschach: Seven Validated Systems* (pp. 55–95). New York: Routledge.

Kleiger, J. H. (1999). *Disordered Thinking and The Rorschach*. Hillsdale, NJ: The Analytic Press.

Kleiger, J. H., & Khadivi, A. (2015). *Assessing Psychosis. A Clinician's Guide*. New York: Routledge.

Klein, M. (1959). Our adult world and its roots in infancy. In M. Masud & R. Khan (Eds.), *Envy and Gratitude and Other Works 1946–1967* (pp. 247–263). London, UK: Hogarth Press.

Laing, R. D. (1960). *The Divided Self*. London, UK: Tavistock Press.

Leichtman, M. (1996). *The Rorschach: A Developmental Perspective*. Hillsdale, NJ: The Analytic Press.

Liddle, P. F. (1987). The symptoms of chronic schizophrenia: A re-examination of the positive-negative dichotomy. *The British Journal of Psychiatry, 151*, 145–151.

McGhie, A., & Chapman, J. (1961). Disorders of attention and perception in early schizophrenia. *British Journal of Medical Psychology, 34*, 103–116.

Meloy, J. R. (1984). Thought organization and primary process in the parents of schizophrenics. *British Journal of Medical Psychology, 57*, 279–281.

Meloy, J. R. (1986). On the relationship between primary process and thought disorder. *Journal of the American Academy of Psychoanalysis, 14*, 47–56.

Meyer, G. J., Viglione, D. J., Mihura, J. L., Erard, R. E., & Erdberg, P. (2011). *Rorschach Performance Assessment System: Administration, Coding, Interpretation, and Technical Manual*. Toledo, OH: Rorschach Performance Assessment System.

Nuechterlein, K. H., & Dawson, M. E. (1984). Information processing and attentional functioning in the developmental course of schizophrenic disorders. *Schizophrenia Bulletin, 10*, 160–203.

Oltmanns, T. F., & Neale, J. M. (1978). Distractibility in relation to other aspects of schizophrenic disorder. In S. Schwartz (Ed.), *Language and Cognition in Schizophrenia* (pp. 117–143). Oxford, UK: Lawrence Erlbaum Associates.

Rapaport, D., Gill, M., & Schafer, R. (1968). *Diagnostic Psychological Testing* (Rev. ed.). R. R. Holt, Ed. New York: International Universities Press. (Original work published in 1946.).

Reininghaus, U., Priebe, S., & Bentall, R. P. (2013). Testing the psychopathology of psychosis: Evidence for a general psychosis dimension. *Schizophrenia Bulletin, 39*, 884–895.

Rochester, S., & Martin, J. R. (1979). *Crazy Talk: A Study of the Discourse of Psychotic Speakers*. New York: Plenum.

Schuldberg, D., & Boster, J. S. (1985). Back to Topeka: Two types of distance in Rapaport's original Rorschach thought disorder categories. *Journal of Abnormal Psychology, 94*, 205–215.

Segal, H. (1973). *Introduction to the Work of Melanie Klein*. London, UK: Hogarth Press.

Shentoub, V. (1987). Thematic apperception test (TAT). Théorie et méthode. *Psychologie française, 32*, 117–126.

Tausk, V. (1933). On the origin of the "influencing machine" in schizophrenia. *Psychoanalytic Quarterly, 2*, 519–556. (Original work published in 1919.)

Viglione, D. J. (2010). *Rorschach Coding Solutions: A Reference Guide for the Comprehensive System* (2nd ed.). San Diego, CA: Author.

Weiner, I. B. (1966). *Psychodiagnosis in Schizophrenia*. New York: Wiley.

Chapter 10

Illogicality
Problems in reasoning and logic

In the previous chapter, I focused on *how* things are said and *how* one selects words and verbalizes ideas in loose, disconnected, and disorganized ways that disrupt communication. I also noted a "soft" distinction between how things are said, on the one hand, and how they are thought about, on the other. Problems with reasoning and logic, collectively referred to as illogicality, pertain to the latter component of thought disorder.

Traditionally, most of the interest in thought disorder has concerned loose and disorganized verbalizations—formal thought disorder. For example, Andreasen's TLC Scale (1979) lists 18 types of thought disorders. However, only one, illogicality, refers to thinking per se. The remaining 17 involve qualities of how the subject verbalizes. Furthermore, recent factor-analytic studies identified separate dimensions of cognitive disorganization (Reininghaus, Priebe, & Bentall, 2013) and disorganized speech (Barch et al., 2013), which place more emphasis on the concept of formal thought disorder and less on properties related to thinking, reasoning, and logic. In delineating different components of disordered thinking, Ali Khadivi and I recently addressed the fact that thinking and reasoning have received less attention in traditional definitions of thought disorder:

A definition of thought disorder is not complete unless we take into consideration how one's beliefs are formulated. We may hear the disjointed way in which individuals express their ideas and the beliefs they hold. However, we are equally interested in the processes of "thinking," "reasoning," and "inference-making," which lead to the unusual ideas and bizarre beliefs that may or may not be expressed in disjointed ways (Kleiger & Khadivi, 2015, p. 28).

What makes illogical thinking illogical?

In order to answer this query, we need to define four related concepts: inference making, reasoning, logic, and causality. Inferences are ideas or conclusions that are based on evidence we perceive. Reasoning is the process of linking and organizing inferences. Logic, a complex mental discipline in and of itself, involves the formal and informal rules one follows when reasoning and drawing conclusions. Causality is the ideational element that connects one occurrence with another, with the first event understood to be partly responsible for the second. Thus, illogicality may be the result of faulty inference making, impaired reasoning, fallacious logic, or mistaken beliefs about causation.

Aristotelian logic is a deductive method of formal logic, best represented by syllogistic reasoning. A syllogism is a simple form of deductive reasoning that involves two premises, one major and one minor, from which a logical conclusion is deduced. Premises may contain facts, speculative statements, or hypotheses. The syllogism "All men are mortal" (major premise), "Jones is a man" (minor premise), "Therefore Jones is mortal" (conclusion) reflects this form of reasoning in which the subjects of both premises ("all men" and "Jones") are related.

Aristotelian logic is based on three fundamental laws (Arieti, 1974): (1) the law of identity, meaning A is always A and never B; (2) the law of contradiction, which states A cannot be A and not A at the same time and place; and (3) the law of excluded middle, which holds that A must be A or not A; it cannot be an intermediate state. In illogical thinking, or what Arieti referred to as "paleologic" thinking, these three laws are annulled. Two premises are equated on the basis of their sharing the same predicate, whereas the properties of the subjects are largely ignored. The law of identity in paleologic thinking allows that A may be B, provided that B shares a common quality with A (e.g. "I am a *virgin*; Mary was a *virgin*; therefore I'm the Virgin Mary"). Likewise, A can be both A and B at the same time. Finally, by condensing several subjects, paleologic thinking neglects the law of excluded middle in that things are often seen as composites of both A and B. In paleologic terms, Descartes' pronouncement becomes "I am, therefore I think" based on the implicit reasoning "Thinking people are (exist); I am (exist); therefore, I think." One can quickly see how fallacious this conclusion is given the fact that not everything that exists is a sentient being.

Arieti (1974) identified three characteristics of the predicates involved in paleologic thinking, which Weiner (1966) elaborated in terms of the Rorschach. "Predicates of quality" describe attributes that are intrinsic to an object, such as thinking or being a virgin are qualities of being human. "Predicates of spatial contiguity" are based on two objects or events sharing a common space. Weiner gave the example of a man seeing several people standing in front of a police station and concluding that they are all policemen *because* of their spatial contiguity to the police station. Likewise "predicates of temporal contiguity" lead the paleologician to assume identity between two objects on the basis of their sharing a similar place in time.

Eilhard von Domarus (1944) used the term "paralogical thinking" to describe thought disorder in schizophrenia that he said was the result of errors in syllogistic reasoning in which two things are identified as being the same on the basis of having common predicates as opposed to similar subjects. The von Domarus principle specifically contradicts the first law, which holds that only when two things have identical subjects, not predicates, can they be the same. Before von Domarus, Freud (1900/1953) described "predicate thinking" as a constituent of primary process, whereby the id identifies two different things as being the same because they share a common predicate. Thus, Miss X presents with the delusion that she is Hillary Clinton because she is a Democrat and so is Mrs. Clinton; therefore Miss X believes that she *is* Hillary Clinton. In addition to violating the law of identity, illogical thought may ignore the law of contradiction, which states that something cannot be two different things at the same time, or more precisely, A cannot be both A and B at the same time and place. Thus, Mr. K (A) might erroneously conclude that he is both himself and LeBron James (B) because both of them reside in Cleveland. The boundary between separate individuals A and B has been collapsed to allow for the coexistence of contradictory, incompatible entities.

Weiner (1966) organized reasoning disturbances under three subcategories, which are each related to some extent to predicate thinking. *Overgeneralization* occurs when the person jumps to erroneous conclusions on the basis of insufficient evidence and attributes meaning that is not justified by the stimulus event. In *Combinative Thinking*, the individual links together separate, conceptually unrelated elements based on temporal or spatial continuity. In other words, based on the perception that two or more elements of a situation occur at the same time or in the same space, one erroneously assumes that they belong together in a meaningful way. Here, one's conclusion is based on perceptual, as opposed to conceptual, reality. Finally, Weiner described *Circumstantial Thinking* as an explicitly stated conclusion based on incidental or nonessential aspects of the situation. Both overgeneralized and combinative thinking reflect the presence of circumstantial thinking, in which conclusions are based on less relevant details. The difference is that in circumstantial reasoning, one makes an explicit statement that exposes the underlying fallaciousness of the reasoning.

An explosion of research in cognitive neuroscience has studied biases in reasoning and inference making from cognitive and neuropsychological perspectives (Garety & Freeman, 2013). Contemporary approaches view illogicality in terms of biases in how individuals reason and attribute causality. These newer lines of investigation have departed from earlier theories of predicate thinking. However, it is not surprising that there are links between the current interest in reasoning biases and older views of the mechanisms of fallacious inference making.

Continuum of illogical thinking

As with all dimensions of psychosis, disturbances in reasoning and logic occur along a continuum from irrational and immature forms of magical thinking, which exist within the normal range, to more severe forms of illogicality that provide the cognitive undergirding for the eventual emergence of delusional beliefs. Take overgeneralization as an example. One does not have to have a thought disorder to engage in occasional overgeneralizing. In addition to normative examples of overgeneralization, milder errors in reasoning that occur outside the psychotic range include: (1) black-and-white, all-or-nothing thinking; (2) catastrophizing;

(3) jumping to conclusions; (4) emotional reasoning; (5) magnification; (6) mind reading; and (7) personalizing (Beck et al., 2009). Other common examples of irrational or immature thinking include assuming causality on the basis of correlation, superstitions, and stereotyping.

Rorschach indicators of illogicality

Weiner (1966) believed that fabulization, confabulation, and absurd Dds (rare details) were Rorschach representations of overgeneralized thinking. As noted in Chapter 4, Rapaport introduced the concept of fabulization to describe varying degrees of affective elaboration that mark a progressive departure, or increase of distance, from the inkblot. Embellished responses such as "hungry animals," or an "ugly person" (as opposed to simply "animals" or a "person") suggest an increased degree of subjectivity and a subtle shift away from the concrete reality of the inkblot. Further noted in Chapters 4 and 8, the scoring concept of confabulation has a long history in Rorschach literature. Rorschach employed the term, but Rapaport broadened its meaning to include embellished responses that could not be justified by realistic aspects of the inkblot. Absurd Dds were the attribution of specific and elaborate meaning to tiny Dds that went far beyond anything that could be justified by aspects of the blot itself. For example, consider Mr. Conklin's response to a tiny fragment of Dd 31 on Card V: "Two people, maybe a man and a woman. They're very close, kind of romantic because they're next to each other and you can see their noses. They're about to kiss each other." I indicated in Chapter 8 that in order to reduce the confusion of attempting to reintroduce an old term like confabulation for such responses, DR is the most representative score for these highly embellished, inappropriately specific, and overly interpreted responses. However, the confabulated DR should be distinguished from the derailed, tangential, or circumstantial DR, which, as described in the last chapter, reflects a different kind of thought disorder process.

Weiner (1966) led the way in considering Incongruous Combinations (INCOMs), Fabulized Combinations (FABCOMs), and Contaminations (CONTAMs) as Rorschach manifestations of combinative thinking because all three involve illogical condensing of separate images and elements. Exner, Weiner, & Schuyler (1976) introduced the term "Inappropriate Combinations" to depict this category. However, in the integrated scoring schema that I presented in Chapter 8, I placed CONTAM responses in a different conceptual category from INCOM and FABCOM combinatory responses because the psychological process that leads to a CONTAM reflects something more than an inappropriate combination of incompatible blot elements. CONTAMs involve a more severe form of condensation in which boundaries between separate details collapse, and one image is superimposed onto the other image. CONTAMs violate the third law of Aristotelian logic, which specifies that A cannot be A and B at the same time.

Finally, circumstantial thinking, according to Weiner (1966), is represented by ALOG in the CS and PEC in the R-PAS. Both scores are Rorschach equivalents of predicate thinking, which are accompanied by an explicit statement regarding the fallacious logic. When Mr. Conklin saw two people on Card V and concluded that they were a man and a woman who were kind of romantic because they were next to each other and were about to kiss, he was exhibiting predicate thinking and received an ALOG/PEC.

Just as the dimension of errors in reasoning can be placed along a continuum from milder to more severe manifestations of illogicality, so can the Rorschach scores that represent these thought processes. To a large extent, distinguishing Level 1 from Level 2 INCOMs and FABCOMs addresses the notion of a continuum of severity. However, I believe that ALOGs and even CONTAMs also can be conceived along a continuum of severity. A key tenet of the Menninger Thought Disturbance Scales, mentioned in Chapter 7, was to define a level of severity *within* each type of scoring category by designating the score as a mild, moderate, or severe manifestation of that particular type of thought disturbance. While subthreshold CONTAMs or ALOG/PECs are not scorable in the CS or R-PAS, it is useful for clinicians to be aware when such subthreshold tendencies occur. For example, when one hears a suggestion of autistic or peculiar logic, which occurs later in the Inquiry/Clarification phase, after the examiner has already queried more than once, ALOG/PEC is not scored. However, we should not overlook the potential germination of this kind of fallacious reasoning, which might become more apparent when the subject is pressed to justify his thinking. Similarly, some responses fall short of criteria for scoring a CONTAM, but a fluid shifting between alternative images occurs in which there is an interpenetration and comingling of images. Although we may decide these responses lack the characteristic fusion quality of a CONTAM, we should pay heed to the fact that the individual is vulnerable to collapsing distinctions between separate frames of reference.

Understanding illogical thinking

Much as it is useful to expand our interpretation of Disorganization scores (DVs and DRs) by viewing them from multiple perspectives as we did in the preceding chapter, we can also conceptualize Illogicality-specific scores (INCOMs, FABCOMs, ALOGS/PECs, and CONTAMs) from different psychological, theoretical, and clinical points of view to add depth to our understanding of these scores and their implications.

Traditional psychological perspectives

Concepts are mental categories for objects, events, or ideas that share a common set of features and allow us to classify objects and events. Concept formation and identification are related cognitive processes that involve generating or identifying a rule or principle for organizing and grouping diverse observations or information. Conceptual thinking refers to our ability to identify, form, and manipulate categories of information, using appropriate levels of generalization and abstraction that conform to reality. Thus, perceiving what looks like wings, a head, a beak, and legs on Card V and calling this "a flying creature" is consistent with the concept of a bird, butterfly, or bat. The elements belong together and are consistent with each of these categories. However, perceiving wings, a head, beaks, and legs and calling this "a person with a beak and wings" violates the conceptual properties of a human being. Here, we have a breakdown in conceptual thinking. Details are combined in a manner that is incompatible with the concept and, hence, with reality. In this particular case, we have an INCOM, which is based on the *perceptual* reality of the inkblot image, not on the *conceptual* reality of the image content. The subject perceives what reasonably looks like wings, a head, a beak, and legs and concludes that it is a person with a beak and wings. What is missing is evidence of corrective monitoring that the person understands that this response violates conceptual reality. FABCOMs can be understood similarly. The grouping or linking of perceptual features of the inkblot leads to an erroneous concept that is incompatible with reality. Thus, in the Card VIII response of "lions walking standing on a butterfly's wings," perceptual reality trumps conceptual reality. Elements of the response, which do not belong together, are inappropriately and illogically synthesized.

Abstract thinking is a cognitive activity that is removed from direct sensory experiences and involves a mental representation of that experience. Concept formation involves representing, or *abstracting*, a unifying principle that is a step removed from the concrete, sensory qualities of the elements themselves. How far that step is from the elements becomes an important characteristic in evaluating the appropriateness of the individual's abstraction. Is it too closely linked to the stimulus properties or too far removed? Has the subject demonstrated too much distance from the stimulus elements? One can hear in this Rapaport's concept of "distance from the inkblot" creeping in again because this is another way of understanding responses that are either overly concrete or, conversely, inappropriately abstract or removed from the stimulus properties of the card. In this regard, the DR-Confabulation response becomes emblematic of an abstraction process gone awry. The overly symbolic DR is a good example of the subject's infusing an inappropriate level of abstraction into the response. For example, the Card IX response, "This represents the inferno, with a gateway into the next realm of life, with all its pain and suffering," is not simply an ABS (Abstraction response) but also reflects an idiosyncratic and overly abstract use of symbols to represent ideas that go well beyond what the features of the inkblot could justify.

Weiner (1966) suggested that two subtypes of idiosyncratic symbolism responses—symbolic interpretation of shading or color and symbolic interpretation of concrete images—may represent deficits in the capacity to form concepts at appropriate levels of abstraction. Weiner also described another category of response that reflects overinclusive conceptual thinking. He called this "abstract preoccupation," in which the subject is overly focused on highly abstract ideas at the expense of attending to more relevant details. These are typically highly confabulated responses in which the subject is preoccupied with vague forces or powers without specific content.

Cognitive neuroscience perspectives

Cognitive neuroscience researchers have studied reasoning biases associated with positive symptoms, particularly the proneness to as well as the formation and maintenance of delusions. Cognitive biases in attribution and reasoning have been associated with delusional thinking. Externalizing and personalizing attribution biases refer to the beliefs that one's negative experiences are caused by external sources and personal significance. Reasoning biases involve how an individual gathers data, weighs evidence, and draws conclusions. The most well-studied reasoning and data-gathering bias in psychosis research is called "jumping to conclusions," or JTC, which is defined as a hasty, impulsive decision-making style characterized by an acceptance of incorrect ideas and the failure to consider alternative explanations. In a current review and meta-analysis of JTC, researchers found that individuals with psychosis make decisions based on less information and that basing conclusions on less evidence is linked to an increased likelihood of having delusions (Dudley et al., 2015). Another review article by leaders in JTC research on delusional beliefs indicated that there is sufficient evidence that JTC and inflexibility of beliefs are stable traits that increase one's susceptibility to the development of delusions (Garety & Freeman, 2013).

The relevance to assessing reasoning errors on the Rorschach becomes clear when we examine the structure of an ALOG or PEC response. The characteristics of the reasoning process that typically gives rise to these scores include immediacy, reductionism, selectivity, and certainty (Kleiger, 1999). Autistic reasoning on the Rorschach, like the JTC reasoning bias, has an immediate quality, as the subject quickly seizes on one element of a situation on which to base a conclusion while prematurely foreclosing and excluding other elements. It follows that this type of reasoning bias is also reductionistic, in that it ignores complexity and bases conclusions on simple, one-dimensional, observations. *Selectivity* is another characteristic. Discrepancies, contradictions, or discontinuities are screened out or ignored, and only those qualities that are consistent with one's conclusion are selected. Selectivity also reflects another kind of cognitive bias, referred to as "confirmation bias" (Nickerson, 1998). Finally, like JTC, ALOG/PEC responses are accompanied by a high degree of certainty, in which the subject explicitly expresses his or her conclusions with conviction. There is little room for doubt.

Anthropological and developmental perspectives

The study of illogicality has extended into the fields of social anthropology and developmental psychology. What adults and Westerners term "magical thinking" is considered normative in some non-Western, native societies and in young children. Unfortunately, the pejorative term "primitive" was liberally used in early anthropological texts to refer to belief structures in indigenous and non-Western societies. When used, this term is placed in quotations to reflect its anachronistic status.

The magic of contiguity

In his study of "primitive" and magical thought, Werner (1948) introduced the term "magic of contiguity" to describe the belief that the properties of one thing, when brought into contact with another entity, could pervade that entity. He described rituals in the Papuan culture wherein an individual rubbed his back and legs against rocks in order to partake of their strength. Contact, or tactile-mediated spatial connection, between the subject's body and a hard substance implies that the desired qualities of hardness are transferred to the body. The combinative activity inherent in this type of thought process speaks to a greater degree of permeability of boundaries (of a near contaminatory quality) than is typically associated with fabulized combinative thinking. If this magical ritual were represented in the form of a Rorschach response, it would probably merit a FABCOM, in that a spatial connection between an animate and an inanimate object occurs with an implicit rupture of boundaries between them. However, beyond discussing this as a conjectured Rorschach response, it is inappropriate to apply our scoring concepts in a cultural context.

Werner pointed out that the magic of contiguity characterizes the reasoning of both the young child and the individual with psychosis. From a developmental perspective, it is appropriate for a youngster to assume that temporal or spatial proximity to magically potent objects will result in the acquisition of the desired or undesired quality. Thus, the two-year-old who combs his hair with a black comb with the hope that it will make his hair black reveals this form of magical combinative thinking.

Parataxic distortion and preoperational thought

Friedman (1952) believed that fabulized combinations and contaminations are products of the "magic of contiguity." Goldfried, Stricker, and Weiner (1971) expanded this connection by bringing in Sullivan's concept of the parataxic mode of functioning. According to Sullivan (1953), parataxic thought occurs in late infancy and involves primitive and erroneous logic that relies on signs, symbols, and signals. Hall and Lindzey (1957) described the parataxic mode as "quasilogical thought." They brought Sullivan's concept of "parataxic distortion" even closer to the Rorschach concept of pathological combinations by stating that the parataxic mode of thinking "consists of seeing causal relationships between events that occur at about the same time but are not logically related" (pp. 140–141).

Although the timing of Piaget's (1959) preoperational period does not coincide precisely with Sullivan's parataxic mode, both of these developmental constructs are characterized by magically contiguous thinking. During the early preoperational period from ages two to four, children view the world egocentrically. They think according to their immediate perceptions, which are processed through an egocentric view of the world. Typically, preoperational youngsters focus on only one attribute of an object at a time. Thus, an event that is spatially or temporally contiguous to a feeling state within the child becomes the most salient feature of a complex event and can become paired with the child's feelings in a causally meaningful way. For example, a scared three-year-old who hears a stranger raise his voice may conclude that the stranger is trying to scare him. As children move beyond preoperational thinking and begin to develop more sophisticated ways of representing the world, they become capable of "decentering" and varying the focus of their attention. Instead of remaining concretely fixated on only one perceptually salient aspect of a situation (e.g. contiguity), they become capable of considering more than one attribute at a time.

By summoning the concepts of parataxic and preoperational thinking, we can begin to view illogicality on the Rorschach as having something in common with superstitious, egocentric, and correlational thinking. Most superstitious beliefs are based on positing a special, meaningful connection between two inherently unrelated events based on temporal or spatial proximity. The hat a player is wearing when he hits a homer becomes a talisman and is forever imbued with special power. In egocentric thinking, the youngster assumes that if mother is upset and in close proximity, then he must have caused her upset. In more scientific circles, correlational thinking erroneously assumes that two things that occur together have a *causal* relationship.

Superstitious beliefs and egocentric and correlational thinking are clear, experience-near examples of inappropriate combinative thinking. Each is based on an immature level of cognition and an overly subjective, egocentric orientation toward the world. It comes as no surprise to find that Exner's normative data (1986, 1993) revealed that both FABCOMs *and* INCOMs occur more frequently in young children and decrease with age.

Despite his view that parataxic thinking occurs in late infancy, Sullivan held that much adult thinking does not extend beyond this more primitive level where causality is assumed to exist between experiences that have nothing to do with each other. Egocentric and correlational thinking are characteristic in individuals whose conviction about the immediacy of their own perceptual experience supersedes their capacity to "decenter" or objectify and consider an event from more than one viewpoint. Combinatory thinking may reflect this form of cognitive rigidity, in which conclusions are based on immediate and obvious perceptions without engaging in thoughtful, reflective activity. Broadly speaking, we are describing an immature cognitive style characteristic of what David Shapiro (1965) called "impulsive styles." In describing the cognitive style of impulsive individuals, diagnostically considered as action-oriented character disorders, Shapiro wrote:

> First, if we say that the impulsive person's attention does not search actively and analytically, we may add that his attention is quite easily and completely captured; he sees what strikes him, and what strikes him is not only the starting point of a cognitive integrative process, but also, substantially, it is its conclusion. In this sense, his cognition may be called *passive*. Second, if he does not search—critically examine this aspect and that aspect—he does not perceive things in their potential and logical significance, but sees them only in their most obvious, immediately personally relevant qualities. In this sense, the impulsive mode of cognition is relatively *concrete* (pp. 150–151).

Developmental theory, thought disorder and the Rorschach

Leichtman (1988, 1996) proposed a developmental theory to explain Rorschach thought disorder scores. Although youngsters typically produce a number of thought disorder scores on the Rorschach, Leichtman stated that developmental normalcy should not be equated with adult psychopathology. Leichtman believed that the developmental theory of Heinz Werner (1948, 1957; Werner & Kaplan, 1963) illuminates the Rorschach response process. According to Werner's theory, "primitive" states of mental functioning tend to be less complex, undifferentiated, diffuse, rigid, and labile. In contrast, more mature states reflect greater differentiation, articulation, integration, flexibility, and stability.

Leichtman (1988) originally proposed a developmental progression of three stages to explain how young children come to be able to take the Rorschach. According to Leichtman, each stage is characterized by shifts in how the Rorschach is given and taken. Each stage is also associated with different test-taking behavior and test responses. Finally, each progressive stage incorporates aspects of the earlier stages. Leichtman called his three stages: I. Perseverative approaches to the Rorschach; II. Confabulatory approaches to the Rorschach; and III. "The Rorschach." His stages are defined by specific patterns, not ages per se.

According to Leichtman, three- and four-year-olds take the Rorschach in a qualitatively different manner, characteristic of his Stage II. Youngsters no longer respond to the blots in a concrete, perseverative manner but are now able to give different responses to each blot, which serves as a springboard for idiosyncratic fantasy. The child's Rorschach may take a more familiar form and may even reveal something about the child's personality functioning. Although the form level of most responses is better than that of the perseverating toddler, most of the responses of the three- to four-year-olds are confabulatory wholes. The child has become enamored of ideas, which take precedence over conceptual reality. The boundary between reality and fantasy is permeable, and affect states tend to influence perception.

Leichtman noted that as children make the transition from stage II to III, there is an increase in the number of responses and in large-detail responses (as opposed to wholes). Klopfer, Spiegelman, and Fox (1956) believed that this transition period was also marked by the introduction of "confabulatory combinations," which they defined as essentially thematically embellished incongruous combinations. Other researchers such as Ames and colleagues (1952) noted that the Rorschachs of five-year-olds are characterized less by confabulations and more by incongruous combinations.

Leichtman believed that the most distinctive Rorschach thought disorder scores are indications of disturbances in the coordination of the symbolic vehicle and the referent object. In other words, in the symbol situation of the Rorschach, there is some discontinuity between the object or concept itself and the way in which it gets mentally represented. The outcome of this lack of coordination between object/concept and symbolic representation includes familiar scores such as INCOMs, FABCOMs, confabulations, and contaminations.

Leichtman observed that a comparative developmental perspective lends support to the ways in which researchers have ordered these four scores along a continuum of psychopathology. Most Rorschach thought disorder researchers view the contamination response as the most severe thought disorder score, followed by confabulations, and fabulized combinations (Blatt & Ritzler, 1974; Johnston & Holzman, 1979). Similarly, normative data demonstrate that these scores occur in a developmental sequence in children's Rorschachs, with scores at the lower end of the continuum (except for contamination responses) occurring at earlier stages and more differentiated and better integrated scores occurring later on. Thus, while Leichtman conceived of the typical Rorschach thought disorder scores as part of a normal developmental progression of increased differentiation and integration in the records of youngsters, he considered them signs of a regressive "de-differentiation and dis-integration" in the records of older children, adolescents, and adults. Leichtman's model represents a shift in thinking about development and psychopathology. Instead of viewing thought pathology as regressive phenomena, Leichtman explains Rorschach thought disorder signs in a progressive and adaptive manner.

Psychoanalytic perspectives

Primary process thinking

Illogicality has traditionally been understood as a manifestation of primary process thinking mediated by the mechanisms of condensation and symbolization. Regardless of whether or not one subscribes to an economic theory of drive energies, primary process thinking is a system of information processing characterized by the fluid shifting of images and ideas. Unlike secondary process thinking, primary process-mediated ideas and their referents lack orderliness and stability. As a result, images and ideas can intermingle with one another and become condensed in ways that are incompatible with external reality. Separate images can become combined or fused, resulting in bizarre hybrids that represent several images or ideas that are either inappropriately linked or merged.

Holt (1956, 1967, 1970, 1977, 2009) believed that the condensation of ideas and images was represented by a continuum of Rorschach scores that reflect arbitrary and inappropriate combinations. He described the most extreme example of condensation as the contamination response, in which overlapping images are fused into a single percept. Holt initially included internal–external responses on this continuum, followed by two scores that reflected the subject's difficulty distinguishing between two percepts for the same blot area. Holt (1977) later introduced the term "interpenetration" to capture this partial fusion process, which could be considered a contamination tendency.

Boundary disturbances and object relations

Boundary disturbances historically have been linked to psychoses, with special reference to pathology in the sphere of the ego. Blatt and Ritzler (1974) conceptualized Rorschach thought disorder scores as different degrees of disruption in boundaries (between self and others and internal and external experiences), thus integrating both Tausk's and Federn's conceptions of ego boundaries with object relational concepts. The focus of Blatt and Ritzler's seminal study involved the diagnostic significance of different levels of boundary disturbances and the relationships between varying degrees of boundary violations, different Rorschach thought disorder scores, and level of psychopathology. They accurately predicted that levels of boundary disturbance would correlate with disruptions in reality testing, impairment in cognitive processes, interpersonal relations, and response to treatment.

Blatt and Ritzler defined three traditional thought disorder scores as different levels of boundary disturbances. As independent percepts, illogically combined because of spatial contiguity, fabulized combinations were posited to represent the process of inferring an inappropriate relationship between unrelated events, experiences, or objects. No merging or fusion of percepts takes place; each can be accurately perceived but are unrealistically related to one another. In confabulation responses, the boundary disruption was said to occur between external perception and internal experience. Thus, Blatt and Ritzler delineated a relationship between reality testing, or the distinction between inner and outer phenomena, and confabulatory thinking. Finally, they inferred that the contamination response reflects a loss of boundary between independent objects, concepts, or images. In object relational terms, contaminatory thinking marks a potential loss of capacity to differentiate self from others.

Lerner, Sugarman, and Barbour (1985) extended Blatt and Ritzler's paradigm to study the developmental continuum of boundary disturbances and levels of thought disorder among neurotic, borderline (outpatient and hospitalized samples), and schizophrenic patients. They found that boundary disturbances (represented by the three categories of thought disorder scores) were present in all four patient groups and that, quantitatively, the hospitalized patients had a greater total of weighted boundary disturbance scores (and thought disorder scores) than the nonhospitalized patients. Their most interesting finding offered confirmation for their original hypothesis that the confabulation score distinguished the inpatient borderlines from all other groups, reflecting a disturbance in maintaining a boundary between inner and outer experiences, whereas the contamination response characterized the schizophrenic group, reflecting a developmentally more severe disturbance in maintaining the boundary between self and other.

Blatt, Tuber, and Auerbach (1990) found one Rorschach measure of the quality of interpersonal relationships to be highly correlated with the severity of psychopathology, and thought disorder scores in particular, in a group of adolescent patients in residential treatment. The Mutuality of Autonomy Scale (MOA; Urist, 1977) is a 7-point ordinal scale that assesses the quality of object relations by evaluating Rorschach interactions between human figures, animals, and objects. The highest MOA scores (5, 6, and 7) are given when the interaction reflects a severe imbalance in power, envelopment and fusion, as well as a heightened degree of malevolence and aggression. Using the MOA, Blatt and colleagues found that malevolent content portrayed in interactions on the Rorschach is significantly related to fabulized combinations, confabulations, and contaminations. The correlation was highest between these malevolent interactions and confabulation scores.

In a similar study, Berg, Packer, and Nunno (1993) used the MOA to examine the relationship between pathology in thinking and object relationships in patients with schizophrenic, borderline, and narcissistic disorders. However, unlike Blatt, Berg and her colleagues looked at the relationship between scores on the MOA and critical Special Scores in the CS. Using a composite measure of Rorschach thought disorder (WSUM6), Berg et al. established empirical support for the observations of earlier theorists (Klein, 1930/1968; Isaacs, 1948; Kernberg, 1967), who held that there was a relationship between pathological object relations and disturbances in thinking. Berg and colleagues found highly significant correlations between composite WSUM6 scores and the most pathological scores on the MOA (5, 6, and 7). In terms of individual scores, the team found the highest correlation between ALOG, FABCOM2, and INCOM 2 scores and MOA 5, 6, and 7 scores, which, according to Berg and her colleagues, suggests that pathological object relations are associated with defensive failures that cannot prevent primary process manifestations from intruding into secondary process thinking.

Examining the degree of overlap between MOA scores and the Special Scores in the CS, Berg and colleagues found that through MOA 6, the two scales measure different facets of psychological functions. However, the severe degree of fusion and aggressive envelopment defined by MOA 7 scores indicate that there will be a significant overlap between MOA 7 and critical Special Scores.

Smith (1980) attempted to synthesize the object relations theories of Klein (1959), Mahler (Mahler, Pine, & Bergman, 1975), Kernberg (1967), and Rinsley (1982) with Rorschach measures of thought organization and reality testing. Smith used object relational concepts to delineate three levels of development within the psychotic range: autism, symbiosis, and differentiation. In accord with Mahler's theory, Smith described the autistic patient as living in an "objectless" world, without concern for external objects. He hypothesized that formal Rorschach scores such as F-responses, which signal a withdrawal of interest from external reality, and contamination scores would characterize this most "primitive" level of functioning. In contrast, symbiotic functioning would be characterized by Rorschach content reflecting objects that are connected, arbitrarily joined together, or by confabulatory responses that manifest a blurring of one's internal representations with one's perceptions of external reality. Thus, Smith proposed that fabulized combinations and confabulations with merger themes would typify the symbiotic level of relatedness.

Disordered thinking and self-experience

A useful way to conceptualize the psychology of the self is in terms of the dimensions of: (1) cohesion versus fragmentation; (2) integration versus splitting; (3) authenticity/realness versus inauthenticity/falseness; (4) vitality versus depletion; (5) internal agency versus external locus of control; (6) differentiation versus fusion; and (7) continuity versus discontinuity (Kohut & Wolf, 1978; Stern, 1985). This list of dimensions captures essential structural components of self-experience that might be reflected in some Rorschach thought disorder categories.

Arnow and Cooper (1988) explored the Rorschach psychology of the self but did not specifically address the interface between disordered thinking and disordered self-experiences. Instead, they conceptualized some of the Rorschach features associated with the self-pathological syndromes described by Kohut and Wolf (1978). For example, they referred to the "overstimulated self" in which the self-object may have excessive needs for self-display and admiration and may end up using the self as an extension. Arnow and Cooper suggested that the grandiose fantasies of these patients might be seen in both the content and structure of the response. Structurally, these individuals may feel the need to provide original and distinct responses that exceed their integrative or synthetic capacities. Again, we could view this as another juncture between an ego capacity and some aspect of self or, as described in the previous section, object relational experience. Arnow and Cooper hypothesized that these grandiose individuals may overstrive to produce unsuccessful combinative responses that are not well justified by the realities of the inkblot. Thus W+ confabulations and fabulized combinations, with poor or unconvincing form level, may reflect the needs of an overstriving grandiose self that is unable to harness or deploy these needs for adaptive purposes.

Arnow and Cooper suggested that Kohut and Wolf's "fragmenting self" may reveal itself in a psychotic confabulatory response such as "It's a person blowing into pieces before my eyes" (Arnow & Cooper, 1988, p. 65). Other expressions of fragmentation may be embedded in various incongruous combinations such as "A person without a head" or Rapaport's "oligophrenic" response, where the subject sees only a portion of an object that is normally seen as a whole entity.

The hypothesized dimension of "integration" versus "splitting" addresses the degree to which discrepant self-experiences (or, for that matter, object representations) are cognitively woven together and affectively tolerated as opposed to walled off and unintegrated. Certain kinds of inappropriate combination responses may reflect splits or a lack of integration in the self. Schafer (1954) listed "integratedness of scores, images, and attitudes" as one of six criteria for judging the overall success or failure of defensive and adaptive operations reflected by an individual Rorschach response. He indicated that the dramatic opposition of images in a single response signals a failure in the individual's adaptive and defensive functioning. Schafer's examples of such a lack of integratedness in Rorschach responses include "A pink polar bear," "A horrible monster with shriveled arms," and "An infant with a fang" (Schafer, 1954, pp. 180–181). Although Schafer approached his analysis from a classical impulse-defense tradition, a self-psychological interpretation of these incongruous combinations might suggest a lack of integration between disparate aspects of self-experience.

The dimension of "differentiation" versus "fusion" reflects an inherent overlap between this key dimension of self-experience and a structural component of relational representation. Internal representations of merger, engulfment, enmeshment, and fusion capture both the gestalt of a paradigmatic object relational experience, and, at the same time, an irreducible subjective sense of self. Thus, as seen in the last chapter, any of the thought disorder scores that have condensation as a base may represent not only relational paradigms but also an ambience of self-experience.

Lerner (1998) conceptualized Rorschach manifestations of authenticity versus inauthenticity when he wrote about the false self. Drawing on the work of Winnicott (1961/1965) and Schachtel (1966), and his earlier work (Lerner & Lerner, 1988), Lerner theorized that the passive compliance with, and accommodation to, environmental demands that is so characteristic of the false self may be reflected in the FCarb response (the Rapaportian subtype of the INCOM response), in which the subject clings to the inappropriate inclusion of color simply because the environment has presented it. Winnicott (1961/1965) suggested that the development of the self is stifled when the individual is unable to maintain a distance from the environment and instead becomes overly dependent on it. Lerner viewed FCarb responses as a loss of adaptive detachment or perspective in which the individual has abandoned a more objective, critical, judgmental attitude. Events in one's life or the dictates of significant objects are not critically examined but accepted based on their most obvious surface qualities. The compliant self passively goes along with the implicit demand to accept an external world that is in some ways incongruous with internal perceptual experience, and is left with a sense of unreality or falseness. Thus, the response "A pink polar bear" may simultaneously reflect a lack of critical thinking and a subjective sense of falseness or unreality.

Mayman (1977) teased out different nuances of meaning of human movement responses on the Rorschach. In addition to explicating the fantasy–ideational, kinesthetic, and relational aspects of M responses, Mayman suggested that certain kinds of human movement responses might reveal something about an individual's capacity for empathy. He distinguished between empathic and narcissistic relatedness based on identification and stated that empathy implies a two-way process in which self–other boundaries are maintained, while identification suggests that the separate existence of the object is not respected. Based on an active identification with others, narcissistic relatedness involves the attribution, or projection, of characteristics of the self onto the other. Thus, based on theory and clinical observations, Mayman reasoned that individuals who relate to others on a narcissistic level tend to produce M responses that are infused with aspects of the individuals themselves. Furthermore, Mayman suggested that these M responses are largely fabulized and described with vividness and conviction. The subject may become absorbed in these Ms, enlivening them with attributes quite distant from the reality of the inkblot. This process was dramatically portrayed by an envious and self-absorbed woman, quite dissatisfied with her life, who responded to Card VII with the following exaggerated confabulatory DR:

> Could be two matrons having a talk over coffee at 10:00 in the morning, and I suppose the bottom is symbolic of the thread that binds them together as homemakers, wives. They're in the same bridge club, bound together by all those ties. Kinda haughty and pretentious with their hands out. They're wealthy too. Pigtails up makes me think of uppity society women.
> (Kleiger, 1999, p. 181)

Psychotherapeutic perspectives

Several writers have moved from their patients' illogical Rorschach responses to the therapeutic implications of such responses (Athey, 1974, 1986; Peebles, 2012; Bram & Peebles, 2014). Athey explored how patients' regressed thought organization as seen on the Rorschach parallels the way they experience object relations in the transference in psychotherapy. In attempting to conceptualize the relationship between thought organization and object relations, Athey found that Blatt and Ritzler's boundary-deficit hypothesis did not go far enough in explicating the specific psychological and relational processes that underlie Rorschach thought disorder indicators. His studies demonstrated the value of using these scores as indices of qualitatively different types of relatedness in treatment. According to Athey, thought disorder indicators are important "in assessing the emergence of qualitatively different levels of regressed psychological processes in the stream of thought and their operation in the patient's experiences with and representations of object relations with other persons during treatment" (1974, p. 162). In particular, Athey sought to conceptualize qualitative distinctions in the organization of thought that can help clinicians anticipate various transference paradigms that might emerge in psychotherapy.

Athey looked at detailed therapy process notes of two patients with schizophrenia, one characterized by the presence of contamination responses and the other by confabulation. Consistent with object relations concepts, he commented on the relational implications of fabulized combinations that occurred in the protocol of one of these patients. Athey suggested that the content of some fabulized combinations might reflect a preoccupation with certain kinds of self–other relationships. For example, the Card VIII response of "A weasel climbing on a butterfly" may reveal a preoccupation with sadomasochistic relational paradigms.

Athey characterized the confabulatory mode as excessive fantasy imposed on a reality that is initially perceived in an accurate manner. He described the transference implications of patient B, whose Rorschach was characterized by numerous confabulation responses, as those of an individual whose perceptions of the therapist were colored by affect-laden fantasies. When this patient became angry, she reacted with an outpouring of affect-dominated fantasies of rejection by the therapist. What initially began as an accurate perception of an interpersonal event was magnified and confabulated into something that departed from reality but was consistent with the patient's interpersonal preoccupation.

Finally, Athey described the contaminatory mode as a loss of distinction between and condensation of different frames of reference. According to Athey, frames of reference are conceptual dimensions by which reality is represented internally as structures. Examples include time (past vs. present vs. future); space (here vs. there); levels of language (reference vs. referent vs. symbol); relational representations (self vs. other, object 1 vs. object 2). Athey characterized the contaminatory transference as an extreme form of fusion with the therapist in which the relationship with a separate figure is condensed and experienced as an alteration in an internal state. He gave the example of a patient who was terrified that she had physically harmed her therapist because she had condensed the *internal fantasy* with the *external reality* of injuring the therapist.

Athey pointed out that different levels of psychotic experience may occur in the confabulatory and contaminatory modes. However, he also indicated that the same patient may fluctuate between different levels of experience, with different relational implications associated with different levels of thought (dis)organization. For example, progression from the contaminatory to the confabulatory mode may signal the capacity to differentiate internal self from other representations. The diagnostician should pay attention to the conditions that facilitate this kind of progressive shift. On the other hand, regression from a fabulized combinatory to confabulatory mode of experience involves losing the reality basis for representing relationships and replacing reality with idiosyncratic affect-laden fantasies. The diagnostic understanding of the conditions that make an individual vulnerable to such a regression in functioning has important treatment implications.

In their individual and joint writings, Peebles (2012) and Bram (Bram & Peebles, 2014) attempted to bring thought disorder scores alive by linking them to specific treatment implications. Peebles wrote about therapy interventions with patients who demonstrate confabulatory, combinative, and contaminatory reasoning in the clinical setting. Included in the writings of Peebles and Bram are behavioral examples of each mode of thinking in a clinical context.

Creative perspectives

Unless we are thinking in terms of developmental or cross-cultural perspectives, as clinicians we typically view illogicality as pathological. However, under certain conditions, departures from conventional logic can be adaptive, and even creative. Consider condensation. As a pathological process, condensation reflects either a regressive wish for merger or a deficit in the ability to suppress the intermingling of incompatible or conflicting impressions (Schwartz & Lazar, 1984). Additionally, pathological condensations involve the unintentional collapse of boundaries between different frames of reference such as time, space, personal identity, and sensory events (actions, thoughts, and feelings). In a clinical context, such perceptual and conceptual condensations are typically the result of a passive and unreflective, as opposed to consciously motivated, process. The key question in distinguishing pathological from adaptive (in particular, creative) condensations concerns the attitude and intentionality of the person employing the mechanism of condensation

If pathological condensations occur without conscious design and in the context of an impaired perspective, most adaptive condensations are fully intended and consciously motivated. In an adaptive sense, condensation is used as a mechanism to express a particular thought, feeling, or experience. In essence, by secondary process design, a primary process mechanism is employed for a specific purpose, whether to convey meaning, solve a problem, make one laugh, or sell a product. The concept of regression in the service of the ego lies at the heart of the intentional deployment of illogical reasoning for adaptive, creative purposes (Kris, 1952).

Adaptive condensation is germane to the topic of creativity and occurs most frequently in works of art and literature. In writing about the creative process, Rothenberg (1971, 1976) coined the term "Janusian thinking" to describe the conscious capacity to conceive and utilize simultaneously two or more contradictory ideas, concepts, or images. Rothenberg believed that this cognitive process, which defies conventional logic, lies at the heart of creative breakthroughs. Rothenberg also introduced another related term reflecting adaptive condensation that he called "homospatial process." He used this term to describe the simultaneous placing of two discrete entities in the same perceptual–cognitive space. Rothenberg first described Janusian thinking in the context of his 1969 study of Eugene O'Neill's play *The Iceman Cometh*. According to Rothenberg, the iceman symbol has at least three meanings: death, Christ, and a sexually potent adulterer. If one substitutes these meanings in the play, the notion of the "iceman coming" produces a number of logically opposite ideas.

Surrealistic artists such as Dali and Magritte frequently merged incompatible images to create disturbing, dreamlike scenes. Dali, in particular, was influenced by Freud's writings on the mechanisms of dreams and unconscious mental processes. A typical Dali technique involved using commonplace objects to set up a chain of metamorphoses that are gradually or suddenly condensed and transformed into a nightmarish image.

Creative condensations abound in poetry, as the poet sees similarities in things that are inherently dissimilar. Condensation underlies the creation of metaphor, and metaphorical language is one of the essential components of poetry. Humor and comedy make liberal use of condensation. Freud (1905/1960) wrote about the psychology of wit and humor after he noticed that certain dreams resembled jokes. Nowhere is creative condensation more apparent than in puns and plays on words. Freud noted that the double meanings found in puns were a preferred technique in jokes.

Of course, the key issue is that of intentionality. Two brief vignettes emphasize how intentionality, or the lack thereof, distinguishes pathological from creative illogicality. The first is a frequently cited, but no less compelling, anecdote that is germane to the issues of both illogicality and disorganization. The story is of a professional conversation between C. G. Jung and James Joyce about the nature of Joyce's daughter's mental illness. Joyce, increasingly distraught over his 21-year-old daughter's apparent descent into schizophrenia, was urged by his patrons in the early 1930s to bring his daughter, Lucia, to meet with the eminent Swiss psychiatrist. Joyce, perhaps in desperation, insisted that Lucia's poetry contained the strands of a new form of literature. Following his examination, Jung, the twentieth doctor to be consulted, told Joyce that Lucia was suffering from dementia praecox and that her poems were "random."

> "How do you know, Dr. Jung?" Joyce asked. Jung replied that her thinking and speech were so deviant and distorted that he could conclude that she was suffering from this particular form of madness. Joyce protested that in his own writing, he purposefully stretched the English language, distorted words, fused thoughts and images. "What is the difference?" he asked. Jung replied that Joyce and his daughter were like two people going to the bottom of a river, but whereas Joyce dove into the deep water, his daughter fell into it. Jung later wrote, "The ordinary patient cannot help himself talking and thinking in such a way, while Joyce willed it and moreover developed it with all his creative forces."
> (Johnston & Holzman, 1979, p. 16, quoting Ellmann, 1959, p. 692)

My favorite example of creativity, illogicality, and intentionality comes from a story of an interview with Bob Zmuda, friend and comic co-conspirator of the late cult comedian Andy Kaufman. During the interview, Zmuda was pointedly asked, "Was Andy Kaufman insane?" With a sober expression, Zmuda paused and responded something to the effect, "Yes, he was ... but he worked awfully hard at it!"

References

Ames, L. B., Learned, J., Metraux, R. W., & Walker, R. N. (1952). *Child Rorschach Responses*. New York: Paul B. Hoeber.

Andreasen, N. (1979). Thought, language, and communication disorders: I. Clinical assessment, definition of terms, and evaluation of their reliability. *Archives of General Psychiatry, 36*, 1315–1321.

Arieti, S. (1974). *Interpretation of Schizophrenia* (2nd ed.). New York: Basic Books.

Arnow, D., & Cooper, S. (1988). Toward a Rorschach psychology of the self. In H. D. Lerner & P. M. Lerner (Eds.), *Primitive Mental States and the Rorschach* (pp. 53–70). New York: International Universities Press.

Athey, G. I. (1974). Schizophrenia thought organization, object relations, and the Rorschach test. *Bulletin of the Menninger Clinic, 38*, 406–429.

Athey, G. I. (1986). Rorschach thought organization and transference enactment in the patient–examiner relationship. In M. Kissen (Ed.), *Assessing Object Relations Phenomena* (pp. 19–50). Madison, CT: International Universities Press.

Barch, D. M., Bustillo, J., Gaebel, W., Gur, R., Heckers, S., Malaspina, D., Owen, M. J., Schultz, S., Tandon, R., Tsuang, M., van Os, J., & Carpenter, W. (2013). Logic and justification for dimensional assessment of symptoms and related clinical phenomena in psychosis: Relevance to DSM-5. *Schizophrenia Research, 150*, 15–20.

Beck, A. T., Rector, N. A., Stolar, N., & Grant, P. (2009). *Schizophrenia: Cognitive Theory, Research, and Therapy*. New York: Guilford Press.

Berg, J. L., Packer, A., & Nunno, V. J. (1993). A Rorschach analysis: Parallel disturbance in thought and in self/object representation. *Journal of Personality Assessment, 61*, 311–323.

Blatt, S. J., & Ritzler, B. A. (1974). Thought disorder and boundary disturbances in psychosis. *Journal of Consulting and Clinical Psychology, 42*, 370–381.

Blatt, S. J., Tuber, S. B., & Auerbach, J. S. (1990). Representation of interpersonal interactions on the Rorschach and level of psychopathology. *Journal of Personality Assessment, 54*, 711–728.

Bleuler, E. (1950). *Dementia Praecox or the Group of Schizophrenias*. (J. Zinkin, Trans.). New York: International Universities Press. (Original work published in 1911.)

Bram, A. D., & Peebles, M. J. (2014). *Psychological Testing That Matters: Creating a Road Map for Effective Treatment*. Washington, DC: American Psychological Association.

Dudley, R., Taylor, R., Wickham, S., & Hutton, P. (2015). *Schizophrenia Bulletin*. DOI: 10.1093/schbul/sbv150.

Ellmann, R. (1959). *James Joyce*. New York: Oxford University Press.

Exner, J. E. (1986). *The Rorschach: A Comprehensive System, Basic Foundations* (Vol. 1, 2nd ed.). New York: Wiley.

Exner, J. E. (1993). *The Rorschach: A Comprehensive System, Basic Foundations* (Vol. 1, 3rd ed.). New York: Wiley.

Exner, J. E., Weiner, I. B., & Schuyler, S. (1976). *A Rorschach Workbook for the Comprehensive System*. Bayville, NY: Rorschach Workshops.

Federn, P. (1952). *Ego Psychology and the Psychoses*. New York: Basic Books.

Freud, S. (1953). The Interpretation of dreams. In the *Standard Edition of the Complete Works of Sigmund Freud* (Vols. 4 & 5). London, UK: Hogarth Press. (Original work published in 1900.)

Freud, S. (1960). Jokes and their relation to the unconscious. In the *Standard Edition of the Complete Works of Sigmund Freud* (Vol. 8, pp. 9–236). London, UK: Hogarth Press. (Original work published in 1905.)

Friedman, H. (1952). Perceptual regression in schizophrenia: An hypothesis suggested by the use of the Rorschach test. *Journal of Genetic Psychology, 87*, 63–98.

Garety, P. A., & Freeman, D. (2013). The past and future of delusions research: From the inexplicable to the treatable. *British Journal of Psychiatry, 203*, 327–333.

Goldfried, M. R., Stricker, G., & Weiner, I. B. (1971). *Rorschach Handbook of Clinical and Research Application*. Englewood Cliffs, NJ: Prentice-Hall.

Hall, C. S., & Lindzey, G. (1957). *Theories of Personality*. New York: Wiley.

Holt, R. R. (1956). Gauging primary and secondary process in Rorschach responses. *Journal of Projective Techniques, 20*, 14–25.

Holt, R. R. (1967). The development of primary process: A structural view. In R. R. Holt (Ed.), *Motives and Thought: Psychoanalytic Essays in Honor of David Rapaport* (pp. 345–383). New York: International Universities Press.

Holt, R. R. (1970). *Manual for the Scoring of Primary Process Manifestations and Their Controls in Rorschach Responses*. New York: Research Center for Mental Health.

Holt, R. R. (1977). A method for assessing primary process manifestations and their control in Rorschach responses. In M. A. Rickers-Ovsiankina (Ed.), *Rorschach Psychology* (2nd ed., pp. 375–420). New York: Krieger.

Holt, R. R. (2009). *Primary Process Thinking: Theory, Measurement, and Research* (Vols. 1 & 2). Lanham, MD: Aronson.

Isaacs, S. (1948). The nature and function of phantasy. *International Journal of Psycho-Analysis, 29*, 73–97.

Johnston, M. H., & Holzman, P. S. (1979). *Assessing Schizophrenic Thinking*. San Francisco, CA: Jossey-Bass.

Kernberg, O. F. (1967). Borderline personality organization. *Journal of the American Psychoanalytic Association, 15*, 641–685.

Kleiger, J. H (1999). *Disordered Thinking and the Rorschach*. Hillsdale, NJ: The Analytic Press.

Kleiger, J. H., & Khadivi, A. (2015). *Assessing Psychosis. A Clinician's Guide*. New York: Routledge.

Klein, M. (1959). Our adult world and its roots in infancy. In *Envy and Gratitude and Other Works 1946–1967* (pp. 247–263). London, UK: Hogarth Press.

Klein, M. (1968), The importance of symbol-formation in the development of the ego. In *Contributions to Psycho-analysis, 1921–1945* (pp. 236–250). London, UK: Hogarth Press. (Original work published in 1930.)

Klopfer, B., Spiegelman, M., & Fox, J. (1956). The interpretation of children's records. In B. Klopfer (Ed.), *Developments in the Rorschach Technique* (Vol. 2, pp. 22–44). New York: Harcourt, Brace & World.

Kohut, H., & Wolf, E. (1978). The disorders of the self and their treatment: An outline. *International Journal of Psychoanalysis, 59*, 413–425.

Kris, E. (1952). *Psychoanalytic Explorations in Art*. New York: International Universities Press.

Leichtman, M. (1988). When does the Rorschach become the Rorschach? Stages in the mastery of the test. In H. D. Lerner & P. M. Lerner (Eds.), *Primitive Mental States and the Rorschach* (pp. 559–600). Madison, CT: International Universities Press.

Leichtman, M. (1996). *The Rorschach: A Developmental Perspective*. Hillsdale, NJ: The Analytic Press.

Lerner, P. (1998). *Psychoanalytic Perspectives on the Rorschach*. Hillsdale, NJ: The Analytic Press.

Lerner, H., & Lerner, P. (1988). Rorschach measures of depression, the false self, and projective identification with narcissistic personality disorders. In H. D. Lerner & P. M. Lerner (Eds.), *Primitive Mental States and the Rorschach* (pp. 71–94). Madison, CT: International Universities Press.

Lerner, P., Sugarman, A., & Barbour, C. G. (1985). Patterns of ego boundary disturbance in neurotic, borderline, and schizophrenic patients. *Psychoanalytic Psychology, 2*, 47–66.

Mahler, M., Pine, F., & Bergman, A. (1975). *The Psychological Birth of the Human Infant*. New York: Basic Books.

Mayman, M. (1977). A multidimensional view of the Rorschach movement response. In M. Rickers-Ovsiankina (Ed.), *Rorschach Psychology* (pp. 229–250). Huntington, NY: Krieger.

Nickerson, R. S. (1998). Confirmation bias: A ubiquitous phenomenon in many guises. *Review of General Psychology, 2*, 175–220.

Peebles, M. J. (2012). *Beginnings: The Art and Science of Planning Psychotherapy* (2nd ed.). New York: Routledge.

Piaget, J. (1959). *The Language and Thought of the Child*. London, UK: Routledge & Kegan Paul.

Reininghaus, U., Priebe, S., & Bentall, R. P. (2013). Testing the psychopathology of psychosis: Evidence for a general psychosis dimension. *Schizophrenia Bulletin, 39*, 884–895.

Rinsley, D. B. (1982). *Borderline and Other Self Disorders: A Developmental and Object-Relations Perspective*. New York: Aronson.

Rothenberg, A. (1969). The iceman changeth: Toward an empirical approach to creativity. *Journal of the American Psychoanalytic Association, 17*, 549–607.

Rothenberg, A. (1971). The process of Janusian thinking in creativity. *Archives of General Psychiatry, 24*, 195–205.

Rothenberg, A. (1976). The process of Janusian thinking in creativity. In A. Rothenberg & C. Hausman (Eds.), *The Creativity Question* (pp. 305–327). Durham, NC: Duke University Press.

Schachtel, E. (1966). *Experiential Foundations of the Rorschach Test*. New York: Basic Books.

Schafer, R. (1954). *Psychoanalytic Interpretation in Rorschach Testing*. New York: Grune & Stratton.

Schwartz, F., & Lazar, Z. (1984). Contaminated thinking: A specimen of the primary process. *Psychoanalytic Psychology, 4*, 319–334.

Shapiro, D. (1965). *Neurotic Styles*. New York: Basic Books.

Smith, K. (1980). Object relations concepts as applied to the borderline level of ego functioning. In J. Kwawer, H. Lerner, P. Lerner, & A. Sugarman (Eds.), *Borderline Phenomena and the Rorschach Test* (pp. 59–87). New York: International Universities Press.

Stern, D. N. (1985). *The Interpersonal World of the Infant*. New York: Basic Books.
Sullivan, H. S. (1953). *The Interpersonal Theory of Psychiatry*. New York: Norton.
Tausk, V. (1933). On the origin of the "influencing machine" in schizophrenia. *Psychoanalytic Quarterly, 2*, 519–556. (Original work published in 1919.)
Urist, J. (1977). The Rorschach Test and the assessment of object relations. *Journal of Personality Assessment, 41*, 3–9.
von Domarus, E. (1944). The specific laws of logic in schizophrenia. In J. S. Kasinin (Ed.), *Language and Thought in Schizophrenia* (pp. 104–114). New York: Norton.
Weiner, I. B. (1966). *Psychodiagnosis in Schizophrenia*. New York: Wiley.
Werner, H. (1948). *Comparative Psychology of Mental Development*. New York: Follett.
Werner, H. (1957). The concept of development from a comparative and organismic view. In D. B. Harris (Ed.), *The Concept of Development* (pp. 125–148). Minneapolis, MN: University of Minnesota Press.
Werner, H., & Kaplan, B. (1963). *Symbol Formation. An Organismic Approach to Language and the Expression of Thought*. New York: Wiley.
Winnicott, D. (1965). Ego distortions in terms of true and false self. In *The Maturational Processes and the Facilitating Environment* (pp. 140–152). Madison, CT: International Universities Press. (Original work published in 1961.)

Chapter 11

Impoverishment in thinking and language

Impoverishment is a quality of dysfunctional thought and verbalization. Like disorganization and illogicality, impoverishment can be a distinct feature of thought disorder. However, whereas disorganization and illogicality are more common, central, and specific features of thought disorder, impoverishment is a broader and less specific category. Individuals demonstrating thought disorder, especially those suffering from schizophrenia, might communicate in impoverished ways; however, a variety of other conditions can be associated with similar kinds of thinking and language manifestations. The aim of this chapter is to examine the category of impoverishment, define its constituent features, review relevant Rorschach characteristics, and bridge impoverishment in thought and speech on the Rorschach to related developmental, psychopathological, and neuropsychological perspectives.

What makes thinking and speech impoverished?

Impoverishment, derived from the word "poverty," means exhausted of resources and vitality, deprived of strength, and depleted of richness. When applied to cognition and language, it can be conceived both in terms of quantity and quality of thoughts, ideas, and speech. In terms of quantity, both ideas and speech can be sparse. Associations between ideas, as well as the flow of ideas, can be limited, with weak or few connections. Outwardly, elements of speech may be simple, meager, and repetitive, lacking in details, elaboration, or diversity of expression. In addition to limited connectivity or synthesis, the impoverished thinker may have difficulty moving beyond concrete qualities of the stimulus field. The ability to represent or symbolize is limited or absent, leaving the impoverished thinker unable to abstract meaning from literal features of objects or the environment.

Constriction in associations and overdependence on concrete aspects of stimuli may also lead to repetitive and stereotyped ideas. Thus, a lack of the flexibility that enables one to move from the concrete to the abstract and find something new in what one perceives leaves the impoverished thinker seeing and saying the same things, even when conditions and stimulus features change.

Cognitive complexity, or lack thereof, is a concept that unifies most of the aspects of impoverishment described above. Complexity is a function of perceptual and ideational differentiation, integration, flexibility, and productivity (Meyer et al., 2011). When cognitive complexity is lacking, information processing and verbalizations tend to be simplistic, constricted, undifferentiated, and repetitive.

Continuum of impoverished thinking

Similar to disorganization and illogicality, impoverished thinking can be viewed along a continuum of severity and associated conditions. However, unlike those other two categories, impoverishment may be a product of a broader range of factors. Issues like intellectual ability, neurological status, education, socioeconomic status, language processing, psychopathology, and willingness to engage and communicate are mediating variables that affect the quality and quantity of ideation and speech. It is also possible to depathologize the concept by viewing brevity and narrowness in thinking and speaking as stylistic differences in cognitive and personality functioning. As is often the case, people may demonstrate similar behavior for different reasons. Such diversity in underlying causes makes it difficult to identify specific Rorschach scoring categories of impoverishment, much less link these specifically to thought disorder. Thus, the question remains: When is impoverished thinking and speech a reflection of intellectual or educational limitations, expressive language disorder, brain damage, depression, traumatic numbing, anxiety, thought disorder, or simply a guarded and defensive approach to accessing and sharing one's thoughts and feelings? In the absence of reliable methods of categorizing impoverished thought disorder on the Rorschach, we can review ways in which the inkblots have been used to capture this more elusive quality of dysfunctional thinking.

Rorschach indicators of impoverished thinking

Rorschach (1921/1942) addressed the issue of impoverishment when he wrote about the response process in certain groups of subjects. He was the first to point out that certain respondents did not seem capable of understanding the interpretive nature of his inkblot experiment. According to Rorschach, "Most organic cases (senile dements, paretics), epileptics, many schizophrenics, most manics, almost all feebleminded subjects, and even many normals are not aware of the assimilative effort. These subjects do not interpret the pictures, they name them" (p. 17). As noted in Chapter 3, Bohm (1958) referred to the implicit task on the Rorschach as "interpretation awareness," wherein the subject is consciously aware that the test is one of interpretation, not literal recognition. Bohm also mentioned that the lowered awareness of interpretation occurs mostly among individuals with schizophrenia or intellectual limitations. In responding to the prompt "What might this be?" such individuals might reveal their lack of interpretation awareness with questions or comments such as, "Is it supposed to be something specific?" or "Will you tell me afterwards what it really is?" (p. 90). Obviously, these questions cannot be scored as such, but they might suggest that the subject is having difficulty with the representative, or interpretive, nature of the task. This signals that the perceptual realities of the inkblot, not what it might represent or symbolize, are dominant. The impoverished thinker gravitates toward attempting to *recognize*, versus interpret, the blots.

As previously noted, Rorschach also introduced a special kind of Dd (small detail score), which he referred to as the "oligophrenic detail" or Do response, to describe another aspect of perceptual and ideational impoverishment. The term "oligophrenic" is both anachronistic and alien to contemporary Western thought. It was originally a Russian diagnosis that referred to congenital mental retardation and was described as a global impairment of cognitive functioning or pervasive organic injury (Gindis, 1988). Rorschach defined Do responses as those in which only a part of an object (typically an animal or human) is seen where most subjects see the whole figure. Rorschach's example was the Card I D4 response of "hands or legs" instead of a whole human (female) body (Rorschach 1921/1942, p. 40). Today, we might refer to such responses as fragmented or unintegrated parts as opposed to synthesized wholes.

Many who followed Rorschach explored the issue of impoverishment in intellectually disabled and neurologically impaired subjects (Piotrowski, 1937; Bohm, 1958). Although they were most interested in establishing differential diagnostic signs that could identify patients with "organic conditions," many of their findings pertained to broader aspects of cognitive impoverishment. With Goldstein (Goldstein & Scheerer, 1941) as a teacher, Piotrowski set out to investigate the effects of brain damage on Rorschach responses. From his efforts emerged a 10-point scale made up of qualitative signs for identifying the presence of brain damage: (1) R, total number of responses, is less than 15; (2) T, average time per response, is more than one minute; (3) M, the number of human movement responses, is less than or equal to one; (4) Cn, color denomination or color naming, is scored if the subject simply names or describes the colors in the blot; (5) F%, good form percentage, is below 70 percent; (6) P%, the percentage of populars, is below 25 percent; (7) Rpt, repetition (perseveration), is scored when the subject gives the same response to several inkblots; (8) Imp, impotence, occurs in the presence of perseveration, and is scored when the subject gives a response despite recognizing that it is inadequate; (9) Plx, perplexity, is scored when the subject shows mistrust about his or her ability and seeks reassurance; (10) AP, automatic phrases, occur when the subject uses the same phrase repeatedly in an indiscriminate manner. Piotrowski regarded the presence of at least five of these signs as a diagnostic indication of personality change that is a result of cortical pathology. He was quite clear, however, in stating that fewer than five signs did not rule out the possibility of brain damage.

In their review of the validity of the Piotrowski signs, Goldfried, Stricker, and Weiner (1971) reported that the most discriminating of the ten signs was impotence and the least were M, P%, and Cn. Impotence significantly distinguished brain-damaged subjects in 10 out of 16 studies, while perseveration, the next most successful sign, was a significant discriminator in 50 percent of the studies. Perplexity and automatic phrases were also said to be among the most effective test signs.

Rapaport, Gill, and Schafer (1946/1968) introduced a continuum of three scores that reflected either an increase or loss of distance: vagueness, confusion, and incoherence. They referred to these scores as, "a continuity in terms of the withering of the response itself, whether due to perceptual or verbal difficulty" (p. 448). In Chapter 9, I discussed incoherence as a characteristic of disorganized verbalization. I focus again on vagueness and confusion responses because they are germane to our discussion of impoverishment. In describing the "withering of the response," Rapaport et al. defined vagueness and confusion as follows:

> Vagueness means that the subject himself is unable to keep a percept alive; in the confusion response, the complete percept is never formed nor entirely communicated; and in the incoherent response, little trace of the original percept is left and communication is totally ineffectual. These comments are easily recognized, and thus are not in need of diagnostic attention; they conceal rather than reveal the essential nature of schizophrenic thought disorder (pp. 448–449).

Rapaport and colleagues provided several examples of each of these scores. In the vague responses, the subject spontaneously communicates feelings about the nebulous quality of percepts that are usually seen clearly by most subjects. For example, the individual might see a commonly perceived image but express some uncertainty. The group said that when vagueness occurs in prepsychotic or psychotic conditions, the subject usually does not express feelings of uncertainty:

> in these cases the first perceptual impression is fleeting and quickly washed away, and despite insistent immediate inquiry the subject is unable to grasp the percept again. The examiner feels in such inquiry as though he were digging in quicksand. Such fleeting impressions are usually embedded in a stream of verbalization where only one or two words, which otherwise might seem simply incoherent, are the clue to the vagueness in a common and well-defined response (p. 449).

Confusion responses, whether expressed explicitly or inferred from the verbalization, reflect the subject's perplexity while giving the response. Rapaport et al. (1946/1968) described how the subject became confused about whether to respond to the card on a conceptual level, to respond strictly to the perceptual qualities of the blot, or to respond on the basis of some subjective experience related to the inkblot. Confusion responses on the Rorschach were thought to reflect confusion in everyday life. However, the problem with this scoring concept was noted by Rapaport and colleagues when they indicated that vague and confused responses could not be sharply defined clinically. According to these researchers, in many cases, the subject's vagueness and confusion were subtle and not readily apparent. Unfortunately, for those of us striving to discern the essence of Rapaport's writings, his definitions of both vagueness and confusion scores were rather vague and confusing themselves.

The TDI, which was based on the scores of Rapaport and his colleagues, followed suit by including thought disorder scoring categories for vagueness, confusion, and incoherence. According to the Holzman TDI research group, both vagueness and confusion responses are relatively rare (M. Coleman and D. Levy, personal communication, June 1992). Nevertheless, they attempted to sharpen the definitions of vagueness and confusion in the TDI. They described vague response as containing too little information to score as a response. Such responses "may be a short, cryptic phrase or a long, meandering, circumstantial paragraph. It may result from the inability to organize and communicate information" (Holzman, Levy, & Johnston, 2005, p. 66). Essentially, a vague response is characterized by poverty of expressed meaning. The TDI scorers noted that the key element in confusion responses was evidence from the verbalizations that the subjects had lost their train of thought and had become baffled by what they were seeing or saying.

By now the reader will surely have noticed that both vagueness and confusion responses harken back to Piotrowski's impotence and perplexity signs. In addition to these two response features, many of Piotrowski's other signs capture much of the constriction and rigidity, along with lack of complexity, productivity, and interpretation awareness, which characterize impoverished cognition and verbalization.

It is especially interesting to note that earlier researchers were struggling to distinguish different forms of schizophrenia from neurological conditions on the basis of their Rorschach profiles. Braekbill and Fine (1956) found that patients with chronic, or "process," schizophrenia demonstrated many of Piotrowski's signs, much more so than patients whose schizophrenia was classified as acute. Lezak (1976) indicated that except when compared against samples of subjects with chronic schizophrenia Piotrowski's signs identified the correct diagnostic category of no less than 51 percent and as many as 97 percent of patients across 11 different studies.

Schuldberg and Boster's 1985 study of Rapaport's concept of "distance" helped clarify Rorschach features of impoverishment. Extremes at the low end of both thought disorder dimensions reflect impoverished thinking and verbalization. Responses falling at the low end of the objective meaning, versus personalized meaning, factor (Dimension 1) included confusion responses and a literal approach to "recognizing," as opposed to interpreting, what the inkblots were. Responses at the low end of Dimension 2 (rigid verbal fluid sets) included perseveration and relationship responses, both of which highlighted the subject's rigidity in responding to the cards.

Weiner (1966) noted that vague and fluid Rorschach percepts often reflect a disturbance in ego boundaries. He discussed the frequent occurrence of vague and amorphous percepts in the records of patients with schizophrenia, which he took to be a product of a deficiency in synthetic capacities of the ego. Vagueness percentage is a variable in R-PAS that reflects simplistic processing. The inability to perceive images in a defined and differentiated manner is reflective of a lack of cognitive complexity, which can result from cognitive deficits, defensive avoidance, impulsivity, stylistic, or situational factors (Meyer et al., 2011).

We have seen how earlier versions of the CS (Exner, Weiner, & Schuyler, 1976; Exner, 1986) included two categories of Special Scores indicative of cognitive rigidity and integrative failures (perseveration, PSV, and confabulation, CONFAB). Hermann Rorschach (1921/1942) had given examples of both perseveration and confabulatory whole responses (essentially what the CS called CONFAB) in protocols of patients with schizophrenia and neurological impairment. Despite the longevity of both scores in Rorschach literature, PSV and CONFAB were dropped from the official list of Special Scores because of their actuarial infrequency (Exner, 1993).

The CS looked beyond Special Scores to identify aspects of cognitive impoverishment. Indices like the Coping Deficit Index (CDI), Lambda, and Processing Efficiency (Zd) also touched on the impoverishment of processing abilities and adaptive functioning, reflecting a lack of psychological resources for thinking about and responding to daily demands. When the CDI was greater than 3, the subject was believed to show ineffective ways of coping with daily experiences. According to Weiner (1998), elevations in CDI were associated with manifestations of helplessness and ineffective problem-solving characteristic of the outdated diagnosis of "inadequate personality." High Lambda scores signified individuals who responded to the inkblots in narrow ways. Such individuals were considered intolerant of complexity, preferring simple and structured situations. Zd reflected how much time and thought individuals expend on processing and interpreting. Low Zd individuals, called "underincorporators," took in less information, examined their experience less thoroughly, and made decisions hastily with minimal cues.

These CS variables measured aspects of information processing or the complexity of cognitive operations. None of these indices was considered diagnostically specific, and certainly none was linked specifically to psychosis or thought disorder. However, as general signs of a paucity of cognitive activity in terms of perception, association, and synthesis, these indices come close to capturing important features of impoverishment.

Although there are no R-PAS Cognitive Scores that specifically represent impoverished thinking, R-PAS places a great deal of importance on the concept of complexity as a feature of differentiated, integrated, flexible, and productive processing activity (Meyer et al., 2011). Subjects who score low on R-PAS variables of complexity, blends, and synthesis are said to be perceiving and thinking in simplistic, constricted, impressionistic, and possibly vague and ineffective ways.

Understanding impoverished thinking

Adducing relevant psychological, developmental, diagnostic, and neurocognitive concepts broadens our perspective of impoverished thinking and verbalization on the Rorschach. These perspectives, though by no means exhaustive, add links that help us understand the various meanings and implications of constriction, rigidity, and concreteness of impoverished Rorschach percepts, processing, and verbalizations.

Psychological perspectives

The inability of patients with brain damage and schizophrenia to think abstractly is articulated in the classic work of Goldstein and Sheerer (1941). They described eight characteristics of the capacity to assume an "abstract attitude":

- detaching the ego from the external world or from internal experience;
- assuming a mental set;
- accounting for and verbalizing actions to oneself;
- shifting reflectively from one aspect of a situation to another;
- holding various aspects of a situation in mind simultaneously;
- grasping the essential nature of the whole, while being able to break apart, separate, and resynthesize the parts;
- abstracting common properties and forming hierarchic concepts;
- planning ahead ideationally and thinking symbolically.

Goldstein and Scheerer's theory of the abstract attitude became one of the early unitary formulations that sought to account for thought disorder in schizophrenia. Proponents believed that schizophrenia patients were unable to move past stimulus-bounded concreteness and achieve an ability to think abstractly. Instead, they were stuck at the level of the stimulus properties themselves, unable to consider and integrate multiple observations into hypotheses that could allow them to move beyond the concrete, reason inductively, and form higher order concepts that could be tested.

Concreteness, or absence of abstract attitude, is the hallmark of Rorschach responses that reflect a lack of interpretation awareness, or Schuldberg and Boster's "object meaning" responses (1985). It is assumed that such concreteness can result from cognitive deficits, defensive or stylistic factors, or immature development.

Developmental perspectives

Leichtman (1996) proposed a developmental framework to explain how children become capable of taking the Rorschach. As described in the previous chapter, his model consisted of the progression of three stages of cognitive development that enable youngsters to manage the symbolic nature of the Rorschach.

Leichtman characterized Stage I Rorschachs as "perseverative" in nature. He noted that researchers and clinicians had long observed that toddlers respond to the ten cards as if there is little difference between them (Klopfer & Margulies, 1941). The young child perseverates due to the difficulty of the task itself. Leichtman explained that a rigid adherence to the same response was a reasonable way of dealing with the uncertainty, ambiguity, and interpretative nature of the Rorschach, which challenges children to think about the inkblots in a symbolic way—a task beyond their cognitive capacities.

> Presented with a strange object, they are asked what it looks like when it does not look like anything, [with] which they are familiar. Moreover, appreciating the connotations examiners wish attributed to the phrase "looks like" requires a command of the nuances of language that is often beyond these subjects, and accomplishing the task set for them requires representations skills they are only beginning to develop (p. 185).

Leichtman elaborated on the views of Klopfer and Margulies by pointing out that this perseverative pattern may be an adaptive problem-solving solution for the toddler. Presented with a difficult and unfamiliar task such as the Rorschach, the youngster may arbitrarily seize upon the first response and then stick with what seemed to work at the beginning of the test. Card I "looks like" nothing other than dirt or a smudge of ink, and Cards II, III, and others really "look like" Card I. Just before turning three, the toddler may exhibit a bit of a shift in his or her perseverative pattern. Although absurd perseverations may still prevail, the two-and-a-half-year-old may either try to refuse some of the cards or give new responses to others.

Leichtman explained the developmental significance of perseverative responding. However, should this mode of processing prevail into later childhood, adolescence, and adulthood, then one would consider perseveration as either a deficit or a marker of neurocognitive regression. For the older subject who responds to a problem-solving task like the Rorschach with frequent perseveration, we might assume that the representational, interpretive nature of the test is more cognitively complex than they can manage.

Psychopathological perspectives: Negative symptoms

Negative symptoms define a distinct domain of psychotic symptomatology. The broad-based impoverishment seen in negative symptoms reduces the complexity and range of communication, affect, social activity, motivation, and psychomotor behavior. Kirkpatrick (2014) described factor-analytic studies that identified two dimensions of negative symptoms. The first is an expressive factor reflecting blunted affect and alogia. The second factor combines anhedonia, avolition, and asociality. Kirkpatrick indicated that preliminary research has suggested that the avolitional factor is a more potent predictor of overall dysfunctionality. Alogia is the term used to describe impoverished speech production. Apathy, avolitionality, and anhedonia reflect lack of motivation and will, as well as loss of interest, enthusiasm, and pleasure in activities. Anergia refers to passivity and lack of initiation in problem-solving activity. Flat affect describes an absence of visible emotional expressiveness and flexibility.

Among the main categories of alogia are brief and unelaborated speech (poverty of speech), vacuous speech devoid of meaningful information (poverty of thought content), and repetitive, rigid, and stereotyped responses (perseveration). Replies to interview or Inquiry questions are brief and constricted, often containing the same limited information.

Poverty of thought (speech)

Verbal responses are decreased and spontaneous elaborations, additions, or explanations are missing. Responses to questions, if given at all, might consist of monosyllabic, one-word answers. The etiology of poverty of thought or speech needs to be determined because it cannot be assumed that this behavior is a pathognomonic negative symptom of schizophrenia. Clearly, depression or suspiciousness may produce extremely constricted responses. In a similar vein, medical origins such as metabolic disturbances and dementia may be the underlying cause for this form of impoverished communication.

Poverty of content

Unlike poverty of speech, poverty of content might contain an abundance of words in response to questions or offered voluntarily. The issue here is poverty of meaning. Responses might be lengthy but reveal rambling and disorganized ideas that are devoid of meaning. With poverty of speech, it is immediately apparent that there is something missing. Communication fails because there is a dearth of words, necessitating frequent prompting from the interviewer/examiner. With poverty of content, listeners may be at first fooled by their communication partner, who appears to be providing sufficient content. However, trying to comprehend, much less summarize, what the individual has said is difficult because there might be no point or goal in the person's communication.

Perseveration

Perseveration is a less frequently described form of alogia than poverty of speech or content. Nonetheless, it is a familiar form of impoverishment that reflects inflexibility in ideation and verbal expression. Perseveration may be detected in either the ideation/content or the words and phrases the individual uses.

Recall that Andreasen (1979) identified two types of thought disorder on her TLC scale. Unlike positive forms of thought disorder, negative thought disorder is characterized by impoverished and contracted thought processes, including thought blocking, poverty of speech, and poverty of content. Andreasen also indicated that negative forms of thought disorder might also be reflected in illogicality and peculiar word usage, including neologisms. Thus, the presence of impoverishment does not preclude the emergence of disorganized words and expressions or nonsensical ideas and inferences.

Negative symptoms are typically associated with schizophrenia and may persist long after florid, or positive, signs of psychosis disappear. Negative symptoms are viewed as either primary or secondary in nature (Carpenter, Heinrichs, & Wagman, 1988). Carpenter's group viewed primary symptoms as direct manifestations of the illness of schizophrenia, as opposed to those negative symptoms that were secondary to a combination of depression, suspicious withdrawal, psychotic symptoms, and extrapyramidal side effects. This model held that individuals who have chronic primary negative symptoms formed a subgroup of schizophrenia patients with "deficit syndrome." Not surprisingly, deficit patients were found to have greater cognitive and neurological impairment than so-called nondeficit patients.

Neuropsychological perspectives: Cognitive impairment

Impoverished cognition and speech may be viewed as manifestations of cognitive impairment associated with psychosis. Current research and diagnostic trends have established cognitive impairment as a core feature of schizophrenia (Harvey, 2013), rendering the question of whether schizophrenia is a brain-based disorder largely moot. Both Kraepelin (1896/1919) and Bleuler (1911/1950) held that more florid, positive features of schizophrenia were secondary to fundamental impairments in cognitive processes. Modern approaches to psychosis have come full circle and regard underlying deficits in cognitive functioning as primary signs of the illness.

However, cognitive impairment is not just confined to schizophrenia. Impairment in cognitive functions is currently regarded as a core domain of all psychosis. The DSM-5 Psychotic Disorder Work Group (Barch et al., 2013) introduced this dimension in response to a large body of research showing that high numbers of individuals with psychosis demonstrated impairment in cognitive functioning. One particularly compelling study found clinically significant cognitive impairment in 84 percent of patients with schizophrenia, 58.3 percent of psychotic major depression patients, and 57.7 percent of patients with psychotic bipolar disorders (Reichenberg et al., 2009).

Studies have established significant associations between negative symptoms, disorganization, and cognitive impairment (O'Leary et al., 2000; Dominguez et al., 2009). In particular, the presence of negative symptoms was significantly negatively correlated with deficits in verbal fluency, verbal learning and memory, intellectual ability, and executive functions. Of these correlations, deficits in verbal fluency and executive functioning (e.g. initiation and flexibility) seem most closely related to impoverished negative symptoms like alogia and perseveration.

An interesting aside was the finding that neither positive symptoms nor depression were significantly correlated with measures of cognitive impairment (Dominguez et al., 2009).

However, we encounter some conceptual confusion in trying to understand impoverished thinking and verbalization from psychopathological (i.e. negative symptoms) and neuropsychological (i.e. cognitive impairment) perspectives. As we have seen, both negative symptoms and cognitive impairment are among core symptom dimensions associated with psychosis, and both have bearing on our understanding of impoverishment. Negative symptoms, typically observed clinically, and cognitive impairment, usually measured psychometrically, share similarities in course, prognosis, and functional skill deficits, not to mention overlapping clinical appearance. Does it make conceptual sense to separate the dimensions of negative symptoms and cognitive impairment, especially when considering the focus of this chapter? Are the differences between these symptom dimensions real or semantic in nature? In reviewing available research, Harvey and colleagues (2006) concluded that although correlated there was sufficient evidence that negative and cognitive symptoms were separable dimensions. Although both dimensions are associated with impoverished thinking and speech, they may have independent etiologies. The researchers concluded that cognitive impairment was correlated with the *ability* to perform everyday living skills, whereas negative symptoms were related to the *likelihood* of actually performing these skills.

Other research findings relevant to understanding impoverishment on the Rorschach link negative symptoms and right hemispheric dysfunction (Cutting, 1994; Kestenbaum-Daniels et al., 1988). Reviewing evidence from neuropsychological, neuropsychiatric, and neurobiological studies, Cutting argued that dysfunction in the right hemisphere underlies symptoms of schizophrenia. He included formal thought disorder, loss of will (avolition), and flattened affect among the symptoms associated with right hemispheric impairment. Cutting discussed the abnormalities in speech and affect in patients with right hemispheric lesions (incoherence, tangentiality, along with a lack of prosody and emotional expressiveness), which he felt were analogous to the features of formal thought disorder and negative symptoms seen in schizophrenia.

Right hemispheric damage typically results in difficulties forming an integrated whole response, referred to as constructional aparaxia. On the Rorschach, those with this impairment would likely be able to perceive individual details but be unable to form a gestalt necessary for a whole response. This is essentially what Kestenbaum-Daniels and her colleagues found in their study comparing Rorschach TDI scores of subjects with right-sided cortical damage to those of subjects with schizophrenia and mania (Kestenbaum-Daniels et al., 1988). The TDI scores of 23 patients with unilateral right hemisphere cortical damage following cerebral vascular accidents were compared to those of similar numbers of both schizophrenic and bipolar manic patient groups. With corrections for number of responses, there were no significant differences in Total TDI scores for the three groups; however, there were distinct qualitative differences between the groups. Using a principal-components analysis, the researchers consolidated all TDI scoring categories into five factors: (1) combinatory thinking (flippant thinking, INCOMs, playful confabulations); (2) fragmented thinking (excessive qualification, concrete thinking, vagueness, fragmentation, confusion); (3) idiosyncratic thinking (peculiar, queer, absurd, neologisms, incoherence); (4) associative looseness (clanging, perseverations, inappropriate distance, looseness, FABCOMs); and (5) arbitrary thinking (ALOG, fluid thinking, confusion). Patients with right-sided damage demonstrated significantly more fragmented thinking than did the patients with schizophrenia or mania. When these subjects gave more than one response per card, they were typically fragments of a whole response (e.g. oligophrenic details) instead of separate responses. For example, a subject may look at Card V and state, "I see wings ... antennae ... and legs" but not intend for these to form an integrated whole.

In the end, an absence of complexity, along with (1) stimulus-bounded concreteness; (2) confusion and perplexity; (3) fragmentation; (4) poverty of speech or meaningful content; (5) reduced verbal fluency, processing speed; and (6) perseveration or an inability in shifting mental sets may reflect impoverishment associated with either cognitive impairment or negative symptomatology, or perhaps both. Whichever explanation, the differential diagnostic and prognostic implications of impoverished thinking, speaking, and communicating are significant.

References

Andreasen, N. (1979). Thought, language, and communication disorders: I. Clinical assessment, definition of terms, and evaluation of their reliability. *Archives of General Psychiatry, 36*, 1315–1321.

Barch, D. M., Bustillo, J., Gaebel, W., Gur, R., Heckers, S., Malaspina, D., Owen, M. J., Schultz, S., Tandon, R., Tsuang, M., van Os, J., & Carpenter, W. (2013). Logic and justification for dimensional assessment of symptoms and related clinical phenomena in psychosis: Relevance to DSM-5. *Schizophrenia Research, 150*, 15–20.

Bleuler, E. (1950). *Dementia Praecox or the Group of Schizophrenias*. (J. Zinkin, Trans.). New York: International Universities Press. (Original work published in 1911.)

Bohm, E. (1958). *Rorschach Test Diagnosis*. New York: Grune & Stratton.

Braekbill, G. A., & Fine, H. J. (1956). Schizophrenia and central nervous system pathology. *Journal of Abnormal Social Psychology, 52*, 310–313.

Carpenter, W. T., Heinrichs, D. W., & Wagman, A. M. (1988). Deficit and nondeficit forms of schizophrenia: The concept. *American Journal of Psychiatry, 145*, 578–583.

Cutting, J. C. (1994). Evidence for right hemispheric dysfunction in schizophrenia. In A. S. David & J. C. Cutting (Eds.), *The Neuropsychology of Schizophrenia* (pp. 231–241). Hove, UK: Erlbaum.

Dominguez, M., Viechtbauer, W., Simons., C. J., van Os., J., & Krabbendam, L. (2009). Are psychotic psychopathology and neurocognition orthogonal? A systematic review of their associations. *Psychological Bulletin, 135*, 157–171.

Exner, J. E. (1986). *The Rorschach: A Comprehensive System, Basic Foundations* (Vol. 1, 2nd ed.). New York: Wiley.
Exner, J. E. (1993). *The Rorschach: A Comprehensive System, Basic Foundations* (Vol. 1, 3rd ed.). New York: Wiley.
Exner, J. E., Weiner, I. B., & Schuyler, S. (1976). *A Rorschach Workbook for the Comprehensive System.* Bayville, NY: Rorschach Workshops.
Gindis, B. (1988). Children with mental retardation in the Soviet Union. *Mental Retardation, 26*, 381–384.
Goldfried, M. R., Stricker, G., & Weiner, I. B. (1971). *Rorschach Handbook of Clinical and Research Application.* Englewood Cliffs, NJ: Prentice-Hall.
Goldstein, K., & Scheerer, M. (1941). Abstract and concrete behavior: An experimental study with special tests. *Psychological Monographs, 53*, 1–151.
Harvey, P. D. (Ed.). (2013). *Cognitive Impairment in Schizophrenia. Characteristics, Assessment, and Treatment.* Cambridge, UK: Cambridge University Press.
Harvey, P.D., Koren, D., Reichenberg, A., & Bowie, C. R. (2006). Negative symptoms and cognitive deficits: What is the nature of their relationship? *Schizophrenia Bulletin, 32*, 250–258.
Holzman, P. S., Levy, D.L., & Johnston, M. H. (2005). The use of the Rorschach technique for assessing formal thought disorder. In R. F. Bornstein & J. M. Masling (Eds.), *Scoring the Rorschach: Seven Validated Systems.* New York: Routledge.
Kestenbaum-Daniels, E., Shenton, M. E., Holzman, P. S., Benowitz, L. I., Coleman, M., Levin, S., & Levine, D. (1988). Patterns of thought disorder associated with right cortical damage, schizophrenia, and mania. *American Journal of Psychiatry, 145*, 944–949.
Kirkpatrick, B. (2014). Progress in the study of negative symptoms, *Schizophrenia Bulletin, 40* (Suppl. 2), 101–106.
Klopfer, B., & Margulies, H. (1941). Rorschach reactions in early childhood. *Rorschach Research Exchange, 5*, 1–23.
Kraepelin, E. (1919). *Dementia Praecox and Paraphrenia.* (R. M. Barclay, Trans.). Chicago, Il: Chicago Medical Books. (Original work published in 1896.)
Leichtman, M. (1996). *The Rorschach: A Developmental Perspective.* Hillsdale, NJ: The Analytic Press.
Lezak, M. (1976). *Neuropsychological Assessment.* New York: Oxford University Press.
Meyer, G. J., Viglione, D. J., Mihura, J. L., Erard, R. E., & Erdberg, P. (2011). *Rorschach Performance Assessment System: Administration, Coding, Interpretation, and Technical Manual.* Toledo, OH: Rorschach Performance Assessment System.
O'Leary, D. S., Flaum, M., Kesler, M. L., Flashman, L. A., Arnt, S., & Andreasen, N. C. (2000). Cognitive correlates of the negative, disorganized, and psychotic symptom dimensions of schizophrenia. *Journal of Neuropsychiatry and Clinical Neurosciences, 12*, 4–15.
Piotrowski, Z. A. (1937). The Rorschach ink-blot method in organic disturbances of the central nervous system. *Journal of Nervous and Mental Disease, 86*, 525–537.
Rapaport, D., Gill, M., & Schafer, R. (1968). *Diagnostic Psychological Testing* (Rev. ed.). R. R. Holt, Ed. New York: International Universities Press. (Original work published in 1946.)
Reichenberg, A., Harvey, P. D., Bowie, C. R., Mojtabai, R., Rabinowitz, J., Heaton, R. K., & Bromet, E. (2009). Neuropsychological function and dysfunction in schizophrenia and psychotic affective disorders. *Schizophrenia Bulletin, 35*, 1022–1029.

Rorschach, H. (1942). *Psychodiagnostics* (5th ed.). Bern, Switzerland: Hans Huber. (Original work published in 1921.)

Schuldberg, D., & Boster, J. S. (1985). Back to Topeka: Two types of distance in Rapaport's original Rorschach thought disorder categories. *Journal of Abnormal Psychology, 94,* 205–215.

Weiner, I. B. (1966). *Psychodiagnosis in Schizophrenia.* New York: Wiley.

Weiner, I. B. (1998). *Principles of Rorschach Interpretation.* Mahwah, NJ: Erlbaum.

Chapter 12

Awareness of perceptual and reasoning errors

When and *With Whom* one shares his or her idiosyncratic ideas or inaccurate impressions relates to the concept of awareness, which is an important component for understanding disordered thinking from a broader, holistic perspective. As noted in the previous chapter, we want to be alert to social–pragmatic aspects of disordered Rorschach responses in order to gauge our patient's social and self-awareness.

Awareness: Insight and social cognition

In the last 25 years, researchers have turned their attention to the role that social and self-awareness and insight play in psychotic disorders (Kleiger & Khadivi, 2015). There have been two major volumes reviewing contemporary studies of the concept of insight in patients with psychotic and nonpsychotic disorders (Amador & David, 2004; Marková, 2005). Amador and colleagues (1991) proposed a multidimensional model of clinical insight, which was narrowed down to two distinct features: (1) awareness and (2) attribution or labeling of psychotic symptoms. This distinction is based on the fact that some patients may be aware of their psychotic experiences but attribute them to reasons other than the presence of a psychotic disorder. Additionally, patients may recognize certain symptoms yet be unaware of others. Marková and Berrios (1992) conceptualized awareness of illness as part of a broader category of self-awareness, as opposed to viewing this as an independent feature of psychotic disturbance. Their concept focuses on changes in the self along a continuum of self-awareness.

In contrast to clinical insight, cognitive insight refers to the broader ability to evaluate abnormal experiences and recognize when one's interpretations are incorrect. Cognitive insight is similar to what we think of as "reality testing." Individuals with impaired cognitive insight may be unable to step back from their psychotic experiences and use feedback to test out and correct their conclusions. Beck and colleagues (2004) distinguished two dimensions of cognitive insight: (1) self-reflectiveness, which includes the capacity of individuals to observe their mental productions and entertain alternative explanations, and (2) self-certainty or overconfidence in the validity of their beliefs and conclusions.

Cognitive insight fits with social cognitive concepts such as "mentalization" and ToM. Social insight and accurate self-appraisal are both conceptually and neurocognitively related to understanding the minds and mental experiences of other people. ToM involves accurate attribution of emotions, knowledge, and intentions to others, whereas cognitive insight involves similar processes with regard to the self.

Deficits in mentalizing capacity may also imply an inability to judge the social inappropriateness of one's bizarre behavior, delusional beliefs, or inappropriate, thought-disordered speech and logic. Related to the unawareness of illness phenomena, individuals with psychosis may lack awareness of how they might sound or appear to other people, who might have trouble understanding what they say or sharing their perceptions of reality. Such individuals may demonstrate what Harrow and Quinlan (1985) referred to as an "impaired perspective," or an inability to take another person's point of view or see oneself through another's eyes. Thus, both ToM and impaired perspective imply an inability to observe psychological or behavioral phenomena from another person's point of view.

Since Harrow and Quinlan wrote about impaired perspective, an increasing number of studies have explored the role of social cognition, mentalization, and ToM in psychosis, particularly schizophrenia (see studies cited in Kleiger & Khadivi, 2015). Quee and colleagues (2010) concluded that social cognition, specifically deficits in emotional recognition and mentalizing, reduce insight in psychotic subjects. Flashman and Roth (2004) hypothesized that impaired ToM might reduce awareness of one's psychotic symptoms and illness if threatening thoughts and intentions were inappropriately attributed to others. Although most of the research on impaired social cognition has focused on schizophrenia, awareness of symptoms has also been examined in bipolar patients. Vaskinn and colleagues (2013) compared insight in their subjects with schizophrenia with insight in those who had bipolar psychoses and found similar deficits in both groups. However, they found that clinical insight was more strongly related to social cognition variables in their schizophrenia sample than in their bipolar I sample. Recently, investigators have looked at the relationship between impaired insight and first episodes of psychosis (Vohs et al., 2015). Researchers found that the ability to form integrated representations of self and others, or "metacognition," is a component variable associated with improved insight.

Intentionality and awareness of disturbance on the Rorschach

An important but often-overlooked aspect of Rorschach interpretation involves understanding our patients' perspectives and intentionality when they reveal and share disturbed responses. When we constructed the Menninger Thought Disturbance scales (Athey, Colson, & Kleiger. 1993), we sought to correlate traditional Rorschach thought disorder scores with test-taking attitudes and psychological experiences that may be associated with thought-disordered responses.

Quantifying what has been, up to now, an elusive variable reflecting the subject's mindset in taking the test and responding to the examiner may help bring into focus important background issues that influence our interpretation of the response itself. Schafer (1954) addressed these factors in his discussion of the interpersonal dynamics in the testing situation:

> It therefore seems important to note whether and to what extent the patient's responses are kind or cruel, proud or disparaging, orderly or sloppy, generous or stingy, trivial or ambitious, flashy or drab, driven or inert, optimistic or pessimistic, and the like. How he presents, evaluates, and treats his responses reflects how he presents, evaluates, and treats himself inwardly and in his relationships (p. 46).

Stated somewhat differently, we want to know how seriously the subject is taking the Rorschach. Does the person "play" with the blots or, although taking them seriously, suddenly lose distance and abruptly depart from a realistic set? Are the patient's lapses in logic and reality testing intentional or unintentional? Relatedly, to what degree is the patient aware that her or his responses are illogical or bizarre and that others might not be able share in their distorted perceptions? In contrast, might the patient be trying to shock or control the examiner by willfully flouting reality and social convention?

Caveats regarding how best to interpret thought-disordered Rorschach responses and their associated scores have regularly appeared in the literature (Exner, 1993; Weiner 1998; Meyer et al., 2011). In discussing disturbances in ideation associated with Level 2 Special Scores and elevated WSUM6, Exner cautioned that although such findings usually involve impaired judgment, bizarre thinking, and disorganized decision-making,

> such conclusion should be tested by reading the responses containing critical Special Scores, mainly to determine the degree to which elements of bizarreness are obvious, as usually is the case in the answers scored as Level 2, or whether they reflect less mature, or even playful forms of organization. It is naïve to assume that all of the responses falling into one category represent equal degrees of slippage or dysfunction (pp. 571–572).

Exner's essential point was that it might be premature to assume severe thought disorder from Level 2 scores, and similarly, to assume impaired reality testing from an accumulation of FQ− responses. First, the examiner needs to gauge the mindset of the person delivering such responses.

Weiner (1998) makes an equally persuasive point that Rorschach data cannot be viewed as definitive evidence of the presence of psychotic phenomena:

> The best way to determine whether people have some symptom is to ask them, just as the presence of some behavior problem, such as substance

abuse, can be identified more reliably by direct inquiry than by any pattern of Rorschach scores (p. 288).

R-PAS developers have also made this cautionary point regarding the interpretation of the SevCog variable, which aims to capture the most severe forms of thought disturbance found in psychotic-level lapses in reasoning, conceptualization, and communication (Meyers et al., 2011). According to the R-PAS group, "one should also consider whether playfulness with the task, deliberate efforts to be shocking or provocative, or a penchant for narrative dramatization might be healthier processes contributing to an elevation" (p. 359).

The lynchpin in determining a subject's mindset when he or she gives a disturbed response is the extent to which the individual is aware that the response is disorganized, illogical, or distorted in form level. What is the best way to find this out? As Weiner indicated, we need to inquire. Thus, examiners should always try to assess a person's level of awareness when they have given us a disturbed response.

Assessing awareness

What is the best way to gauge our patients' level of awareness when they have given responses containing thought-disordered and minus-form-level responses? We are interested in determining their mindsets: what they were thinking and how they intended to respond. Most important, we want to know how cognizant they are that others may find their response strange and confusing.

Sometimes if one listens closely to a disturbed response, the patient's degree of awareness is implicit in his spontaneous wording during the Free Association. More often than not, however, we need to wait until the Inquiry or Clarification phase to judge whether or not patients are aware of the disturbed nature of what they have told us they saw during the Free Association. The Inquiry, after all, is the patient's opportunity to engage the ego and demonstrate his capacities to mentalize, self-monitor, take a critical perspective, and hear his responses through another's ears. When presented with her responses in the Inquiry, does the patient tell us that "It really does not look like that," or "I know that's crazy and impossible," or "I didn't actually mean it to be a bat with alligators on its wings"? By doing so, the patient implicitly conveys a latent awareness that the response had something in it that did not make sense and that he or she is trying to address this. Thus, these individuals are demonstrating a more intact social–cognitive perspective that is available to them when asked to think more about and then explain their response.

However, in many cases, the patient does not respond to inherent cues in the Inquiry to stand back and observe her or his thinking and perception. When this happens, secondary inquiries can be helpful to gently probe a patient's level of awareness of the disturbed responses.

Testing of limits

Klopfer and colleagues (1954) pointed the way with their presentation of methods for testing of limits after the responses have been gathered and the Inquiry completed. Bruno Klopfer, the phenomenologist, was keenly interested in viewing the response as the patient experienced it. He focused more on understanding what might facilitate a patient's being able to see human movement or color when they had not initially given any responses containing these determinants. Thus, in a series of graded questions, the examiner queried whether, after taking a second look, the patient could see any cards in which there might be humans or people moving.

Regarding the testing of limits in psychodiagnostic testing, Berg (1984) wrote about expanding the parameters in testing situations to enable the examiner to move beyond standard administrative procedures in order to understand aspects of the patient's experience not captured by test scores alone. Of particular interest was Berg's discussion of examiner interventions that might facilitate the patient's self-reflection about his or her responses.

Few have contributed more to extended inquiry methods than Handler (2002, 2007, 2008), who championed the notion that our understanding of a patient's responses transcends the scores we assign to them. With his creative testing-of-limits procedures, Handler attempted to reduce interpretive errors by asking patients to explain their thought-disordered responses and provide an alternative response that most people might be able see or understand. In the case of bizarre images, Handler would ask where the patient would see such an image. According to Handler, "The ability to give more traditional responses tells me the patient is not as seriously disturbed as he or she appeared to be, judging from the Free Association and Inquiry" (2008, p. 531). Handler's observation fitted with studies showing that increased awareness of one's disturbed experiences is associated with reduced severity of psychotic symptoms and an increased capacity to benefit from treatment (Strauss, 1969; Cullberg, 2006; Naeem, Kingdon, & Turkington, 2008; Brabban, Tai, & Turkington, 2009).

The need to test the limits of thought-disordered responses has been a particular interest of mine (Kleiger, 2012, 2013). However, it was not until the work of a team of Israeli researchers that assessing a patient's awareness of her or his disturbed responses was subjected to empirical analysis. As noted previously, Rothschild-Yakar and colleagues (2015) and Lacoua, Koren, and Rothschild-Yakar (2015) extended Handler's testing-of-limits queries by developing a structured post-testing method to determine patients' awareness of their disturbed responses both in terms of perceptual accuracy and the nature of reasoning underlying the patients' verbalizations. These researchers employed their new measure of awareness of perceptual and ideational deviations to determine the relationship of self-reflectivity and psychosis risk in a nonclinical sample of adolescents. They first administered the Rorschach according to the CS. In the subsequent testing-of-limits phase, the examiners asked subjects to refer to the similarities and differences between their own perceptions and ideation, reflected in their disturbed responses, and those they imagined other people would have. Regarding minus-form-level responses, examiners asked the following questions about each response: "To what extent would others see in the blot what you have seen (citing the response)?" Participants responded on a 7-point scale, ranging from 0 (they will not see it/it's hard to see) to 6 (they will see/it's easy to see). Regarding responses receiving Special Scores, examiners asked: "Without connection to the form of the inkblot, to what extent will others think about the idea that you thought about (citing the response)?" Participants responded on a 7-point scale, ranging from 0 (they will not think about this idea—it's exceptional) to 6 (they will think about it—it's a simple and commonplace idea). The researchers found significant correlations between their awareness variables and subjects' scores on measures of psychosis risk (Miller et al., 2003). Their findings were consistent with those of other studies, which demonstrated the link between impaired insight and first episodes of psychosis (Vohs et al., 2015).

Rothschild-Yakar also extended her investigation beyond traditional measures of reality testing and thought disturbance in predicting psychosis risk to social–cognitive and object relational realms. In terms of thinking about thought disorder in a broader sense, she highlighted the importance of object relations and ToM as components for studying the impact of their thoughts on others.

The results of the preliminary research of Rothschild-Yakar et al. and Lacoua, Koren, and Rothschild-Yakar set the stage for future prospective studies of the predictive validity of awareness measures on the Rorschach. In particular, these researchers are determined to study the role that awareness, ToM, and internalized object relations play in actual conversion to psychosis in vulnerable individuals.

Clinical examples: Kurt, Johannes, and Chandra

Kurt was a 23-year-old whose odd and aggressive behavior left his parents and treaters concerned about the possibility of a disturbance in his thinking and reality testing. Kurt's therapist wondered whether he was capable of insight. The question of whether Kurt was aware of his odd and inappropriate behavior was reflected in his spontaneous response to Card IV in the Free Association phase: "A person going down a slide because of the way his legs were spread out. It looked like a demon with three legs but I didn't want to say that because you'd think I was some kind of insane kook." Kurt's words reflect an implicit awareness of how the examiner and others might have heard his response and viewed his behavior.

Johannes was an older adolescent whose therapist also wondered about the risk for psychosis. Johannes was withdrawn, had refused to go to school, and had recently shown poor judgment by engaging in petty theft. When handed Card VI, he paused and responded: "Some kind of rock thing with arms reaching out. Not sure but the rock is in the middle and these are its arms" (INC2).

In the Inquiry, Johannes modified his response by spontaneously adding, "It looks like that, but it doesn't make much sense." At this, the examiner asked,

"How might others view your answer? What would they think?" Johannes demonstrated some awareness of what others might think about his response by stating, "They probably wouldn't see it this way, cuz that can't be real. If they heard me say this [a rock with arms reaching out], they would probably think I was nuts." Thus, by taking Johannes' comments in the Inquiry and probing a bit further, we were able to establish that despite his vulnerability Johannes appeared to retain some capacity to mentalize how others might hear his responses and what they would think of him.

It was necessary to employ a post-testing inquiry with Chandra, a psychotically prone adolescent (Kleiger & Khadivi, in press). Although she was not demonstrating positive symptoms suggestive of an active psychosis, there were enough concerns about her functioning to arrange an evaluation. Chandra gave several Level 2 thought disorder responses on her Rorschach, which raised questions about the tenuous nature of her ability to think in a logical and reality-based manner. Chandra's Rorschach was administered according to R-PAS procedures. In the Clarification phase, she did not give any indication that she was aware of the disturbed nature of her responses. Because of time constraints, the following response to Card VII was selected for a secondary inquiry: "Looks like two girls that are looking at each other intensely. Looks like they are surprised. Looks like they have worms coming out of their heads" (FAB2).

With Chandra, the examiner employed a testing-of-limits method similar to that developed by the Israeli group. However, instead of 7-point rating scales to assess form level and thinking separately, the examiner employed a simple 3-point scale (0—Others would not see it this way; 1—Others might agree to a limited extent; 2—Others would see it the same way) and asked Chandra to rate her response. Thus, following the completion of the formal Clarification phase, the examiner asked Chandra, "Regardless of the shape of the blot, what might others think about your response of 'two girls that are looking at each other intensely ... Looks like they have worms coming out of their heads?" Without much pause, Chandra gave her response a rating of 2 and then explained, "It does make sense because logically it looks like worms are coming out of their heads and they're staring at each other. So I guess other people would see this too." Chandra's response suggested an inability to take distance from her thought-disordered response and achieve a realistic social perspective. Chandra ended up being hospitalized not long after the evaluation when she began complaining that her mother was trying to poison her.

Kurt and Johannes retained some capacity to step back and reject or modify their original disturbed responses. Their ability to engage in this type of self-reflectivity tells us something about their capacity to mentalize. Unfortunately, Chandra seemed unable to do this. She gave a severe Level 2 response, and despite hearing it again in the Inquiry/Clarification and once more in a testing-of-limits query, she did not budge. It looked like what she saw. Others would logically reach the same conclusion.

Determining the patient's mindset that lies behind the response and the score is of critical importance in evaluating indications of thought disorder on the Rorschach. Listening carefully to how a patient describes or spontaneously modifies a disturbed response in the Free Association or noting how he/she tries to undo, or engage in "damage control," during Inquiry provides cues to the individual's level of awareness of how his or her ideas might sound to another person. When necessary, testing the limits of the patient's awareness of disturbed responses after the completion of the formal Inquiry helps in assessing the *When and With Whom* aspect of disordered thinking and, specifically, helps examiners determine their patient's capacity to mentalize and hear him- or herself through the ears of another. How patients respond to such invitations to step back and evaluate their disturbed responses has diagnostic and prognostic significance that go beyond what the scores, by themselves, can tell us.

References

Amador, X. F., & David, A. S. (2004). *Insight and Psychosis: Awareness of Illness in Schizophrenia and Related Disorders.* Oxford, UK: Oxford University Press.

Amador, X. F., Strauss, D., Yale, S., & Gorman, J. (1991). Awareness of illness in schizophrenia. *Schizophrenia Bulletin, 17*, 113–130.

Athey, G. I., Colson, D., & Kleiger, J. H. (1993). *Manual for Scoring Thought Disorder on the Rorschach.* Unpublished manuscript, The Menninger Clinic, Topeka, KS.

Beck, A. T., Baruch, E., Balter, J. M., Steer, R. A., & Warman, D. M. (2004). A new instrument for measuring insight: The Beck Cognitive Insight Scale. *Schizophrenia Research, 68*, 319–329.

Berg, M. (1984). Expanding the parameters of psychological testing. *Bulletin of the Menninger Clinic, 48*, 10–24.

Brabban, A., Tai, S., & Turkington, D. (2009). Predictors of outcome in brief cognitive behavior therapy for schizophrenia. *Schizophrenia Bulletin, 35*, 859–864.

Cullberg, J. (2006). *Psychoses: An Integrative Perspective.* Hove, UK: Routledge.

Exner, J. E. (1993). *The Rorschach: A Comprehensive System, Basic Foundations* (Vol. 1, 3rd ed.). New York: Wiley.

Flashman, L. A., & Roth, R. M. (2004). Neural correlates of unawareness of illness in psychosis. In X. F. Amador & A. S. David (Eds.), *Insight and Psychosis: Awareness of Illness in Schizophrenia and Related Disorders* (2nd ed., pp. 157–176). Oxford, UK: Oxford University Press.

Handler, L. (2002). Non-traditional approaches to the administration and interpretation of projective tests. Paper presented at the 17th International Congress of Rorschach and Projective Methods, Rome, Italy.

Handler, L. (2007). Therapeutic assessment with children and adolescents. In S. Smith & L. Handler (Eds.), *The Clinical Assessment of Children and Adolescents: A Practitioner's Handbook* (pp. 53–72). Mahwah, NJ: Lawrence Erlbaum Associates.

Handler, L. (2008). A Rorschach journey with Bruno Klopfer: Clinical application and teaching. *Journal of Personality Assessment, 90*, 528–535.

Harrow, M., & Quinlan, D. (1985). *Disordered Thinking and Schizophrenic Psychopathology.* New York: Garden Press.

Kleiger, J. H. (2012). Differential diagnosis of disordered thinking: What the Rorschach tells us. Workshop presented at the Summer Seminars of the International Society of the Rorschach, San Remo, Italy.

Kleiger, J. H. (2013). Mining for gold: Simple techniques for eliciting what is latent and unexpressed in standard Rorschach responses. Paper presented at the annual meeting of the Society for Personality Assessment, San Diego, CA.

Kleiger, J. H., & Khadivi, A. (2015). *Assessing Psychosis. A Clinician's Guide.* New York: Routledge.

Kleiger, J. H., & Khadivi, A. (in press). When wolves fall from the sky: Emerging psychosis in an adolescent. In J. Mihura & G. Meyer (Eds.), *Applications of the Rorschach Performance System.* New York: Guilford Press.

Klopfer, B., Ainsworth, M., Klopfer, W., & Holt, R. (1954). *Developments in the Rorschach Technique* (Vol. 1). New York: Harcourt, Brace & World.

Lacoua, L., Koren, D., & Rothschild-Yakar, L. (2015). Poor awareness of problems in thought and perception and risk indicators of schizophrenia-spectrum disorders. A correlational study of nonpsychotic adolescents in the community. Paper presented at the annual meeting of the Society for Personality Assessment, Brooklyn, NY.

Marková, I. S. (2005). *Insight in Psychiatry.* Cambridge, UK: Cambridge University Press.

Marková, I. S., & Berrios, G. E. (1992). The assessment of insight in clinical psychiatry: A new scale. *Acta Psychiatrica Scandinavia, 186,* 1185–1188.

Meyer, G. J., Viglione, D. J., Mihura, J. L., Erard, R. E., & Erdberg, P. (2011). *Rorschach Performance Assessment System: Administration, Coding, Interpretation, and Technical Manual.* Toledo, OH: Rorschach Performance Assessment System.

Miller, T. J., McGlashan, T. H., Rosen, J. L., Cadenhead, K., Ventura, J., McFarlane, W., Perkins, D.O., Pearlson, G. D., & Woods, S. (2003). Prodromal assessment with the Structured Interview for Prodromal Symptoms: Predictive validity, interrater reliability, and training to reliability. *Schizophrenia Bulletin, 29,* 703–715.

Naeem, F., Kingdon, D., & Turkington, D. (2008). Predictors of response to cognitive behaviour therapy in the treatment of schizophrenia: A comparison of brief and standard interventions. *Cognitive Therapy and Research, 32,* 651–656.

Quee, P. J., van der Meer, L., Bruggeman, R., de Haan, L., Cahn, W., Krabbendam, L., Mulder, N. C. L., Wiersma, D., & Aleman, A. (2010). Insight in psychosis: The role of neurocognition and the additional explained variance of social cognition and symptom dimensions. *Schizophrenia Research, 117,* 333.

Rothschild-Yakar, L., Lacoua, L., Brener, A., & Koren, D. (2015). Impairments in interpersonal representations and deficits in social cognition as predictors of risk for schizophrenia in non-patient adolescents. Paper presented at the annual meeting of the Society for Personality Assessment, Brooklyn, NY.

Schafer, R. (1954). *Psychoanalytic Interpretation in Rorschach Testing.* New York: Grune & Stratton.

Strauss, J. S. (1969). Hallucinations and delusions as points on continua function: Rating scale evidence. *Archives of General Psychiatry, 21,* 581–586.

Vaskinn, A., Sundert, K., Ueland, T., Agartz., I., Melle, I., & Andreassen, O. A. (2013). Social cognition and clinical insight in schizophrenia and bipolar disorder. *The Journal of Nervous and Mental Disease, 201,* 445–451.

Vohs, J. L., Lysaker, P. H., Liffick, E., Francis, M. M., Leonhardt, B. L., James, A., Buck, K. D., Hamm, J. A., Minor, K. S., Mehdiyoun, N., & Breier, A. (2015). Metacognitive capacity as a predictor of insight in first-episode psychosis. *Journal of Nervous and Mental Disease, 203,* 371–378.

Weiner, I. B. (1998). *Principles of Rorschach Interpretation.* Mahwah, NJ: Erlbaum.

Part IV

Differential diagnosis of psychotic phenomena on the Rorschach

Chapter 13

Primary psychoses and the Rorschach

I noted earlier that even the most passionate Rorschach critics (Wood et al., 2003) agreed that one of Hermann Rorschach's most enduring contributions was his discovery that his "inkblot experiment" was highly sensitive to the fault lines in his patients' thinking and their vulnerability to psychosis (Kleiger, 2015). This essential finding—first detected by Rorschach, further developed by the likes of Rapaport, Bohm, and Holt and well represented in contemporary Rorschach systems like the CS and R-PAS—received its strongest empirical support from Mihura and colleagues (2013), who found that variables assessing cognitive and perceptual processes were robust means for detecting and distinguishing patients with psychotic disorders from patients with other forms of disturbance.

In this chapter, I review literature that can help diagnosticians identify some of the differential patterns of disorganization, illogicality, and impoverishment found in the Rorschachs of patients suffering from, or at risk for, primary psychotic disorders. The term "primary" is a bit misleading because we may distinguish between diagnostic categories in which psychosis is an inherent feature of the disorder and those in which it might or might not be present. Thus, schizophrenia-spectrum disorders are considered "primary" psychoses. In contrast, depression, bipolar, and substance-induced psychoses may be a result of another primary disturbance (i.e. in mood or substance usage). However, I have chosen to use the term "primary" in this chapter to group together disorders that may present with a broad range of psychotic symptom dimensions in contrast to other disorders that may include isolated, encapsulated, transient, and milder features of "secondary" psychotic-like phenomena (the subject matter of the next chapter).

In order to do justice to the issue of identifying Rorschach features in primary psychoses, two essential points need to be made. First, it is not only foolhardy but also inaccurate to pretend that a differential diagnosis can be made on the basis of clinical phenomenology alone, whether we are talking about symptoms or psychological testing responses (Paris, 2013). Clinical diagnosis needs to be based on multiple methods, including different signs and symptoms, charting of the duration and history of disturbances, and various methods of assessment. Although we might discern some useful differential diagnostic signposts, thought-disordered Rorschach responses are not like fingerprints that can be unequivocally linked to specific forms of psychosis. We need to be aware of the limitations of our techniques. In the past, too many mistakes have been made in overly ambitious and overly optimistic assumptions of the diagnostic potency of the Rorschach. At most, the Rorschach provides a representational assessment of disorganization, illogical reasoning, and, to some extent, impoverishment (as a result of negative symptoms and/or impaired cognition). We have no unequivocal representational measures of delusions per se on the Rorschach; however, based on second-order inferences, we might suggest a vulnerability to delusional beliefs on the basis of Rorschach indications of illogicality or impaired reality testing. Rorschach indications of depression and mania, both added to the list of symptom dimensions in the DSM-5, can also be inferred from scoring variables, qualities of verbalization, and thematic content. The essential point is that the assessment of disorganization, illogicality, and impoverishment, when grouped with other findings, might help in making a differential diagnosis.

The second point is that contemporary understanding of psychosis is in flux. Nowhere is this more apparent than in the reorganization of psychotic disorders in the DSM-5 (American Psychiatric Association, 2013; Barch et al., 2013). Psychotic disorders are assessed along eight symptom dimensions (hallucinations, delusions, disorganized speech, abnormal behavior, negative symptoms, impaired cognition, depression, and mania) and along four levels of severity (0—not present to 4—present and severe). Major psychoses include the schizophrenia spectrum and a host of other conditions such as delusional disorders and psychoses resulting from psychoactive substances like amphetamines, cocaine, hallucinogens, and cannabis. Psychotic symptoms can also be secondary to a mood disorder or appear in a more limited way in other conditions as well. Finally, psychotic symptomatology may be detected in nascent form in those conditions that suggest a high risk for psychotic decompensation. Contemporary diagnostic standards have moved away from a strict categorical classification of discrete entities with clear boundaries. Currently, we speak in terms of symptom dimensions and diagnostic spectrums.

To make this discussion consistent with how psychosis is currently understood, I have organized this chapter along the lines of the DSM-5. I begin with the schizophrenia spectrum and related psychotic disorders and then turn to psychotic subtypes of depression and bipolar disorder. I include the provisional category of Attenuated Psychotic Disorder and close with a review of clinical and research findings relevant to the Rorschach's assessment of patients with drug-induced psychoses.

Schizophrenia spectrum and other psychotic disorders

In contrast to the DSM-IV (American Psychiatric Association, 1994) and its predecessors, the preeminence of schizophrenia as a categorical diagnosis has been scaled back. Schizophrenia is no longer conceived of as a discrete entity made up of subtypes, but as a spectrum comprised of heterogeneous symptom dimensions along a continuum of severity that includes schizotypal personality. Gone are traditional subtypes such as paranoid, disorganized, residual, and catatonic disorders. In their place is a broad spectrum of Schizophrenia and Other Psychotic Disorders. As part of this reorganization, schizoaffective and delusional disorders have lost their categorical privilege as discrete diagnostic entities. They are now subsumed under the "Other Psychotic Disorders" rubric. While they retain separate diagnostic criteria, they are considered close relatives of the schizophrenia family.

The schizophrenia spectrum

Rorschach manifestations within the schizophrenia spectrum have been studied far more than those occurring in other forms of psychoses. Before looking at Rorschach studies, it is useful to review characteristic aspects of psychosis in the schizophrenia spectrum. First, let's define the spectrum. Conservatively, the spectrum includes schizophrenia, schizophreniform disorder, schizotypal, and possibly schizoid personality. Included in the broader continuum of schizophrenia are the biological relatives of schizophrenia such as schizoaffective disorder, which, however, also has ties to affective disorders. Delusional disorder, although it shares some common features with schizophrenia, does not appear to be genetically bound to the spectrum (Manschreck, 2007).

Disturbances within the schizophrenia spectrum are characterized by the presence of disorganization, illogicality, and impoverishment. Looking at the dimensional structure of psychoses on the PANSS (Kay, Fishbein, & Opler, 1987), Reininghaus, Priebe, and Bentall (2013) found that psychosis in schizophrenia-spectrum patients was characterized by greater amounts of positive and negative symptoms and cognitive disorganization. The positive dimension included hallucinations, delusions, unusual thought content, grandiosity, and suspiciousness, all of which might reflect underlying illogicality leading to a disturbance in thought content. The negative dimension reflected the presence of blunted affect, emotional withdrawal, poor rapport, lack of spontaneity, disturbance of volition, and social avoidance, all of which are consistent with the notion of impoverishment in cognitive, emotional, and social functioning. Finally, the cognitive disorganization factor reflected loading from PANSS items, including conceptual disorganization, difficulties in abstract thinking, stereotyped thinking, mannerisms and posturing, disorientation, poor attention, and preoccupation.

The presence of positive and negative symptoms in schizophrenia is well established. Schizophrenia spectrum patients may present with varying levels of hallucinatory and delusional experiences and bizarre beliefs. They may also demonstrate deficits in emotional expression, ideational productivity and richness, and social–occupational functioning. In terms of cognitive disorganization, there is a great deal of research to substantiate that schizophrenia spectrum psychosis is characterized by more severe disorganization in thinking and speech. To understand this better, it is instructive to look more closely at aspects of cognitive disorganization in schizophrenia.

Cognitive disorganization in schizophrenia can be understood in terms of impairments in information processing and attentional focus. There is an extensive body of literature that looks at the key role of deficits in attention and information processing in schizophrenia (Bleuler, 1911/1950; Cameron, 1938; Shakow, 1950, 1962; Payne, Mattusek, & George, 1959; Venables, 1960; McGhie & Chapman, 1961; Braff & Geyer, 1990; Braff, Grillon, & Geyer, 1992; Judd et al., 1992). Cameron noted the difficulties that schizophrenic subjects have in focusing on relevant stimuli. Shakow concluded that schizophrenic individuals have problems maintaining focus or a major cognitive set. McGhie and Chapman underscored the problems that schizophrenic patients have attending to and organizing sensory data in order to reduce the "chaotic flow of information reaching consciousness" (p. 111). These researchers demonstrated that individuals with schizophrenia have difficulty attending to the most relevant aspects of a stimulus field and screening out irrelevant stimuli. Perry and Braff (1994) demonstrated a significant relationship between information processing deficits, cognitive fragmentation, and thought disorder in schizophrenia. They hypothesized that when attentional and information-processing functions are disturbed, individuals may be flooded by poorly modulated stimuli, leading to increased distractibility, cognitive fragmentation, and thought disorder.

In his theoretical contribution to understanding the nature of thought pathology in schizophrenia, Meissner (1981) discussed the link between attentional processes and concept formation. Meissner contrasted schizophrenic and paranoid processes in terms of the ability to organize perceptual stimuli into conceptual categories. According to Meissner, the paranoid process is characterized by forming and maintaining rigid conceptual categories that are refractory to the corrective influence of perceptual input. The schizophrenic process, on the other hand, reflects a deficit in conceptual organization, leading to cognitive confusion, fragmentation, and disorganization. Whereas the paranoid individual, according to Meissner, organizes stimuli in a rigid and "hyper-conceptualized" manner, the schizophrenic does so in a loose or "hypo-conceptualized" way.

As a consequence of this deficit in the capacity to form conceptual categories, individuals with schizophrenia have trouble organizing, regulating, and integrating perceptual material into conceptual categories. Meissner added that if the ability to organize perceptual information into conceptual categories is lacking, then attention is left without regulation and is subject to increased variability, instability, and distraction. As a result, stimuli competing for attention are not organized conceptually or hierarchically, leading to fluid attentional focus and an impairment in the ability to screen out irrelevant stimuli.

Rorschach variables

Signs of cognitive disorganization, illogicality, and impoverishment have been found with varying degrees of severity in the Rorschach records of patients who fall within the schizophrenia spectrum. Seminal studies of differential Rorschach patterns of disordered thinking showed that while schizophrenia subjects did not achieve significantly higher Total TDI scores than acutely manic or schizoaffective patients, their thought-disordered responses differed qualitatively (Solovay, Shenton, & Holzman, 1987). Compared to other psychotic groups, Rorschach thought-disordered responses of schizophrenia patients were found to be more disorganized, confused, ideationally fluid, and containing more peculiar and queer words and expressions. In post hoc comparisons of scoring factors in manic and schizophrenia subjects, Fluid Thinking (relationship verbalizations, fluidity, and contaminations), Confusion (word-finding difficulty, confusion, absurd responses, incoherence, and neologisms), and Idiosyncratic Verbalizations (peculiar verbalizations) emerged as the factors that best distinguished subjects with schizophrenia. Shenton et al. (1989) also found that biological relatives of patients with chronic schizophrenia and schizoaffective disorder (manic type) had significantly more peculiar verbalizations than relatives of other psychotic patients.

The finding that individuals within the schizophrenia spectrum showed peculiar language on the Rorschach was supported by another study that used the TDI to assess thought disorder in psychometrically identified schizotypic individuals (Coleman, Levy, & Lezenweger, 1996). These subjects were nonpsychiatric undergraduates who scored high on a 35-item Perceptual Aberration Scale (PerAb; Chapman & Chapman, 1987), which measures body image and perceptual distortions associated with schizotypy, a less malignant and more common variant of schizophrenia (Meehl, 1962). High PerAb scores defined the schizotype group (not necessarily diagnosable as schizotypal personalities), which scored significantly higher on the TDI (total mean TDI = 8.83, SD = 15.30) than the low PerAb group (Total TDI = 3.65, SD = 4.97). The groups also differed in terms of the number of idiosyncratic verbalizations, with the schizotypic group giving significantly more responses containing peculiar language and odd expressions (peculiar and queer responses). The authors concluded that the schizotypic individuals displayed qualitatively similar thought disorder scores to those of schizophrenia subjects and their first-degree relatives, adding support to the biogenetic link between the two phenomena.

Although, as indicated earlier, no single individual score holds an exclusive relationship with any specific diagnosis, in addition to responses containing idiosyncratic language, there is some evidence that less common scores such as contaminations (CONTAM), neologisms (DV2), and verbal incoherence (DR2) might be associated more often with schizophrenia. For example, Koistinen (1995) found that the most severe level of TDI scores (1.0) occurred predominantly among schizophrenic subjects. In addition to the specificity of the contamination response, neologisms and incoherent responses occurred principally in the records of patients with schizophrenia. Even when contrasting the records of those with schizophrenia to those who had a range of schizophrenia-spectrum diagnoses (schizoaffective disorder, schizophreniform disorder, schizotypal disorder, delusional disorder, and psychotic disorder, NOS), these three 1.0-level scores were found to be most specific to the Rorschachs of schizophrenia patients. A review of Koistinen's data indicates that none of his schizophrenia-spectrum subjects produced a neologism, and only one schizoaffective subject gave a contamination response. Unfortunately, like contamination, the frequency of the other 1.0-level severity scores is similarly rare. For example, of Koistinen's 542 subjects, 1.0-level scores occurred only 13 times (2.4 percent). Furthermore, although they virtually never occurred in the records of nonschizophrenia subjects, they made up only 18.2 percent of the thought disorder scores among schizophrenic subjects. Thus, the problem with these findings is that contaminations (and all of the 1.0-level scores in the TDI) are so rare. Even if they come close to the level of specificity with schizophrenia, their rarity makes them less sensitive markers.

Despite qualitative similarities of thought disorder within this broad and heterogeneous spectrum, there is a continuum of severity ranging from biological relatives of schizophrenia patients to schizotypal individuals to schizophrenia out- and inpatients (Exner, 1986; Coleman, Levy, & Lenzenweger, 1996; Perry et al., 2003). In a study contrasting thought disorder in borderline, schizotypal, and schizophrenia subjects, Exner (1986) found similar numbers of thought disorder Special Scores among his schizotypal (5.6) and hospitalized schizophrenia subjects at admission and just before discharge (7.3 and 7.17, respectively). In contrast, borderline subjects had a significantly lower mean number (3.44) of critical Special Scores, suggesting a closer relationship between the schizotypal and schizophrenic groups. When contrasted on the weighted sum of the Special Scores (WSUM6), the differences between the borderline and the other two groups were even more dramatic. Although the schizotypal group's mean WSUM6 was almost twice as high as that of the borderline group, it was also significantly lower than that of the schizophrenic groups both at admission and before discharge. The data suggest that schizotypal individuals give about as many thought-disordered responses as do schizophrenic subjects but at a lower level of severity.

This study was also published before Exner began distinguishing between Level 1 and Level 2 Special Scores, which allow for further refinement in the scoring of pathological Rorschach responses. Interestingly, the data suggested that in terms of the kinds of disordered thought processes, schizotypal subjects demonstrated significantly more DVs than the borderline group and even more than subjects in the schizophrenic sample. In terms of reality testing, Exner showed that both the schizotypal and borderline groups had similar form-level percentages (X+%) of 69 percent, significantly greater than the admission and discharge schizophrenia groups whose X+% scores were 54 percent and 51 percent, respectively. The mean minus-form-level percentages (X-%) for the groups, in ascending order of severity, were 13 percent for borderlines, 18 percent for schizotypals, and 31 percent and 34 percent for these two schizophrenia groups at admission and discharge. Exner's data suggested that in terms of disordered thinking and reality testing, schizotypal individuals occupied a middle range of severity between schizophrenia and borderline personality disorders. In other structural respects, the schizotypal and schizophrenia groups were indistinguishable, supporting the hypothesis that both groups are phenotypically related. Like individuals with schizophrenia, patients who are schizotypal tended to be introversive, detached, ideationally oriented, and affectively constrained.

Using the EII as a measure of thought and perceptual disturbance, Perry et al. (2003) found elevations of the EII in schizophrenia-spectrum groups compared to "normal" controls. Samples of spectrum subjects included (1) undergraduates with elevated scores on either Chapman and Chapman's (1987) PerAb or MagId (Magical Ideation) scales, (2) first-degree relatives of schizophrenia patients, (3) subjects diagnosed with schizotypal personality disorder, (4) schizophrenia outpatients, (5) schizophrenia acute inpatients, and (6) schizophrenia chronic-care inpatients. Researchers found a significant increase in EII scores along the schizophrenia spectrum according to degree of pathology. Normal comparisons had lower EII scores than family members, students with elevated PerAb and MagId scales, schizotypal individuals, and all groups of schizophrenia subjects. Consistent with earlier research showing similarities between schizotypal and schizophrenia subjects, Perry et al.'s schizotypal group did not differ significantly from schizophrenia outpatients in terms of their levels of disturbed thinking and perception. Nonetheless, there was a trend toward lower scores for schizotypal subjects when compared to inpatients with schizophrenia. There were significant differences between the groups for five of the six variables that make up the EII, with scores increasing in the pathological direction across the spectrum. In particular, WSUM6 and FQ- scores increased at the .001 level of significance across severity levels on the spectrum.

Recent international studies have confirmed that both the CS and R-PAS scores effectively discriminate schizophrenia from nonpsychotic subjects (Benedik et al., 2013; Dzamonja-Ignjatovic et al., 2013). Benedik et al. found that the TP Comp (Thought Perception Composite) and EII-3 were slightly superior than the PTI and EII-2 in identifying subjects with schizophrenia. Furthermore, as noted in previous chapters, Biagiarelli and colleagues (2015) found significant correlations between the PTI and PANSS, specifically noting the relationship of X-% with negative symptoms, M- with delusional thinking, and WSUM6 with thought disorder.

Gomilla (2011) used the CS to examine the differences in the Rorschachs of male patients with chronic and acute schizophrenia. Patients with schizoaffective and psychotic mood disorders were excluded from the study. All patients were taking antipsychotic medication. Chronic patients had been hospitalized for a minimum of two years and, as expected, were characterized by a reduction in their cognitive abilities. Both groups had elevated numbers of DR2, INCOM2, FABCOM2, and CONTAM scores. Although both groups of schizophrenia patients gave severely thought-disordered responses, Gomilla indicated that the acute group produced more florid records consisting of a slightly greater number of DR2s and CONTAMs.

Another recently published study compared the effectiveness of the CS and TDI in distinguishing a small sample of patients with early-onset schizophrenia from a group of nonpsychotic patients experiencing hallucinations (Andersen et al., 2016). Even though the two groups could not be distinguished by the total amount of thought disorder in their records, the schizophrenia group was characterized by a greater number of .75- and 1.0-level scores on the TDI (absurd responses, fluidity, incoherence, ALOG, and contaminations) and by the presence of contaminations on the CS. In addition to identifying Rorschach scores more specific to schizophrenia, the study provided an interesting contrast between the TDI and CS. The authors cautiously argued that the TDI is superior to the CS when assessing early-onset schizophrenia.

Schizoaffective disorder

The diagnostic integrity of schizoaffective disorder has for years been surrounded by controversy regarding its place in diagnostic nomenclature and the very nature of its existence. Researchers in psychopathology have attempted to discover whether schizoaffective disorder is a variant of schizophrenia or an affective disorder, a separate diagnostic phenomenon, a midpoint along a continuum between schizophrenia and bipolar illness, or a combination of schizophrenia and affective disorder.

Prior to the 1980s, the Rorschach literature contributed little to this debate. It was not until 1987 that Rorschach researchers investigated schizoaffective psychosis in a rigorous empirical manner. Shenton, Solovay, and Holzman (1987) contrasted the quality of TDI scores between a carefully selected group of schizoaffective and schizophrenic subjects Because of the variability in the schizoaffective group, subjects were divided into schizoaffective–manic and schizoaffective–depressed subgroups. The researchers also contrasted TDI scores from these groups with those from their manic group (Solovay, Shenton, & Holzman, 1987). The results of their study showed that schizoaffective–manic subjects resembled both schizophrenic and manic subjects in the quality of their thought disorder patterns on the TDI. Response productivity also showed a similar pattern, with the manic group giving the highest number of responses and the schizoaffective–depressed and schizophrenic groups giving the lowest number.

Schizoaffective–manic subjects resembled manic subjects in more superficial ways compared to their similarities with schizophrenic subjects. Although the schizoaffective–manic subjects demonstrated combinatory activity and some irrelevant intrusions like the manic subjects, they were most similar to the schizophrenic group in terms of their confusion, idiosyncratic thinking, and disorganization, albeit more verbal and expansive than the schizophrenic subjects. However, unlike the bipolar manic group, the schizoaffective–manics were less humorous and playful in their combinatory activity, which often struck the listener as peculiar, distant, and overly private.

The schizoaffective–depressed subjects differed generally from each of the clinical groups and resembled the normals in many ways. They produced more contracted records, devoid of more dramatic combinatory activity and idiosyncratic verbalizations. However, they were strikingly similar to the schizophrenic group on an Absurdity factor from the principle components-factor analysis. This factor included loadings from response categories such as neologisms and absurd responses. This noteworthy feature led researchers to claim that schizoaffective–depressed patients can be distinguished from constricted normals and patients with primary depressions (Holzman, Shenton, & Solovay, 1986).

Lending further support to their typology of disordered thinking, Shenton conducted additional research demonstrating that the quality of thought disorder in the groups of first-degree relatives was similar to that of the schizoaffective, schizophrenic, and manic subjects themselves (Shenton et al., 1989). It is interesting that the relatives of schizoaffective–manic subjects showed the highest quantity of thought disorder and the highest number of idiosyncratic verbalizations, followed by relatives of the state hospital schizophrenics. As expected, relatives of schizoaffective–depressed subjects showed the lowest amount of thought disorder (next to normals); however, their constricted records revealed isolated examples of disordered thinking.

The same qualitative distinctions on the TDI among schizoaffective and schizophrenic patients have not been found elsewhere. As mentioned above, the study by Khadivi, Wetzler, and Wilson (1997) did not support the fine discriminations that the researchers at McLean Hospital found between the different groups of psychotic patients. In particular, Khadivi's group did not find that their schizoaffective subjects demonstrated more combinatory activity, idiosyncratic verbalizations, and confusion. However, it should be noted that their sample size was small and did not distinguish schizoaffective–manic from depressed subjects.

Delusional disorder

Delusional disorders (formerly referred to as "Paranoia" or "Paranoid Disorders") need to be distinguished from delusional beliefs that can occur in other psychiatric or medical conditions. In fact, delusions have been observed to occur in over 75 different clinical conditions (Manschreck, 1979, 1995; Maher & Ross, 1984). What we are talking about here is a discrete psychotic syndrome characterized by a stable and well-defined delusional system that occurs within a relatively normal-functioning personality. Although the individual may eventually become overwhelmed and dominated by the delusional beliefs, they may exist in "encapsulated" form for much of the time.

Compared to schizophrenia and mood disorders, delusional disorders are relatively uncommon. Positive symptoms, other than the delusions themselves, are not typical (Manschreck, 2007). Furthermore, the individual's speech, attentional processes, perception, and conceptual abilities are intact. Reininghaus, Priebe, and Bentall (2013) found that scores for patients with delusional disorders were lower on negative and cognitive disorganization factors. Thus, we should expect to see fewer signs of impoverishment and cognitive disorganization in delusional disorders than we encounter in the schizophrenia spectrum.

Persecutory and paranoid delusions are most often found among patients diagnosed with delusional disorders. However, it is important to distinguish the dimension of delusional thinking from paranoid thinking (or paranoid cognitive style). Not all delusional disorders need be based on a paranoid style of thinking. The recognition that encapsulated delusions did not have to be paranoid in nature eventually led framers of the DSM to change the name of the syndrome from "Paranoid" to "Delusional" Disorder.

Because of its rarity, delusional disorder is less studied than others among the primary psychoses. As such, apart from some case reports (Exner & Erdberg, 2005; Hussein, 2015), pure paranoia and delusional disorders have received little attention in the Rorschach literature. In the past, authors focused primarily on Rorschach differences between schizophrenia patients with and without paranoid features, finding fewer signs of pathology in paranoid schizophrenia (Belyi, 1991; Auslander, Perry, & Jeste, 2002). Despite a dearth of data regarding delusional disorders, we can examine the cognitive–psychological characteristics and Rorschach indices of paranoid thinking. Likewise, we can ponder the issue of whether the Rorschach provides clues regarding an individual's vulnerability to forming delusional beliefs. Granted, we cannot clearly identify a delusion on the Rorschach as we can in a clinical interview; however, a central question concerns whether signs of illogicality, detectable on the Rorschach under the right conditions, might predispose an individual to delusional thinking.

Rorschach indicators of a paranoid style

Rapaport, Gill, and Schafer (1946/1968) delineated a number of Rorschach structural features indicative of a paranoid style. They found the emotional constriction and guardedness of the paranoid to be reflected in (1) a low total number of responses; (2) a propensity to reject cards because of refusal to see anything in the inkblot; (3) fewer color responses, and a greater number of form-dominated and general form responses versus those dominated by color, suggesting heightened concern over emotional control. Rapaport also indicated that a high number of space responses (S) would be characteristic of paranoid conditions, reflecting the individual's oppositionality and underlying hostility. One would expect these space responses, and most other responses, to be accurately perceived (higher F+%) because of the paranoid person's rigidity and sharp attunement to external reality.

Regarding overtly disordered thinking, Rapaport and his associates indicated that "these patients are very sparing in their use of any of these pathological verbalizations" (p. 435). According to Rapaport's group, confabulations are unlikely to occur in paranoid states; however, some queer and relationship verbalizations may be seen. In terms of relationship verbalizations, Rapaport was talking about the paranoid subject's tendency to try to discover the purpose of the test or search for hidden meaning in the Rorschach cards.

Schafer (1948) presented a case of a patient who suffered from an enduring encapsulated delusion that did not lead to widespread disorganization or deterioration. In attempting to generalize about Rorschach indices, Schafer suggested that such patients may give a few strained symbolic responses in a rather constricted record. He elaborated on these indices in his later work (1954) and added a number of features he thought diagnostic of paranoia. Schafer agreed that paranoid patients will demonstrate their emotional constriction and restraint by achieving high F%s, a low number of color responses, more FC than CF + C responses, and a tendency to reject cards. He added that their tendency to ferret out hidden details would be demonstrated by using a greater number of unusual details of the inkblot to form their images.

Unlike Rapaport, who did not feel that the paranoid state was conducive to the production of many M scores, Schafer believed that these patients could give a number of Ms, some of which might be distorted in form. Schafer also suggested that there may be a tendency to ascribe human movement to tiny details of the inkblot. An example of this response was given by a constricted and guarded patient who studied the tiny details on top of what is usually perceived as a human head or face (D9) on Card VII and responded, "This is a town full of people. They are carrying on their business. These people are looking at these others over here." Even with a high-powered microscope, one would not be able to detect any convincing rationale for humans engaging in activity. This response would not only be scored M-, but there is also a distinct confabulatory quality.

Again, unlike Rapaport, Schafer believed that confabulations could occur in paranoid conditions. Predicated on the tendency to blur reality with fantasy, Schafer reasoned that confabulatory elaboration is a prominent aspect of pathological projection. He stated that confabulatory embellishment requires setting up arbitrary connections between details of the blot. Schafer added that confabulations in an overcautious and guarded setting may be especially indicative of paranoia. Overcautiousness could be expressed through the patient's efforts to retain control by limiting the number of responses, by rejecting cards, or by being overly vague and noncommittal about what he or she sees in the inkblots.

One of Schafer's (1954) unique contributions was to describe the importance of thematic content as a source for making inferences about structural and dynamic issues. Regarding paranoia, Schafer indicated that content reflecting themes of self-protection and external threat could signal the potential to employ projective defenses. Imagery indicative of self-protection could reflect themes of flight, hiding, or exertion of superior power. Content such as shields, armor, shells, and grandiose images of powerful figures could reflect self-protective concerns. Imagery suggesting external threat may reflect aggressive, accusatory, or erotic themes. This includes such contents as sinister, evil, or threatening figures; leering faces, eyes, pointing fingers; policemen, detectives, judges, and so on.

Schachtel (1966) and Rapaport, Gill, and Schafer (1946/1968) described a particular type of shading response in which the subject used shading to delineate form or shape. Both sources indicate that the F(c) response was indicative of perceptual sensitivity. Rapaport stressed the watchful and cautious quality of the response, while Schachtel emphasized the "stretching out of feelers in order to explore nuances" (p. 251). As such, the F(c) response has come to be associated with a watchful, hypervigilant stance, possibly suggestive of a paranoid style.

Putting this all together, we can see how the paranoid style (apart from the concurrence of delusional thinking) manifests itself in responses in which the subject looks cautiously for unusual details (Dds), including white space; often uses shading to carve out internal shapes in the blot; may perceive human movement that has a distorted and confabulatory quality; and may elaborate themes that suggest external danger or a need for protection. The following response given by an angry paranoid man indicates this constellation of features in one response to Card VIII: "If you look in here (inside of D5) you can see a guy with a hood. Looks like an executioner with hate in his eyes. Ready for the kill. Also looks kinda like a KKK guy with a sheet over his head."

Finally, the Hypervigilance Index (HVI) in the CS and the Vigilance Composite (V-Comp) in the R-PAS assess effortful, detail-oriented sensitivity and attention to cues. Conceptually, these variables may pick up a subject's watchfulness, wariness, and suspiciousness. Exner (1993) reported that the HVI was found to be positive in 88 percent of paranoid schizophrenic subjects and in 90 percent of subjects with paranoid personalities.

Delusional thinking and the Rorschach

If a delusion is a false belief based on incorrect reasoning, we might expect disturbances in logical thinking to lie at the base of delusion formation. As discussed in Chapter 10, one form of illogical reasoning is conceptualized as predicate thinking, which is best captured by ALOG and PEC responses. Like delusions, ALOG/PEC responses reflect the subject's sense of certainty about his or her idiosyncratic interpretation of reality, which is usually based on only limited information while overlooking more obvious and relevant cues.

However, like Rapaport, Exner stated that ALOG responses are most common among patients with schizophrenia. Neither of these researchers presented data suggesting that this score specifically represents a delusional process in and of itself. In other words, ALOG is generally associated more with severe psychosis, schizophrenia in particular, than with delusional thinking per se.

Several studies challenged the hypothesis that predicate thinking underlies the formation of delusions (Nims, 1959; Williams, 1964). Researchers failed to demonstrate that delusional subjects reason any differently than do nondeluded ones Thus, for the most part, psychosis researchers have concluded that the formation of delusions is not due to some defect in formal reasoning that is absent in nondeluded subjects. Although I know of no Rorschach studies that have attempted to link ALOG responses with nonschizophrenic delusional disorders, it is probably safe to conclude that, based on the available evidence, we should not expect patients with delusional disorders to give more ALOGs than nondeluded subjects.

Absent any evidence of specific impairment of reasoning ability in delusional patients, Maher (1974, 1988; Maher & Ross, 1984) proposed that delusions are rational and systematic explanations of anomalous experiences that are arrived at by the same process that scientists use to account for their observations. Maher argued that delusional theories arise when the subject is presented with a puzzle or discontinuity that requires some form of explanation. The puzzle activates a "search mode" that impels the subject to find an explanation. When an explanation has been developed, it is accompanied by significant feelings of relief and reduction of tension. Data that are discrepant with this explanation evoke cognitive dissonance and are not welcome.

Chapman and Chapman (1988) agreed that Maher's model held promise for describing the underlying process of delusion formation in nonschizophrenia delusional subjects, but they also adduced evidence that subjects scoring high on scales measuring distortions in perception and magical thinking demonstrated an upsurge of cognitive slippage when discussing psychotic or psychotic-like experiences such as delusions or aberrant beliefs. These same subjects did not show cognitive slippage when discussing other experiences, even nonpathological anxiety-arousing ones. When asked about their deviant experiences, these subjects tended to express themselves vaguely, demonstrate word-finding difficulty, and become tangential. The Chapmans, together with Edell (Chapman, Edell, & Chapman, 1980), found that subjects who had more delusional and aberrant beliefs than control subjects also showed more cognitive slippage. However, the mild cognitive deviancy appeared primarily when the subjects were discussing their anomalous experiences.

What this suggests is that the Rorschach will not likely be sensitive to underlying delusional mechanisms unless the subject's delusional ideas are somehow aroused by the inkblot stimuli. However, Biagiarelli and colleagues (2015) found significant correlations between M– and delusions, as indexed by the PANSS. Despite this suggestive finding, M– should not be considered a sensitive and specific measure of delusionality. Too many other patients give M– in the absence of psychosis or delusional symptoms. Furthermore, Mihura et al.'s meta-analytic research (2013) did not support an interpretative relationship between M– and psychosis.

In many cases, individuals with delusions do not reveal any formal disturbance in thinking or reality testing on the Rorschach. This may be especially true if the subject is responding to the inkblots in a cautious and constricted manner. This prediction seems consistent with the suggestions of Rapaport and Schafer, who both indicated that delusional patients may be difficult to detect on testing. According to Rapaport, "Patients with paranoid conditions may or may not be coarctated, because their ideational productivity takes the form of delusions, they remain exceedingly coherent, and great segments of their intellectual functioning are unimpaired by the delusion formation" (Rapaport et al., 1946/1968, p. 391). Schafer added, "These cases are among the most difficult to diagnose on the basis of test results. Many of them are indistinguishable from normals" (1948, p. 91).

Bipolar disorder: Manic psychosis

"Manic-depressive insanity" was part of Kraepelin's (1921) early diagnostic schema. Clinicians have always considered psychosis as one possible manifestation of mania; however, it seems that most of the diagnostic emphasis historically was placed on the striking affective and behavioral characteristics of manic individuals. With the exception of the concepts of "pressured speech" and "flight of ideas," the quality of thought in mania received comparatively little attention from early psychiatric experts.

However, a strikingly different picture began to emerge in the 1970s. Lipkin, Dyrud, and Meyer (1970) found that the cognitive phenomenology of mania overlapped considerably with that of schizophrenia. Carpenter, Strauss, and Muleh (1973) looked specifically at the quality of thought processes and reported a high frequency of first-rank Schneiderian symptoms of schizophrenia in manic individuals. Andreasen and her colleagues conducted a number of studies comparing thought processes in manics and schizophrenics (Andreasen & Powers, 1974; Andreasen, Tsuang, & Canter, 1974; Andreasen, 1979a, 1979b; Andreasen & Akiskal, 1983). The collective conclusions of Andreasen's studies were that (1) manic subjects had high levels of thought disorder characterized by overinclusive and bizarre conceptual thinking, whereas schizophrenic subjects were more underinclusive and bizarre in their concept formation; (2) based on responses to a Proverbs Test, clinicians diagnosed thought disorder more frequently in manic subjects than in those with schizophrenia; and (3) Bleulerian and Schneiderian symptoms are not specific to schizophrenia but occur in many manic subjects as well. Taken together, these studies contributed significantly to greater diagnostic precision and reliability for both schizophrenia and manic–depressive illness. The studies conducted by Morrison and Flanagan (1978) and Pope and Lipinski (1978) influenced the evolution of the modern DSM systems by concluding that many patients with bipolar (manic) illnesses were commonly misdiagnosed as schizophrenic on the basis of their having disturbances in formal thought processes.

It is useful to spend a few minutes examining the phenomenological nature of disordered thinking in manic conditions and contrasting this with schizophrenia. Nowhere are questions of differential diagnosis more common than between these two clinical syndromes. Against a backdrop of what distinguishes thought disorder in schizophrenia and mania, we can begin to review what is known about the Rorschach manifestations of these and other forms of primary psychoses.

Distinguishing thought disorder in schizophrenia and mania

Verbal productivity has been found to be a distinguishing feature of thought disorder, with manics exceeding schizophrenics in the volume of speech productivity alone (Harvey, Earle-Bover, & Wielgus, 1984; Oltmanns et al., 1985). Although formal thought disorder in both groups is characterized by disorganization, the distinguishing features are impoverishment and coherence. For example, Andreasen (1983) contrasted the "empty disorganized" speech in schizophrenia with the "fluent disorganized" speech in mania. Researchers have also focused on speech deviance, which is more coherent and cohesive in mania compared to schizophrenia (Wykes & Leff, 1982; Hoffman, Stopek, & Andreasen, 1986). Other key distinguishing features include the presence of more playful and combinatory thinking in mania (Holzman, Levy, & Johnston, 1986; Solovay, Shelton, & Holzman, 1987) and more impoverished and idiosyncratic speech in schizophrenia (Cuesta & Peralta, 2011). Docherty, De Rosa, and Andreasen (1996) also found more evidence of ambiguous word usage in mania and more missing information references in the speech of schizophrenia subjects.

Regarding other psychotic symptoms, for early-onset bipolar patients with manic psychosis, the most common psychotic features are delusions of grandeur (62 percent), persecution (60 percent), and influence (38 percent), with 41 percent of patients demonstrating positive formal thought disorder (Kennedy et al., 2005). In addition to being characterized as distractible, self-referential, and grandiose, mental activity in mania has been described as expansive, rapid, pressured, circumstantial, and tangential (Belmæker & van Praag, 1980). In her study of affective disorders and creativity, Jamison (1993) found that both creative and hypomanic thinking is characterized by fluency, rapidity, and flexibility. A greater speed of thinking leads to a greater quantity of thoughts and associations that may produce some unique ideas and associations. However, whereas healthy creative individuals may demonstrate a richness in their unusual associations, manic subjects may have difficulty maintaining a focus and filtering out distractions that give their associations a bizarre quality (Andreasen & Powers, 1974).

Jamison mentioned another key aspect of manic thought: the ability to combine ideas or categories of thought to form new and original connections (combinative thinking). Using object-sorting tests, researchers have showed that manic subjects demonstrate overinclusiveness in their conceptual thinking through the tendency to combine test objects into categories in a way that broadens, shifts, and blurs conceptual boundaries (Andreasen & Powers, 1974). Harrow and colleagues (1982) also demonstrated that manic subjects tend to be more active and behaviorally overinclusive than schizophrenic individuals. However, manic thought may not simply be overinclusive; it may be bizarre and idiosyncratic as well (Harrow et al., 1982). Harrow and his colleagues also used a proverb and object-sorting test to assess bizarre and idiosyncratic thinking in manic, schizophrenic, and nonpsychotic patients. They found that 94 percent of their manic subjects, compared to

79 percent of their schizophrenic subjects, demonstrated moderate to severe "bizarre–idiosyncratic thought" (their name for diverse types of speech and behavior associated with positive thought disorder or florid psychosis).

Despite the possible presence of bizarreness, overinclusiveness, and first-rank symptoms, manic speech has also been described as more reality based and logical enough to invite involvement by others (Janowsky, Leff, & Epstein, 1970). Harrow and his group also noted how manic subjects attempted to interact with others, albeit in bizarre and inappropriate ways, whereas schizophrenic individuals tended to be more private, autistic, and inwardly directed. Perhaps it is this interactivity that, according to Janowsky, Leff, & Epstein, makes people dismiss the schizophrenic individual as "crazy" and accept the manic patient's pseudology more easily. Echoing this idea, Lipkin, Dryud, and Meyer (1970) reported that:

> The ideation of the patient with a manic episode, although at times delusional, shows reasonably good form; and the associations, although often occurring as a flight of ideas or even clang associations, have a different quality than the puzzling symbolic looseness of associations demonstrated in schizophrenia (p. 266).

Hoffman, Stopek, and Andreasen (1986) conducted a discourse analysis to contrast the different processing requirements that manic and schizophrenic speech impose on the listener. Their linguistic analysis of speech samples of manic, schizophrenic, and normal subjects provided some support for the claim that manic thought/speech disorder is in some ways less incoherent or alienating than that found in schizophrenics. Hoffman and his team based their investigation on the psycholinguistic studies of Deese (1978, 1980), which proposed that an extended, multisentence text will be experienced as coherent if the listener can organize the propositions expressed by the text into a hierarchical discourse structure. If a speech segment can be organized by the listener into a propositional hierarchy, with some of the propositions dependently linked to others, then all of the propositions expressed by the speaker can be logically related to one another.

Hoffman, Stopek, and Andreasen determined that, unlike schizophrenia subjects, manic speakers can construct complex, well-organized discourse plans that sound incoherent only when the speaker abruptly shifts from one plan to another. As a result of this finding, they concluded that the disorganized, but more comprehensible, speech of the subjects with mania would be characterized by a "structural shift" from one well-formed message or discourse plan to another, whereas the disorganization of the speaker with schizophrenia was characterized more by a "structural deficiency" in generating any clear plan whatsoever.

These reports suggest that illogical and incoherent speech in mania may somehow be less alienating and less difficult for the listener to understand (or simply tolerate) than the speech and logic of schizophrenic individuals. It may be that the interpersonal orientation of the manic also helps make it easier for the listener to attend than the more distant demeanor of the subject with schizophrenia. The delusions of manic patients often reflect themes of ecstasy and communion as opposed to the more ominous and fearful delusions of the schizophrenic patients, who seem oriented more toward seclusiveness and segregation. Perhaps it is also the infectious mood of the manic subject that is more amusing and less frightening than the affective flatness or incongruity of the schizophrenic that increases the listener's tolerance for deviance. Andreasen and Pfohl (1976) conducted a linguistic analysis of manic speech and found it to be colorful and filled with adjectives and action verbs; however, curiously, it reflected more interest in things than in people.

Rorschach indices of manic thought disorder

In my earlier work (Kleiger, 1999), I reviewed pioneering studies describing Rorschach characteristics of patients with mania. Most of these older studies listed Rorschach variables that usually had to do with the number of responses, location color, movement, and form level. Because thought disorder was not considered emblematic of mania, few Rorschach researchers addressed the quality of thinking in subjects with mania. An exception was Weiner, who stated, "They [manics] employ both movement and color freely, extend their interpretations far beyond conventional animal and popular percepts, and obvious D locations, and embellish their responses with numerous fanciful specifications, combinations, and peripheral associations" (Weiner, 1966, p. 433).

Unquestionably, the most detailed and rigorous Rorschach analysis of disordered thinking in mania was conducted by Holzman's TDI research group (Solovay, Shenton, & Holzman, 1987). The mean TDI score for their 20 manic subjects was 25.02 ($\pm$ 16.15) compared to a mean of 35.58 ($\pm$ 38.77) for the group of 43 schizophrenic subjects. Although the schizophrenic group was rated as significantly more disorganized (in terms of GAS ratings) and with more chronicity than the manic group, there was not a significant difference between Total TDI scores. This was apparently due to the greater variation within the schizophrenia sample. In a principal components-factor analysis, one factor correctly identified 73.3 percent of the manic group. Termed "Combinatory Thinking," this factor comprised the following individual TDI scores (and their respective loadings): playful confabulation (0.83), Incom (.60), flippant response (.58), and fabulized combination (.53). An additional factor that distinguished the manic group from the schizophrenic group was called "Irrelevant Intrusions" (made up of flippant and looseness responses). In terms of severity levels, the schizophrenic group showed thought disorder at all four levels of severity on the TDI. In contrast, none of the manic subjects demonstrated thought disorder scores at the most severe level of 1.0. Both groups had equivalent amounts of thought disorder at the .25 and .75 levels, while the manic group produced more thought disorder scores at the .50 level than did the schizophrenic group. It is the .50-level scores that include such factors as playful confabulations and Fabcoms.

Based on their data, Solovay, Shenton, and Holzman (1987) concluded that:

> manic thought disorder manifests itself as ideas loosely strung together and extravagantly combined and elaborated ... One prominent outcome of such an arbitrary integrative process is the appearance of irrelevant intrusions into social discourse that at times may appear inappropriately flippant and playful (p. 19).

Khadivi, Wetzler, and Wilson (1997) cross-validated some of these key findings as they pertained to manic subjects. Contrasting six overarching thought disorder categories (Combinatory Thinking, Idiosyncratic Verbalization, Autistic Thinking, Fluid Thinking, Absurdity, and Confusion), among paranoid schizophrenic, manic, and schizoaffective subjects, they found that the manic group showed significantly more combinatory thinking than the other two groups. They concluded that combinatory thinking reflects a tendency to connect things normally kept apart. Here, the subject's effort to integrate disparate elements outstrips adherence to reason, reality, and intellectual capacity. Khadivi and his colleagues associated this combinatory process with distractibility or problems in maintaining one's focus. They noted that since manic individuals are driven to respond to unrelated stimuli, they become overinclusive and are unable to screen out irrelevant stimuli. The authors also conjectured that this combinatory quality may be related to the concept of "flight of ideas."

Singer and Brabender (1993) used the CS to examine differences and similarities between bipolar manic, bipolar depressed, and unipolar depressed subjects. Consistent with one earlier study, they found more cognitive slippage in subjects with bipolar depression compared to those with unipolar depression (Donnelly, Murphy, & Scott, 1975). Brabender and Singer also found that the bipolar manics had significantly higher SUM6 and WSUM6 Special Scores, more scores at Level 2, higher SCZI, and a higher X-% than the other two groups. Within the manic group, 77 percent had at least one DR1, 56 percent had one or more DR2s, 50 percent had INCOMs, 56 percent FABCOMs, and 22 percent ALOGs. Interestingly, none of the manics had Level 2 Deviant Verbalizations (DV2), which would include neologisms or extremely odd word usage. This is quite consistent with TDI studies showing that idiosyncratic verbalizations are less reflective of manic thinking.

Kimura and colleagues (2013) conducted a similar study to Brabender and Singer's with Japanese patients and controls. They contrasted Rorschach thought disorder indices in bipolar and unipolar depressives with a group of nonpatient controls. Their main finding was that the bipolar depressive group scored higher on WSUM6 than both the unipolar and control groups. Furthermore, DR2 scores occurred roughly three times as frequently in the bipolar group than in the unipolar and control groups. Kimura's study showed the presence of significant disordered thinking in bipolar depressed patients who were not in a manic phase. Two related studies found higher levels of Rorschach thought disorder in euthymic bipolar patients (Mandel et al., 1984) and in the healthy offspring of bipolar patients

(Osher et al., 2000), suggesting that disordered thought, as defined by elevations on WSUM6, might serve as an endophenotypic marker of bipolar disorder.

In summary, there is convincing evidence of a "manic Rorschach thought disorder profile" characterized primarily by combinatory thinking, playful confabulations, and flippant remarks, which may be present to some extent in patients across the bipolar spectrum. In addition to structural findings, qualitative features such as pressured, rapid speech, use of active verbs, affective language, and ambitious integrative efforts may bolster the characteristic thought disorder signs to strengthen diagnostic inferences. There is also evidence that bipolar depressives can be identified (and distinguished from unipolar depressives) on the basis of combinatory activity, poorer form level, and constriction.

Major depression with psychotic features

Major unipolar depression with psychotic features has received less attention than other psychotic disorders and often goes unrecognized (Smith et al., 2007). In a large epidemiological survey (Ohayon & Schatzberg, 2002), 18.5 percent of individuals who met criteria for major depression were also classified as having a psychotic component to their depression. Delusions are generally more common than hallucinations and most often reflect themes of guilt, punishment, persecution, and, to a lesser extent, illness, poverty, and nihilism (Kuhs, 1991). Because depressed patients may be less inclined to share their thoughts, clinicians need to pay attention to other symptoms and behavior, including psychomotor disturbance (agitation or retardation), cognitive impairment, hypochondriasis, anxiety, and paranoid ideation (Smith et al., 2007). It is also important to point out that negative symptoms have not commonly been found among these patients (Husted, Beiser, & Iacono, 1995).

Disordered thinking and depression

Winokur, Clayton, and Reich (1969) identified thought content and process disturbances in a heterogeneous group of depressive subjects. Roughly 20 percent of the total depressive sample of 89 subjects were found to have moderate to severe formal thought disorder (including such thought disorder manifestations as paralogical or unrelated responses, tangentiality, flight of ideas, neologisms, echolalia, perseveration, clanging, and word salad). Of their 47 confirmed unipolar subjects, a surprisingly high 40 percent had moderate to severe formal thought disorder.

Ianizito, Cadoret, and Pugh (1974) studied disorders of thought content and form in unipolar depressives and found that 78 percent of unipolar patients who demonstrated moderate to severe disturbances in the formal structure of their thinking had poor outcomes as measured by longer lengths of stay and referral for ECT. Thus, the authors concluded that formal thought disorder at the time of admission may predict a severe episode of depression that might be more refractory to treatment.

Sprock and colleagues (1983) looked at cognitive functioning in subjects complaining of depression. Specifically, they investigated the presence of thought disorder in patients with chronic pain who complained of depressive symptoms. These subjects were not considered to be suffering from primary affective illness; instead they were classified as "depressed" on the basis of rating themselves extremely depressed on the Beck Depression Inventory. The researchers found three significant areas of deficit on a tachistoscopic procedure designed to test information processing speed: (1) abstracting ability; (2) associative intrusions; and (3) speed of processing. Impairment in each area was significantly correlated with ratings of depression. The Category Test has also been used to study abstraction ability in both unipolar and bipolar depressives (Donnelly et al., 1980; Savard, Rey, & Post, 1980). In these studies, investigators discovered a significant degree of abstraction impairment in hospitalized depressives of both types compared with nondepressed controls.

Silberman, Weingartner, and Post (1983) looked for evidence of illogical reasoning and inefficient use of feedback by the depressed sample on an impersonal, abstract, problem-solving task. Using a procedure in which subjects must generate, test, and ultimately narrow down a problem-solving hypothesis based on feedback from the examiner, Silberman and colleagues found that a combined sample of unipolar and bipolar depressives demonstrated significantly impaired performances. Specifically, the depressed group had more trouble focusing and tended to make more perseverative errors than a nondepressed control group. Perseveration was said to occur when subjects stuck to incorrect solutions despite being given negative feedback. Interestingly, the researchers found that their depressed subjects performed qualitatively similar to subjects with right- and left-temporal lobectomies. They concluded that some organic dementias with perseverative tendencies might be useful as models for aspects of the dementia associated with depression.

Carter (1986) conducted a study to assess the presence of formal thought disorder in psychotically depressed individuals. In particular, she was interested in contrasting the nature of disordered thinking in psychotic depression and chronic paranoid schizophrenia. Carter found that the psychotic depressive subjects demonstrated as much idiosyncratic thinking (including such qualities as looseness, incoherence, and illogicality) as subjects classified as paranoid schizophrenic. Carter concluded that the presence of psychosis equalizes thought disorder among different diagnostic groups. Like Harrow et al. (1982), she believed that the kinds of positive thought disorder found in her subjects were products of a psychotic state and that distinctions between different diagnostic groups were less significant. In essence, Carter was saying that the presence of thought disorder in psychotic depressives was a product not of depression but of the associated psychotic decompensation. She suggested that a general psychoticism profile would include idiosyncratic thinking, restricted abstraction ability, linguistic errors, content deficiencies, intermixing, and loss of goal directedness.

Kay (1986) took issue with Carter's conclusions that thought disorder is not qualitatively associated with diagnosis but is primarily a product of psychotic decompensation. Among other things, Kay criticized Carter's decision to contrast psychotic depressives with paranoid schizophrenics, who have demonstrated less severe cognitive impairment than those with other subtypes of schizophrenia. Paranoid schizophrenia yields relatively fewer signs of positive thought disorder in interviews and testing ratings than nonparanoid subtypes. Thus, as Kay argued, it should not be surprising that a schizophrenic subgroup known for its lesser degree of thought impairment would fail to demonstrate more positive thought disorder than another actively psychotic group.

Rorschach findings

Although empirical support for a general thought disorder profile for depression remains ambiguous, there are some useful Rorschach findings that may prove helpful in making differential diagnostic decisions between such clinical syndromes as bipolar versus unipolar depression and psychotic depression versus other psychotic disorders.

Singer and Brabender (1993) pointed out that the issue of distinguishing bipolar from unipolar depressives has been largely neglected in the Rorschach literature. They found that bipolar depressives had a significantly greater mean SUM6 and WSUM6 than their unipolar counterparts. Regarding the presence of Special Scores, the bipolar group demonstrated significantly more Level 1 DR and INCOM responses than the unipolar depressives. In fact, the bipolar depressives did not differ significantly from the bipolar manics on these two measures. It was particularly noteworthy that 60 percent of the bipolar depressives gave DRs, compared to 77 percent of the manics and only 14 percent of the unipolars. Singer and Brabender found that the responses of the bipolar depressives were qualitatively "less fantastic, less playful, and less sanguinely toned than the bipolar manic subjects" (p. 342).

As mentioned earlier in this chapter, the manic subjects scored significantly higher on WSUM6 (with a greater number of Level 2 Special Scores) and SCZI than either the bipolar or unipolar depressives. The bipolar and unipolar groups did not differ on frequency of Level 2 scores. The researchers concluded that Level 2 Special Scores are the realm of the manic bipolar subjects (72 percent of the manics had more than one Level 2 score compared to 33 percent of the bipolar depressives and 18 percent of the unipolars).

In addition to having more Level 1 INCOMs and DRs than the unipolars, the bipolar depressed group obtained a higher percentage of minus-form-level responses than the unipolar group (X-% = 21 vs. 14 for unipolars), leading the authors to conclude that when depression:

> is manifest (either from the Rorschach or from other modes of observation) and a relatively high number of Special Scores is present, particularly in combination with a deficit in reality testing, the hypothesis of the presence of a bipolar disorder should be raised (p. 343).

Looking more closely at Singer and Brabender's data on unipolar depressives, one can see that they demonstrated a relatively low frequency of disordered thinking. In every category, they showed fewer Special Scores than bipolar subjects. In most categories, their frequency of Special Scores is similar to that of nonpatient adults (Exner, 1993).

Attenuated Psychosis Syndrome (APS)

Over the past 20 years, researchers around the world have become keenly interested in the early detection and intervention of patients considered at high risk for transitioning to psychosis (Kleiger & Khadivi, 2015). These high-risk syndromes have been termed "at-risk mental states" or ARMS (McGorry, Yung, & Phillips, 2001), "ultra-high-risk" or UHR (Yung & McGorry, 2007), "clinical high-risk" or CHR (Addington & Heinssen, 2012), and "psychosis-risk syndrome" or PRS (McGlashan, Walsh, & Woods, 2010). The explosion of interest in these high-risk conditions prompted the DSM-5 panels to propose Attenuated Psychosis Syndrome (APS) as a provisional condition requiring further study (American Psychiatric Association, 2013).

A pioneer in this field, Allison Yung and her colleagues (1998) defined a set of criteria that predicted psychosis onset within a year of identification. They identified three high-risk clusters or syndromes that reflect a combination of recent functional deterioration plus trait-based characteristics or one of two state-based symptom groups. Recent functional decline was defined as a change in mental state of at least one month in duration and clearly associated with deterioration in premorbid levels of functioning. Yung et al.'s groups included a: (1) Genetic Risk and Deterioration Syndrome, when there is a genetic risk for psychosis (i.e. first-degree relative diagnosed with a schizophrenia-spectrum disorder and/or the individual meets the criteria for schizotypal personality disorder); (2) Brief Intermittent Psychotic State (BIPS) or Brief Limited Intermittent Psychotic State (BLIPS), for patients characterized by the presence of one or more positive psychotic symptoms, including formal thought disorder, that cross the threshold for psychosis but occur at a frequency too brief to meet official diagnostic criteria of a psychotic disorder; and the more common (3) Attenuated Positive Symptom State (APSS), which describes patients who demonstrate nonpsychotic, pre-delusional thoughts, subthreshold hallucinatory perceptual anomalies, and pre-thought-disordered speech organization. The APSS syndrome reportedly characterizes most high-risk patients (McGlashan, Walsh, & Woods, 2010). McGlashan and colleagues developed a set of subpsychotic, attenuated criteria that correspond to different dimensions of psychotic level symptomatology.

Key features of DSM-5's APS include a variety of "psychosis-like" symptoms falling below the threshold for a full psychotic disorder. Among the proposed criteria are: (1) attenuated forms of either hallucinations, delusions, or disorganized speech; (2) symptoms occurring at least once a week for the past month; (3) symptoms worsening in the past year; (4) symptoms that are distressing and disabling; (5) symptoms not better explained by another mental disorder, including psychotic depression or bipolar disorders; and (6) criteria for a full-blown psychosis have never been met. In addition to being less severe and frequent, insight and reality testing are relatively intact.

Although attenuated syndromes have been associated more with schizophrenia than mania, there is some evidence to suggest that both disorders share some prodromal features. However, unusual ideas were more associated with schizophrenia prodrome, whereas obsessions, compulsions, and difficulties with memory, concentration, thinking, mood lability, suicidality, restlessness, fatigue, and agitation were all more consistent with a mania prodrome (Correll et al., 2007).

Clinical assessment of Attenuated Psychosis Syndromes (APS)

Development of assessment instruments to detect psychosis-risk patients has been a key part of research programs. A number of instruments, based on comprehensive interviews and rating scales, were developed to identify high-risk patients (see Kleiger & Khadivi, 2015). However, there are two problems, one scientific and the other practical, that affect the viability of these assessment instruments. The first problem is that, with a few exceptions, practicing diagnosticians have been less involved in developing or utilizing these methods for identifying psychosis-risk patients in routine clinical settings. The instruments, generally lengthy and impractical to administer in an office setting, often require extensive training and various members of the research team to collect the data. Also, as with most research-based assessment instruments, these methods are not published and widely available for clinicians to use in their diagnostic practices. For these reasons, assessment instruments, though comprehensive in scope, are generally unsuitable, impractical, or unavailable to the practicing clinician facing diagnostic decisions regarding the psychotic potential in the patients they evaluate. Instead, clinicians typically rely on unstructured clinical interviews and standard psychological testing instruments to determine whether a patient might be at risk for developing a psychosis.

The second problem with large-scale research instruments, and the concept of attenuated psychosis in general, is the high false-positive rates associated with prediction studies. Rates for converting to psychosis among patients identified as high-risk range from 20 percent to 50 percent in several long-term prospective studies (Shrivastava et al., 2011). The negative consequences of high false-positive identifications include unfortunate stigmatizing, unnecessary treatment, and possibly ineffective treatment (Paris, 2013).

In general, psychological tests have not been among the methods used in large-scale detection studies. Not only are these not the instruments of choice in psychosis-risk studies, but also few contemporary prediction studies have been published using traditional psychological assessment instruments. However, as Mihura and her colleagues noted, "given that a notable strength of the Rorschach is its ability to detect psychosis, primary and secondary prevention research might refine its ability to detect high-risk psychosis cases" (Mihura et al., 2013, p. 579). As noted in Chapter 2, investigators have begun to use the Rorschach to identify variables associated with psychosis risk (Kimhy et al., 2007; Ilonen et al., 2010; Lacoua, Koren, & Rothschild-Yakar, 2015). Kimhy and colleagues found that clinically high-risk patients displayed substantial deficits in reality testing or perceptual accuracy (FQ of responses) that were comparable to the levels of poor FQ found in patients with schizophrenia. Poor FQ was a more significant factor than Rorschach indices of disordered thinking, which were generally more intact in high-risk patients compared to their psychotic counterparts. Kimhy et al. concluded that poor FQ of Rorschach responses may represent a trait-like marker in patients at clinical high risk, which could be identified before the occurrence of disturbances in thought organization. They also found that individuals in the high-risk group who had first-degree relatives with a history of psychosis had poorer FQ than high-risk individuals with no such family history. Studying comorbidity in UHR individuals, Inoue, Yorozuya, & Mizuno (2014) also found more evidence of poor Rorschach FQ and less indication of disordered thought processes among their high-risk subjects.

However, other research teams found problems with both FQ and disordered thinking in the Rorschachs of individuals identified as being at high-risk for psychosis (Ilonen et al., 2010; Lacoua, Koren, & Rothschild-Yakar, 2015). These findings fit with DSM-5 descriptions of disorganized communication that manifest as odd speech (vague, metaphorical, overelaborate, stereotyped), unfocused speech (confused, muddled, too fast or too slow, wrong words, irrelevant context, off track), meandering speech (circumstantial, tangential). When the disorganization is moderately severe, the individual frequently gets into irrelevant topics but responds easily to clarifying questions (American Psychiatric Association, 2013, p. 784).

To make diagnostic inferences that your patient might have APS, you will need sufficient information that the individual has deteriorated over the last year. Assessing for the presence of milder hallucinatory symptoms and delusional or quasi-delusional beliefs is necessary. On the Rorschach, pay attention to dips in form accuracy and milder manifestations of disorganization and illogicality. Thus, we might expect to find slippage in the form of more Level 1 than Level 2 DRs, INCOMs, and FABCOMs. Testing the limits of the patient's awareness of both FQ- and thought-disordered responses will be important for assessing the degree of insight present.

Drug-induced psychoses

According to the DSM-5, psychotic disorders can occur in association with a broad range of prescription and nonprescription substances. A great deal of interest has focused around so-called "drug-induced psychosis" as a result of methamphetamine, cocaine, hallucinogenic, and cannabis intoxication. Patients with drug-induced psychoses present to emergency medical services with an array of psychotic symptoms that make it difficult to distinguish primary from substance-induced psychosis.

A number of factors complicate the assessment of the role of these substances in determining psychotic symptoms (Kleiger & Khadivi, 2015). For example, patients may not agree to the toxicology procedures necessary to establish a causal connection. Some drugs like K-2 and Ecstasy are not routinely assessed in standard toxicology screenings. In many acute care settings, patients are discharged before the recommended four-week period of drug-free observation. As a result of these complicating factors, patients are frequently misdiagnosed (Addington & Addington, 1998).

Another complicating issue is whether patients with primary and drug-induced psychoses can be distinguished on the basis of clinical symptomatology. Symptoms of drug-induced psychosis are similar to those of an acute schizophrenia-spectrum psychosis. Delusions and hallucinations are common occurrences in patients with cocaine and amphetamine-induced psychoses (Fujii & Sakai, 2007; Jacobs & Haning III, 2007; Bramness et al., 2012). Delusions of grandiosity and paranoia occur in 93 percent of cocaine-induced psychoses (Fujii & Sakai, 2007). Both methamphetamine psychosis (MAP) and cocaine types of substance-induced psychosis also manifest auditory hallucinations and, to a lesser extent, visual and tactile hallucinations (formication). In a comprehensive review of the literature, Acklin (2017) indicated that the symptoms of MAP are indistinguishable from the positive symptoms of acute paranoid schizophrenia. Ideas of reference and delusions of persecution are most often exhibited in psychoses associated with methamphetamine use (in Jacobs & Hanning III, 2007). Acklin noted that pre-psychotic experiences may include ideas of reference and abnormal mood states, which then shift to more floridly psychotic states characterized by delusions of reference, persecution, and poisoning, along with auditory and visual hallucinations. Acklin reviewed recent findings regarding the phenomenology of MAP, which has been described as a "toxic psychotic state" characterized by paranoia and fear.

Psychotic symptoms associated with cannabis appear to be somewhat different (Núñez Domínguez, 2007). Manic excitement and paranoia are common, accompanied by grandiosity, hostility, confusion, hallucinations, and experiences of depersonalization and derealization. As with psychosis induced by cocaine and amphetamines, delusions associated with cannabis psychosis are predominantly paranoid and grandiose in nature. In contrast to psychoses associated with other substances, cannabis hallucinations may be less common.

Earlier reports were essentially that "psychosis is psychosis," and that patients presenting with substance-induced psychoses could not be distinguished on the basis of clinical phenomenology from those individuals with schizophrenia-spectrum psychoses (Janowsky & Risch, 1979). However, the literature presents somewhat equivocal conclusions regarding whether patients with substance-induced psychosis exhibit formal thought disorder. In a small sample study, Harris and Batki (2000) found that patients with both cocaine and amphetamine-induced psychoses obtained scores on the Thought Disturbance scale of the PANSS that were equivalent to the 80th percentile of schizophrenia subjects' scores. Compared to schizophrenia subjects, those with MAP had high levels of positive symptoms and lower, but not insignificant, levels of negative symptoms. Again, despite possible subtle distinctions in clinical presentation, it appears that MAP can masquerade as schizophrenia.

Núñez Domínguez (2007) indicated that patients presenting with cannabis-induced psychosis may demonstrate disturbances in thought processes such as flight of ideas. However, more consistent findings have suggested differences, including the absence of formal thought disorder in patients with drug-induced psychoses (Bell, 1965; Rosenthal & Miner, 1997; Yui et al., 2000). These studies focused more on the prominence of delusions and hallucinations than on the presence of cognitive disorganization or peculiarities in language. Furthermore, the DSM-5 mentions delusions and hallucinations, but not disorganized speech, as essential diagnostic features of substance-induced psychotic disorders. Additionally, studies have shown that negative symptoms are also generally not present in these patients (Janowsky & Risch, 1979; Harris & Batki, 2000).

The relationship between drug abuse and psychosis is complex. Perhaps the most significant challenge in understanding and diagnosing substance-induced psychoses is that patients suffering from psychotic disorders have increased susceptibility to abusing drugs like cannabis and methamphetamines (Bramness et al., 2012). There is a high prevalence of substance usage in patients with schizophrenia and bipolar disorder (Regier et al., 1990). Patients with primary psychotic disorders may abuse these drugs, which trigger or exacerbate their symptoms of psychosis. Furthermore, schizotypal and similarly psychotically prone individuals may convert to full-blown psychosis after habitual use of cannabis and methamphetamines. Finally, roughly one-fourth of patients who have previously had a drug-induced psychosis may become psychotic years later. Bramness and colleagues (2012) proposed a diathesis stress model to explain the relationships between amphetamines and psychosis. According to their model, lower exposure to the drug (i.e. lower doses) is likely to precipitate psychosis in psychotically vulnerable individuals, whereas higher exposure is less likely to lead to psychosis in individuals who have no such vulnerability. However, repeated exposure to amphetamines can actually increase vulnerability over time and heighten risk for psychotic decompensation even in the absence of acute exposure.

The role of psychological assessment and the Rorschach

Can psychological assessment, and the Rorschach in particular, play a role in evaluating individuals who present with drug-induced psychosis? Clearly, we need to acknowledge both the limits of our instruments and the importance of using multiple methods of assessment, observation, history gathering, and laboratory studies. It is doubtful that any one psychological assessment method can distinguish between patients whose psychosis is the result of substance overuse and those with primary psychotic disorders. Moreover, few would assume that this should be our role. However, once patients suspected of drug-induced psychoses are medically stabilized, testing can play a role in establishing a baseline of their cognitive functioning and identifying psychosocial vulnerabilities (Kleiger & Khadivi, 2015).

Given that many of the studies mentioned found fewer incidences of formal thought disorder or negative symptoms in drug-induced psychosis, it is reasonable to think that we might expect fewer Rorschach representations of these features in such individuals. However, as Acklin (2017) noted, published Rorschach studies of MAP are difficult to find. Proceeding cautiously, with the knowledge that empirical evidence of Rorschach manifestations of substance-induced psychoses is lacking, we might predict that these psychotic individuals will not evidence signs of peculiar language, disorganization, concreteness, and constriction. Thus, Rorschach records would possibly contain fewer DVs, derailed DRs, and indications of impoverishment. Instead, we might expect that these individuals will exhibit behavioral signs of agitation, anxiety, suspiciousness, and excitability. Hallucinations and delusions cannot be identified on the Rorschach; however, we might find evidence of jumping to conclusions in the form of an ALOG/PEC. Response content may reveal themes of guardedness, paranoia, and persecution. Additionally, we might encounter grandiosity in the form of lengthy, embellished responses with highly symbolic content.

In his recent chapter, Acklin (2017) largely debunked any speculation that individuals with MAP and schizophrenia would produce qualitatively different thought disorder profiles. Acklin compared two diagnostic cases, one diagnosed with DSM-IV Schizophrenia (Paranoid Type) and the other with Methamphetamine Dependence and Methamphetamine-induced Psychotic Disorder. Comparing MMPI-2 and R-PAS Rorschach variables, Acklin demonstrated that the records of these two individuals were indistinguishable on indices of thought disorder and reality testing. Both men showed dramatic elevations in critical variables in the Perception and Thinking Problems Domain. EII-3, TP Comp (Thought & Perception Composite), SevCog (Severe Cognitive Codes), and FQ- exceeded the 99th percentile. Acklin found two interesting differences in M- and P (Populars). The MAP subject scored significantly higher on both, suggesting he gave more conventional responses but also more distorted representations of human movement. Acklin concluded that given the similarities in clinical and psychodiagnostic presentations, examiners will need to rely on extra-Rorschach information, specifically a patient's clinical and substance abuse history.

Medication effects on Rorschach indices of disordered thinking

Psychiatric colleagues often ask assessment psychologists whether their patients should be tested while off neuroleptic medication. Obviously, the clinical need to prescribe medication for an acutely psychotic and agitated patient supersedes the value of waiting until the person can be scheduled for testing. Nonetheless, just as neuroleptic medication has an effect on reducing positive symptoms, so does it reduce indications of more florid signs of thought disorder on psychological testing (Kleiger & Khadivi, 2015). A number of studies found that Rorschach indices of disordered thinking, as measured by the TDI, decreased over the course of treatment with anti-psychotic medication (Hurt, Holzman, & Davis, 1983; Spohn et al., 1986). The scores associated with severe thought disorder and psychotic distortions of reality were likely to be reduced or eliminated. However, residual, less dramatic indications of thought pathology were found to persist (Spohn et al., 1986; Gold & Hurt, 1990). Finding milder, .25-level instances of cognitive slippage in the records of medicated schizophrenia patients led Spohn to conclude that more severe levels of Rorschach thought disorder were related to the presence of a psychotic state, while milder scores represented trait-like features of the illness of schizophrenia (Holzman, Levy, & Johnston, 2005).

References

Acklin, M. W. (2017). Madness and mayhem, and murder: A comparative Rorschach case study of methamphetamine psychosis and paranoid schizophrenia. In R. E. Erard and F. B. Evans (Eds.), *The Rorschach in Multimethod Forensic Practice*. New York: Routledge.

Addington, J., & Addington, D. (1998). Effect of substance misuse in early psychosis. *The British Journal of Psychiatry, 172* (Suppl. 33), 134–136.

Addington, J., & Heinssen, R. (2012). Prediction and prevention of psychosis in youth at clinical high risk. *Annual Review of Clinical Psychology, 8,* 269–289.

American Psychiatric Association. (1994). *Diagnostic and Statistical Manual of Mental Disorders* (4th ed.). Washington, DC: Author.

American Psychiatric Association. (2013). *Diagnostic and Statistical Manual of Mental Disorders* (5th ed.). Washington, DC: Author.

Andersen, D. B., Vernal, D. L., Bilenberg, N., Væver, M. S., & Stenstrøm, A. D. (2016). Early-onset schizophrenia: Exploring the contributions of the Thought Disorder Index to clinical assessment. *Scandinavian Journal of Child and Adolescent Psychiatry and Psychology, 4,* 23–30.

Andreasen, N. C. (1979a). Thought, language, and communication disorders: I. Clinical assessment, definition of terms, and evaluation of their reliability. *Archives of General Psychiatry, 36,* 1315–1321.

Andreasen, N. C. (1979b). Thought, language, and communication disorders: II. Diagnostic significance. *Archives of General Psychiatry, 36,* 1325–1330.

Andreasen, N. C. (1983). The clinical differentiation of affective and schizophrenic disorders. In M. R. Zales (Ed.), *Affective and Schizophrenic Disorders: New Approaches to Diagnosis and Treatment*. New York: Brunner/Mazel.

Andreasen, N. C., & Akiskal, H. S. (1983). The specificity of Bleulerian and Schneiderian symptoms: A critical reevaluation. *Psychiatric Clinics of North America, 6,* 41–53.

Andreasen, N. C., & Pfohl, B. (1976). Linguistic analysis of speech in affective disorders. *Archives of General Psychiatry, 33,* 1361–1367.

Andreasen, N. C., & Powers, P. S. (1974). Overinclusive thinking in mania and schizophrenia. *British Journal of Psychiatry, 125,* 452–456.

Andreasen, N. C., Tsuang, M. T., & Canter, A. (1974). The significance of conceptual style. *Archives of General Psychiatry, 32*, 70–73.

Auslander, L. A., Perry, W., & Jeste, D. V. (2002). Assessing disturbed thinking and cognition using the Ego Impairment Index in older schizophrenia patients: Paranoid vs. nonparanoid distinction. *Schizophrenia Research, 53*, 199–207.

Barch, D. M., Bustillo, J., Gaebel, W., Gur, R., Heckers, S., Malaspina, D., Owen, M. J., Schultz, S., Tandon, R., Tsuang, M., van Os, J., & Carpenter, W. (2013). Logic and justification for dimensional assessment of symptoms and related clinical phenomena in psychosis: Relevance to DSM-5. *Schizophrenia Research, 150*, 15–20.

Bell, D. S. (1965). Comparison of amphetamine psychosis and schizophrenia. *British Journal of Psychiatry, 111*, 701–707.

Belmæker, R. H., & van Praag, H. M. (Eds.). (1980). *Mania: An Evolving Concept*. New York: Spectrum.

Belyi, B. I. (1991). Interpretation of Rorschach ink blots by patients with delusional forms of schizophrenia. *Zhrunal Nevropatologii i Psikhiatrii, 91*, 97–104.

Benedik, E., Coderl, S., Bon, J., & Smith, B. L. (2013). Differentiation of psychotic from nonpsychotic inpatients: The Rorschach Perceptual Thinking Index. *Journal of Personality Assessment, 95*, 141–148.

Biagiarelli, M., Roma, P., Comparelli, A., Andrados, P., Di Pomponio, I., Corigliano, V., Curto, M., & Ferracuti, S. (2015). Relationship between the Rorschach Perceptual Thinking Index (PTI) and the Positive and Negative Syndrome Scale (PANSS) in psychotic patients: A validity study. *Psychiatry Research, 225*, 315–321.

Bleuler, E. (1911). *Dementia Praecox or the Group of Schizophrenias*. (J. Zinkin, Trans.). New York: International Universities Press, 1950.

Braff, D. L., & Geyer, M. A. (1990). Sensorimotor gating and schizophrenia: Human and animal model studies. *Archives of General Psychiatry, 47*, 181–188.

Braff, D. L., Grillon, C., & Geyer, M. A. (1992). Gating and habituation of the startle reflex in schizophrenic patients. *Archives of General Psychiatry, 49*, 206–215.

Bramness, J. G., Gundersen, Ø. H., Guterstam, J., Rognli, E. B., Konstenius, M., Løberg, E. M., Medhus, S., Tanum, L., & Franck, J. (2012). Amphetamine-induced psychosis—a separate diagnostic entity or primary psychosis triggered in the vulnerable? *BMC Psychiatry*, http://www.biomedcentral.com/1471-244X/12/221.

Cameron, N. (1938). Reasoning, regression and communication in schizophrenics. *Psychological Monographs, 50*, 1–340.

Carpenter, W. T., Strauss, J. S., & Muleh, S. (1973). Are there pathognomonic symptoms in schizophrenia: An empiric investigation of Schneider's first-rank symptoms. *Archives of General Psychiatry, 28*, 847–852.

Carter, M. L. (1986). The assessment of thought deficit in psychotic unipolar depression and chronic paranoid schizophrenia. *Journal of Nervous and Mental Disease, 174*, 336–341.

Chapman, L., & Chapman, J. P. (1987). The search for symptoms predictive of schizophrenia. *Schizophrenia Bulletin, 13*, 497–553.

Chapman, L., & Chapman, J. P. (1988). The genesis of delusions. In T. Oltmanns & B. Maher (Eds.), *Delusional Beliefs*. New York: Wiley.

Chapman, L., Edell, W. S., & Chapman, J. P. (1980). Physical anhedonia, perceptual aberration and psychosis proneness. *Schizophrenia Bulletin, 6*, 639–653.

Coleman, M. J., Levy, D. L., & Lenzenweger, M. F. (1996). Thought disorder, perceptual aberrations, and schizotypy. *Journal of Abnormal Psychology, 105*, 469–473.

Correll, C. U., Penzner, J. B., Frederickson, A. M., Richter, J. J., Auther, A. M., Smith, C. W., Kane, J. M., & Cornblatt, B. A. (2007). Differentiation in the preonset phases of schizophrenia and mood disorders: Evidence in support of a bipolar mania prodrome. *Schizophrenia Bulletin, 33*, 703–714.

Cuesta, M. J., & Peralta, V. (2011). Testing the hypothesis that formal thought disorders are severe mood disorders. *Schizophrenia Bulletin, 37*, 1136–1146.

Deese, J. (1978). Thought into speech. *American Science, 66*, 314–321.

Deese, J. (1980). Pauses, prosody, and the demands of production in language. In H. W. Dechert & M. Raupach (Eds.), *Temporal Variables in Speech: Studies in Honor of Frieda Goldman-Eisler* (pp. 69–84). The Hague: Mouton.

Docherty, N. M., DeRosa, M., & Andreasen, N. C. (1996). Communication disturbances in schizophrenia and mania. *Archives of General Psychiatry, 53*, 358–364.

Donnelly, E. G., Murphy, D. L., & Scott, W. H. (1975). Perception and cognition in patients with bipolar and unipolar depressive disorders. A study in Rorschach responding. *Archives of General Psychiatry, 32*, 1128–1131.

Donnelly, E. F., Waldman, I. N., Murphy, D. L, Wyatt, R., J. & Goodwin, F. K. (1980). Primary affective disorder: Thought disorder in depression. *Journal of Abnormal Psychology, 89*, 315–319.

Dzamonja-Ignjatovic, T., Smith, B. L., Jocic, D., & Milanovic, M. (2013). A comparison of new and revised Rorschach measures of schizophrenic functioning in a Serbian clinical sample. *Journal of Personality Assessment, 95*, 471–478.

Exner, J. E. (1986). Some Rorschach data comparing schizophrenics with borderline and schizotypal personality disorders. *Journal of Personality Assessment, 50*, 455–471.

Exner, J. E. (1993). *The Rorschach: A Comprehensive System, Basic Foundations* (Vol. 1, 3rd ed.). New York: Wiley.

Exner, J. E., & Erdberg, P. (2005). *The Rorschach: A Comprehensive System, Advanced Interpretation* (Vol. 2, 3rd ed.). New York: Wiley.

Fujii, D. E., & Sakai, E. Y. (2007). In C. D. Fujii & I. Ahmed (Eds.), *The Spectrum of Psychotic Disorders* (pp. 382–391). New York: Cambridge University Press.

Gold, J. M., & Hurt, S. W. (1990). The effects of haloperidol on thought disorder and IQ in schizophrenia. *Journal of Personality Assessment, 54*, 390–400.

Gomilla, M. V. (2011). The Rorschach Test in the differential diagnosis of 245 schizophrenic inpatients. *Annuary of Clinical and Health Psychology, 7*, 79–93.

Harris, D., & Batki, S. L. (2000). Stimulant psychosis: Symptom profile and acute clinical course. *The American Journal of Addictions, 9*, 28–37.

Harrow, M., Lanin-Kettering, I., Silverstein, M. L., & Meltzer, H. Y (1982). Thought pathology in manic and schizophrenic patients. *Archives of General Psychiatry, 39*, 665–671.

Harvey, P. D., Earle-Bover, E. A., & Wieglus, M. S. (1984). The consistency of thought disorder in mania and schizophrenia. An assessment of acute psychotics. *Journal of Nervous and Mental Diseases, 172*, 458–463.

Hoffman, R. E., Stopek, S., & Andreasen, N. C. (1986). A comparative study of manic vs. schizophrenic speech disorganization. *Archives of General Psychiatry, 43*, 831–838.

Holzman, P. E., Levy, D. L., & Johnston, M. H. (2005). The use of the Rorschach technique for assessing format thought disorder. In R. F. Bornstein & J.M. Masling (Eds.), *Scoring the Rorschach: Seven Validated Systems*. New York: Routledge.

Holzman, P. E., Shenton, M. E., & Solovay, M. R. (1986). Quality of thought disorder in differential diagnosis. *Schizophrenia Bulletin, 12*, 360–371.

Hurt, S. W., Holzman, P. S., & Davis, J. M. (1983). Thought disorder: The measurement of its changes. *Archives of General Psychiatry, 40*, 1281–1285.

Hussein, O. (2015). From persecution to depression: A case of chronic depression—associating the Rorschach, the TAT, and Winnicott. *Journal of Personality Assessment, 97*, 230–240.

Husted, J. A., Beiser, M., & Iacono, W. G. (1995). Negative symptoms in the course of first-episode affective psychosis. *Psychiatric Research, 56*, 145–154.

Ianzito, B. M., Cadoret, R. J., & Pugh, D. D. (1974). Thought disorder in depression. *American Journal of Psychiatry, 131*, 703–707.

Ilonen, T., Heinimaa, M., Korkeila, J., Svirskis, T., & Salokangas, R. K. R. (2010). Differentiating adolescents at clinical high risk for psychosis from psychotic and non-psychotic patients with the Rorschach. *Psychiatry Research, 179*, 151–156.

Inoue, N., Yorozuya, Y., & Mizuno, M. (2014). Identifying comorbidities of patients at ultra-high risk for psychosis using the Rorschach Comprehensive System. Paper presented at the XXI International Congress of Rorschach and Projective Methods, Istanbul, Turkey.

Jacobs, L., & Hanning III, W. (2007). Methamphetamine. In D. Fujii & I. Ahmed (Eds.), *The Spectrum of Psychotic Disorders* (pp. 392–405). New York: Cambridge University Press.

Jamison, K. R. (1993). *Touched with Fire*. New York: Free Press.

Janowsky, D. S., Leff, M., & Epstein, R. S. (1970). Playing the manic game. *Archives of General Psychiatry, 22*, 252–261.

Janowsky, D. S., & Risch, C. (1979). Amphetamine psychosis and psychotic symptoms. *Psychopharmacology, 65*, 73–77.

Judd, L. L., McAdams, L., Budnick, B., & Braff, D. L. (1992). Sensory gating deficits in schizophrenia: New results. *American Journal of Psychiatry, 149*, 488–493.

Kay, S. R. (1986). Thought deficit in psychotic depression and chronic paranoid schizophrenia: Methodological and conceptual issues. *Journal of Nervous and Mental Disease, 174*, 342–347.

Kay, S. R., Fiszbein, A., & Opler, L. A. (1987). The Positive and Negative Syndrome Scale (PANSS) for schizophrenia. *Schizophrenia Bulletin, 13*, 261–276.

Kennedy, N., Everitt, B., Boydell, J., van Os, J., Jones, P. B., & Murray, R. M. (2005). Incidence and distribution of first-episode mania by age: Results from a 35-year study. *Psychological Medicine, 35*, 855–863.

Khadivi, A., Wetzler, S., & Wilson, A. (1997). Manic indices on the Rorschach. *Journal of Personality Assessment, 69*, 365–375.

Kimhy, D., Corcoran, C., Harkavy-Friedman, J. M., Ritzler, B., Javitt, D. C., & Malaspina, D. (2007). Visual form perception: A comparison of individuals at high risk for psychosis, recent onset schizophrenia and chronic schizophrenia, *Schizophrenia Research, 97*, 25–34.

Kimura, H., Akemi, O., Kawashima, R., Inoue, T., Nakagawa, S., Suzuki, K., Asakura, S., Tanaka, T., Kitaichi, Y., Masui, T., Kitagawa, N., Kako, Y., Abekawa, T., Kusumi, I., Yamanaka, H., Denda, K., & Koyama, T. (2013). Differences between bipolar and unipolar depression on Rorschach testing. *Neuropsychiatric Disease and Treatment, 9*, 619–627.

Kleiger, J. H. (1999). *Disordered Thinking and the Rorschach*. Hillsdale: NJ: The Analytic Press.

Kleiger, J. H. (2015), An open letter to Hermann Rorschach: What has become of your experiment? *Rorschachiana, 36*, 221–241.

Kleiger, J. H., & Khadivi, A. (2015). *Assessing Psychosis. A Clinician's Guide.* New York: Routledge.

Koistinen, P. (1995). *Thought Disorder and the Rorschach.* Oulu: Oulun Yliopistd.

Kraepelin, E. (1921). *Manic-Depressive Insanity and Paranoia.* Edinburgh: E. & S. Livingston.

Kuhs, H. (1991). Depressive delusion. *Psychopathology, 24,* 106–114.

Lacoua, L., Koren, D., & Rothschild-Yakar, L. (2015). Poor awareness of problems in thought and perception and risk indicators of schizophrenia-spectrum disorders. A correlational study of nonpsychotic adolescents in the community. Paper presented at the annual meeting of the Society for Personality Assessment, Brooklyn, NY.

Lipkin, K. M., Dyrud, J., & Meyer, G. G. (1970). The many faces of mania: Therapeutic trial of lithium carbonate. *Archives of General Psychiatry, 22,* 262–267.

Maher, B. A. (1974). Delusional thinking and perceptual disorder. *Journal of Individual Psychology, 30,* 98–113.

Maher, B. A. (1988). Anomalous experience and delusional thinking: The logic of explanations. In T. F. Ottmanns & B. A. Maher (Eds.), *Delusional Beliefs* (pp. 15–33). New York: John Wiley & Sons.

Maher, B. A., & Ross, J. S. (1984). Delusions. In H. E. Adams & P. B. Sutker (Eds.), *Comprehensive Handbook on Psychopathology* (pp. 383–409). New York: Plenum Press.

Mandel, B., Last, U., Belmæker, R. H., & Rosenbaum, M. (1984). Rorschach markers in euthymic manic-depressive illness. *Neuropsychobiology, 12,* 96–100.

Manschreck, T. C. (1979). The assessment of paranoid features. *Comprehensive Psychiatry, 20,* 370–377.

Manschreck, T. C. (1995). Pathogenesis of delusion. *The Psychiatric Clinics of North America, 18,* 213–229.

Manschreck, T. C. (2007). Delusional Disorder. In D. Fujii & I. Ahmed (Eds.), *The Spectrum of Psychotic Disorders* (pp. 116–133). New York: Cambridge University Press.

McGhie, A., & Chapman, J. (1961). Disorders of attention and perception in early schizophrenia. *British Journal of Medical Psychology, 34,* 103–116.

McGlashan, T. H., Walsh, B., & Woods, S. (2010). *The Psychosis-Risk Syndrome: Handbook for Diagnosis and Follow-up.* New York: Oxford University Press.

McGorry, P. D., Yung, A., & Phillips, L. (2001). Ethics and early intervention in psychosis: Keeping up the pace and staying in step. *Schizophrenia Research, 51,* 17–29.

Meehl, P. E. (1962). Schizotaxia, schizotypy, schizophrenia. *American Psychologist, 17,* 827–838.

Meissner, W. W. (1981). The schizophrenic and paranoid process. *Schizophrenia Bulletin, 7,* 611–631.

Mihura, J. L., Meyer, G. J., Dumitrascu, N., & Bombel, G. (2013). The validity of individual Rorschach variables: Systematic reviews and meta-analyses of the comprehensive system. *Psychological Bulletin, 139,* 548–605.

Morrison, J. R., & Flanagan, T. A. (1978). Diagnostic errors in psychiatry. *Comprehensive Psychiatry, 19,* 109–117.

Nims, J. P. (1959). Logical reasoning in schizophrenia: The von Domarus Principle. Unpublished doctoral dissertation, University of Southern California, Los Angeles.

Núñez Domínguez, L. A. (2007). Cannabis-induced psychosis. In D. Fujii & I. Ahmed (Eds.), *The Spectrum of Psychotic Disorders* (pp. 369–381). New York: Cambridge University Press.

Ohayon, M. M., & Schatzberg, A. F. (2002). Prevalence of depressive episodes with psychotic features in the general population. *American Journal of Psychiatry, 151*, 1855–1861.

Oltmanns, T. E, Murphy, R., Berenbaum, H., & Dunlop, S. R. (1985). Rating verbal communication impairment in schizophrenia and affective disorders. *Schizophrenia Bulletin, 11*, 292–299.

Osher, Y., Mandel, B., Shapiro, E., & Belmæker, R. H. (2000). Rorschach markers in offspring of manic-depressive patients. *Journal of Affective Disorders, 59*, 231–236.

Paris, J. (2013). *The Intelligent Clinician's Guide to the DSM-5*. New York: Oxford University Press.

Payne, R. W., Mattusek, P., & George, E. I. (1959). An experimental study of schizophrenic thought disorder. *Journal of Mental Science, 105*, 627–652.

Perry, W., & Braff, D. L. (1994). Information-processing deficits and thought disorder in schizophrenia. *American Journal of Psychiatry, 151*, 363–367.

Perry, W., Minassian, A., Cadenhead, K., Sprock, J., & Braff, D. (2003). The use of the Ego Impairment Index across the schizophrenia spectrum. *Journal of Personality Assessment, 80*, 50–57.

Pope, H. G., & Lipinski, J. F. (1978). Diagnosis in schizophrenia and manic-depressive illness: A reassessment of the specificity of "schizophrenic" symptoms in light of current research. *Archives of General Psychiatry, 35*, 811–828.

Rapaport, D., Gill, M., & Schafer, R. (1968). *Diagnostic Psychological Testing* (Rev. ed.). R. R. Holt, Ed. New York: International Universities Press. (Original work published in 1946.)

Regier, D. A., Farmer, M. E., Rae, D. S., Locke, B. Z., Keith, S. J., & Judd, L. L. (1990). Comorbidity of mental disorders with alcohol and other drug abuse: Results from the Epidemiological Catchment Area (ECS) Study. *Journal of the American Medical Association, 264*, 2511–2518.

Reininghaus, U., Priebe, S., & Bentall, R. P. (2013). Testing the psychopathology of psychosis: Evidence for a general psychosis dimension. *Schizophrenia Bulletin, 39*, 884–895.

Rosenthal, R. N., & Miner, C. R. (1997). Differential diagnosis of substance-induced psychosis and schizophrenia in patients with substance use disorders. *Schizophrenia Bulletin, 23*, 187–193.

Savard, R. J., Rey, A. C., & Post, R. M. (1980). Thinking in depression. *Archives of General Psychiatry, 4*, 456–459.

Schachtel, E. (1966). *Experiential Foundations of the Rorschach Test*. New York: Basic Books.

Schafer, R. (1948). *The Clinical Application of Psychological Tests*. New York: International Universities Press.

Schafer, R. (1954). *Psychoanalytic Interpretation in Rorschach Testing*. New York: Grune & Stratton.

Shakow, D. (1950). Some psychological features of schizophrenia. In M. L. Reyment (Ed.), *Feelings and Emotions* (pp. 383–390). New York: McGraw-Hill.

Shakow, D. (1962). Segmental set: A theory of the formal psychological deficit in schizophrenia. *Archives of General Psychiatry, 14*, 79–83.

Shenton, M. E., Solovay, M. R., & Holzman, P. (1987). Comparative studies of thought disorders: II. Schizoaffective disorder. *Archives of General Psychiatry, 44*, 21–30.

Shenton, M.E., Solovay, M. R., & Holzman, P. (1989). Thought disorder in the relatives of psychotic patients. *Archives of General Psychiatry, 46*, 897–901.

Shrivastava, A., McGorry, P. D., Tsuang, M., Woods, S. W., Cornblatt, B. A., Corcoran, C., & Carpenter, W. (2011). Attenuated psychosis symptoms syndrome as a risk syndrome of psychosis, diagnosis in DSM-V: The debate. *Indiana Journal of Psychiatry, 53*, 57–65.

Silberman, E. K., Weingartner, H., & Post, R. M. (1983). Thinking disorder in depression. *Archives of General Psychiatry, 40*, 775–780.

Singer, H. K., & Brabender, V. (1993). The use of the Rorschach to differentiate unipolar and bipolar disorders. *Journal of Personality Assessment, 60*, 333–345.

Smith, E. G., Burke, P. R., Grogan, J. E., Fratoni, S. E., Wogsland, C. S., & Rothschild, A. J. (2007). Psychosis in major depression. In D. Fujii & I. Ahmed (Eds.), *The Spectrum of Psychotic Disorders* (pp. 156–194). New York: Cambridge University Press.

Solovay, M. R., Shenton, M. E., & Holzman, P. S. (1987). Comparative studies of thought disorders: I. Mania and schizophrenia. *Archives of General Psychiatry, 44*, 13–20.

Spohn, H. E., Coyne, L., Larson, J., Mittleman, F., Spray, J., & Hayes, K. (1986). Episodic and residual thought pathology in chronic schizophrenics: Effect of neuroleptics. *Schizophrenia Bulletin, 12*, 394–407.

Sprock, J., Braff, D. L., Saccuzzo, D. P., & Atkinson, J. H. (1983). The relationship of depression and thought disorder in pain patients. *British Journal of Medical Psychology, 56*, 351–360.

Venables, P. H. (1960). The effect of auditory and visual stimulation on the skin potential response of schizophrenics. *Brain, 83*, 77–92.

Weiner, I. B. (1966). *Psychodiagnosis in Schizophrenia*. New York: Wiley.

Williams, E. B. (1964). Deductive reasoning in schizophrenia. *Journal of Abnormal Social Psychology, 69*, 47–61.

Winokur, G., Clayton, P., & Reich, T. (1969). *Manic Depressive Illness*. St. Louis, MO: C. V. Mosby.

Wood, J. M., Nezworski, M. T., Lilienfeld, S. O., & Garb, H. N. (2003). *What Is Wrong with the Rorschach? Science Confronts the Controversial Inkblot Test*. New York: Wiley & Sons.

Wykes, T., & Leff, J. (1982). Disordered speech: Difference between manics and schizophrenics. *Brain and Language, 15*, 117–124.

Yui, K., Ikemoto, S., Ishiguro, T., & Gooto, K. (2000). Studies of amphetamine or methamphetamine psychosis in Japan: Relation of methamphetamine psychosis to schizophrenia. *Annals of New York Academy of Science, 914*, 1–12.

Yung, A. R., Phillips, L. J., McGorry, P. D., McFarlane, C.A., Francey, S., Harrigan, S., Patton, G.C., & Jackson, H. J. (1998). Prediction of psychosis. A step towards indicated prevention of schizophrenia. *British Journal of Psychiatry, 172* (Suppl. 33), 14–20.

Yung, A. R., & McGorry, P. D. (2007). Prediction of psychosis: Setting the stage. *British Journal of Psychiatry, 191* (Suppl. 51), 1–8.

Chapter 14

Secondary psychotic phenomena and the Rorschach

The widening scope of symptom dimensions and continua of severity means that various indications of psychosis, including disturbances in thinking, can be found in patients who are not presenting with primary or substance-induced psychosis. Our interest in Rorschach manifestations of disordered thinking includes a review of characteristics of disorganized, illogical, and impoverished thinking in those typically nonpsychotic disorders whose clinical features might, on occasion, approach or enter a psychotic realm.

Beginning with disordered thinking in borderline personality organization, a broader category than the contemporary DSM definition of Borderline Personality Disorder (BPD), I review relevant Rorschach characteristics of trauma and dissociative disorders, which are among the clinical syndromes that may share features of psychotic-like phenomena and disordered thinking. Finally, I discuss the psychotic features and disordered forms of thought that one might encounter in individuals with severe Obsessive–Compulsive-spectrum disorders.

Borderline disorders

The title of Cauwels's 1992 book, *Imbroglio*, captures the complex and sometimes confusing concept of borderline personality. Despite the decades of controversy and the countless volumes written to sharpen the concept, there still does not exist unanimous agreement of just what the borderline concept "borders" on or between. The most salient confusion is whether borderline refers to a discrete personality disorder (i.e. BPD) or to an overarching level of personality functioning (i.e. borderline personality organization). The former is a narrower clinical phenomenon coming from a tradition of descriptive psychiatry (Grinker, Werble, & Drye, 1968; Gunderson & Singer, 1975; Gunderson, 1977, 1984) and formally recognized as a "personality disorder" since the advent of the DSM-III (American Psychiatric Association, 1980). The latter concept, which subsumes the former, originated from the psychoanalytic literature grounded in the theories of ego psychology and object relations (Knight, 1953; Kernberg, 1967).

Psychosis, disordered thinking, and borderline psychopathology

Regardless of which tradition one favors, all definitions of borderline disorders include some mention of the propensity for psychotic, or primary process, thinking. Knight (1953) described "ego weaknesses" in normal-appearing patients undergoing transient psychotic episodes. Knight suggested that the borderline patient could demonstrate a spectrum of thought pathology ranging from subtle peculiarities of expression to fully autistic thought content. Knight wrote, "Occasional blocking, peculiarities of word usage, obliviousness to obvious implications, contaminations of idioms, arbitrary inferences, inappropriate affect, and suspicion-laden behavior and questions are a few possible examples of such unwitting betrayals of ego impairment of psychotic degree" (p. 103).

Kernberg (1967) developed his seminal theory of borderline personality organization while at Menninger, a decade after Knight introduced the concept and two decades after Rapaport, Gill, and Schafer (1946/1968) introduced the concept of the diagnostic testing battery. Kernberg considered projective testing an important method for identifying primary process thinking and weakening of reality testing in patients with borderline structures. He downplayed the presence of a formal thought disorder in these patients and stated that reality testing, though usually intact, may weaken under the press of heightened emotionality, alcohol or drugs, or in the throes of a psychotic transference. Both borderline and psychotic patients are vulnerable to psychotic transferences. But, according to Kernberg, lapses in reality testing for the borderline individual tend to be circumscribed to the treatment setting and do not generally affect the patient's functioning outside of treatment.

Stone (1980) described "soft signs" of disordered thinking characteristic of borderline patients. Whereas the psychotic patient may have delusions, the borderline may have "overvalued ideas" and magical thinking. Stone included among these soft signs such phenomena as heightened superstitiousness, vague or murky speech, attention to irrelevancies, rigid attitudes, tangentiality, and circumstantiality. Episodic depersonalization and derealization, psychotic transference reactions, distorted perceptions of others, and brief paranoid experience were the most common experiences in inpatient and outpatient borderlines. For example, Chopra and Beatson (1986) found that all of their inpatient borderline subjects had some type of brief psychotic experience, and at least 77 percent of their borderline patients had brief paranoid or other psychotic experiences and/or symptoms of depersonalization and derealization. On the other hand, only 53 percent reported transient auditory or visual hallucinations.

Gunderson (1984) viewed the tendency toward psychotic thinking as a chief characteristic of BPD. He stressed that the psychotic symptoms in borderline patients were typically ego dystonic and mild, characterized by paranoid ideation, psychotic-like reactions to drugs, depersonalization, or derealization. Brief psychotic-like reactions was finally added as criterion for BPD in the DSM-IV

(American Psychiatric Association, 1994) in the form of "transient stress related paranoid ideation or dissociative symptoms." Gunderson characterized the phenomenology of psychotic reactions in borderline patients by describing five qualities of experience: (1) affective phenomena; (2) disturbances in the sense of reality; (3) audio-visual perceptual distortions; (4) paranoid beliefs; and (5) self-boundary confusion. Affective phenomena involve unrealistic preoccupations with inner badness, worthlessness, or sinfulness reaching delusional proportions. Disturbances in one's sense of reality include signs and symptoms of derealization and depersonalization characterized by out-of-body experiences and perceptual changes in the size and shape of one's body. Roughly 75 percent reported dissociative experiences and paranoid ideas (Zanarini, Gunderson, & Frankenburg, 1990).

Auditory and visual pseudoperceptions may or may not involve actual hallucinatory experience. Usually the patient experiences transitory perceptual distortions that are brief and unelaborated. Examples might include hearing sound or hearing one's name called. However, one study found that 29 percent of a borderline sample reported auditory hallucinations that were distressing and had persisted since childhood (Yee et al., 2005).

Borderline-level paranoid beliefs include ideas of reference, around which some reality testing is maintained. For example, the patient may believe that he is being talked about but then reminds himself that this is probably his imagination. Finally, self-boundary confusion essentially involves a type of boundary impairment associated with a certain level of reality testing difficulty—in particular, the failure to distinguish "inner from outer." While maintaining a sense of separateness from the other and an accurate perception of the external world, the borderline patient may confuse his thoughts with those belonging to the other.

Gunderson described conditions under which borderline patients are most vulnerable to brief psychotic decompensation. These are characterized chiefly by threats to important primary object ties. He further indicated that regressive shifts in thinking reflect the emergence of primary process thinking, overelaborate affects, and a breakdown in reality testing.

Rorschach thought disorder and the borderline psychopathology

Early studies of borderline psychopathology and the Rorschach were confounded by a lack of conceptual clarity regarding the differences between "borderline schizophrenia" and borderline personality organization (Kleiger, 1999). Rapaport et al. (1946/1968) did not use the term borderline to describe their group of 33 "preschizophrenic" patients, who in some ways presaged the contemporary bifurcation of the borderline concept into separate borderline and schizotypal personalities. Referring to their sample of "preschizophrenics," Rapaport et al. identified one subtype as an "overideational" group and the other as a "coarctated" one. The overideational preschizophrenics demonstrated an "enormous wealth of fantasy, obsessive ideation, and preoccupation with themselves and their bodies" (p. 436). Their responses were frequently characterized by a tendency to embellish their ideas with vivid affective elaboration, to combine their associations, and to use odd language. The coarctated preschizophrenics, on the other hand, tended to respond to the inkblots in a more constricted, impoverished manner, giving odd responses that reflected a sense of alienation. The responses were delivered in a flat, dull manner, often revealing form level that was characteristically poor. Today, we would view this latter group as belonging more to the schizophrenia than borderline spectrum of psychopathology.

Several excellent reviews of Rorschach characteristics of borderline personality or organization have highlighted a number of findings in the literature (Blais & Bistis, 2004; Mihura, 2006). These include studies that have focused on (1) the "good Wechsler/bad Rorschach" paradigm; (2) the presence of mild to moderate levels of thought and FQ disturbances; (3) the qualitative nature of thought disturbances and boundary disturbances; and (4) the thematic content in borderline Rorschachs.

Good Wechsler/bad Rorschach

The first of these research trends involved comparisons between the Wechsler and Rorschach, the so-called "good WAIS/bad Rorschach" hypothesis best represented in the work of Singer (1977), who asserted that an adequate performance on the WAIS, together with a Rorschach characterized by "highly elaborated, idiosyncratic associative content and peculiar reasoning ... is almost axiomatic that a borderline diagnosis should follow" (p. 194). Despite differences in the literature, some general conservative conclusions seem warranted. First, it is reasonable to say that borderline-level individuals will probably struggle more with the ambiguity of the Rorschach than with the familiarity and conventionality of the Wechsler tests. As such, their Rorschachs will reveal more signs of disordered thinking than will their responses on the Wechsler. However, as noted by Blais and Bistis (2004), the magnitude of these findings varies according to which groups the borderline subjects are being compared. While borderline individuals may produce fewer signs of disordered thinking on the WAIS compared to psychotic patients, their WAIS scores do not differ in the degree of thought disturbance from other patients with personality disorders. Furthermore, the assumption that their Wechslers should be intact, "clean," and free of signs of disturbed thinking is questionable. As Berg (1984) observed, the WAIS tests of borderline patients may be "speckled with lapses in logical thinking" (p. 123), especially on tasks that require more extensive use of language and verbal reasoning such as the Comprehension and Similarities subtests. Most important, what this simplistic hypothesis overlooks are the intriguing qualitative differences in the nature of thought disorder profiles between psychotic and borderline patients.

Mild–moderate disturbances in FQ and thinking

Another commonly accepted finding is that borderline individuals produce mild to moderate thought-disordered responses and obtain form-level scores that are lower than nonpatients but higher than psychotic individuals. Blais and Bistis (2004) and Mihura (2006) reviewed studies showing moderate X+ and F+% responses of borderline subjects (.65 to .70) and a greater frequency of Fu than F– responses (Singer & Larson, 1981; Steiner et al., 1984; Exner, 1986).

Regarding levels of thought disorder, Rapaport stated that overideational preschizophrenic patients produced more moderate signs of disturbed thinking compared to patients with schizophrenia (Rapaport et al., 1946/1968). Later studies used both the TDI and the old SCZI from the CS and found that borderline subjects had fewer severe 1.0-level scores on the TDI (Harris, 1993) and lower scores on the SCZI than psychotic subjects. Hilsenroth, Fowler, and Pawader (1998) also determined that the mean SCZI for borderline patients was 3.0, significantly lower than the mean of 4.5 in patients with psychosis. Furthermore, psychotic patients were more likely to meet all six of the SCZI criteria than were borderline individuals. Since the SCZI is no longer part of the CS, its relevance to this discussion is somewhat outdated. However, the PTI has been shown to be highly correlated with the SCZI (Hilsenroth et al., 2007). Thus, based on research findings, it is reasonable to look for milder levels of thought disturbance (Level 1> Level 2), moderate FQ–%, and FQu>FQ– in the records of borderline patients (Blais & Bistis, 2004).

Borderline-level thought disorder scores

Another line of research concerns empirical findings regarding formal Rorschach variables associated with borderline-level thought disorder (in particular form-level and specific thought disorder scores). Disordered thinking in borderline protocols is generally less severe than that in psychotic patients. Beginning with Rapaport, most researchers have found fabulized combinations and confabulations to be the most typical of these moderate-level scores. Singer (1977) emphasized the borderline's tendency to embellish ideas with affect or overly specific attributions and to combine images based on proximal contiguity. However, there has been some disagreement regarding whether combinatory or confabulatory thinking is most characteristic of thought disorder on the borderline Rorschach.

Some studies have emphasized that FABCOMs are the hallmark of the borderline Rorschach (Larson, 1974; Gunderson & Singer, 1975; Singer, 1977; Singer & Larson, 1981; Patrick and Wolfe, 1983). Rapaport et al. (1946/1968) indicated that "overideational preschizophrenic" subjects had a greater number of fabulized responses and FABCOMs than confabulations. Other groups of researchers found that their borderline samples were distinguished by varying degrees of confabulatory thinking (Lerner, Sugarman, & Barbour, 1985; Wilson, 1985). To be more specific, Wilson (1985) demonstrated that his borderline subjects (DSM-III BPD and schizotypals) had higher confabulation tendency scores, as well as higher Fabulized Combination Benign scores than his neurotic and psychotic groups. At the same time, Lerner, Sugarman, & Barbour (1985) found that inpatient borderlines (DSM-III BPD and schizotypal personality disorders) gave more confabulations than neurotics, outpatient borderlines (not operationally defined), or schizophrenic subjects.

Based on their research, Lerner, Sugarman, & Barbour (1985) and Sugarman (1986) theorized that confabulation scores reflect a borderline-level structural impairment in the formation of the "inner/outer" boundary. Furthermore, Lerner and Sugarman reasoned that borderline individuals do not fully recognize the inkblots as having an existence separate from themselves. Sugarman suggested that borderlines tend to shape external reality according to their inner needs and relational paradigms. Thus, both Lerner and Sugarman viewed borderline-level ego disturbances as indicative of a developmental arrest at the level of transitional objects, and that patients giving confabulations are treating the inkblots as transitional phenomena, investing them with attributes coming from themselves.

In writing about the phenomenology of borderline experience, Cauwels (1992) quoted a borderline patient who spoke about her tendency to *perceive* accurately but *misinterpret* what she perceives:

> People say I distort a lot, and one of my major problems is hypersensitivity. But I know that a lot of what I pick up on is true. My interpretation of it and reaction to it may be off, but my initial perception is accurate ... Now what I might do is think that someone's anger, for instance, is caused by me. My perception of the anger is true, but my interpretation of it is a distortion (p. 78).

Additional research on social cognition and borderline personality has found that borderline individuals may make incorrect social attributions, which they hold with higher levels of confidence than control subjects (Shilling et al., 2012). This combination of reasonably accurate perception together with misinterpretation—or overly subjective or inferential judgment—seems to capture the borderline tendency to combine accurate (or unusual) form with moderate degrees of confabulatory thinking. According to Blais and Bistis (2004), scoring categories will typically include Level 1 INCOMs, FABCOMs, and DRs. Likewise, borderline individuals' perception of reality will not be significantly impaired; however, they are prone to misinterpret, or, more specifically, overinterpret what they do perceive.

Borderline thematic content

The final line of investigation has looked at qualitative aspects of responses in the Rorschachs of borderline individuals. Certain kinds of response content not only reflect the intrusion of primary process material but also, I believe, help distinguish certain formal scores (e.g. combinatory and confabulatory responses) in borderlines from those that occur in other types of disorders. For example, affect-laden fantasies reflecting themes of malevolence, aggression, loss, reunion, or merger may characterize some of the responses of borderline patients. Themes cluster into two primary content categories relevant to the dynamics of borderline functioning: malevolence/aggression and symbiosis/separation. Whether these themes are reflected in the content of an ordinary or fabulized response, a FABCOM, or a confabulation, borderline patients have an uncanny way of focusing their attention on primitive affect-laden psychological issues.

Several investigators have found greater malevolence in the test imagery of borderline subjects compared to other groups of patients (Lerner & St. Peter, 1984; Stuart et al., 1990; Westen et al., 1990; Nigg et al., 1992). Lerner and St. Peter found that borderlines produced more malevolent human representations than did schizophrenia subjects. Stuart et al. reported similar findings in their group of borderline subjects, who produced more malevolent figures than did subjects with major depression and normal controls. According to their findings, borderlines also perceive human action as more highly motivated than do either depressives or normal subjects. Stuart and her colleagues (1990) gave the following examples of highly motivated malevolent activity that occurred within the context of either a combinatory or confabulatory response:

> These are two people that are half male and half female, and they're mixing a potion in a large bowl. Looks like it might be some kind of evil ritual. Their hearts are exposed (p. 313).

> These two pieces here [look like] you know, like in Casper the Ghost? These look like the bad guys that are trying to get [Casper] to do mean things (pp. 313–314).

Another typical aggressive, fabulized response (and INCOM) of borderline-level severity can be seen in a common response to Card X: "Angry insects, yelling at each other."

Researchers have found similar phenomena in other tests with borderline subjects. For example, Westen et al. (1990) used the TAT to demonstrate that borderlines construct more malevolently toned relational paradigms than do major depressives. Nigg et al. (1992) used the Early Memories test to show that borderline patients represent early care-giving figures more malevolently, sadistically, and as having been unhelpful. Consistent with this hypothesis, other studies have demonstrated that borderline individuals attribute negative and malevolent qualities to human figures (Barnow et al., 2010).

Regarding themes of symbiosis and separation, Kwawer (1980) developed a Rorschach scale to assess borderline interpersonal relations and found that borderline subjects gave at least one response that symbolized symbiotic relatedness and difficulties in separating and differentiating from a primary object. Included among his scoring categories were responses reflecting themes of engulfment;

symbiotic merging; violent symbiosis, separation, and reunion; malignant internal processes, including primitive incorporation; birth and rebirth; metamorphosis and transformation; narcissistic mirroring; separation–division; boundary disturbance; and womb imagery.

Using her developmental object relations scale, Coonerty (1986) found that borderline subjects produced significantly more responses indicative of separation–individuation concerns than did a sample of schizophrenic subjects, whose concerns reflected pre-separation issues. Practicing subphase phenomena (Mahler, Pine, & Bergman, 1975) were characterized by responses that reflected narcissistic mirroring, pairing, and omnipotence or insignificance. In contrast, rapprochement-level responses reflected themes of figures who were enmeshed, stuck, and unable to separate. Figures could be depicted as having unstable form or affect and were seen as struggling either to come together or separate, with resulting damage to one or both. Consistent with Mahler's theory of separation–individuation, Coonerty found that her borderline subjects were rated higher on both the practicing (narcissism) and rapprochement scales of her instrument than were the schizophrenic subjects.

Researchers have correlated specific Rorschach scales having to do with unmodulated aggression and undifferentiated self–other paradigms with core factors of DSM-IV BPD (Blais, Hilsenroth, & Castlebury, 1997; Blais et al., 1999). Among those measures that were most highly correlated with BPD were Holt's Level 1 Aggression Scale (Holt, 1977, 2009) and Urist's Mutuality of Autonomy Scale (1977). Compared to other personality disorders, BPD patients showed greater disruptions in Rorschach object relations scales (more malevolent engulfment and destruction) and the presence of primitive aggressive imagery.

Differential diagnosis

The borderline concept has been regarded as a fickle one, viewed and defined differently by different experts. As with efforts to categorize other complex phenomena, the borderline concept has lent itself to "lumping" and "splitting" approaches. We have seen how some have strived to construct broad categories that lump together seemingly heterogeneous disorders into a borderline realm of functioning, while others have sought to split up this heterogeneity and limit the construct only to a narrow range of individuals. Regardless of whether one prefers to be a borderline "lumper" or "splitter," these conceptual difficulties become especially apparent when one is using the Rorschach to assess so-called borderline phenomena.

One of the persistent difficulties has to do with the relationship between borderline disorders and related diagnostic syndromes. Regardless of whether one employs the narrow or broad definition of "borderline," the issue of comorbidity makes differential diagnosis especially challenging. In terms of Rorschach indices of disordered thinking, how can we be sure whether the patient's combinatory, confabulatory, aggressively tinged, charged, or symbiotic responses reflect a primary borderline personality disturbance and not a bipolar-spectrum disorder, a schizotypal personality, or the psychic imprint of chronic trauma?

Trauma and dissociation

Psychological trauma has a profound effect on the structure and content of the survivor's internal world, leading to acute and, in some cases, chronic, deformations in character development, cognitive functioning, affect tolerance, reality testing, self-experience, and object relational paradigms. Additionally, hallucinatory experiences and psychotic-like thinking have long been described in traumatized people who were clinically normal prior to their traumatic experiences (Weisath, 1989). Regarding the impact of trauma, the nexus between early, severe trauma and the development of psychotic phenomena has attracted a great deal of interest, as researchers have begun to interpret dimensions of psychosis as a spectrum of responses to early traumatic experiences (Read et al., 2005; Larkin & Morrison, 2006).

Rorschach studies of trauma

The Rorschach has been described as an ideal trigger for traumatic memories and feelings (van der Kolk & Ducey, 1989; Carlson & Armstrong, 1994). Stated eloquently by Kaser-Boyd and Evans, "The abstract images, coupled with dark and vibrant colors, call out images of danger and harm in individuals who experienced trauma and evoke the subjective experience of trauma" (2008, p. 255). An array of studies and reviews of heterogeneous survivors of childhood, combat, and other forms of adult trauma has amassed a constellation of Rorschach variables that operationally define the signs and symptoms of post-traumatic responses, including diagnosable PTSD (Carr, 1984; van der Kolk & Ducey, 1989; Armstrong & Lowenstein, 1990; Cerney, 1990; Hartman et al. 1990; Armstrong, 1991; Kaser-Boyd, 1993; Levin, 1993; Briere, 1997; Kaiser-Boyd & Evans, 2008; Viglione, Towns, & Lindshield, 2012). Based on aggregate research findings, Viglione and associates (2012) presented five interpretive categories: (1) cognitive constriction; (2) trauma-related imagery; (3) trauma-related cognitive disturbances; (4) stress response; and (5) dissociation. Although each is important, the first three are most pertinent to our interests in psychotic phenomena and disordered thinking in the Rorschachs of trauma patients.

Cognitive constriction—reflecting efforts to control, simplify, and narrow one's perceptual focus and thinking—represents the signs of traumatic avoidance characteristic of one phase of PTSD. Viglione described forms of constriction seen on the Rorschach as structurally and thematically "impoverished" (Viglione, Towns, & Lindshield, 2012). Among the Rorschach indications of impoverishment, one expects fewer responses, a higher F% (Lambda in the CS), a lower number of blends, reduced organizational activity, and repetitive, possibly perseverated, content focusing on animals and animal details. As discussed in Chapter 11, signs of impoverishment on the Rorschach may or may not represent the negative dimension of psychosis or, more specifically, manifestations of negative thought disorder. Referring to these signs of impoverishment as "negative symptoms of PTSD" (e.g. numbing, withdrawal, emotional constriction), Kaser-Boyd and Evans (2008, p. 260) drew attention to how one might mistakenly interpret cognitive constriction on the Rorschach as negative signs of psychosis.

Trauma-related imagery and cognitive disturbances include content and formal variables. Trauma imagery is best represented by the Trauma Content Index (TCI; Armstrong & Loewenstein, 1990) or the somewhat broader Critical Contents variable found in the EII and R-PAS (Perry & Viglione, 1991; Viglione et al., 2011). Of course, trauma-related cognitive disturbances are reflected by elevations on scoring variables and indices representing problems in reality testing, disorganization, and illogicality. The combination of thematic and formal variables may represent the traumatic flooding phase of post-traumatic conditions, possibly thought of as "positive symptoms" of PTSD. Reviews of literature support the presence of disturbances in reality testing and thinking (Kleiger, 1999; Kaser-Boyd & Evans, 2008; Viglione, Towns, & Lindshield, 2012). As noted above, the concurrence of such positive signs of trauma on responses containing critical contents or trauma imagery might represent encapsulated psychotic-like phenomena on the Rorschach.

Traumatic thought disorder

Armstrong (1994b) introduced the term "traumatic thought disorder" (TTD) to describe the unique sort of confabulatory responses produced by traumatized patients. She defined TTD as a dynamic, state-dependent phenomenon triggered by the traumatic stimulus. Most characteristic of this process is its affectively driven loss of distance, or flooding, as the subject becomes immersed in the blot characteristics and the response that follows. According to Armstrong, the response itself can be disorganized and perseverative and can have the quality of an encapsulated traumatic reaction. There is typically a striking loss of reality testing as the intensity of the imagery triggered by the inkblot overshadows the subject's critical capacity to perceive reality accurately. Graphic and primitive imagery tinged with aggression, sadism, and sexual–anatomical violence reminiscent of Holt's Level 1 Aggression scales may color the patient's confabulatory immersion in the blot.

It is useful to note that such confabulatory-DR immersions in trauma survivors may reflect a loss of interpretation awareness. Because the inkblots might serve as triggers for trauma-related imagery (which the subject has possibly controlled or avoided until seeing the blots), responses of trauma patients may lose the "as if," representative characteristic of the typical response process. Trauma researchers reject the traditional explanation that the primitive imagery and extreme loss of distance represented in these responses reflect the "breakthrough of primary process" material or signal the presence of a borderline-level thought disorder or, worse, an incipient psychotic regression. Instead, researchers like Armstrong, Levin, Briere, and van der Kolk view such responses as unmetabolized reexperiencing of the traumatic event. According to Carlson and Armstrong (1994), the Rorschach ceases to be a projective test and instead becomes a trigger for reliving the trauma. van der Kolk argued that trauma survivors lose the capacity to represent traumatic experiences symbolically and instead express graphic unfiltered images of trauma concretely on the Rorschach. Thus, according to Armstrong (1994b), the TTD, with its trauma-laden confabulatory quality that contains self-reference and graphically primitive imagery, is almost seen as a Rorschach equivalent of a flashback experience.

The following examples from traumatized patients illustrate the convergence of FQ-, DR-Confabulation, and trauma-related imagery in a single response. The first patient, Ms. C., a survivor of severe childhood incest, was diagnosed with severe complex PTSD and a dissociative disorder. She was evaluated on an inpatient unit after she had cut herself so badly that she required more than 120 stitches.

> Card II: "The first thing I see is my art which tends to be black and covered in blood!" [Inquiry] "That's what I did before; I cut myself and had a black marker which I wrote with. I cut myself and covered the black with blood."

The second patient, Mr. K., was a combat veteran presented by Kaser-Boyd and Evans (2008). He had described horrific images of combat with mutilated bodies, torn apart by high-caliber weapons.

> Card VII: "This looks sort of like a face. Like the skin area around, exactly what it would look like if they peeled off the skin, except they didn't take off the nose which would be here in the empty space) and that would be the beard. The skin of the face, peeled open. Here the ears would go and the eyes, but they just took the skin off." (Kaser-Boyd & Evans, 2008, p. 270)

Combinatory thinking in trauma records

In her study of a heterogeneous group of adult trauma survivors, Levin (1993) found an increased number of FABCOM2 responses among her samples. In an effort to explain this finding, Levin and Reis (1996) suggested that combinatory responses may be a metaphor for the incongruity of the survivor's traumatic experiences. For example, the response "a foot sticking out of the ground" is combinatory but, according to the traumatologist's argument, may represent an implausibility of the survivor's experience captured by an actual witnessing of a scene of violence and death. On a more symbolic level, the combinatory response such as "looks like a weasel climbing on a butterfly" is probably less reflective of a literal trauma experience and more indicative of a sadomasochistic relational paradigm, perhaps itself the product of some sort of interpersonal trauma bonding.

Levin and Reis also compared the frequency of FABCOMs among groups of "pure trauma" adults, combat veterans, and patients suffering from dissociative disorders. The descriptive statistics showed little difference in mean number of FABCOMs, with the dissociative group giving an average of .40 compared with the two trauma groups, which averaged between .52 and .56. Although substantially greater than the adult nonpatient mean of .17, the FABCOM averages of these trauma-related groups were smaller than those of Exner's (1986) BPD (.62) and schizotypal (.79) groups and roughly equivalent to the mean of his depressed inpatients (.52).

Levin also noted the increased number of perseveration responses (PSV) among her adult trauma survivors. Together with a positive HVI (Exner, 1993) and graphic depiction of traumatic content, Levin understood elevations in perseveration scores as a composite of variables that depict the survivor's psychological guardedness and preoccupation with repetitive traumatic themes.

Rorschach studies of dissociative disorders

Closely related to trauma, dissociative disorders have also received special attention in the Rorschach literature (Wagner & Heise, 1974; Lovitt & Lefkof, 1985; Armstrong & Loewenstein, 1990; Armstrong, 1991, 1994a; Scroppo et al., 1997; Brand, Armstrong, & Loewenstein, 2006; Brand et al., 2009). Most thoroughly represented by the work of Armstrong and Brand, dissociative patients (dissociative disorders/MPD) have been shown to have distinctive Rorschach profiles similar to but also different from those of other trauma groups. According to Armstrong (1991), dissociative disorders/MPD subjects gave at least one developmentally advanced human movement response (M+). Although their overall good form-level percentage (X+%) was not significantly different from that found in schizophrenic samples, the dissociative disorders/MPD group produced more unusual (Xu) responses than severely distorted ones (X-). Furthermore, they gave extremely high numbers of responses with aggressive, anatomical, blood, morbid, or sexual content. Finally, dissociative disorders/MPD subjects often gave playful and artistic responses and FABCOMs that reflected the experience of dividedness or multiplicity. Scroppo et al. (1997) confirmed these findings in their sample of dissociative identity disordered (DID) subjects who gave significantly more FABCOMs, lower X+%s, and more responses containing morbid, bloody, or anatomical contents than a control group.

In terms of the thematic nature of the combinatory activity, Armstrong (1991) gave the following example of a combinatory response to Card VII that depicts the theme of multiplicity:

> These are two girls and they're the same person, but there are two of them and they're always checking each other. And this is another part of the female

anatomy that they share. This is where the vagina is, why the two of them know they're the same person. And it's why you know they're girls (p. 543).

The bizarre combinatory quality of this response is quite apparent but so is the confabulatory tendency ("they're always checking each other") and the strained logic ("This is where the vagina is ... it's why you know they're girls). This significantly thought-disordered response is also consistent with Armstrong's finding of an elevated SCZI and WSUM6 in these patients.

Compared to military and nonmilitary survivors of trauma, and to Exner's borderline and schizotypal samples, Armstrong's dissociative disorders/MPD subjects had the highest WSUM6 mean (WSUM6 = 19.73). Reminiscent of Levin's explanation of the greater presence of FABCOMs in her adult trauma survivors, Armstrong (1991) concluded that elevated thought disorder indices in dissociative disorders/MPD patients not only reflect the disorganizing impact of traumatic reexperience but also the fact that

> Multiplicity is, at one level, an illogical self-construction that affirms the primacy of fantasy over logical, external restrictions. The Rorschach, as a measure of phenomenologic experience, captures the efforts of MPD patients to bend the constraints of linear logic and language to express their internal reality (p. 543).

Putman (1997) has labeled this phenomenon "dissociative thought disorder" to describe the kind of "trance logic" that is typical of dissociative patients who have the ability to tolerate mutually contradictory propositions without seeming awareness of their logical discordance.

In a series of studies with dissociative disorders (comprised of patients with DID and DDNOS diagnoses), Brand and colleagues (Brand, Armstrong, and Loewenstein, 2006; Brand et al., 2009) compared Rorschach findings from the dissociative disorders group with multiple groups of PTSD, depressed, borderline, and psychotic patients. The researchers found that reality testing of the dissociative disorders group was similar to that of the psychotic group, suggesting a vulnerability to confusing internal and external stimuli. However, unlike the psychotic group, dissociative disorders patients had significantly lower scores on variables of disturbed thinking (WSUM6). Thus, although prone to misperceiving the locus of the stimuli, whether it was internal or external, dissociative disorders patients were better able to think in logical and organized ways. Further distinguishing patients with dissociative disorders from those with borderline or psychotic disorders were differences in the number of human movement responses, affective responsiveness, and complexity-related variables. Unlike borderline patients, dissociative disorders were more introversive, showed more detached self-reflection (higher number of FD responses). Additionally, they showed more avoidance of emotional stimuli (lower Affective Ratio or Afr) but less ability to back away from complexity (lower Lambda or F%). According to the collective studies of Brand and Armstrong, dissociative disorders patients with trauma histories present a unique composite of Rorschach features accompanying their disturbances in reality testing and traumatic thought disorders.

Obsessive–compulsive spectrum disorders

Like most former categorical diagnoses, Obsessive–Compulsive Disorder (OCD) is now conceptualized as a neurobiological process that exists along a spectrum of related disorders including hoarding, trichotillomania, and body dysmorphic disorder (BDD). In considering the possible presence of psychotic phenomena associated with OCD, hoarding, and BDDs, the concept of insight into one's obsessions, preoccupations, and compulsive mandates is key. According to the DSM-5 (American Psychiatric Association, 2013), in making a diagnosis of these spectrum disorders one must specify whether the patient has good or fair insight, poor insight, or absent insight/delusional beliefs. This last designation means that the person is completely convinced that the OCD-related beliefs are true. Thus, with OCD, hoarding, and BDD, there is room to consider the presence of delusionality; hence, there is a psychotic component to these spectrum conditions.

A number of pre-Freudian writers observed the close connection between obsessive–compulsive phenomena and delusional states (Hunter & MacAlpine, 1963). Even Freud (1908/1958) noted that obsessive–compulsive and body dysmorphic symptoms may not always occur in the context of a neurosis but in some cases may be a form of psychosis. In one of his most famous case studies, Freud described how the Wolfman was obsessed with imagined defects on his nose (Gardiner, 1959). In general psychiatry, the association between obsessive–compulsive disorders and schizophrenia also has a long lineage of scientific inquiry (Bumke, 1906; Mignard, 1913; Eggers, 1969; Sullivan, 1956). Early interests in this area concerned (1) the comorbidity of obsessive–compulsive syndrome with schizophrenia, (2) the occurrence of obsessional symptoms in schizophrenia (Pious, 1950; Rosen, 1957; Huber and Gross, 1989), and (3) the progression of OCD to schizophrenia (Gordon, 1926; Muller, 1953; Rudin, 1953; Kringlen, 1965; Ackhova, 1976; Birnie & Littmann, 1978). Among the implications of these studies was that OCD and schizophrenia were intimately related and that shifts from one condition to the other were relatively common.

More contemporary researchers argued that OCD represents a spectrum of disorders ranging in severity from anxiety disorders to psychoses (Weiss, Robinson, & Winnik, 1969; Robinson, Winnik, & Weiss, 1976; Insel & Akiskal, 1986). Weiss, Robinson, and Winnik described the longitudinal course of 36 OCD patients whose obsessional symptoms reached delusional proportions. What was particularly interesting about these individuals was that they did not have premorbid compulsive traits. Furthermore, their delusional obsessions were ego syntonic and aggressive in nature. Weiss, Robinson, and Winnik proposed the diagnostic category of "obsessive psychosis" to distinguish these patients from those suffering from schizophrenia.

Insel and Akiskal (1986) reviewed the literature on psychotic symptoms and OCD and concluded that OCD and schizophrenia are separate syndromes and that schizophrenia deterioration in well-established OCD is extremely rare. However, they agreed that some form of psychotic decompensation among OCD patients is not that unusual. They reviewed follow-up studies with OCD patients who eventually became psychotic and discovered that as many as 20 percent may indeed develop psychotic symptoms. Insel and Akiskal concluded that the kind of psychosis that could become superimposed on OCD was related to either a paranoid state or a mood disorder. According to these researchers, the shift from an obsessional idea to a delusional belief occurs when resistance to an obsessional idea or urge is given up and

> may take either (1) an affective form, when the fear of contamination is replaced by the delusional guilt that one has contaminated others, or (2) a paranoid form, when doubts about having committed some reprehensible act are replaced by the delusion that one is being subjected to persecution as if one had actually committed such acts (p. 1529).

Although Insel and Akiskal observed that the distinction between delusional OCD patients and those suffering from primary delusional disorders may be difficult, they suggested that the OCD patient may be more likely to fear hurting others, while the paranoid (delusional) patient is more afraid of being harmed by someone else.

Two additional teams of researchers proposed diagnostic categories for patients whose obsessional symptoms reached delusional severity. Researchers identified a group of near-delusional OCD patients with what they called "chronic deteriorative OCD" (Rasmussen & Tsuang, 1986). Others used the term "schizo-obsessive" to describe this group of patients (Jenike, Baer, & Carey, 1986; Hwang & Hollander, 1993). In general, such individuals were characterized by social isolation, odd speech, paranoia, and depersonalization. Furthermore, as a group, they were younger than the typical nonpsychotic OCD patients. In terms of treatment response, Jenike's schizo-obsessive patients were more refractory to pharmacological and behavioral treatments. The patients described by Jenike, Baer, and Carey seemed to fall closer to the schizophrenia spectrum, whereas the obsessive psychotics described by Weiss, Robinson, and Winnik and Insel and Akiskal appeared to be more similar to patients with encapsulated delusional disorders.

Recent studies identified two different types of obsessive–compulsive syndromes and their relationship to OCD symptoms and schizotypy (Lee, Kim, & Kwon, 2005; Lee & Telch, 2005). The model classifies OCD into two subtypes: reactive obsessions (RO) and autogenous obsessions (AO). According to Lee and Kwon, ROs have more realistic concerns about contamination, doubts, mistakes, and accidents and are associated with perfectionism. In contrast, AOs involve highly aversive, unrealistic thoughts, images, and impulses that are threatening—including sexual, aggressive, blasphemous, and repulsive ideas and images that the patient perceives as ego dystonic and unacceptable. Some sort of symbolic trigger or external threat, like dirt, may evoke ROs' fear of contamination and need for compulsive hand washing. In contrast, no such symbolic link exists between a stimulus cue and AOs. For example, something like the letter S may trigger the thought to kill one's sister in an AO (Lee, Kim, & Kwon, 2005). Thus, AOs are associated more with magical thinking, idiosyncratic perceptions, and schizotypal traits. For ROs, the relationship with schizotypal personality is negligible.

Rorschach studies

The terms "obsessive psychosis," "schizo-obsessive," and "OCD-spectrum disorder without insight/delusional beliefs" imply that the patient's beliefs and compulsions have reached delusional proportions. However, as with patients suffering from encapsulated delusional disorders, the Rorschach may not always be sensitive to their circumscribed delusionality. As noted in the last chapter, the presence of an encapsulated delusion may not be associated with signs of disorganization or illogicality on the Rorschach. Nonetheless, some studies have identified distinguishing features of OCD-spectrum patients with poor insight.

In a small sample of carefully diagnosed OCD patients, Coursey (1984) found that 20 percent of his subjects gave responses with scorable thought disorder. Lee and colleagues (2005) used the CS Rorschach to examine the differences between reactive and autogenous obsessional patients. The researchers compared both groups of obsessional patients with samples of individuals suffering from other anxiety disorders (ANX) and schizophrenia (SZ). Compared to both the RO and ANX subjects, the AO and SZ groups received higher and comparable scores on the SCZI. Furthermore, AO and SZ subjects had higher numbers of M-, FQ-, and Level 1 and 2 INCOMs, FABCOMs, and DRs. The researchers concluded that compared to patients with other anxiety disorders and ROs, individuals with autogenic obsessions demonstrated more evidence of disordered thinking.

References

Achkova, M. (1976). Neurotic-like and psychopathic-like forms of schizophrenia in children and teenagers (in Bulgarian). *Nevrologia, Psikhiatria i Neurokhirurgia* (Sofia), *15*, 326–332.

American Psychiatric Association. (1980). *Diagnostic and Statistical Manual of Mental Disorders* (3rd ed.). Washington, DC: Author.

American Psychiatric Association. (1994). *Diagnostic and Statistical Manual of Mental Disorders* (4th ed.). Washington, DC: Author.

American Psychiatric Association. (2013). *Diagnostic and Statistical Manual of Mental Disorders* (5th ed.). Washington, DC: Author.

Armstrong, J., (1991). The psychological organization of multiple personality disordered patients as revealed in psychological testing. *Psychiatric Clinics of North America, 14*, 533–546.

Armstrong, J. (1994a). Reflections on multiple personality disorder as a developmentally complex adaptation. *The Psychoanalytic Study of the Child, 49,* 349–370. New Haven, CT: Yale University Press.

Armstrong, J. (1994b). Disordered thinking, disordered reality: Issues and insights from dissociative and traumatized patients. Presented at Thought Disorder Conference, The Menninger Clinic, Topeka, KS.

Armstrong, J., & Loewenstein, R. J. (1990). Characteristics of patients with multiple personality and dissociative disorders on psychological testing. *Journal of Nervous and Mental Diseases, 178,* 448–454.

Barnow, S., Arens, E. A., Sieswerda, S., Dinu-Biringer, R., Spitzer, C., & Lang, S. (2010). Borderline personality disorder and psychosis: A review. *Current Psychiatry Reports, 12,* 186–195.

Berg, M. (1984). Borderline psychopathology as displayed on psychological tests. *Journal of Personality Assessment, 47,* 120–133.

Birnie, W. A., & Littman, S. K. (1978). Obsessionality and schizophrenia. *Canadian Psychiatric Association Journal, 23,* 77–81.

Blais, M. A., & Bistis, K. (2004). Projective assessment and borderline psychopathology. In M. J. Hilsenroth & D. L. Segal (Eds.), *Comprehensive Handbook of Psychological Assessment* (Vol. 2, pp. 485–499). Hoboken, NJ: Wiley.

Blais, M. A., Hilsenroth, M., & Castlebury, F. (1997). Content validity of the DSM-IV borderline and narcissistic personality disorder criteria sets. *Comprehensive Psychiatry, 38,* 31–37.

Blais, M. A., Hilsenroth, M., Fowler, J. C., & Conboy, C. A. (1999). A Rorschach exploration of the DSM-IV borderline personality disorder. *Journal of Clinical Psychology, 55,* 563–572.

Brand, B. L., Armstrong, J. G., & Loewenstein, R. J. (2006). Psychological assessment of patients with dissociative identity disorder. *Psychiatric Clinics of North America, 29,* 145–168.

Brand, B. L., Armstrong, J. G., Loewenstein, R. J., & McNary, S. W. (2009). Personality differences on the Rorschach of dissociative identity disorder, borderline personality disorder, and psychotic patients. *Psychological Trauma: Theory, Research, Practice, and Policy, 1,* 188–205.

Briere, J. (1997). *Psychological Assessment of Adult Posttraumatic States.* Washington, DC: American Psychological Association.

Bumke, O. (1906). Die psychischen zwanger-scheinungen (The manifestations of psychic compulsion). *Allgemeine Zeitschrift fur Psychiatrie und Psychisch-Gerichtliche Medizin, 63,* 138–148.

Carlson, E. B., & Armstrong, J. (1994). The diagnosis and assessment of dissociative disorders. In S. J. Lynn & J. L. Rhue (Eds.), *Dissociation: Clinical and Theoretical Perspectives* (pp. 159–174). New York: Guilford Press.

Carr, A. (1984). Content interpretation re: Salley and Teillings' Dissociated rage attacks in a Vietnam veteran: A Rorschach study. *Journal of Personality Assessment, 48,* 42–421.

Cauwels, J. M. (1992). *Imbroglio: Rising to the Challenges of Borderline Personality Disorder.* New York: Norton.

Cerney, M. (1990). The Rorschach and traumatic loss: Can the presence of traumatic loss be detected from the Rorschach? *Journal of Personality Assessment, 55,* 781–789.

Chopra, H. D., & Beatson, J. A. (1986). Psychotic symptoms in borderline personality disorder. *American Journal of Psychiatry, 143,* 1605–1607.

Coonerty, S. (1986). An exploration of separation individuation in the borderline personality disorder. *Journal of Personality Assessment, 50*, 501–511.

Coursey, R. D. (1984). The dynamics of obsessive-compulsive disorder. In T. R. Insel (Ed.), *New Findings in Obsessive-Compulsive Disorder* (pp. 104–121). Washington, DC: American Psychiatric Press.

Eggers, C. (1969). Zwang und jugendliche psychosen (Compulsions and juvenile psychoses). *Praxis der Kinderpsychologie und Kinderpsychiatrie, 118*, 202–208.

Exner, J. E. (1986). Some Rorschach data comparing schizophrenics with borderline and schizotypal personality disorders. *Journal of Personality Assessment, 50*, 455–471.

Exner, J. E. (1993). *The Rorschach: A Comprehensive System: Vol. 1. Basic Foundations* (3rd ed.). New York: Wiley.

Freud, S. (1959). Character and anal erotism. In the *Standard Edition of the Complete Works of Sigmund Freud* (Vol. 9, pp. 167–175). London, UK: Hogarth Press. (Original work published in 1908.)

Gardiner, M. (1959). *The Wolf-man and Sigmund Freud*. London, UK: Karnac Books.

Gordon, A. (1926). Obsessions in their relation to psychoses. *American Journal of Psychiatry, 5*, 647–659.

Grinker, R. R., Werble, B., & Drye, R. C. (1968). *The Borderline Syndrome*. New York: Basic Books.

Gunderson, J. G. (1977). Characteristics of borderline. In P. Hartocollis (Ed.), *Borderline Personality Disorders: The Concept, the Syndrome, the Patient* (pp. 173–192). New York: International Universities Press.

Gunderson, J. G. (1984). *Borderline Personality Disorder*. Washington, DC: American Psychiatric Press.

Gunderson, J. G., & Singer, M. T. (1975). Defining borderline patients: An overview. *American Journal of Psychiatry, 132*, 1–10.

Harris, O. (1993). The prevalence of thought disorder in personality-disordered outpatients. *Journal of Personality Assessment, 61*, 112–120.

Hartman, W., Clark, M., Morgan, M., Dunn, V., Fine, A., Perry, G., & Winsch, D. (1990). Rorschach structure of a hospitalized sample of Vietnam veterans with PTSD. *Journal of Personality Assessment, 54*, 149–159.

Hilsenroth, M., Eudell-Simmons, E. M., DeFife, J. A., & Charnas, J. W. (2007). The Rorschach Perceptual-Thinking Index (PTI): An examination of reliability, validity, and diagnostic efficiency. *International Journal of Testing, 7*, 269–291.

Hilsenroth, M., Fowler, J. C., & Pawader, J. R. (1998). The Rorschach Schizophrenia Index (SCZI): An examination of reliability, validity, and diagnostic efficiency. *Journal of Personality Assessment, 70*, 514–534.

Holt, R. R. (1977). A method for assessing primary process manifestations and their control in Rorschach responses. In M. A. Rickers-Ovsiankina (Ed.), *Rorschach Psychology* (2nd ed., pp. 375–420). New York: Krieger.

Holt, R. R. (2009). *Primary Process Thinking: Theory, Measurement, and Research* (Vols. 1 & 2). Lanham, MD: Aronson.

Huber, G., & Gross, G. (1989). The concept of basic symptoms in schizophrenic and schizoaffective psychoses. *Recent Progress in Medicine, 80*, 646–652.

Hunter, R., & MacAlpine, I. (1963). *Three Hundred Years of Psychiatry*. London, UK: University Press.

Hwang, M. Y., & Hollander. E. (1993). Schizo-obsessive disorders. *Psychiatric Annals, 23*, 396–400.

Insel, T. R., & Akiskal, H. S. (1986). Obsessive-compulsive disorder with psychotic features: A phenomenologic analysis. *American Journal of Psychiatry, 143*, 1527–1533.

Jenike, M. A., Baer. L., & Carey, R. J. (1986). Co-existent obsessive-compulsive disorder and schizotypal personality disorder: A poor prognosis indicator (letter). *Archives of General Psychiatry, 43*, 296.

Kaser-Boyd, N. (1993). Rorschachs of women who commit homicide. *Journal of Personality Assessment, 60*, 458–470.

Kaser-Boyd, N., & Evans, F. B. (2008). Rorschach assessment of psychological trauma. In C. B. Gacono & F. B. Evans (Eds.), *The Handbook of Forensic Rorschach Assessment* (pp. 255–277). New York: Taylor & Francis.

Kernberg, O. F. (1967). Borderline personality organization. *Journal of the American Psychoanalytic Association, 15*, 641–685.

Kleiger, J. H. (1999). *Disordered Thinking and the Rorschach*. Hillsdale, NJ: The Analytic Press.

Knight, R. P. (1953). Borderline states. *Bulletin of the Menninger Clinic, 17*, 1–12.

Kringlen, E. (1965). Obsessional neurotics: A long term follow-up. *British Journal of Psychiatry, 111*, 709–722.

Kwawer, J. (1980). Primitive interpersonal modes, borderline phenomena, and Rorschach content. In J. Kwawer, H. Lerner, P. Lerner, & A. Sugarman (Eds.), *Borderline Phenomena and the Rorschach Test* (pp. 89–106). New York: International Universities Press.

Larkin, W., & Morrison, A. P. (Eds.). (2006). *Trauma and Psychosis: New Directions for Theory and Therapy*. New York: Routledge.

Larson, D. G. (1974). The Borderline Syndrome in the Rorschach: A Comparison with Acute and Chronic Schizophrenics. Thesis, University of California, Psychology Department, Berkeley, CA.

Lee, H. J., Kim, Z. S., & Kwon, S. M. (2005). Thought disorder in patients with obsessive-compulsive disorder. *Journal of Clinical Psychology, 61*, 401–413.

Lee, H. J., & Telch, M. J. (2005). Autogenous/reactive obsessions and their relationship with OCD symptoms and schizotypal personality features. *Journal of Anxiety Disorders, 19*, 793–805.

Lerner, H., & St. Peter, S. (1984). Patterns of object relations in neurotic, borderline, and schizophrenic patients. *Psychiatry, 47*, 77–92.

Lerner, H., Sugarman, A., & Barbour, C. G. (1985). Patterns of ego boundary disturbance in neurotic, borderline, and schizophrenic patients. *Psychoanalytic Psychology, 2*, 47–66.

Levin, P. (1993). Assessing post-traumatic stress disorder with the Rorschach projective technique. In J. P. Wilson & B. Raphael (Eds.), *International Handbook of Traumatic Stress Syndromes* (pp. 189–200). New York: Plenum.

Levin, P., & Reis, B. (1996). The use of the Rorschach in assessing trauma. In J. Wilson & T. Keane (Eds.), *Assessing Psychological Trauma and PTSD* (pp. 529–543). New York: Guilford Press.

Lovitt, R., & Lefkof, G. (1985). Understanding multiple personality disorder with the comprehensive Rorschach system. *Journal of Personality Assessment, 59*, 289–294.

Mahler, M., Pine, F., & Bergman, A. (1975). *The Psychological Birth of the Human Infant*. New York: Basic Books.

Mignard, M. (1913). De l'obsession: Émotive ou délire d'influence (On obsession: Emotional or delusion of influence). *Annales Médecine Psychologique* (Paris), *71*, 333–343.

Mihura, J. L. (2006). Rorschach assessment of borderline personality disorder. In S. K. Huprich (Ed.), *Rorschach Assessment of Personality Disorders* (pp. 171–203). Mahwah, NJ: Erlbaum.

Muller, C. (1953). Der ubergong von zwangsnekrose in schizophrenic im licht der katumnese (Transformation of compulsive neurosis into schizophrenia in light of the case history). *Schweizer Archiv für Neurologie und Psychiatrie, 72*, 218–225.

Nigg, J. T., Lohr, N. E., Westen, D., Gold, L. J., & Silk, K. R. (1992). Malevolent object representations in borderline personality disorder and major depression. *Journal of Abnormal Psychology, 101*, 61–67.

Patrick, J., & Wolfe, B. (1983). Rorschach presentation of borderline personality disorder: Primary process manifestations. *Journal of Clinical Psychology, 39*, 442–447.

Perry, W., & Viglione, D. J. (1991). The Ego Impairment Index as a predictor of outcome in melancholic depressed patients treated with tricyclic antidepressants. *Journal of Personality Assessment, 56*, 487–501.

Pious, W. (1950). Obsessive-compulsive symptoms in an incipient schizophrenic. *Psychoanalytic Quarterly, 19*, 327–339.

Putnam, F. (1997). *Dissociation in Children and Adolescents*. New York: Guilford Press.

Rapaport, D., Gill, M., & Schafer, R. (1968). *Diagnostic Psychological Testing* (Rev. ed.). R. R. Holt, Ed. New York: International Universities Press. (Original work published in 1946.).

Rasmussen, S. A., & Tsuang, M. (1986). Clinical characteristics and family history in DSM-III obsessive-compulsive disorder. *American Journal of Psychiatry, 143*, 317–322.

Read, J., van Os, J. V., Morrison, A. P., & Ross, C. A. (2005). Childhood trauma, psychosis and schizophrenia: A literature review with theoretical and clinical implications. *Acta Psychiatrica Scandinavica, 112*, 330–350.

Robinson, S., Winnik, H. Z., & Weiss, A. A. (1976). Obsessive psychosis: Justification for a separate clinical entity. *Israeli Annals of Psychiatry, 14*, 39–48.

Rosen, I. (1957). The clinical significance of obsessions in schizophrenia. *Journal of Mental Science, 103*, 773–785.

Rudin, G. (1953). Ein beitrag zur frage der zwangskrankheit (A contribution to the question of compulsive disease). *Archiv fur Psychiatrie und Nervenkrankheiten, 191*, 14–54.

Scroppo, J. C., Drob, S. L., Weinberger, J. L., & Eagle, P. (1997). Identifying dissociative identity disorder: A self-report and projective study. *Journal of Abnormal Psychology, 107*, 272–284.

Shilling, L., Wingenfeld, K., Löwe, B., Moritz, S., Terfehr, K., Köther, U., & Spitzer, C. (2012). Normal mind-reading capacity but higher response confidence in borderline personality patients. *Psychiatry and Clinical Neurosciences, 66*, 322–327.

Singer, M. T. (1977), The Rorschach as a transaction. In M. Rickers-Ovsiankina (Ed.), *Rorschach Psychology* (pp. 455–485). Huntington, NY: Krieger.

Singer, H. K., & Larson, D. G. (1981). Borderline personality and the Rorschach test. *Archives of General Psychiatry, 38*, 693–698.

Steiner, M., Martin, S., Wallace, J., & Goldman, S. (1984). Distinguishing subtypes within the borderline domain: A combined psychoneuroendocrine approach. *Biological Psychiatry, 19*, 907–911.

Stone, M. H. (1980). *The Borderline Syndromes: Constitution, Personality, and Adaptation.* New York: McGraw-Hill.

Stuart, J., Westen, D., Lohr, N. E., Silk, K. R., Becker, S., Vorus, N., & Benjamin, J. (1990). Object relations in borderlines, major depressives, and normals: Analysis of Rorschach human responses. *Journal of Personality Assessment, 55*, 296–314.

Sugarman, A. (1986). An object relations understanding of borderline phenomena on the Rorschach. In M Kissen (Ed.), *Assessing Object Relations Phenomena* (pp. 77–88). Madison, CT: International Universities Press.

Sullivan, H. S. (1956). *Clinical Studies in Psychiatry.* H. S. Perry, M. L. Gawel, & M. Gibbon, Eds. New York: W. W. Norton.

Urist, J. (1977). The Rorschach Test and the assessment of object relations. *Journal of Personality Assessment, 41,* 3–9.

van der Kolk, B., & Ducey, C. (1989). The psychological processing of traumatic experience: Rorschach patterns in post-traumatic stress disorder. *Journal of Traumatic Stress, 2,* 359–374.

Viglione, D. J., Perry, W., Giromini, L., & Meyer, G. J. (2011). Revising the Rorschach Ego Impairment Index to accommodate recent recommendations about improving Rorschach validity. *International Journal of Testing, 11,* 349–364.

Viglione, D. J., Towns, B., & Lindshield, D. (2012). Understanding and using the Rorschach Inkblot Test to assess post-traumatic conditions. *Psychological Injury and Law, 5,* 135–144.

Wagner, E., & Heise, M. (1974). A comparison of Rorschach protocols of three multiple personalities. *Journal of Personality Assessment, 38,* 308–331.

Weisath, L. (1989). A study of behavioral responses to an industrial disaster. *Acta Psychiatrica Scandinavica, 355,* 13–71.

Weiss, R., Robinson, S., & Winnick, H. Z. (1969). Obsessive psychosis: Psychodiagnostic findings. *Israeli Annals of Psychiatry, 7,* 175–178.

Westen, D., Lohr, N., Silk, K., Gold, L., & Kerber, K. (1990). Object relations and social cognition in borderlines, major depressives, and normals: A TAT analysis. *Psychological Assessment: A Journal of Consulting and Clinical Psychology, 2,* 335–364.

Wilson, A. (1985). Boundary disturbances in borderline and psychotic states. *Journal of Personality Assessment, 49,* 346–355.

Yee, L., Korner, A. J., McSwiggan, S., Meares, R. A., & Stevenson, J. (2005). Persistent hallucinosis in borderline personality disorder. *Comprehensive Psychiatry, 46,* 147–154.

Zanarini, M. C., Gunderson, J. G., & Frankenburg, F. R. (1990). Cognitive features of borderline personality disorder. *American Journal of Psychiatry, 147,* 57–63.

Chapter 15

Malingered psychosis and disordered thinking

Detecting malingering in clinical and forensic evaluations is a not an uncommon concern for practitioners (Rogers et al., 1998). As with all detection strategies, detecting malingered psychosis is a complex clinical process that requires a systematic, multimodal approach that looks for convergence and inconsistencies between history, collateral sources of information, behavioral observations, and diagnostic testing (Ganellen et al., 1996). Furthermore, as demonstrated by Resnick and Knoll (2008), the detection of malingered psychosis requires extensive knowledge about the phenomenology of psychotic symptomatology.

Regarding psychological assessment, what role might the Rorschach play in the detection of malingered psychotic symptoms, and thought disorder in particular? Can thought disorder be simulated on the Rorschach; and if so, what signs or patterns might we look for that would help us distinguish feigned from actual psychotic phenomena? These questions have been of interest to researchers for decades, with studies providing various conclusions and cautionary notes.

Before discussing the Rorschach's role in detecting malingered psychotic symptomatology, it is useful to begin with some conceptual and clinical issues pertaining, first, to suspected malingering and then to what is known about the differences between dissimulated and genuine psychotic symptoms. Once the stage has been set with sufficient background information, we can review literature regarding the potential contributions and limitations of the Rorschach in the detection of feigned psychotic symptoms.

Suspecting malingering

The suspicion that an individual might be feigning psychotic symptoms begins with an understanding of those conditions that give rise to the suspicion in the first place. Cunnien (1997) presented a threshold model that begins with contextual and clinical factors that might alert an examiner to the possibility of malingering. The chief factor in raising a diagnostician's suspicion is the presence of a motive and potential for secondary gain, such as seeking to evade criminal responsibility. Efforts to feign psychosis were found in 8 percent of defendants referred for pretrial assessments (Cornell & Hawk, 1989). Secondary factors include: (1) symptom complaints that exceed physical findings; (2) symptoms that worsen when the individual is being observed; (3) exaggeration or "overacting" of symptoms; (4) marked inconsistencies and contradictions; (5) bizarre, nonsensical symptoms that are unbearable, uncontrollable, do not respond to conventional treatments, or resolve too quickly; and (4) lack of cooperation with the assessment and treatment (Resnick & Knoll, 2008).

Exaggeration of psychotic symptoms is a prominent clue that an individual might be feigning "craziness" (Harris, 2000; Resnick & Knoll, 2008). The psychosis simulator might believe that the more bizarre his behavior and the more outlandish his claims, the greater likelihood of convincing evaluators that he is, in fact, suffering from a psychotic disorder. Throughout the literature, overplaying or exaggeration of symptoms is described as a hallmark clue of potential malingering of psychosis. Additionally, unlike the actual psychotic sufferer, the malingerer may also be eager to call attention to her bizarre and putative psychotic symptoms.

In keeping with the notion that malingerers may seek to embellish their symptoms, positive features of psychosis (the more dramatic the better) lend themselves more to dissimulating efforts than formal thought disorder and negative symptoms. According to Sherman, Trief, and Sprafkin (1975), malingerers have more difficulty feigning the disorganized form and idiosyncratic process of psychotic thinking than they do imitating the content of a bogus delusion. For example, derailment, tangentiality, and incoherently disorganized speech are more difficult to feign. Additionally, malingerers are less likely to demonstrate perseverative speech. In a study of speech characteristics in feigned and genuine schizophrenia, Najolia (2013) found that her dissimulating subjects could not mimic the subtle features of formal thought disorder. In other words, they did not display confused references and lack of grammatical clarity, despite that the majority of them later indicated that they were indeed trying to fake formal thought disorder.

More obvious positive symptoms like hallucinations and delusions are easier to feign than negative symptoms. Malingerers are less apt to mimic subtle negative symptoms like flat affect, alogia, and avolition (Resnick & Knoll, 2008). Najolia (2013) found that her subjects who tried to simulate the speech characteristics of schizophrenia ended up mumbling more and slurring their speech. However, these subjects showed something like alogia because of their long pauses while speaking.

Additionally, consistent with existing literature, Resnick and Knoll (2008) and Najolia (2013) found that subjects seeking to feign psychosis performed more poorly on cognitive tasks. Thus, consistent with their efforts to draw attention to their incapacity, simulators of psychosis might endeavor to present themselves as more cognitively impaired than is characteristic of people with actual schizophrenia.

Regarding the quality of positive symptom simulation, Resnick and Knoll (2008) summarized research findings that distinguished actual from simulated hallucinations and delusions. Briefly, malingering should be expected when auditory hallucinations are (1) continuous rather than intermittent; (2) vague or inaudible; (3) contain stilted or odd language; (4) consist mainly of commands that must be obeyed; (5) occur without delusions; and (6) cannot be diminished with coping strategies. Delusional complaints should be suspect when their onset is abrupt rather than gradual, and when the subject is eager to call attention to his delusion. Moreover, behavior that is inconsistent with delusional claims should cause clinicians to be suspicious of dissimulation. Relatedly, bizarre delusional content is most often accompanied by disorganized thinking. Thus, when an individual claims to have bizarre delusions without evidence of a formal disturbance in thinking or speech, the index of suspicion for malingering is raised.

One might anticipate that malingerers of psychosis would reveal their feigned symptom presentations on the Rorschach in a similar manner that they reveal them in a clinical interview situation. If this were the case, then we would expect to find testing equivalents of some of these same distinguishing clinical features on the Rorschach.

Rorschach detection of malingered psychosis: Empirical studies

Detecting malingered psychosis with the Rorschach, like detection strategies with any clinical procedure, is a complex process that defies a simple search for test signs and instead requires a strategic approach incorporating a variety of test and nontest variables. The most effective detection strategies are those involving standardized methods that are conceptually based, empirically validated, systematically differentiating, and delineating a specific response style (Rogers, 2008). Given these criteria, how effective has the Rorschach been in helping to detect malingered psychosis?

Despite earlier research that concluded that the Rorschach could not be faked (Fosberg, 1938, 1941, 1943), more contemporary studies have found that under some conditions the Rorschach *is* susceptible to simulation of psychosis (Elhai, Kinder, & Frueh, 2004; Ganellen, 2008; Sewell, 2008). In fact, it is currently accepted that it is difficult to distinguish the Rorschachs of dissimulating subjects who have knowledge about psychosis from subjects who are clinically psychotic. Several recent literature reviews agreed that Rorschach studies of malingering fell short of satisfying all of Rogers's search strategy criteria (2008) and that there were no empirically specific indicators of malingering on the Rorschach (Elhai, Kinder, & Frueh, 2004; Ganellen, 2008; Sewell, 2008). In general, most studies failed to identify a set of Rorschach variables that could reliably distinguish between psychotic and dissimulating subjects. Furthermore, when differences in key variables pertaining to psychosis and thought disorder were found, classification was marred by unacceptably high rates of false positives and negatives. However, these literature reviews also raised a number of questions about the nature of the existing studies themselves. For example, not all of the studies reviewed used standardized scoring systems to evaluate Rorschach protocols

(Albert, Fox, & Kahn, 1980). Furthermore, too many studies assumed that experimental dissimulation was equivalent to clinical malingering of psychosis.

Although these major reviews of the status of malingering and the Rorschach agreed that detection strategies should always involve: (1) multi-method assessments; (2) include collateral information; and (3) look for discontinuities among all of the data, the authors reached different conclusions about whether to throw out the baby with the bath water. For example, Sewell (2008), in perhaps the most severe indictment of the Rorschach's contribution to detecting malingered psychosis, indicated that because of a lack of empirical evidence, the Rorschach had little to offer. However, his pessimistic conclusion is, in part, based on a selective referencing of the work of other contributors. For example, in quoting Exner (1991) and referencing Elhai, Kinder, & Frueh (2004), Sewell left the impression that none of these researchers found any value in using the Rorschach to aid in detecting malingering. Such is not the case. While recognizing the empirical limitations of the Rorschach in detection studies, Exner, Kinder, and Frueh (2004) and Ganellen (2008) agreed that there were several empirically valid findings that could prove useful to clinicians who used the Rorschach as part of a multi-method, context-sensitive detection strategy (Mihura, 2012).

Rorschach indications of malingered psychosis: Clinical clues

It is true that certain types of Rorschach responses can be manipulated to evade the clinical detection of malingering. As noted above, the majority of studies have shown that conventional Rorschach indices of thought disorder and impaired reality testing have not been all that successful in distinguishing individuals with clinical psychosis from subjects who are simulating psychosis, especially when those individuals have knowledge about psychotic symptomatology. However, these findings do not mean that clinicians should dispense with the Rorschach when trying to tease out whether a subject might be attempting to feign psychosis. The absence of empirically proven decision rules for separating those who are clinically psychotic from those who are malingering does not preclude looking at some of the response and behavioral features that have been shown to be associated with malingered Rorschachs. For example, Schretlen (1997) listed signs that might raise suspicion when assessing an individual in a context in which malingering is being considered:

- fewer responses;
- frequent card rejections;
- paucity of popular responses;
- numerous dramatic, morbid, or bizarre responses;
- repeated questions about the purpose of the testing or pained compliance.

These and other clinical signs have appeared in the literature over the last several decades. Seamons and colleagues (1981) used a counterbalanced design with clinical and nonclinical samples of offenders instructed to feign mental illness and normalcy. Judges found a high number of "dramatic responses" in the records of subjects judged to be simulating mental illness. Dramatic responses were defined as those containing themes of depression, sex, blood, gore, mutilation, confusion, hatred, fighting, and decapitation. Dissimulating subjects had significantly more dramatic responses and inappropriate combinations and fewer Populars. This finding has received support from several studies (Frueh & Kinder, 1994; Netter & Viglione, 1994; Ganellen et al., 1996). Netter and Viglione identified common dissimulation strategies such as:

- pretending the image on the card was alive;
- creating a dramatic story;
- making aggressive, provocative, and critical comments;
- spoiling a popular response;
- making reference to hearing voices;
- longer reaction times (particularly on Card V).

Ganellen et al. (1996) separated forensic subjects into "honest" and "malingering" groups based on the MMPI F scale T-scores greater than or equal to 90. They found no differences between the groups on the SCZI, R, number of Populars, X+ or X–%, or Level 2 Special Scores. However, like others, they observed highly significant differences on a measure of Dramatic Content, including responses containing blood, sex, fire, explosions, and aggressive or morbid content and themes. Ganellen's group took their conclusions a step further by recommending a combination of MMPI and Rorschach variables when considering the likelihood of malingered psychosis. These researchers suggested that a pattern of extreme elevations on MMPI scales F, Pa, and Sc, along with lower scores on L and K, together with Rorschachs containing few structural indications of psychosis and overly dramatic content, may depict intentional malingering of psychosis.

McDougall (1996) used a discriminant function analysis to distinguish subjects with schizophrenia from dissimulating subjects. She identified 11 variables as malingering indicators and three as nonmalingering indicators. Most of these indicators were Rorschach scoring variables. However, like Netter and Viglione's indicators (1994), some variables were related to extra-test behavior. McDougall's indicators of malingering included:

- two or more instances of circumstantiality;
- two or more instances of the card "coming alive";
- two or more distress comments;
- WSUM6 > 5 + ModWSUM6;
- two or more simple responses containing multiple Special Scores;
- Card V reaction time >10 seconds;
- Card V Popular with a Special Score;
- two or more FABCOMs;

- no unspoiled Popular on Cards IV and V;
- at least four or more Special Scores on Cards IV, V, and VI than on Card I;
- three or more Dramatic Content scores (Mor, Blood, Sex, Fire, Ex, AG).

Indicators of nonmalingering included:

- D1 Popular response on Card VIII with no Special Score;
- D1 Popular on Card X with no Special Score;
- two or more responses in which the subject acknowledged that the response might not be plausible.

Although McDougall obtained an overall correct classification rate of 78.3 percent, with only 11 percent of the simulators misclassified as having schizophrenia, the false-positive rate (schizophrenia subjects misclassified as malingering) was over 42 percent. Despite this unacceptable false-positive rate, McDougall's approach identified a number of novel signs and combinations of variables that may prove useful in clinical settings.

Departing from disappointing nomothetic approaches, Exner and Erdberg (Exner, 1991; Exner & Erdberg, 2005) used a single case study method of known malingerers to highlight those variables most reflective of feigning psychosis. Over a 15-year-period, Exner's Rorschach Research Foundation acquired 31 protocols of adjudicated malingers. Of the 21 defendants involved in criminal proceedings, only two received scores of 6 on the revised SCZI, " but both records were so bizarre that they were unbelievable and both were highly inconsistent with the cooperativeness of the subject during the testing" (Exner, 1991, p. 438). Despite the absence of a homogeneous set of structural variables, Exner indicated that all of the malingering defendants showed the following features:

- A large number of lengthy bizarre responses. The Free Association responses of malingerers contained roughly twice as many words (25–40 words) compared to a sample of nonpatient adults (13.2 words). Although subjects in upper socioeconomic groups with superior intelligence also give lengthy verbalizations, they do not contain the bizarre content found in malingerers.
- Bizarreness in words and content is mixed with good FQ.
- A large number of Special Scores reflecting efforts to appear bizarre, which are associated with DR comments and phrases scores.

Exner concluded that "Overall, if anything is to be gleaned from these 31 cases, it is the fact that the record 'doesn't sound right' in light of other information, mainly history data available concerning the subject" (p. 439).

Exner and Erdberg (2005) presented the Rorschach and MMPI-2 of a suspected malingerer who received a score of 4 on the PTI. However, the authors concluded that "his Rorschach findings are characterized by such extreme findings as to create suspicion about the genuineness of his psychopathology. His WSUM6 of 95, the presence of 14 Level 2 Special Scores, and five M- scores in a 19 response record are especially noteworthy" (p. 428).

Exner and Erdberg noted that most of the subject's Level 2 Special Scores occurred in responses that had appropriate FQ. Furthermore, the quality of these Special Score responses was overly dramatic, "raising a question about whether someone with this magnitude of cognitive dysfunction could actually complete the Rorschach" (p. 428).

What is most striking about these idiographic observations of malingered psychosis on the Rorschach is how closely they match what forensic researchers have written about interview-based characteristics of individuals feigning psychosis (Kucharski et al., 1998; Harris, 2000; Resnick & Knoll, 2008). All stress the feature of symptom exaggeration or overacting. As Resnick and Knoll (2008) put it, malingerers are notorious overactors, who "mistakenly believe that the more bizarre their behavior, the more convincing they will be" (p. 60). They provided an evocative quote about how the malingerer "crowds the canvas, piles symptom upon symptom and so outstrips madness itself, attaining to a but clumsy caricature of his assumed role" (Jones & Llewellyn, 1917, p. 80). Additionally, malingerers tend to call attention to their symptoms and present contradictions and inconsistencies in their symptom descriptions. Furthermore, they may become hostile and provocative during the interview or respond in a slow manner, presumably to give themselves more time to think about how to successfully deceive the interviewer.

Note the similarity to what researchers have said about Rorschach response features of malingered psychosis. Netter and Viglione (1994) not only pointed out the overdramatizing of negative contents and calling attention to their symptoms (e.g. claiming to hear voices), but also to their hostile, provocative comments and long reaction times. Finally, the marked inconsistencies and contradictions noted by interviewers like Resnick and Knoll (2008) are similar to the discontinuities found in malingered Rorschachs, in which Level 2 Special Scores often occurred in Popular responses with better FQ (Exner, 1991; Ganellen et al., 1996).

Specificity and sensitivity of thought disorder scores

Thus far, most of the emphasis has been on malingered psychosis as a whole, as opposed to establishing a narrower focus on malingered thought disorder on the Rorschach. While it is true that many of the studies reviewed have used composite variables like total number of Level 2 Special Scores, WSUM6, and SCZI, less has been said about the Special Scores themselves. The exception to this last point is the observation that malingered records contain more dramatic responses. Overly dramatic answers have been defined as responses containing blood, gore, violence, sex, and morbid themes. However, dramatic contents may also be presented in bizarre, overly elaborated verbalizations, which could be scored as DR2s. A number of researchers noted the presence of confabulated DRs in the records of individuals feigning psychosis (Exner, 1991; Netter & Viglione,

1994; McDougall, 1996). However, Ganellen et al. (1996) did not find this to be the case. They found that subjects defined as honest or as malingering could not be distinguished on the basis of DR. However, if there are any special scoring categories that could be manipulated for dramatic effect they are probably DR, followed by INCOM and FABCOM. Seamons et al. (1981) found a greater number of inappropriate combinations in their mental illness simulators. The individual attempting to present a bizarre record in order to feign psychosis may not simply overrely on violent and graphic thematic content but may also elaborate bizarre ideas in a confabulatory manner. For example, consider the following two examples of severely confabulated DR2s. Which responses were produced by a malingering subject and which by an individual with an emerging psychosis?

Subject 1:

Card. II. *This is like the Catholics, I'd rather not talk about it, It's Christ, he's pierced & dying, there's blood all over.*

Card VII. *It's two figures representing the people of different nations, they see each other but there is a dividing line to show how they're apart. They're supposed to be together but they're held apart.*

Card IX. *This lousy pink is like an unborn child and all these things around it are trying to poison it, they're waiting to devour it and the ovaries in the middle, like poisoned amoebae and they are ready to get at it.*

Subject 2:

Card II. *I think I can see a rabbit if I look at it from side, I think a rabbit who is either being slaughtered or has finished a race. Some sort of fight or physical activity, vomiting, definitely in some sort of physical pain. I feel that pain is ... fake. I think it's just trying to show that it's in pain and looks like a rabbit because it has resembling ears.*

Card II. *This reminds me of I think ... either animals or people. I feel like they'd maybe be from different areas or maybe the same area but they're um ... my first instinct was they're fighting but now they look very old and look like making a resolution and both have very different ideas and are agreeing on one thing. I feel both are very strong-headed, hot-headed people but being calm when agreeing on one thing ... My first impression was also blood, red at bottom and their heads were red splotches at the top. Yea, I think they're different people, yea very different.*

Card III. *Someone ... um ... either like calling out a start of a war. I think either a very happy thing or a very tragic thing. Definitely starting something the person's face I feel like they're starting a thing they don't want to start, like a very tragic thing but looking at it as a whole, looked like it started something very happy.*

Distinguishing the malingering subject from the clinically disturbed subject on the basis of a few Level 2 DRs such as these is extremely difficult and also not in keeping with standards of clinical practice, which would discourage making differential diagnostic decisions on the basis of isolated test data. What makes it even more difficult to distinguish between these subjects is that both sets of responses contain highly charged, contradictory, dramatic thematic content verbalized in a confabulated, overly embellished manner. In most respects, these subjects cannot be differentiated on the basis of their DR2s. However, if you chose Subject 2 as the individual with an emerging psychosis, you would be correct. Subject 1 is taken from Exner and Erdberg's Case Examples (2005, pp. 420–421).

Two possible clues to making this distinction include the DV1 in Subject 2's first response to Card II ("resembling ears") and the implicitly bizarre logic in her second response to Card II, where she described the figures as "strong-headed, hot-headed people." She later shared her impression that "their heads were red splotches at the top," which suggests that she conflated the color red with the concept of being "hot-headed." The expression "strong-headed" is also a bit peculiar. Furthermore, although Subject 1 showed some contradictory ideas in his Card VII response (e.g. "They're supposed to be together but they're held apart"), each of Subject 2's responses contains inherently nonsensical contradictions, suggesting marked ideational ambivalence, à la Bleuler (1911/1950). One final clue might be Subject 1's words on Card II, "I'd rather not talk about it," which hints at a feigned loss of distance, designed to call attention to the fact that this idea ("Catholics") had some sort of private religious significance to him that he could not bear to talk about.

These potential distinguishing features illustrate that while overly dramatic content and embellished verbalizations may occur in the records of clinical subjects and feigners of psychosis, alike, it is more difficult for the malingerer of psychosis to feign features of formal thought disorder. Resnick and Knoll (2008) indicated that symptoms like derailment, neologisms, loose associations, and word salad were rarely simulated. I would add to this subtle slips in logic, as in the case of the color red concretely representing "hot-headedness." In general, Subject 1's language is clearer than Subject 2's. Although Subject 1's content is bizarre and dramatic, it is less fluid.

In addition to subtle differences in language and logic, we would not expect to see contamination responses in the malingered Rorschach. Contaminations are low-frequency responses to begin with. They reflect a collapse of ideational and perceptual boundaries that point to a severe disturbance in the structure of the person's thinking.

If the malingering subject wants to be noticed, the way to do this is through feigning positive symptoms. In the interview, this takes the form of malingered hallucinations and delusions and on the Rorschach overly dramatic responses that may (or may not) be expressed as confabulated DRs. Regarding feigned negative symptoms, Resnick and Knoll (2008) indicated that symptoms such as flat affect, alogia, avolition, and impaired interactions are less likely to be malingered than positive symptoms. Impoverishment is also less likely to be simulated on the Rorschach. As such, we expect to find fewer subtle indications of negative thought disorder and cognitive impairment. As the work of Schuldberg and Boster (1986) showed, there may be fewer responses that are concrete, constricted, perseverative, and fragmented in the records of individuals trying to feign psychosis.

Final comments

Some things are clearer than others when attempting to detect malingered psychosis or thought disorder on the Rorschach. Although composite indices like the PTI, WSUM6, number of Level 2 Special Scores, or the outdated SCZI have not proven to be substantial markers, we do have some clues to mark the trail. Clinicians should neither be overly confident nor unduly pessimistic when looking to the Rorschach to help them distinguish the clinically psychotic individual from the malingerer. Care in conducting a multi-method assessment—which includes multiple tests, interviews, and collateral observations and records—is indispensible in looking for patterns and discontinuities that are helpful in detecting malingering.

One final point is worth noting. Most of the seminal research on malingering and the Rorschach was conducted 20 or more years ago. In two decades, the Rorschach researchers have made significant advances, best typified by the development of the R-PAS (Meyer et al., 2011). Not only does the R-PAS have a broader cadre of variables in the domain of Perception and Thinking Problems, but the R-PAS method itself has removed one of the major confounds identified in the malingered Rorschach literature. Elhai, Kinder, and Frueh (2004) indicated that R was a confounding variable in research on malingering and the Rorschach.

It is hoped that new attention will be paid to the subject of malingering psychosis on the Rorschach. Now that the R-PAS is gaining a foothold in the clinical Rorschach field it is time for an old topic to be reexamined. Additionally, studies using forensic subjects, not just experimental simulators, and employing more sophisticated discriminative function analyses will add empirical heft and conceptual clarity to the malingering psychosis phenomenon, which, according to Resnick and Knoll (2008), is likely to increase in the future.

References

Albert, S., Fox, H. M., & Kahn, M. W. (1980). Faking psychosis on the Rorschach: Can expert judges detect malingering? *Journal of Personality Assessment, 44*, 115–119.

Bleuler, E. (1911). *Dementia Praecox or the Group of Schizophrenias*, trans. J. Zinkin. New York: International Universities Press, 1950.

Cornell, D. G., & Hawk, G. L. (1989). Clinical presentation of malingerers diagnosed by experienced forensic psychologists. *Law and Human Behavior, 13*, 375–383.

Cunnien, A. J. (1997). Psychiatric and medical syndromes associated with deception. In R. Rogers (Ed.), *Clinical Assessment of Malingering and Deception* (2nd ed., pp. 26–44). New York: Guilford.

Elhai, J. D., Kinder, B., & Frueh, B. (2004). Projective assessment of malingering. In M. J. Hilsenroth & D. L. Segal (Eds.), *Comprehensive Handbook of Psychological Assessment: Personality Assessment* (Vol. 2, pp. 553–561). New York: Wiley.

Exner, J. E. (1991). *The Rorschach: A Comprehensive System, Advanced Interpretation* (Vol. 2, 2nd ed.). New York: Wiley.

Exner, J. E., & Erdberg, P. (2005). *The Rorschach: A Comprehensive System, Advanced Interpretation* (3rd ed.). New York: Wiley.

Fosberg, I. A. (1938). Rorschach reactions under varied instructions. *Rorschach Research Exchange, 3*, 12–31.

Fosberg, I. A. (1941). An experimental study of the reliability of the Rorschach psychodiagnostic technique. *Rorschach Research Exchange, 5*, 71–84.

Fosberg, I. A. (1943). How do subjects attempt to fake results on the Rorschach test? *Rorschach Research Exchange, 7*, 119–121.

Frueh, B. C., & Kinder, B. N. (1994). The susceptibility of the Rorschach Inkblot Test to malingering or combat-related PTSD. *Journal of Personality Assessment, 62*, 280–298.

Ganellen, R. J. (2008). Rorschach assessment of malingering and defensive response sets. In C. B. Gacono & F. B. Evans (Eds.), *The Handbook of Forensic Rorschach Assessment* (pp. 89–119). New York: Taylor & Francis.

Ganellen, R. J., Wasyliw, O. E., Haywood, T. W., & Grossman, L. S. (1996). Can psychosis be malingered on the Rorschach? An empirical study. *Journal of Personality Assessment, 66*, 65–80.

Harris, M. R. (2000). The malingering of psychotic disorders. *Jefferson Journal of Psychiatry, 15*, 12–23.

Jones, A., & Llewellyn. J. (1917). *Malingering*. London, UK: Heinemann.

Kucharski, L. T., Ryan, W., Vogt, J., & Goodloe, E. (1998). Clinical symptom presentation in suspected malingerers: An empirical investigation. *Journal of the American Academy of Psychiatry and the Law, 26*, 579–585.

McDougall, A. (1996). Rorschach indicators of simulated schizophrenia. *Dissertation Abstracts International, 57*, 2159.

Meyer, G. J., Viglione, D. J., Mihura, J. L., Erard, R. E., & Erdberg, P. (2011). *Rorschach Performance Assessment System: Administration, Coding, Interpretation, and Technical Manual*. Toledo, OH: Rorschach Performance Assessment System.

Mihura, J. L. (2012). The necessity of multiple test methods in conducting assessments: The role of the Rorschach and self-report. *Psychological Injury and Law, 5*, 97–106.

Najolia, G. M. (2013). An examination of speech characteristics under conditions of affective reactivity and variable cognitive load as distinguishing feigned and genuine schizophrenia. Unpublished Dissertation, Louisiana State University.

Netter, B. E. C., & Viglione, D. J. (1994). An empirical study of malingering schizophrenia on the Rorschach. *Journal of Personality Assessment, 62*, 45–57.

Resnick, P. J., & Knoll, J. L. (2008). Malingered psychosis. In R. Rogers (Ed.), *Clinical Assessment of Malingering and Deception* (3rd ed., pp. 51–68). New York: Guilford.

Rogers, R. (2008). Detection strategies for malingering and defensiveness. In R. Rogers (Ed.), *Clinical Assessment of Malingering and Deception* (3rd ed., pp. 14–35). New York: Guilford.

Rogers, R., Salekin, R. T., Sewell, K. W., Goldstein, A., & Leonard, K. (1998). A comparison of forensic and nonforensic malingers: A prototypical analysis of explanatory models. *Law and Human Behavior, 22*, 353–367.

Schretlen, D. J. (1997). Dissimulation on the Rorschach and other projective measures. In R. Rogers (Ed.), *Clinical Assessment of Malingering and Deception* (2nd ed., pp. 208–222). New York: Guilford.

Schuldberg, D., & Boster, J. S. (1985). Back to Topeka: Two types of distance in Rapaport original Rorschach thought disorder categories. *Journal of Abnormal Psychology, 94,* 205–215.

Seamons, D. T., Howell, R. J., Carlisle, A. L., & Roe, A. V. (1981). Rorschach simulation of mental illness and normality by psychotic and nonpsychotic legal offenders. *Journal of Personality Assessment, 45,* 130–135.

Sewell, K. W. (2008). Dissimulation on projective measures. In R. Rogers (Ed.), *Clinical Assessment of Malingering and Deception* (3rd ed., pp. 207–217). New York: Guilford.

Sherman, M., Trief, P., & Sprafkin, Q. R. (1975). Impression management in the psychiatric interview: Quality, style, and individual differences. *Journal of Consulting and Clinical Psychology, 43,* 867–871.

Chapter 16

Rorschach indications of psychotic phenomena in children and adolescents

Devoting a chapter to the Rorschach assessment of psychotic phenomena in children and adolescents is a necessary yet daunting task. It is necessary both because children and adolescents suffer from early-onset psychoses with disordered thinking and because the Rorschach plays an important role in the assessment of this population. A comprehensive review of either thought disorder or the Rorschach would be incomplete without addressing clinical manifestations and diagnostic issues in younger patients. However, perhaps in no other area is the diagnostic task more complex and the research so limited as it is with children and adolescents. As we shall see, despite the importance and relevance of the good diagnostic work, assessing thought disorder and other psychotic phenomena in youth presents a number of challenges.

Prevalence, complexities, confounds, and limitations

As with adults, in children we can distinguish the presence of psychotic symptoms, on the one hand, and actual psychotic disorders, on the other. Despite conventional perceptions, psychotic symptoms are not uncommon in children (Cepeda, 2007). According to Birmaher (2003), prevalence of psychotic symptoms in children and adolescents ranges between 4 and 8 percent, respectively. Although psychotic phenomena are relatively common, psychotic disorders are not. In children, as well as adults, mood disorders are the most frequent clinical problem that may have associated psychotic symptoms (Cepeda, 2007). The nature of psychotic symptoms varies considerably among children and adolescents. As might be assumed, hallucinations are the most common psychotic symptoms, followed by delusional thinking. Hallucinations were reported by 80 percent of young patients presenting with psychotic symptoms. Nearly 74 percent reported command auditory hallucinations. Delusional beliefs were less common, by comparison, reported by 22 percent of patients in this group. Somewhat surprising is that "thought disorder" is comparatively infrequent, reported by about 3 percent of child/adolescent with psychotic symptoms (Cepeda, 2007). Presumably, what is meant by "thought disorder" is the more restrictive, categorical symptom having to do with disorganized speech. Thus, from a clinical perspective, diagnosable psychotic disorders may be rare in youngsters; however, reported hallucinatory and delusional experiences are common in young patients whose mood disorders include psychotic-like features. What seems to be missing in this vulnerable young patient group are frequent disturbances in the form of thought or organization of speech.

More so than with adults, psychotic phenomena and disorders in children are either overlooked, dismissed, normalized, or misdiagnosed. Extremes of dismissal or normalization (e.g. "she'll grow out of it" or "kids have active imaginations") and overdiagnosis or pathologizing (e.g. conflating Rorschach scores relating to disordered thinking or poor FQ with "psychosis") are not unusual. Contributing to the diagnostic conundrum are three major confounding variables: the role of development, the frequency of comorbid conditions, and the presence of myriad medical, neurological, and toxic factors that can produce psychotic symptoms that may masquerade as psychological or functional in etiology.

Finally, when it comes to psychodiagnosis, and the Rorschach in particular, we enter a forest where the trail is harder to detect. Although literature regarding children's Rorschach responses has existed for decades, many are case reports or studies with low sample sizes, design limitations, or antiquated scoring systems (Klopfer & Margulies, 1941; Klopfer, Spiegelman, & Fox, 1956). Contemporary studies using current systems and more sophisticated designs are not that common. Researchers have used the TDI to study Rorschach manifestations in children between the ages of 5 and 16 who were either psychotic or had mothers diagnosed with schizophrenia or bipolar mania (Arboleda & Holzman, 1985). The TDI has also been used to study adolescent-onset schizophrenia and major depression with psychotic features (Makowski et al., 1997). Studies using the CS to explore psychotic phenomena and disordered thinking in children have been quite limited. Smith and his colleagues examined the PTI, SCZI, M-, and X-% in a heterogeneous sample of inpatients aged 8 to 18 (Smith et al., 2001). Unfortunately, as the authors acknowledged, their sample size was small, racially homogeneous, and most important, included fewer than 5 percent of patients who were diagnosed with psychotic disorders. Another recent study compared the diagnostic accuracy of the TDI with WSUM6 of the CS in a small sample of adolescents aged 12 to 18, over half of whom had a diagnosis of schizophrenia (Andersen et al., 2016). Apart from these few studies, we currently lack well-designed studies that look more closely at the Rorschach's role in assessing psychotic phenomena in the young and its contribution to differential diagnosis.

The role of development

Normal developmental processes may muddy the waters when assessing psychotic phenomena in children (Kleiger & Khadivi, 2015). Without considering the role of cognitive and language development, one might confuse developmental immaturity with psychopathology. For example, between the ages of five and seven, children come to develop stable concepts, manage symbolic media, separate fantasy from reality, establish cohesive links from one idea to the next, and begin to understand the perspective of the listener. Younger children readily engage in magical thinking and have difficulties grasping the stability of concepts or understanding the perspective of the listener. Without these developmental achievements, which make reality testing and mature communication possible, it is difficult to determine the presence of psychotic phenomena. Whereas younger children have yet to develop these requisite cognitive (reasoning) and language capacities, some older children may be delayed in developing the ability to distinguish fantasy from reality and communicate their ideas in an orderly manner. In such cases, developmental delays, and not psychosis per se, may be a better way of understanding what, at first, presents as psychotic-like phenomena.

Another way to approach the issue of development is to look at the Rorschach from an ontological perspective. As we have seen, Leichtman (1996) provided a way to conceptualize the processes underlying common Rorschach thought disorder scores from a developmental perspective. Up until the ages of five or seven, disordered Rorschach responses are best understood as manifestations of the developmental limitations or achievements of the youngsters taking the test. Thus, as noted in Chapter 11, perseverative thinking is developmentally appropriate for two- to three-year-olds who lack the capacity to think representationally. Similarly, confabulation and combinative thinking on the Rorschach for children before the age of five are considered signs of cognitive development and not of disordered thinking.

Comorbidity and atypical presentations

Comorbid and atypical presentations of other psychological disorders further complicate the assessment process with children. First, most children presenting with psychotic symptoms will also complain of or exhibit other symptoms and disorders. In particular, mood-related symptoms, fears and anxiety, inattention, social difficulties, and dysregulated behavior may be present in the child who concurrently exhibits psychotic symptomatology. Nearly 100 percent of children aged 4 to 15 who were carefully diagnosed with either schizophrenia or schizoaffective disorder had at least one comorbid disorder such as ADHD or an oppositional defiant, depressive, or anxiety disorder (Ross, Heinlein, & Tregallas, 2006).

In addition to the frequency of comorbidity, a broad range of childhood problems may either masquerade as psychoses or, conversely, mask the presence of underlying psychotic phenomena (Cepeda, 2007; Kleiger & Khadivi, 2015; McCarthy, 2015). Regarding the issue of masquerading, a range of undetected neurodevelopmental disorders, intellectual disabilities, trauma-related disturbances, anxiety, and mood disorders may include difficulties in reality testing, reasoning, and speaking. In some cases, what at first suggests psychotic phenomena might be an atypical feature of another disorder that when effectively treated may lead to the resolution of psychotic symptoms. For some of these children, what initially seemed psychotic was actually not. For others, their psychotic-like symptoms are better understood as transient byproducts of another primary disorder.

Cepeda (2007) reviewed categories of "benign psychoses" that may lead clinicians to overinterpret the diagnostic significance of transient and circumscribed symptoms. Included in this category are the phenomena of imaginary friends and hallucinations secondary to sleep or sensory deprivation or bereavement.

Alternatively, some youngsters may present with an array of symptoms that, at first, do not suggest underlying psychotic phenomena. Intense fears, obsessional preoccupations, rituals, social withdrawal, anger, irritability, inattention, and disruptions in sleep and appetite may all be calling cards for what turns out to be underlying psychotic-like experiences. The alert child clinician knows that presenting symptoms seemingly unrelated to underlying psychotic phenomena might be associated with hallucinatory or delusional symptoms that are difficult for the child to communicate (Kleiger & Khavidi, 2015).

Medical, neurological, and toxic disturbances

Ruling out the presence of a metabolic, neurological, or toxic etiology is critical for all patients, but especially for children presenting with psychotic symptoms (Cepeda, 2007; Kleiger & Khadivi, 2015). Cepeda presents an exhaustive review of medical conditions associated with delirium and psychosis and provides guidelines for differentiating between primary and secondary psychoses associated with an underlying medical or toxic origin. Not surprisingly, hallucinations and delusions are more common in psychoses secondary to medical etiology, whereas thought disorder is rare. Cepeda points out that hallucinatory phenomena are often visual in nature and that delusions are simple and unorganized.

Rorschach literature

In addition to the scarcity of contemporary Rorschach studies of children and adolescents with psychotic symptoms or disorders, the adequacy of norms for younger subjects has been an unsettled issue. Up until the early 2000s, most had considered CS norms for children and adolescents to be adequate. However, an international database of nonpatient adult and child samples highlighted distinct differences in the standard norms of the CS (Meyer, Erdberg, & Shaffer, 2007), which led to unresolved controversy regarding which set of norms clinicians should use when interpreting child and adolescent Rorschachs. In particular, researchers discovered a large divergence in FQ-related scores between the 2003 CS norms (Exner, 2003) and those of the 2007 composite international norms (Meyer, Erdberg, & Shaffer, 2007). In essence, using CS norms results in poorer FQ scores, which may lead clinicians to overinterpret difficulties with reality testing and thinking. At the same time, some might argue that the more "permissive" international norms have the potential to overlook these kinds of problems in thought organization and reality testing as well (Viglione & Giromini, 2016).

Currently, R-PAS researchers have developed a transitional set of norms for children and adolescents based on statistical procedures to generate normative expectations. The foundation for these norms is the international data sets, as opposed to the older norms from the CS. These transitional norms are currently being used in R-PAS interpretations with children aged 6 to 17 (Meyer et al., 2011).

Primary psychoses and secondary psychotic phenomena: Clinical features and Rorschach contributions

Despite the limited research in the area of psychosis, children, and the Rorschach and the complications stemming from development, comorbidity, and possible medical etiologies, how useful is the Rorschach in identifying, interpreting, and understanding psychotic phenomena in children and adolescents? Furthermore, are there enough empirical studies and published clinical reports to provide clues to differential diagnoses? In the following sections, I summarize available clinical and Rorschach findings that pertain to differential diagnoses among the schizophrenia spectrum, affective psychoses, neurodevelopmental, trauma-related conditions, and personality disorders. However, I offer two caveats.

First, as noted above, the literature in this area is limited. As much as we might hope that science can help clinicians distinguish Rorschach manifestations of disordered thinking in children and adolescents with schizophrenia from those with psychotic mood disorders, the research is sparse compared to that of adults. For example, studies often have very few inpatient subjects diagnosed with specific kinds of psychoses like schizophrenia. Instead of having separate groups of patients with schizophrenia-spectrum disorders, bipolar disorders, and those who are psychotically depressed, psychotic youngsters are generally aggregated into the same sample group, administered the Rorschach, and compared to nonpatients or patients with other psychiatric disorders. While this approach is useful for studying dimensions like thought disorder across different groups of patients, it makes it harder to conduct a more fine-grained discrimination of differential patterns of Rorschach thought disorder among various categories of psychosis in children and adolescents (i.e. schizophrenia spectrum vs. bipolar mania vs. psychotic unipolar depression). In other words, when used with children, the Rorschach is more successful in addressing dimensional questions (i.e. how disordered, disorganized, illogical, or impoverished is this child's thinking?) than categorical questions (i.e. are the qualitative features of the Rorschach more suggestive of schizophrenia or an affective psychosis?).

The second caveat has to do with another type of differential diagnosis—distinguishing childhood psychosis from personality disorders. Despite a long tradition of talking about personality disorders in children, I find it difficult to diagnose personality disorders in the context of a child's developing personality. Thus, questions of whether psychotic phenomena reflect the presence of a nascent personality disorder or an early-onset psychosis may make some clinical sense but are fraught with conceptual and diagnostic difficulties.

Early-onset schizophrenia

Clinical features

Early-onset schizophrenia (before the age of 12 or 13) is considered both extremely rare and quite malignant (Cepeda, 2007; Kleiger & Khadivi, 2015; McCarthy, 2015). Fewer than 5 percent of children referred to NIMH for questionable psychoses were confirmed to have childhood-onset schizophrenia, or COS (Sporn & Rapoport, 2001). This rare condition is associated with a lower level of premorbid functioning and a poorer prognosis (Rapoport & Gogtay, 2011). Although by the time they reach clinical attention, children endorse positive symptoms and disorganized thinking like adults with schizophrenia, they may report more visual hallucinations than adults (Rapoport & Gogtay, 2011). However, these are typically not the initial symptoms in COS. The most common symptom and behavioral presentations include a set of nonspecific developmental delays, school and social problems, learning disabilities, oppositionality, and affective dysregulation (Schaeffer & Ross, 2002).

Rorschach contributions

Two TDI studies contribute to the literature. Arboleda and Holzman (1985) compared Rorschach TDI scores in four groups of children aged 5 to 16 years. The groups included normal controls, inpatient psychotic children, inpatient nonpsychotic children, and high-risk children (children whose mothers were diagnosed with either schizophrenia-spectrum or affective, primarily bipolar, psychoses). Nine of the hospitalized children had heterogeneous diagnoses—which included schizophrenia, major affective psychoses, and pervasive developmental disorders. Another nine patients in this group did not have psychotic diagnoses but were described as the "spectrum group" on the basis of evidencing clinical signs of thought disorder, having psychosis in relatives, or receiving neuroleptic medication. High-risk and psychotic children had similarly high levels of TDI scores compared to the other two groups. Both groups demonstrated scores reflecting: (1) word-finding difficulties; (2) clang responses; (3) loose associations; (4) tendency to fluid responses; (5) confabulations; and (6) contaminations. The qualitative nature of the high-risk children was strikingly similar to that of the children in the hospitalized psychotic-spectrum group. Both groups also gave more pathological responses, scored at .75 and 1.0 levels of severity.

Although this study did not examine the qualitative differences between groups of schizophrenia-spectrum and bipolar psychoses, it was a significant contribution in two respects. First, it established some normative data for nonpatient children on the TDI and discussed the developmental nature of immature and magical thinking that could be picked up by the TDI in normal children. Second, the study broke new ground by demonstrating how thought disorder might serve as a marker for psychotic vulnerability in high-risk children who had psychotic first-degree relatives but were not themselves showing clinical signs of psychosis.

The differential diagnostic question was taken up by Makowski and colleagues (1997), who compared qualitative features of thought disorder in adolescents with early-onset schizophrenia to those with psychotic depression and another nonpsychotic inpatient group. The average age of the subjects was 15 years. TDI scores were higher for all hospitalized adolescents compared to those of a control group. The most striking finding was that the thought disorder in the adolescent-onset schizophrenia group was qualitatively different from that in the psychotically depressed group but quite similar to that found in adult-onset schizophrenia. TDI scores in the adolescent schizophrenia group were characterized by significant amounts of idiosyncratic word usage (queer verbalizations), illogical reasoning (ALOG), confusion responses, loss of realistic attunement to the task (flippancy and loss of distance), and looseness.

A recent study by a group of Danish researchers examined the TDI and the WSUM6 and PTI from the CS in a small sample of 23 patients aged 12 to 18 years, referred to the clinic because of psychotic or psychotic-like symptoms (Andersen et al., 2016). Diagnoses were based on clinical interviews and the PANSS (Kay et al., 1987). Seventy percent of the sample met ICD-10 criteria for schizophrenia, and five of these patients were prescribed neuroleptic medication when referred for assessment. The other patients received diagnoses of unspecified behavioral and emotional disorders or personality disorders. The schizophrenia group had mean scores on the TDI of 31.1 ($\pm$ 26.8) and WSUM6 of 35.6 ($\pm$ 30.9). It is interesting that neither the Total TDI nor WSUM6 discriminated between the two groups, although the WSUM6 came close (p = .062). The Total TDI correlated with WSUM6. However, the Total TDI did not coordinate with the PANSS General Psychopathology score, whereas the WSUM6 did. The most pathological responses (those at the .75 and 1.0 levels) were restricted to patients diagnosed with schizophrenia; however, six patients from this group had no pathological responses. The authors attributed this negative finding to three issues: (1) a problem of power, given the small sample sizes; (2) the fact that one third of these patients had already been placed on neuroleptic medication, which has a dampening effect of more florid signs of thought disorder; and (3) the fact that some of these patients may have demonstrated negative, versus positive, forms of thought disorder. Nonetheless, the researchers indicated that only patients in the schizophrenia group gave absurd, incoherent, fluid, contamination, and autistic responses. In addition, only word-finding difficulties were found in patients in this group. Of further interest, when the responses were scored using CS Special Scores, contamination was only found in the schizophrenia group.

The authors cautiously concluded that the TDI is a preferred method of assessing thought disorder on the Rorschach with early-onset schizophrenia because it provides a more detailed and nuanced assessment of disordered thinking.

Exner and Erdberg (2005) reviewed a number of studies that used the CS to examine thought disorder in adolescents. Armstrong, Silberg, and Parente (1986) found that adolescent patients with psychotic disorders, including schizophrenia spectrum and psychotic depression, were associated with higher levels of thought disorder as measured by both the TDI and SCZI. Studies also showed that intellectual level is an important intervening variable, as highly intelligent and creative adolescents tended to produce more DV and DR responses (Gallucci, 1989; Franklin & Cornell, 1997). These studies also concluded that the presence of Level 2 Special Scores was rare in the highly intelligent and creative group and may serve as a basis for determining when the adolescents' Rorschach responses indicate creativity or psychopathology.

Exner, Thomas, and Mason (1985) demonstrated the stability of Rorschach variables associated with reality testing and disordered thinking. Their study initially tested 29 adolescents with schizophrenia, aged 12 to 15 years, and then reassessed them 11 to 14 months later. Despite treatment, which presumably included neuroleptic medication for many of these patients, there were no significant differences between the two administrations on X-, M-, or WSUM6. The authors concluded that the severity of structural psychopathology, as indexed by the Rorschach FQ- and WSUM6, had been refractory to clinical intervention efforts.

Finally, as noted earlier Smith et al. (2001) found M- to be a more sensitive measure of disordered thought in children and adolescents than SCZI, PTI, or X%. Exner and Erdberg (2005) concluded their review by stating "within the Rorschach, M- and Level 2 Special Scores are of particular note" (p. 393). However, as reported previously, M- as an index of disordered thinking did not hold up well in Mihura's meta-analysis (Mihura et al., 2013).

Affective psychoses

Clinical features

Psychoses associated with mood disorders are far more common among children and adolescents than COS, with prevalence rates in the general population of close to 3 percent in school-age children and 6 percent for adolescents (McCarthy & Dobroshi, 2015). The severity of major depression in younger patients is highly correlated with the later development of psychotic features. Thus, severe, early-onset depression can be considered an important risk factor. Additionally, as described by McCarthy and Dobroshi (2015), there is also a risk that these children with severe depression with psychotic features will eventually develop bipolar disorder.

Psychotic symptoms associated with bipolar disorder occur with greater frequency in childhood and adolescence than during any other developmental period (Carlson, 2013). Research efforts have sought to identify prodromal features for bipolar disorders, but the results have been mixed (Sossin, 2015). Sossin summarized the features related to higher risk for bipolar disorder, which include mood lability, anxiety, excitement, loud speech, stubbornness, decreased sleep, difficulties with thinking, and a deficit in facial affect recognition. Of course, all of these features are not specific to bipolar youth; however, when there is a family history of bipolar disorder, these symptom and temperamental features become more significant. In general, compared to children with COS, children with bipolar disorders demonstrated better premorbid social and academic functioning (Cepeda, 2007).

Cepeda (2007) summarized research showing that psychotic symptoms may occur in close to 60 percent of children who exhibit bipolar mania. In Cepeda's study, 87 percent presented with elated mood, 85 percent with grandiosity, and 55 percent had grandiose delusions. Adolescents with psychotic bipolar disorder often exhibit visual and auditory hallucinations and delusions with less bizarre content than children with COS (McCarthy & Dobroshi, 2015). Some have argued that, as with adult patients, speech/thinking in psychotic bipolar youth is more organized and structured compared to that of children with schizophrenia (Cummings & Mega, 2003). In terms of general diagnostic features, Carlson (2005) used the acronym HIPERS to aid in the identification of mania in children:

H: Hyperactivity and high energy
I: Irritability
P: Psychosis–Grandiosity
E: Elated mood
R: Rapid speech, racing thoughts, flight of ideas
S: Reduced sleep need

Rorschach contributions

The Rorschach literature on thought disorder patterns among bipolar and psychotically depressed children and adolescents is unfortunately quite slim. As reported above, Makowski et al. (1997) compared adolescents diagnosed with schizophrenia to those with psychotic depression. Both groups received elevated total TDI scores, but their scores tended to be qualitatively different. The researchers factor analyzed their data and identified seven empiric factors. Although there was overlap between the two groups of psychotic adolescents, the group with major depression with psychotic features was characterized by idiosyncratic symbolism, confabulation, INCOMs, and contaminations. Makowski concluded that scores associated with the depressive psychosis group reflected a style of thinking in which responses are embellished arbitrarily with personal meaning.

Contemporary, well-designed Rorschach studies of bipolar disorders in children and adolescents are difficult to find. Apart from studies on disordered thinking in asymptomatic offspring of bipolar parents, I could not find any studies that looked specifically at the Rorschachs of children actually diagnosed with bipolar disorders. Excluding case reports or unpublished dissertations, which also are not that common, I found one brief report that looked at a small sample of asymptomatic children, aged 7 to 16, of parents who were diagnosed as manic-depressive by DSM-III criteria (Osher et al., 2000). The data showed that when compared to nonpatient controls, the offspring of bipolar parents showed significantly higher WSUM6 and Level 2 Special Scores. Whether their WSUM6 indices were characterized more by one type of score versus another was not reported in the findings. This study extended the authors' previous research, which sought to discover psychological markers of bipolar disorders on the Rorschach.

Trauma-induced disorders

Clinical features

The relationship between childhood trauma and the development of psychotic symptoms or disorders was discussed at length in the previous chapter. Trauma-induced psychotic symptoms in children may be transient byproducts of abuse by adults or bullying by peers. As preadolescents, these individuals are twice as likely to experience psychotic symptoms like hallucinations and delusions (Radmanovic, 2012). Cepeda (2007) indicated that hallucinations and delusions of traumatized children and adolescents are often directly associated with the traumatic events and the perpetrator. These youngsters may hear the perpetrators making derogatory comments or frightening them. Victims may also experience the presence of the perpetrator through all senses, fearing that the perpetrator will return to traumatize them again. Voices have the quality of intrusive thoughts or concerns, where the child is essentially reexperiencing fragmentary aspects of the traumatic stimuli. Command hallucinations to harm oneself or others are not unusual and may occur frequently at night. In hospitalized samples of children with PTSD, between 20 percent and 76 percent endorse hallucinations. When dissociative disorder is also diagnosed, psychosis is present in up to 95 percent of these children (Cepeda, 2007). Disorganized speech (formal thought disorder) is generally not characteristic of these children (Radmanovic, 2012).

Rorschach contributions

Unlike that of other childhood disorders, the literature on PTSD is more plentiful and of higher empirical and clinical quality. Holaday (2000) summarized a series of studies examining the effects of trauma on children and adolescents through their Rorschach responses. Comparing the Rorschachs of 35 children with PTSD (mean age 10) to 35 children with Oppositional Defiant Disorder (ODD; mean age 11) against CS norms for children, Holaday found significant differences in a number of variables related to reality testing and thought disturbance. Specifically, SCZI, WSUM6, and X+% were found to be significantly different between these two groups. What makes Holaday's study particularly compelling is her use of a relevant clinical control group (children with ODD), as opposed to simply comparing the PTSD children to CS norms, which, as indicated above, some have called into question. In addition, Holaday may have been among the first psychologists to write about the problems with SCZI. As described earlier, when she submitted her manuscript for publication in 1988, Holaday suggested that the SCZI be renamed the Perception and Thinking Index (PATI) in order to remove the inaccurate diagnostic implications of SCZI. Finally, Holaday provided a rich conceptual discussion of why traumatized children might show disruptions in reality testing and logical thinking on a procedure like the Rorschach:

> Trauma interrupts the child's naïve belief that the world is dependable and predictable and the people in it follow logical rules based on trust and fairness, and it also disrupts the belief that there is appropriate punishment for people who do bad things. When young victims cannot comprehend or make sense of what happened to them, life becomes irrational, illogical and confusing. Reality is no longer understood in the same way as it was before the trauma (p. 155).

Viglione's 1990 case study of a traumatized child made a substantial contribution to the Rorschach literature on trauma and the differential diagnosis of disordered thinking based on the Rorschachs of children. Viglione's thesis was that disordered thinking in children, as expressed through the Rorschach, might represent an adaptive response to overwhelming stress and not necessarily a more severe psychotic disturbance. Others have also written about the adaptive nature of primary process thinking in children's Rorschach responses, (Russ, 1988; Murray, 1992). In a series of three Rorschachs administered to a child between the ages of 11 and 15, Viglione showed how his patient's initially disturbed Rorschach represented an adaptive regression to his mother's suicide attempt and how much of what looked like thought disorder in the boy's first Rorschach disappeared on subsequent testing, seven months and four years later. Viglione concluded that some initial evidence of cognitive slippage on the Rorschach may be a positive prognostic indicator that the child is processing the trauma in an automatic, reparative manner. He went on to state that in more severe, nontrauma-based disturbances, one might expect to see more Level 2 Special Scores and a lack of content representative of the traumatic event.

Neurodevelopmental disorders: Autism spectrum, ADHD, and learning disabilities

Autism spectrum: Clinical features

In the past autism was frequently misdiagnosed as childhood schizophrenia; however, it is now well recognized as a distinct neurodevelopmental spectrum of symptoms varying in level of severity. Although there may be some overlap in behavioral rigidity, hallucinatory phenomena, magical beliefs, perseveration, and tangentiality, disordered thinking is not a typical feature of children within the autism spectrum. However, researchers have recognized a smaller group of children with what has been termed "multiple complex developmental disorder" or "multiplex developmental disorders" (Kumra et al., 1998; Zalsman & Cohen, 1998). These children have multiple social, emotional, and cognitive developmental delays that are subsumed under the umbrella of the autism spectrum. What makes this group unique is the presence of more pronounced psychotic symptoms. In these cases, a comorbid diagnosis of psychosis is warranted in addition to a diagnosis of an autism-spectrum disorder.

Those unfamiliar with the spectrum of autism may mistake some superficial similarities as signs of psychosis. Both schizophrenia and autism-spectrum disorders may include unusual speech patterns, odd ideas, social withdrawal, and flat affect. Abnormalities in pragmatic language—such as poor topic maintenance, difficulties with coherence, and lack of reciprocity—may strike clinicians as signs of a formal thought disorder rather than manifestations of social language impairment symptomatic of autism. Additionally, an overfocus on unusual interests may make one think about the possibility of delusions, while idiosyncratic sensory experiences or hypersensitivities might suggest hallucinations. Furthermore, poor mentalizing skills and impairments in social perception may lead diagnosticians to view the youngster as paranoid rather than autistic. Executive deficits in initiation, activation, and motivation may present in a similar manner to negative symptoms of schizophrenia.

Rorschach contributions

Using the CS, Holaday (2001) compared the Rorschachs of 24 boys with Asperger's Disorder, ages 7 to 18, to a matched group of same-aged boys with emotional and behavioral disorders. Holaday found that the Asperger's group had fewer cooperation responses (COP) and fewer human movement (M), and human responses (H) as well as higher scores on the CDI than either the matched contrast group or established CS age-specific norms. The data highlighted impoverishment in relational capacities and coping resources and limited ideational resources available for fantasy and ego-directed thinking. Among the guidelines proposed for identifying Asperger boys, Holaday included COP=0, CDI >3, H <2, M <2, along with an absence of texture (T=0) and lower than expected color responses (WSUMC). Surprisingly, none of the variables having to do with reality testing (X+ or X-%) or thought organization (WSUM6 or PTI) were among distinguishing scores.

The absence of scores reflecting poor reality testing and disordered thinking is at odds with findings from other case reports, which found elevations on X–, WSUM6, and PTI in youngsters with autism-spectrum-like features (Bernabei et al., 1999; Yalof, 2006). Bernabei and colleagues compared the Rorschachs of two children, ages six and seven, one with autism and the other with pervasive developmental disorder. The team found striking contrasts. One child demonstrated the kind of concrete and rigid response style that Schuldberg and Boster (1985) described as at one pole of dimensional deconstruction of Rapaport's concept of "distance from the blot." This child showed little capacity to respond to the Rorschach in a representational manner. In contrast, the other child showed the opposite. His record was replete with Special Scores, especially DR2s, suggesting that he fell in the "fluid and highly personalized" quadrant of Schuldberg and Boster's schema. The authors concluded that these two little boys with autism-spectrum disorders occupied opposite poles in terms of their imaginative capacities, with one child demonstrating impoverished cognitive resources and an absence of imaginative capacities, while the other showed a distortion of his thought processes and reality testing.

In writing about a latency-stage boy with features of both nonverbal learning disability and Asperger's, Yalof (2006) was at first struck by his patient's claim that he could hear his mother's voice when alone, and by his fears of being whisked away by ghosts. The boy spoke about the "curse" of his imagination and the "fragile line" between his fantasies and reality. Initially, Yalof wondered if the patient might have schizophrenia (personal communication, May 29, 2016). Elevated scores on Rorschach indices of disordered thinking seemed to support initial concerns about some sort of psychotic process. However, in his rich and clinically sophisticated integrative case study, Yalof linked his young patient's elevated PTI and WSUM6 (which included an ALOG and several Level 2 INCOMs and FABCOMs) not only to the boy's problem in distinguishing between reality and fantasy, but also to how the patient sought refuge in his fantasies. Yalof explained how the youngster seemed to use fantasy as a means of comforting or stimulating himself. Sometimes his fantasies served as a form of adaptive self-expression, allowing him to express privately what others might have viewed as unconventional. Yet despite the functions that fantasy immersion might have served for this boy, Yalof concluded that any adaptive gains came at a significant cost to his reality testing.

ADHD, conduct disorders, and learning disabilities: Clinical features

Two key issues may potentially complicate the diagnosis of ADHD in children. First, comorbidity or confusion with other psychiatric and developmental disorders is extremely high. Uncomplicated, or so-called "pure culture," cases often do not reach the psychologist's office and are instead assessed and managed by pediatricians. More often than not, when psychologists evaluate children for ADHD-related concerns, their inattention, impulsivity, hyperactivity, and executive deficits are either comorbid with or symptomatic of another disturbance. In other words, when evaluating children for the presence of ADHD, it is important to be aware that problems with hyperactivity, concentration, and impulsivity can be the result of anxiety, mania, or psychosis, to name but a few of the possible underlying sources (Cepeda, 2007). Similarly, children presenting with conduct problems and learning disabilities may often suffer from other problems as well. Clearly, psychotic symptoms are typically not among diagnostic criteria for any of these syndromes; however, in many of these many cases, the copresence of anxiety and mood-related issues, and occasional concomitant psychotic-like phenomena may not be unusual.

Differentiating pediatric bipolar disorder from ADHD may be challenging. However, clinicians pay attention to symptoms like pressured speech, hypomania, decreased need for sleep, and flight of ideas, along with a strong family history of bipolarity, to make the differential diagnosis (Cepeda, 2007). Akiskal (2005) also commented on the striking presence of grandiosity and euphoria in male bipolar children.

Rorschach contributions

A number of Rorschach studies have pointed out that children with ADHD show impaired perceptual accuracy (Acklin, 1990; Bartell & Solanto, 1995; Cotugno, 2006). In distinguishing children with LD/ADHD from those with psychosis, Murray (1992) agreed that scores on Rorschach indices of poor reality testing and disordered thinking might be elevated in the former group. Murray indicated that even when LD/ADHD children receive Special Scores, the form level of these responses is good to moderately poor and the Special Scores have a fantasy, cartoon-like quality that reflect things they have seen in the popular media. INCOMs and FABCOMs might be more common in the records of these nonpsychotic children with ADHD. In contrast, Murray emphasized how psychotic children's thought-disordered responses are more idiosyncratic and malignant where boundaries are collapsed in a more primitive manner.

Darleen: Is this psychosis?

The choppy waters of assessing disordered thinking in the Rorschachs of children and adolescents is often navigated by looking at clinical cases that frequently reflect the confounding factors of comorbidity and development discussed throughout this chapter. Darleen, a 12-year-old adopted child in a single-parent household, presented with a range of chronic social and academic difficulties. Referred for an evaluation both to update her Individualized Education Program and assist her therapist in diagnostic understanding and treatment planning, this lanky, bespectacled girl was seen for a comprehensive assessment of her neurocognitive, academic, and personality functioning. Since the age of eight, she had been treated for ADHD and language-based learning disabilities. Speech and language evaluations ruled out expressive and receptive language disorders but identified longstanding weaknesses in language pragmatics. Early sensory integration problems resulted in years of occupational therapy. Darleen also struggled with difficulties making friends and in recent years had withdrawn from her peer group. Like many such youngsters, Darleen spent much of her time in Internet chat rooms or playing online games.

In addition to wanting an updated assessment of her cognitive and academic functioning, her mother and therapist had some concerns about her thinking and ability to distinguish fantasy from reality. Six months prior to her testing, Darleen told a school counselor that she thought she was a vampire. The school notified the mother and therapist. Several months later, Darleen appeared to drop this belief but became preoccupied with having special powers to read others' minds and control the weather. During the interview, she indicated that her mother and therapist knew little of this because she was only beginning to figure this out herself. Darleen later revealed that she was a queen of a legion of creatures, some alive and others who had risen from the dead. On occasion, she claimed to hear a demon's voice. She said that she sometimes saw figures wearing strange uniforms walking around her on the sidewalk.

Darleen spoke about her special powers and odd beliefs in a monotone. She appeared to want to talk only about this and resisted efforts to shift her attention to the testing that we were scheduled to do. She established fleeting eye contact but seemed to have difficulty sustaining an appropriate social gaze. Twice when she entered my office for a testing session, she began speaking as if she were in the middle of a sentence. Numerous times throughout the process, I found myself becoming uncertain of what she had just said and needed to ask for clarification.

The mother provided the information that was known about Darleen's birth parents. The birth mother reportedly suffered from ADHD and anxiety, but her father (Darleen's biological grandfather) had been diagnosed with schizophrenia in his late teens. Additionally, the birth mother's aunt (the biological grandfather's sister) was said to have had traits suggestive of higher functioning autism. Finally, Darleen's mother confirmed the presence of mild birth trauma during a difficult forceps delivery.

Both Darleen's mother and her school counselor provided unexpected information regarding Darleen's recent functioning at home and in school. Despite earlier concerns about her inattentiveness, social isolation, and odd beliefs about becoming a vampire, the adults who had daily contact with Darleen noted how well she appeared to be doing within the last month. Neither her mother nor her counselor had noticed anything unusual—no decline in Darleen's hygiene, no disturbance of her sleep, or increased social withdrawal. A month ago, with gentle goading from her mother and her therapist, Darleen had agreed to try out for the school volleyball team. To their surprise and pleasure, she made the team and was beginning to talk more with her peer group in and outside of school.

On performance testing, Darleen obtained a WISC-V FSIQ at the 32nd percentile while demonstrating cognitive impairment on tests of nonverbal problem solving, working memory, and processing speed. Despite the mother's and counselor's reports of Darleen's improvement, another teacher rated her in the clinically significant range on BASC-3 (Reynolds & Kamphaus, 2015) scales of Atypicality and Withdrawal. She obtained a single scale elevation on the SCZ scale of the PAI-A (Morey, 2007), with a high score on the Psychotic Experiences subscale.

Darleen gave 25 responses on her R-PAS-administered Rorschach. Scores on all variables in the Perceptual and Thinking Problems domain were more than 3.0 standard deviations above the mean for adolescents her age. Standard scores for two critical indices, SevCog and FQ-%, were 150 and 134, respectively. Among her Cognitive Scores were on Level 2 deviant verbalization (DV2), two Level 2 fabulized combinations (FAB2), one peculiar Logic (PEC), and two contaminations (CON). Table 16.1 illustrates the nature of her more disturbed responses.

As one can see, Darleen's worst responses are alarming. One contamination response is rare; two are even more unlikely. Although there are no scores that reach pathognomonic certainty, contamination scores might come close. The severe collapse of boundaries that we see in responses III-5 and VII-13 might alert us to the presence of psychotic confusion in maintaining a distinction between incompatible frames of reference, including self and others.

Table 16.1 Sampling of Darleen's Rorschach responses

Card	Response	Clarification	R-PAS Coding
I-2	This could be angels summoning flying "dracoids"	These are the angels in the middle (D4) and the creatures, here on the sides (D2) (Dracoids?) Yes, a special reptilian variety	W (H), (A) Sy 2 – Ma, FMa DV2, COP, AGC
III-5 V	Here, at the bottom, a bat cave	Right here (D7). It's a bat, the claws; it's a cave. (Bat cave). Yea, the wings (Dd31) is the dark cave	D7 A, NC u Y CON, AGC
VII-13	Smoke. Clouds coming up. Or girls. Kinda smoke girls, made out of smoke cuz if they're dark like that it would be some kind of smoke	Yep, (Smoke girls?) You can see they're facing each other (Dd22) with the smoke going up inside.	W H, NC Vg 2 o Y PEC, CON
IX	Generals at the top with a bloody demon dropping from their swords		D3, 6 H, (H), Bl, Sy 2 u m, CF, FAB2, MOR, AGC

Following Viglione's model (1990), which views Rorschach material in the context of the child's environmental stresses and manifest behavior, we know that there were no environmental stresses that would have suggested that Darleen's disturbed Rorschach might have been a response to traumatic events. From a behavioral perspective, we have mixed input from parents and teachers. Darleen's parents and school counselor reported that since joining the volleyball team and socializing with peers Darleen seemed less distracted and more responsible. However, one of her teachers reportedly observed odd and inappropriate social behavior in the classroom (talking to herself, expressing unusual ideas), along with floridly bizarre beliefs in her special powers (which she revealed to me during the interview). Finally, we have dramatic evidence of highly disturbed thinking and reality testing on her Rorschach. Her disturbed responses earned several Level 2 scores, including two rare contaminations. Thus, we have some convergent clinical and testing information that strengthens an impression that Darleen is experiencing severe psychotic symptoms. However, we are troubled by the apparent fact that according to two adults who see her daily she actually appeared to be functioning more adaptively in her social environment. Further complicating the diagnostic picture was the presence of longstanding difficulties with social communication and peer relationships. Thus, in the presence of psychotic-like symptoms evident from performance testing and clinical interview, on the one hand, and reports of adaptive functioning by mother and counselor, on the other, there was evidence of difficulties with social cognition and rigidity.

If there is one clear conclusion to be reached from the array of clinical and assessment information, it was that reaching a definitive diagnostic impression was premature. Feedback could be provided to the school concerning Darleen's educational needs, while simultaneously working closely with Darleen's therapist to provide feedback to the family and to recommend a diagnostic and medical consultation from a child psychiatrist. In addition to a medication consultation, Darleen needed a thorough physical and neurological work-up to rule out possible medical factors contributing to her symptoms.

The data strongly supported the presence of significant psychotic symptoms, but Darleen's age and absence of clear signs of functional deterioration made a schizophrenia prodrome seem less convincing. Could her positive experiences with her entry into the social world because of her volleyball experience have forestalled a more precipitous psychotic episode? On the other hand, might her bizarre set of magical beliefs reflect the beginning of a delusional system that provided Darleen with an explanation for her confusing experiences and anxiety earlier in the year? Had she settled on a psychotic explanation that helped reduce her anxiety at the sacrifice of staying grounded in reality? Beyond questions of psychosis, does Darleen have a disorder within the autism spectrum, or possibly a multiple complex developmental disorder, reflecting the comorbid existence of a longstanding spectrum disorder with rapidly developing psychosis?

In all diagnostic work, especially when evaluating the possible presence of an emerging psychotic disorder in a young patient, caution and provisional impressions are the rule. Candid discussions with parents and treaters are important. Overaggressive and premature diagnostic closure is unhelpful. So is turning a blind eye to a set of symptoms that clearly require monitoring and further consultations. However, as long as the child is not in crisis, is engaged in effective treatment, and has been referred for additional medical/medication consultations, then an ongoing diagnostic process should proceed in a careful and extended manner.

References

Acklin, M. W. (1990). Personality dimensions in two types of learning-disabled children: A Rorschach study. *Journal of Personality Assessment, 54*, 67–77.

Akiskal, H. S. (2005, December). The nature of preschool mania. (Commentary). *The Journal of Bipolar Disorders, 4*, 17.

Andersen, D. B., Vernal, D. L., Bilenberg, N., Væver, M. S., & Stenstrøm, A. D. (2016). Early-onset schizophrenia: Exploring the contributions of the Thought Disorder Index to clinical assessment. *Scandinavian Journal of Child and Adolescent Psychiatry and Psychology, 4*, 23–30.

Arboleda, C., & Holzman, P. S. (1985). Thought disorder in children at risk for psychosis. *Archives of General Psychiatry, 42*, 1004–1013.

Armstrong, J., Silberg, J. L., & Parente, F. J. (1986). Patterns of thought disorder on psychological testing: Implications for adolescent psychopathology. *Journal of Nervous and Mental Disease, 174*, 448–456.

Bartell, S. S., & Solanto, M. V. (1995). Usefulness of the Rorschach Inkblot Test in assessment of attention deficit hyperactivity disorder. *Perceptual and Motor Skills, 80*, 531–541.

Bernabei, P., Palli, F. G., Levi, G., Mazzoncini, B., & Cannoni, E. (1999). Disturbance of imagination and symbolization in pervasive developmental disorders: Preliminary study utilizing the Rorschach Inkblot Test. *Perceptual and Motor Skills, 89*, 917–930.

Birmaher, B. (2003). Treatment of psychosis in children and adolescents. *Psychiatric Annals, 33*, 257–264.

Carlson, G. A. (2005). Diagnosing bipolar disorder in children and adolescents. In S. P. Kutcher (Ed.), *Child and Adolescent Psychopharmacology News, 10*, 1–6.

Carlson, G. A. (2013). Affective disorders and psychosis in youth. *Child and Adolescent Psychiatric Clinics of North America, 22*, 569–580.

Cepeda, C. (2007). *Psychotic Symptoms in Children and Adolescents. Assessment, Differential Diagnosis, and Treatment*. New York: Routledge.

Cotugno, A. J. (2006). Personality attributes of attention deficit hyperactivity disorder (ADHD) using the Rorschach Inkblot Test. *Journal of Clinical Psychology, 51*, 554–562.

Cummings, J. L., & Mega, M. S. (2003). *Neuropsychiatry and Behavioral Neuroscience*. Oxford: Oxford University Press.

Exner, J. E. (2003). *The Rorschach: A Comprehensive System, Basic Foundations* (Vol. 1, 4th ed.). New York: Wiley.

Exner, J. E., & Erdberg, P. (2005). *The Rorschach: A Comprehensive System, Advanced Interpretation* (Vol. 2, 3rd ed.). New York: Wiley.

Exner, J. E., Thomas, E. A., & Mason, B. J. (1985). Children's Rorschach: Description and prediction. *Journal of Personality Assessment, 49*, 13–20.

Franklin, K. W., & Cornell, D. G. (1997). Rorschach interpretation with high-ability adolescent females: Psychopathology or creative thinking? *Journal of Personality Assessment, 68*, 184–196.

Gallucci, N. T. (1989). Personality assessment with children of superior intelligence: Divergence vs. psychopathology. *Journal of Personality Assessment, 53*, 749–760.

Holaday, M. (2000). Rorschach protocols from children and adolescents diagnosed with posttraumatic stress disorder. *Journal of Personality Assessment, 75*, 143–157.

Holaday, M. (2001). Rorschach protocols from children and adolescents with Asperger's disorder. *Journal of Personality Assessment, 76*, 482–495.

Kay, S. R., Fiszbein, A., & Opler, L. A. (1987). The Positive and Negative Syndrome Scale (PANSS) for schizophrenia, *Schizophrenia Bulletin, 13*, 261–276.

Kleiger, J. H., & Khadivi, A. (2015). *Assessing Psychosis. A Clinician's Guide*. New York: Routledge.

Klopfer, B., & Margulies, H. (1941). Rorschach reactions in early childhood. *Rorschach Research Exchange, 5*, 1–23.

Klopfer, B., Spiegelman, M., & Fox, J. (1956), The interpretation of children's records. In B. Klopfer (Ed.), *Developments in the Rorschach Technique* (Vol. 2, pp. 22–44). New York: Harcourt, Brace & World.

Kumra, S., Jacobsen, L. K., Lenane, M., Zahn, T.P., Wiggs, E., Alaghband-Rad, J., Castellanos, F. X., Frazier, J. A., McKenna, K., Gordon, C. T., Smith, A., Hamburger, S., & Rapoport, J. L. (1998). Multidimensionally impaired disorder: Is it a variant of very early-onset schizophrenia? *Journal of the American Academy of Child and Adolescent Psychiatry, 37*, 91–99.

Leichtman, M. (1996). *The Rorschach: A Developmental Perspective*. Hillsdale, NJ: The Analytic Press.

Makowski, D., Waternaux, C., Lajonchere, C. M., Dicker, R., Smoke, N., Kopelwiez, H., Minn, D., Mendell, N. R., & Levy, D. L. (1997). Thought disorder in adolescent-onset schizophrenia. *Schizophrenia Research, 23*, 147–166.

McCarthy, J. B. (2015). Contemporary views of psychotic disorders. In J. B. McCarthy (Ed.), *Psychosis in Childhood and Adolescence* (pp. 25–46). New York: Routledge.

McCarthy, J. B., & Dobroshi, Z. (2015). Mood disorders and psychosis. In J. B. McCarthy (Ed.), *Psychosis in Childhood and Adolescence* (pp. 107–122). New York: Routledge.

Meyer, G. J., Erdberg, P., & Shaffer, T. W. (2007). Toward international normative reference data for the Comprehensive System. *Journal of Personality Assessment, 89*, S201–S216.

Meyer, G. J., Viglione, D. J., Mihura, J. L., Erard, R. E., & Erdberg, P. (2011). *Rorschach Performance Assessment System: Administration, Coding, Interpretation, and Technical Manual*. Toledo, OH: Rorschach Performance Assessment System.

Mihura, J. L., Meyer, G. J., Dumitrascu, N., & Bombel, G. (2013). The validity of individual Rorschach variables: Systematic reviews and meta-analyses of the comprehensive system. *Psychological Bulletin, 139*, 548–605.

Morey, L. C. (2007). *The Personality Assessment Inventory—Adolescent Professional Manual*. Lutz, FL: Psychological Assessment Resources.

Murray, J. (1992). Toward a synthetic approach to the Rorschach: The case of a psychotic child. *Journal of Personality Assessment, 58*, 494–505.

Osher, Y., Mandel, B., Shapiro, E., & Belmæker, R. H. (2000). Rorschach markers in offspring of manic-depressive patients. *Journal of Affective Disorders, 59,* 231–236.

Radmanociv, M. B. (2012). First-psychotic episode in childhood and adolescence. *Psychiatria Danubina, 24,* 388–391.

Rapoport, J. L., & Gogtay, N. (2011). Childhood onset schizophrenia support for a progressive neurodevelopmental disorder. *International Journal of Developmental Neuroscience, 29,* 251–258.

Reynolds, C. R., & Kamphaus, R. W. (2015). *BASC-3: Behavior Assessment System for Children* (3rd ed.). Upper Saddle River, NJ: Pearson Education, Inc.

Ross, R. G., Heinlein, S., & Tregellas, H. (2006). High rates of comorbidity are found in childhood-onset schizophrenia. *Schizophrenia Research, 88,* 90–95.

Russ, S. W. (1988). Primary process thinking, divergent thinking, and coping in children. *Journal of Personality Assessment, 52,* 539–549.

Schaeffer, J. L., & Ross, R. G. (2002). Childhood-onset schizophrenia: Premorbid and prodromal diagnostic and treatment histories. *Journal of the American Academy of Child and Adolescent Psychiatry, 41,* 538–545.

Schuldberg, D., & Boster, J. S. (1985). Back to Topeka: Two types of distance in Rapaport's original Rorschach thought disorder categories. *Journal of Abnormal Psychology, 94,* 205–215.

Smith, S.R., Baity, M.R., Knowles, E.S., & Hilsenroth, M.J. (2001). Assessment of disordered thinking in children and adolescents: The Rorschach Perceptual-Thinking Index. *Journal of Personality Assessment, 77,* 447–463.

Sossin, K. M. (2015). Risk factors for autism and psychosis. In J. B. McCarthy (Ed.), *Psychosis in Childhood and Adolescence* (pp. 62–89). New York: Routledge.

Sporn, A., & Rapoport, J. L. (2001, April). Childhood onset schizophrenia. Mini-review. *Child and Adolescent Psychopharmacology News,* 1–6.

Viglione, D. J. (1990). Severe disturbance or trauma-induced adaptive reaction: A Rorschach child case study. *Journal of Personality Assessment, 55,* 280–295.

Viglione, D. J., & Giromini, L. (2016). *Journal of Personality Assessment, 98,* 391–397.

Yalof, J. (2006). Case illustration of a boy with nonverbal learning disorder and Asperger's features: Neuropsychological and personality assessment. *Journal of Personality Assessment, 87,* 15–34.

Zalsman, G., & Cohen, D. J. (1998). Multiplex developmental disorder. *The Israel Journal of Psychiatry and Related Sciences, 35,* 300–306.

Final Thoughts
Empirical, conceptual, and practical considerations

As in earlier chapters, I will organize my final comments about the state of Rorschach assessment of psychotic phenomena around empirical, conceptual, and practical themes. In each case, I balance a look at the current state of the art with a look toward the future in terms of how the assessment of psychosis with the Rorschach can be improved and further developed.

Empirical considerations

Rapaport, and Rorschach before him, made the first efforts to investigate psychotic mental processes with the Rorschach in a scientific manner. As always, criticism of Rapaport's methodology is axiomatic, but Rapaport, Schafer, and Gill are to be credited not only for their conceptual advances, but also for their attempts to study psychotic mental functioning empirically. Holt took the scientific study of primary process thinking much further, and Holzman and colleagues represent the apex of rigorous empirical investigations of thought disorder with their TDI metric. In a parallel manner, Exner, Weiner, and the R-PAS developers have grounded their studies of psychotic phenomena with the Rorschach in an empirical tradition. Despite criticisms about what is wrong or lacking in the Rorschach, advocates of the CS and R-PAS have steadfastly demonstrated the scientific validity of the Rorschach in assessing psychotic phenomena.

Moving forward, I expect to see future studies with the R-PAS and hope also to see further research with the CS in the assessment of psychotic phenomena. Specifically, I am eager for researchers to turn their attention to more cutting-edge issues like identifying psychosis risk and assessing insight into awareness of disturbances in thinking and reality testing. For the R-PAS, improved norms and expanded scores in the Perception and Thinking Domain should encourage researchers to study psychosis risk prospectively to see which scores and combination of scores and indices aid in predicting conversion to psychosis in vulnerable patients. Although some work has been started in this area (Kimhy et al., 2007; Ilonen et al., 2010; Inoue, Yorozuya, & Mizuno, 2014; Lacoua, Koren, & Rothschild-Yakar, 2015), these studies all used the CS. Using both the TDI and R-PAS in such investigations could contribute to the early detection field, especially when studies move beyond correlational to prospective research.

Similar studies using the R-PAS, CS, and TDI methods could also investigate testing-of-limits procedures for gaining insight into our patients' awareness of the disturbed responses they give. Rothschild-Yakar and colleagues (2015) have opened this important area of psychosis assessment to empirical study. Adding new post-clarification or inquiry techniques to assist in judging patients' abilities to step back and demonstrate their awareness and capacities to mentalize how others might react to their disturbed thinking and perceptual distortions will be of great value to assessment psychologists.

Future Rorschach studies in differential diagnosis will aid clinicians tasked with making these kinds of diagnostic decisions. The pioneering research with the TDI established a benchmark for these kinds of investigations, which looked to identify thought disorder "signatures" for patients with different kinds of psychoses. CS studies have not focused on these kinds of studies in the same way. With the R-PAS gaining a foothold in assessment practice and research, there is renewed opportunity to establish Rorschach profiles for individuals whose psychotic symptoms are more emblematic of schizophrenia spectrum as opposed to bipolar spectrum psychoses. To further this line of investigation, two specific areas of inquiry might be pursued.

The first would be to develop a hypomanic index (A. Khadivi, personal communication, May 14, 2013). Such an index would not be intended to conflate a clinical diagnosis with the identification of personality and symptom characteristics but would aim to highlight those formal and thematic features of an individual's Rorschach that identify heightened affectivity associated with hypomanic or manic processes.

The second differential diagnostic issue would involve trying to empirically operationalize psychotic impoverishment on the Rorschach. Currently, assessment specialists rely on their clinical acumen and knowledge of psychopathology (as they always should) to detect signs of impoverishment, whether understood as manifestations of negative symptoms or cognitive impairment. Clearly, the problem has been to identify a set of Rorschach features that is more specific to psychotic impoverishment, which could be distinguished from more general disengagement stemming from disinterest, depression, or defensiveness. In the CS, the CDI has been viewed as a broad measure of deficits in social skills, immaturity, and problems in coping with everyday living. The R-PAS Engagement and Cognitive Processing Domain addresses many features of impoverishment having to do with complexity, cognitive energy, productivity, flexibility, and synthesis. We would expect the CDI and R-PAS variables having to do with complexity and engagement to be significant in those individuals experiencing negative symptoms and impaired cognition; however, once again, positive findings on these measures are not diagnostically specific. Thus, can an impoverishment index be developed that can distinguish the presence of negative symptoms and cognitive impairment from other, nonpsychotic, conditions associated with constricted and barren Rorschach records?

Although malingering on the Rorschach has been well studied, the development of R-PAS again has opened the way for new investigations of malingered psychosis on the Rorschach. As seen in Chapter 15, researchers have been unable to identify a valid set of Rorschach malingering measures that hold up under scientific scrutiny. A set of clinical signs has been suggested; however, a new look at establishing valid Rorschach measures of malingered psychosis would be invaluable to clinical and forensic psychologists. Researchers determined to study malingered psychosis using R-PAS variables should consider using actual forensic samples, as did Ganellen and colleagues (1996) with the CS, as opposed to nonclinical psychosis simulators.

Finally, Rorschach psychosis studies with adolescents and children are particularly thin. As reviewed in the last chapter, efforts have been made to investigate psychotic phenomena in younger patients using the TDI and CS; however, more quality research in this critical, yet challenging, area is needed. Once again, the advent of the R-PAS with its updated international norms for youngsters should aid researchers in studying psychotic phenomena in children and adolescents. Another area in which there is a dearth of current studies has to do with the autism spectrum. Apart from case studies, since Holaday's 2001 CS study of Asperger's children, there have been few empirical Rorschach investigations of autism spectrum children—specifically how they might look different from those children with primary psychotic conditions.

Ultimately, it is humbling to realize how much we, I, do not understand about psychosis, psychotic-like phenomena, and exactly what the Rorschach can and cannot tell us. The wish that individual scoring categories might have privileged links to specific diagnostic groups has so far proven to be elusive, if not a fantasy. Just as the nature of clinical phenomena like hallucinations and delusions are no longer seen as pathognomonic of any specific diagnostic group, it is mostly likely the same with our Special Scores, Cognitive Codes, as well as composites like EII-3, TP-Comp, WSUMCog, PTI, and X-%. Nonetheless, further studies, both nomothetic and idiographic, might help clinicians understand how these scores and composites appear in differing levels of severity and frequency in different kinds of clinical conditions.

Conceptual considerations

The focus of my work, as put forth in this volume and others (Kleiger, 1992a, 1992b, 1999), has been to move beyond the sometimes closed world of scores and indices and look for links between empirically established scores and clinical and theoretical concepts that can enliven our understanding of what these scores might mean. In *Disordered Thinking and the Rorschach* (1999), I wanted to move beyond static individual scores to the psychological processes underlying these scoring categories. However, in describing "confabulatory, combinatory, paleological, and contaminatory thinking" as I did, the focus remained on the language of Rorschach scores, which, in the end, can disconnect us from broader clinical concepts. Thus, my effort in this book has been to organize what we know about various Special Scores and Cognitive Codes, as well as confabulatory, combinatory, paleological, and contaminatory thinking, into broader dimensions of disordered thinking having to do with disorganization, illogicality, and impoverishment. I have also attempted to suggest further possible second-order linkages between categories of disorganization, illogicality, and impoverishment and psychological, neurocognitive, developmental, and psychoanalytic concepts that might add subtle and more finely tuned understanding when we attempt to decipher a patient's disordered responses on the Rorschach.

I realize that my effort to build these kinds of conceptual bridges will appeal to some, while perhaps leaving others to question the absence of empirical "beef" in these efforts to build such conceptual scaffolding (Kleiger, 1992b). Obviously, balance and proportionality are needed. I have tried to incorporate empirical underpinnings throughout this book, seeking to ground clinical inferences in established science. Where the links are weaker, I hope that I have acknowledged this and made my suggested associations hypothetical or conjectural.

Practical considerations

I have the highest respect for the contributions of Holt and Holzman and their colleagues, who have elevated the scientific study of disordered thinking and psychotic phenomena on the Rorschach. Unfortunately, to someone whose principal identity has always been that of a practitioner, the TDI and the Pripro are not friendly to the clinical diagnostician. Whenever I make such a comment, I am compelled to defend the intentions of Holt and Holzman's groups. Neither set out to develop clinical instruments. Holt (2009) was clear in stating that his Pripro was not designed to be used in clinical assessment. The TDI is a bit different because the most highly trained individuals have been successful in using it clinically to aid in differential diagnosis. However, in my opinion, reaching this level of expertise with a sophisticated instrument like the TDI is far more difficult than simply reading an explanation of the different scoring categories. Mastery of the TDI requires a significant amount of practice, and more important, establishing suitable reliability with the developers of the instrument at Harvard. More problematic regarding the TDI, however, is the fact that the developers administer the Rorschach according to the Rapaport method. As stated in Chapter 5, doing research with TDI when one has administered the Rorschach according to the CS or R-PAS raises methodological questions. Does the Rapaport method, in which the inquiry is conducted after each card and with the card out of sight, yield similar protocols as the CS or R-PAS? So far, to my knowledge, this question has not been studied. Thus, comparing TDI scores to those scores obtained with the CS or R-PAS might have a bit of an apples-versus-oranges quality.

In the future, I predict we shall see further inroads by R-PAS, which I believe holds the most promise for assessing psychotic phenomena and for the future of the Rorschach in general. Just as the CS "breathed new life into the Rorschach," so has the R-PAS. Furthermore, the expanded set of scoring variables in the Perception and Domain sector further refines the identification of psychotic phenomena in Rorschach protocols.

I also predict that we shall see increased use of abbreviated Rorschach techniques such as those used by the TDI group (Carpenter et al., 1993) and those being developed by R-PAS clinicians (Eblin et al., 2014) and by Choca, Rossini, and Garside (2016). Clinical innovations are always enthusiastically welcomed, especially when they can make an instrument like the Rorschach, with its robust ability to identify psychotic phenomena, available to a wider swath of psychologists who may not have the time to routinely administer the standard procedure. However, just as developments like the CS and now R-PAS offer clinicians more efficient and scientifically sound means for assessing psychotic phenomena, I hope that practitioners and those who teach students will not lose sight of more traditional approaches. In other words, for those of us using either the R-PAS or the CS, our diagnostic work is always enriched by never losing sight of the seminal contributions of Rapaport, Schafer, and Holt, to name only a few. Likewise, if clinicians adopt four-card methods for assessing psychotic phenomena or more general aspects of personality functioning, it will be important to understand the limitations of newer, abbreviated methods and to know when older, traditional approaches, though not without their warts and economical disadvantages, can provide richer clinical diagnostic understanding about our patients' thinking, internal experiences, reality testing, and awareness of their disturbances in each of these areas.

References

Carpenter, J. T., Coleman, M. J., Watemaux, C., Perry, J., Wong, H., O'Brian, C., & Holzman, P. S. (1993). The Thought Disorder Index: Short for assessments. *Psychological Assessment, 5*, 75–80.

Choca, J., Rossini, E., & Garside, D. (2016). The Practical Rorschach: Adjusting the Rorschach for the 21st Century. Symposium presented at the annual meeting of the Society for Personality Assessment, Chicago, IL.

Eblin, J. J., Meyer, G. J., Mihura, J. L., & Viglione, D. J. (2014). Development and Preliminary Validation of a Brief Behavioral Measure of Psychotic Propensity. Unpublished Manuscript.

Ganellen, R. J., Wasyliw, O. E., Haywood, T. W., & Grossman, L. S. (1996). Can psychosis be malingered on the Rorschach? An empirical study. *Journal of Personality Assessment, 66*, 65–80.

Holaday, M. (2001). Rorschach protocols from children and adolescents with Asperger's disorder. *Journal of Personality Assessment, 76*, 482–495.

Holt, R. R. (2009). *Primary Process Thinking: Theory, Measurement, and Research* (Vols. 1 & 2). Lanham, MD: Aronson.

Ilonen, T., Heinimaa, M., Korkeila, J., Svirskis, T., & Salokangas, R. K. R. (2010). Differentiating adolescents at clinical high risk for psychosis from psychotic and non-psychotic patients with the Rorschach. *Psychiatry Research, 179*, 151–156.

Inoue, N., Yorozuya, Y., & Mizuno, M. (2014). Identifying comorbidities of patients at ultra-high risk for psychosis using the Rorschach Comprehensive System. Paper presented at the XXI International Congress of Rorschach and Projective Methods, Istanbul, Turkey.

Kimhy, D., Corcoran, C., Harkavy-Friedman, J. M., Ritzler, B., Javitt, D. C., & Malaspina, D. (2007). Visual form perception: A comparison of individuals at high risk for psychosis, recent onset schizophrenia and chronic schizophrenia. *Schizophrenia Research*, *97*, 25–34.

Kleiger, J. H. (1992a). A conceptual critique of the EA: es comparison in the Comprehensive Rorschach System. *Psychological Assessment, 4*, 288–296.

Kleiger, J. H. (1992b). A response to Exner's comments on "A conceptual critique of the EA: es comparison in the Comprehensive Rorschach System." *Psychological Assessment, 4*, 301–302.

Kleiger, J. H. (1999). *Disordered Thinking and the Rorschach*. Hillsdale, NJ: The Analytic Press.

Lacoua, L., Koren, D., & Rothschild-Yakar, L. (2015). Poor awareness of problems in thought and perception and risk indicators of schizophrenia-spectrum disorders. A correlational study of nonpsychotic adolescents in the community. Paper presented at the annual meeting of the Society for Personality Assessment, Brooklyn, NY.

Rothschild-Yakar, L., Lacoua, L., Brener, A., & Koren, D. (2015). Impairments in interpersonal representations and deficits in social cognition as predictors of risk for schizophrenia in non-patient adolescents. Paper presented at the annual meeting of the Society for Personality Assessment, Brooklyn, NY.

Index

.25 level, Thought Disorder Index (TDI) 68–9
.50 level, Thought Disorder Index (TDI) 70–1
.75 level, Thought Disorder Index (TDI) 71
1.0 level, Thought Disorder Index (TDI) 72
3-card sets 105–6
4-card sets 106
5-card sets 105–6
10-card sets 105–6

AB (Abstraction) 88–9
abbreviated card set methods 105–6
abstract attitude 174
abstract preoccupation 150
abstract thinking 150
Abstraction (AB) 88–9
absurd Dds 148
absurd responses 50; Thought Disorder Index (TDI) 71
absurdity 75
absurdity factor, schizoaffective-depressed patients 201
Acklin, M. W. 217, 219
adaptive regression 60
Adaptive Regression Score (ARS) 58
ADHD (Attention Deficit Hyperactivity Disorder), children/adolescents 272–3
adolescents: ADHD 272–3; affective psychoses 267–9; assessing psychotic phenomena *see* psychotic phenomena in children and adolescents; conduct disorders 272–3; early-onset schizophrenia 265–7; learning disabilities 272–3; neurodevelopmental disorders 270–3; Rorschach 264–5; trauma 269–70

affective psychoses, children/adolescents 267–9
Akiskal, H. S. 241
ALOG (autistic logic) 47, 87, 115–16; delusional thinking 204; Thought Disorder Index (TDI) 71
alogia 175–6
ALOG/PEC 149
Amador, X. F. 182
Andreasen, N. 13–15, 145, 176, 206, 207, 208, 209
anergia 176
anthropological and developmental perspectives, illogicality 151–5
AO (autogenous obsessions) 241–2
apathy 176
APS (attenuated psychosis syndrome) 214–16
APSS (Attenuated Positive Symptom State) 214
Arboleda, C. 74, 265
Arieti, S. 47, 146
Aristotelian logic 146
Arlow, J. A. 139
ARMS (at-risk mental states) 214
Armstrong, J. 236, 237, 238–9
Arnow, D. 158
ARS (Adaptive Regression Score) 58
artists 163
assessing: awareness 185–9; contributions of Rapaport and Holt systems 58–62; thought disorder 27–32
Assessing Schizophrenic Thinking 65
assessments 29–32
associative distance 111
asyndesis 131
Athey, G. I. 160–1
at-risk mental states (ARMS) 214

Attenuated Positive Symptom State (APSS) 214
attenuated psychosis syndrome (APS) 214–16
atypical presentations, psychotic phenomena in children and adolescents 262–3
auditory pseudoperceptions 229
Auerbach, J. S. 157
authenticity versus inauthenticity 159
autism 158, TRAUT system 103–5
autism spectrum, children 270–2
autistic logic (ALOG) 47, 87, 115–16; delusional thinking 204; Thought Disorder Index (TDI) 71
autistic verbalization 75
autogenous obsessions (AO) 241–2
awareness 182–3; assessing 185–9
awareness of disturbances 183–5; integrated Rorschach model 119
awareness of illness 182

Barbour, C. G. 232
Batki, S. L. 218
BDD (body dysmorphic disorder) 240
Beatson, J. A. 228
Beck Depression Inventory 212
Benedik, E. 199
benign psychoses 263
Bentall, R. P. 22, 135–6, 195, 201–2
Beres, D. 139
Berg, J. L. 157, 186, 230
Berrios, G. E. 182
beta elements 140
Biagiarelli, M. 205
Bion, W. R. 140–1
bipolar disorder 213; manic psychosis 206–11
BIPS (Brief Intermittent Psychotic State) 214
Birmaher, B. 260
Bistis, K. 231
BIT (bizarre-idiosyncratic thinking) 16
bizarre delusions 250
bizarre-idiosyncratic thinking (BIT) 14, 16, 208
Blais, M. A. 231
Blatt, S. J. 156, 157
Bleuler, Eugen xiii, 12
BLIPS (Brief Limited Intermittent Psychotic State) 214
body dysmorphic disorder (BDD) 240

Bohm, E. 40, 169
borderline disorders 227–35
Borderline Personality Disorder (BPD) 227
borderline psychopathology, thought disorder 229–34
borderline thematic content 232–4
borderline-level paranoid beliefs 229
borderline-level thought disorder scores 231–2
Boster, J. S. 44, 172, 174, 272
boundary disturbances 156–8
BPD (Borderline Personality Disorder) 227
Brabender, V. 210, 213
Braekbill, G. A. 172
Braff, D. 196
Bram, A. D. 162
Brand, B. L. 238
Brenner, C. 139
Brief Intermittent Psychotic State (BIPS) 214
Brief Limited Intermittent Psychotic state (BLIPS) 214

C., Ms., trauma 237
Cadoret, R. J. 211
Cameron, N. 196
Cancro, R. 16
Caplan, R. 16
Card I 48, 175
Card II 49, 50, 237, 256
Card IV 39, 48, 50, 187
Card IX 39, 47, 49, 150
Card V 39, 47, 179
Card VI 187
Card VII 188, 203, 237, 238–9
Card VIII 49, 134–5, 160, 204
Carlson, E. B. 237, 268
Carpenter, W. T. 177, 206
Carter, M. L. 212
categories of DV (deviant verbalization) 44–50
Category Test 212
causality 145–6
Cauwels, J. M. 232
CDI (Coping Deficit Index) 173
Cepeda, C. 263, 268
Chaika, E. O. 13
chain association 126
Chandra 188
Chapman, J. P. 196, 205
Chapman, L. 205

Index   289

children: ADHD 272–3; affective psychoses 267–9; assessing psychotic phenomena *see* psychotic phenomena in children and adolescents; conduct disorders 272–3; Darleen 273–7; early-onset schizophrenia 265–7; learning disabilities 272–3; neurodevelopmental disorders 270–3; and the Rorschach 154–5; Rorschach 264–5; trauma 269–70
Choca, J. 106
Chopra, H. D. 228
CHR (clinical high-risk) 214
chronic deteriorative OCD 241
Circumstantial DRs 85
circumstantial response DRs 112
Circumstantial Responses 85
circumstantial thinking 147
circumstantiality 133
clanging 132
clangs, Thought Disorder Index (TDI) 69
Clayton, P. 211
clinical assessments, APS (attenuated psychosis syndrome) 215–16
clinical clues, indications of malingered psychosis 251–4
clinical considerations, Thought Disorder Index (TDI) 78–9
clinical diagnosis 193
clinical examples, assessing awareness 187–9
clinical high-risk (CHR) 214
clinical utility, CS and R-PAS 100
coarctated preschizophrenics 230
coded responses, disorganization 126–8
Cognitive Codes 98
cognitive codes, R-PAS 95
cognitive complexity 169
cognitive constriction 235
cognitive disorganization, schizophrenia 133, 196
cognitive impairment 177–9
cognitive insight 182–3
cognitive neuroscience perspectives, illogicality 151
cognitive slippage 205
Coleman, Michael 73, 79
combinative thinking 147
combinatory reasoning 114–15
combinatory responses 38
combinatory thinking 75, 209; trauma 237–8

communication, thought disorder 12–14
comorbidity 234; psychotic phenomena in children and adolescents 262–3
Comprehensive System *see* CS (Comprehensive System)
The Comprehensive Textbook of Psychiatry 12
conceptual models for organizing dimensions of thought disorder 109–10
conceptual reality 150
conceptual thinking 149–50
concreteness 174
COND (condensed reasoning) 116–17
condensation 54–5, 162, 163
condensed reasoning (COND) 116–17
conduct disorders, children/adolescents 272–3
CONFAB (confabulation) 87–8, 100, 173
confabulation 46–7; Thought Disorder Index (TDI) 71
confabulation tendency 51
confabulatory combinations 155
confabulatory DRs 113
confabulatory reasoning 115
confabulatory whole response 46
confabulatory-combined whole answer 38–9
confusion 48–9, 75, 128; Thought Disorder Index (TDI) 70
confusion responses 171–2
constructional aparaxia 178
CONTAM (contamination) 86, 149
contaminated whole response 39
contamination 39, 86; malingered psychosis 256; Thought Disorder Index (TDI) 72
contamination tendency 51
contaminatory thinking 156
content perseveration 87–88
content variables 54
continuum of severity, disorganization 129
continuums: of illogicality 147–8; impoverished thinking 169; thought disorder 19
contradictions 55
control and defense variables 55–6
Coonerty, S. 234
Cooper, S. 158
Coping Deficit Index (CDI) 173
COS (childhood-onset schizophrenia) 265
Coursey, R. D. 242
creative perspectives, illogicality 162–4

CS (Comprehensive System) 82, 97–100, 173, 263–4, 280–1; Inadequate M responses 89; inappropriate combinations 85–6; inappropriate logic 87; levels of variable severity 90–1; scoring 82–93; special content scores 88–9; Special Scores 87–8; unusual verbalizations 83–5
Cunnien, A. J. 248
Cutting, J. C. 178

Darleen 273–7
DD (Demand for Defense) 57
Dd (small detail score) 170
DE (defense effectiveness) 58
De Rosa, M. 207
decentering 153
deciphering thought disorder 43
defense effectiveness (DE) 58
defensive activity 56
DeFife, J. A. 60
Delta Index 66
delusional disorders 195, 201–6
delusional operations 89
delusional states, OCD (Obsessive-Compulsive Disorder) 240
delusional thinking, Rorschach and 204–6
delusions 151, 211; drug-induced psychoses 217
Demand for Defense (DD) 57
depression 211–214
derailment 15, 132
detecting: malingered psychosis 250–1; psychosis with R-PAS 94
development, psychotic phenomena in children and adolescents 261–2
developmental perspectives, impoverished thinking 174–5
developmental theory 154–5
Deviant Response (DR) 84–5; disorganized speech 111–14
deviant verbalization *see* DV (deviant verbalization)
diagnosis, clinical diagnosis 193
Diagnostic Psychological Testing 59
diagnostic spectrums 194
dialipsis 72
differential diagnosis 234–5
differentiation, versus fusion 159
discourse coherence 134
discrete personality disorder 227

disordered thinking 1–2, 11, 12, 16, 19, 22–3; assessing *see* assessing thought disorder; depression 211–214; differential diagnosis and pathognomic signs 19–21; holistic model of disordered thinking 17–19; neuropsychological approaches 21–2; self-experience and 158–60
disordered thought content 16
disorders of content 16
disorganization 125; coded responses 126–8; continuum of severity 129; indicators of 127–9; integrated Rorschach model for conceptualizing thought disorder 110–14; linguistic perspectives 133–5; neuropsychological perspectives 135–6; overview 141; psychoanalytic perspectives 137–41; psychological perspectives 130–1; psychopathological perspectives 131–3; psychotherapeutic perspectives 136–7
disorganized speech 15, 125–6, 133; integrated Rorschach model for conceptualizing thought disorder 110–11
Disorganized Speech (Thinking) 2
Disorganized Thinking (Speech) 126
displacement 54–5, 138
Displacement DRs 126–8
dissociation, trauma 235
dissociative disorders 238–40
distance 172
distance from inkblots, Rapaport, David 43–4
distant association 126–7
distractible speech 132
disturbances: integrated Rorschach model 119; thought disorder 17
disturbances in ideation 184
disturbed responses 185
Do responses 118, 170
Dobroshi, Z. 267
Docherty, N. M. 207
Dominguez, Núñez 218
DR (Deviant Response) 84–5; disorganized speech 111–14; malingered psychosis 254–5
DR2s, malingered psychosis 255–6
dramatic contents 254
dramatic responses, malingered psychosis 252
dreaming 54

drug-induced psychoses 216–19
Dryud, J. 208
DSM 5, APS (attenuated psychosis syndrome) 214
DSM-III 109
DV (deviant verbalization) 42–51, 83–5; categories of 44–50; disordered thinking 110–11; disorganization 110–11
Dyrud, J. 206

Early Memories test 233
early-onset schizophrenia 265–7
Edell, W. 74, 205
editing 21
ego functioning, formal thought disorder (FTD) 138–9
Ego Impairment Index-3 (EII-3) 95
ego weaknesses 228
egocentric thinking 153
EII 199
EII-2 199
EII-3 (Ego Impairment Index-3) 95
Elhai, J. D. 257
embellished responses 148
empiric factors 74–5
empirical studies, detecting malingered psychosis 250–1
empirical-sign method 40
Epstein, R. S. 208
Erard, Bob 93–4
Erdberg, Phil 93–4, 253–4, 267
Evans, F. B. 235, 237
Exner, John 82–3, 93, 184, 204, 253–4, 267, 280
experiments 37–9
extreme loss of distance 51

FABCOMs (fabulized combinations) 38–9, 46, 86, 115, 238; CS (Comprehensive System) 91; Thought Disorder Index (TDI) 71, 77; trauma 237–8
FABs (fabulized combinations) 115
fabulized combination 38–9
fabulized responses 45–6
factor-analysis studies, Thought Disorder Index (TDI) 74–5
Fine, A. 172
Flanagan, T. A. 206
Flashman, L. A. 183
flat affect 176
flight of ideas 210
flippant response DRs 112

flippant responses, Thought Disorder Index (TDI) 69
fluid thinking 75
fluid verbalization DRs 112
fluidity, Thought Disorder Index (TDI) 71
form level 56–7
formal thought disorder (FTD) 15–17; ego functioning 138–9
formal variables 54–5
Formless M response 89
FQ, poor FQ 216
FQ Percentages 96
fragmentation 129; Thought Disorder Index (TDI) 71
fragmenting self 158
Free Association 186, 189
Freud, Sigmund 137, 146, 240
Friedman, H. 152
Frueh, B. C. 257
FTD (formal thought disorder) 15–17
fusion, versus differentiation 159

Ganellen, R. J. 252, 255
Genetic Risk and Deterioration Syndrome 214
Gill, Merton 43, 171, 202, 204, 280
Goldstein, K. 170, 174
Gomilla, M. V. 199
good Wechsler/bad Rorschach 230
Gorham Proverbs Test 30
Grebb, J. A. 16
Gunderson, J. G. 228–9

Hall, C. S. 152
Handler, L. 186
Harris, D. 218
Harrow, M. 17, 19, 183, 207
Hartmann, H. 139
Havel, Joan 53
Hertz, Margarite 82–3
HIPERS 268
history of thought disorder 12
Hoffman, R. E. 208
Holaday, M. 269–71, 282
holistic model of disordered thinking 17–19
Holt, Robert 43, 51–58, 156, 234, 280, 283; Displacement DRs 126–7; primary process thinking 138
Holt systems, assessing contributions of 58–62

Holzman, Philip 13, 65–66, 197, 200, 210, 265, 280
homospatial process 162
How dimension, thought disorder 17
Human Movement responses 89
human movement responses 160
HVI (Hypervigilance Index) 204
HYPERs (hyper-attentional errors) 104
Hypervigilance Index (HVI) 204
hypo-attentional errors (HYPOs) 104
hypomanic index 281
HYPOs (hypo-attentional errors) 104

The Iceman Cometh 162–3
identity 146
idiosyncratic symbolism 89; Thought Disorder Index (TDI) 70
idiosyncratic verbalization 75
illogical thinking 145–7
illogicality 4, 18, 145–7; anthropological and developmental perspectives 151–5; cognitive neuroscience perspectives 151; continuum 147–8; creative perspectives 162–4; indicators of 148–9; integrated Rorschach model for conceptualizing thought disorder 114–17; psychoanalytic perspectives 155–60; psychotherapeutic perspectives 160–2; traditional psychological perspectives 149–51
image fusion 55
Imbroglio 227
impaired perspective 183
impairment, cognitive impairment 177–9
imponderables 40
impoverished thinking 4; continuums 169; developmental perspectives 174–5; indicators of 169–73; integrated Rorschach model for conceptualizing thought disorder 117–18; neuropsychological perspectives 177–9; psychological perspectives 174; psychopathological perspectives 175–7
impoverishment 168–9; trauma 236
impulsive styles 153–4
Inadequate M responses, CS (Comprehensive System) 89
inadequate personality 173
inappropriate activity 55
inappropriate combinations 148; CS (Comprehensive System), 85–6
inappropriate commentary 84
inappropriate distance, Thought Disorder Index (TDI) 68
inappropriate logic 87
inappropriate phrase DRs 112
inappropriate phrases 84
INC (incongruous combinations) 114
incoherence 48–9, 132; Thought Disorder Index (TDI) 72
INCOM (Incongruous Combination) 85–6; CS (Comprehensive System) 91; Thought Disorder Index (TDI) 69, 77
incongruous combinations (INC) 114
increased distance 85
indicators of: disorganization 126–9; illogicality 148–9; impoverished thinking 169–73; malingered psychosis 251–4; nonmalingering 253; paranoid styles 202–4
indices of manic thought disorder 209–11
inferences 145
inkblots 37–9; 47–50
Inoue, N. 216
Insel, T. R. 241
insight 10
integrated Rorschach model for conceptualizing thought disorder 110; awareness of disturbances 119; disorganization 110–14; illogicality 114–17; impoverished speech and thinking 117–18
integration versus splitting 159
intentionality 163, 183–5
interpenetration 156
interpersonal dynamics in testing situations 184
interpersonal relationships 157
interpretation awareness 169
Interpretation of Dreams 137
interpretive distance 111
issues in assessing thought disorder 27–9

Jamison, K. R. 207
Janowsky, D. S. 208
Janusian thinking 162
Jenike, M. A. 241
Johannes 187–8
Johnston, M. H. 65–6
Joyce, James 163
Joyce, Lucia 163
JTC (jumping to conclusions) 151
Jung, C. G. 163

K, Mr., trauma 237
Kaser-Boyd, N. 235, 237
Kaufman, Andy 163–4
Kay, S. R. 212–13
Kernberg, O. F. 228
Kestenbaum-Daniels, E. 178
K-FTDS (Kiddie Formal Thought Disorder Rating Scale) 16
Khadivi, Ali 145, 201, 210
Kiddie Formal Thought Disorder Rating Scale (K-FTDS) 16
Kimhy, D. 216
Kimura, H. 210
Kinder, B. N. 257
Kirkpatrick, B. 175
Kleiger, J. H. 17, 88
Klein, Melanie 139–40
Kleinian concepts 139–40
Klopfer, Bruno 186
Knight, R. P. 228
Knoll, J. L. 249, 254, 256
Kohut, H. 158
Koistinen, P. 74, 77, 198
Koren, D. 186
Kraepelin, E. 12, 136, 206
Kurt 187–8
Kwawer, J. 233
Kwon, S. M. 241

Lacoua, L. 186
Lambda 173
language, thought disorder 12–14
Language and Reasoning codes, R-PAS (Rorschach Performance Assessment System) 95
language production system 134
learning disabilities, children/adolescents 272–3
Lee, H. J. 241, 242
Leff, M. 208
Leichtman, M. 154–5, 174–5
Lerner, P. 51, 159, 232, 233
Level 1, CS (Comprehensive System) 90
Level 1 Aggression Scale 234
Level 2, CS (Comprehensive System) 90
Level 2 scores 184
levels of variable severity, CS (Comprehensive System) 90–1
Levin, P. 237–8
Levy, Dr. Deborah 65, 79
Lezak, M. 172
Liddle, P. F. 109, 133

Lindzey, G. 152
linguistic perspectives, disorganization 133–5
linguists, thought disorder 13
Lipinski, J. F. 206
Lipkin, K. M. 206, 208
location scores 39
logic 145, 146
looseness, Thought Disorder Index (TDI) 70
Loss of Appropriate Set 84

M- 96, 205
M responses 160
magic of contiguity 152
magical thinking 151
MagId (Magical Ideation) 199
Maher, B. A. 205
major depression with psychotic features 211–14
Makowski, D. 266
malapropisms 127
malevolence/aggression 233
malingered psychosis 248–257
malingering, suspecting 248–50
mania 206–11; differential diagnosis and pathognomic signs 19–21
manic psychosis 206–11
MAP (methamphetamine psychosis) 217, 219
Markova, I. S. 182
Mason, B. J. 267
Mayman, M. 51, 160
McCarthy, J. B. 267
McDougall, A. 252–3
McGhie, A. 196
McGlashan, T. H. 214
Mechanical Perseveration 87–8
mechanisms of primary process thinking 138
medication, effects on Rorschach 219–20
Meissner, W. W. 196
Meloy, J. R. 88, 138
Menninger Thought Disturbance scales 183
metabolic, psychotic phenomena in children and adolescents 263
metacognition 183
methamphetamine psychosis (MAP) 217
Meyer, Greg 93–4, 206, 208
Mihura, Joni 31, 93–4, 231

mild-moderate disturbances in FQ and thinking, borderline disorders 231
Mizuno, M. 216
MMPI 252
MOA (Mutuality of Autonomy Scale) 157, 234
mode of apperception 38
modifications of Rapaport system 50–1
Morrison, J. R. 206
Muleh, S. 206
multiple complex developmental disorder 271
multiplex developmental disorders 271
multiplicity 239
Mutuality of Autonomy Scale (MOA) 157, 234

Najolia, G. M. 249
negative symptoms 175–178
negative thought disorder 14–15
neologisms 84, 132; Thought Disorder Index (TDI) 72
Netter, B. E. C. 252, 254
neurodevelopmental disorders, children/adolescents 270–3
neurological, psychotic phenomena in children and adolescents 263
neuropsychological approaches 21–2
neuropsychological perspectives: disorganization 135–6; impoverished thinking 177–9
neuropsychological testing 29–30
neutralization index 53
Nigg, J. T. 233
nonmalingering, indicators of 253
normative base, Thought Disorder Index (TDI) 73–4
Nunno, V. J. 157

object relations 156–8
Object Sorting Tests 30
obsessive psychosis 240
OCD (Obsessive-Compulsive Disorder) 240–2
ODD (oppositional defiant disorder) 269–70
Odd Use of Language 84
oligophrenic details 118, 170
oppositional defiant disorder (ODD) 269–70
organic conditions 170
Other Psychotic Disorders 194–5

overgeneralization 147
overideational preschizophrenics 230
overly abstract elaborations 89
overly symbolic DRs 114
overstimulated self 158

Packer, A. 157
paleologic thinking 146
paleological reasoning 47
PANSS 195
paralogical thinking 47
paranoia 201
paranoid beliefs, borderline disorders 229
paranoid disorders 201
paranoid styles, indicators of 202–4
parataxic distortion 152–4
passive M responses 89
PATI (Perception and Thinking Index) 270
PECs (Peculiar Logic) 115–16; delusional thinking 204
peculiar reasoning 115–16
peculiar verbalizations 47–8, 69, 84, 127–8
pediatric bipolar disorder 273
Peebles, M. J. 162
Peebles-Kleiger 88
PerAb (Perceptual Aberration Scale) 197
Perception and Thinking Domain, R-PAS (Rorschach Performance Assessment System) 95–6
Perception and Thinking Index (PATI) 270
Perceptual Aberration Scale 197
perceptual and through processes 114
perceptual reality 150
Perceptually Based codes, R-PAS (Rorschach Performance Assessment System) 95
Perceptual-Thinking Index (PTI) 91–3
performance-based psychological assessment methods 29–30
Perry, J. 196, 199
perseveration 176–7, 212; Thought Disorder Index (TDI) 69
perseveration (PSV) 87–8
perseveration of ideas 15
personality disorder 227
Pfohl, B. 209
Piaget, J. 153
Piotrowski, Z. A. 170, 172
Piotrowski signs 170
playful combinations 115

playful confabulation, Thought Disorder Index (TDI) 71
poetry 163
poor FQ 216
Pope, H. G. 206
position response 39
positive thought disorder 14–15, 131
Post, R. M. 212
post hoc factors 75
poverty of content 176
poverty of speech 14–15
poverty of thought 176
poverty of thought content 14
predicate thinking 47, 146–7
predicates of quality 146
predicates of spatial contiguity 146
predicates of temporal contiguity 146
premises 146
preoperational thought 152–4
preschizophrenics 229–30
pressure of speech 132
Priebe, S. 195, 201–2
primary process scoring system 52–8
primary process thinking 137, 138, 155–6
primary psychoses 193–4; APS (attenuated psychosis syndrome) 214–16; bipolar disorder 206–11; delusional disorders 201–6; depression 211–14; drug-induced psychoses 216–19; schizoaffective disorder 200–1; schizophrenia spectrum 195–200
primitive 151–2
Pripro Scoring System 53, 60, 283
Processing Efficiency (Zd) 173
projective identification 140
projective tests 30, 228
Proverbs Test 30
PSV (perseveration) 87–8, 238
psychoanalytic perspectives 137–41
Psychodiagnostik 40
psychological assessments, drug-induced psychoses 218–19
psychological perspectives: disorganization 130–1; illogicality 149–51, 155–60; impoverished thinking 174
psychopathological perspectives: disorganization 131–3; impoverished thinking 175–7
psychosis 10–11; detecting with R-PAS 94
psychosis-risk syndrome 214

psychotherapeutic perspectives: disorganization 136–7; illogicality 160–2
psychotic disorders 194
psychotic features, depression 211–14
psychotic phenomena 1
psychotic phenomena in children and adolescents 260–4
psychotic symptoms 194
PTI (Perceptual-Thinking Index) 91–3
PTSD (post-traumatic stress disorder) 235; children 269
Pugh, D. D. 211
puns 127
pure culture 272
Putman, F. 239

quasilogical thought 152
Quee, P. J. 183
queer responses 84; Thought Disorder Index (TDI) 70
queer verbalizations 47–8, 127–8
Quinlan, D. 19, 183

Rapaport, David 42–3, 139, 171, 202–4, 280; DV (deviant verbalization) 42–51
Rapaport systems, assessing contributions of 58–62
reactive obsessions (RO) 241–2
readability 128
reality 9
reality testing 9–10, 182
reasoning 145
reasoning biases 151
reasoning disturbances 147
regression 162
Reich, T. 211
Reininghaus, U. 195, 201–2
Reis, B. 237–8
relationship errors (RELERs) 104
relationship verbalization, Thought Disorder Index (TDI) 70
relationships, interpersonal relationships 157
RELERs (relationship errors) 104
reliability, Thought Disorder Index (TDI) 72–3
Resnick, P. J. 249, 254, 256
response atrophy 48
response verbalizations 48
Ritzler, B. A. 156
RO (reactive obsessions) 241–2

Robinson, S. 240
Rorschach assessment xiii, 30–2
Rorschach, Hermann xiii, 37
Rorschach indices of manic thought disorder 209–11
Rorschach Performance Assessment System *see* R-PAS (Rorschach Performance Assessment System)
Rorschach variables, schizophrenia spectrum 196–200
Roth, R. M. 183
Rothenberg, A. 162
Rothschild-Yakar, L. 186–7, 281
R-PAS (Rorschach Performance Assessment System) 82, 93–100, 173, 257, 280–1, 283–4; clinical utility 100; cognitive codes 95; detecting psychosis 94; Perception and Thinking Domain 95–6; SevCog (Severe Cognitive Codes) 185
R-PAS Engagement and Cognitive Processing Domain 281

Scale for the Assessment of Thought, Language, and Communication (TLC) 13–14
Schachtel, E. 204
Schafer, Roy 43, 51, 159, 171, 184, 204, 206, 280
schizoaffective disorder 195, 200–1
schizoaffective-depressed patients 201
schizoaffective-manic patients 200
schizo-obsessive 241
schizophrenia 12, 194–5; cognitive disorganization 196; cognitive impairment 177–9; disordered thinking 19–21; distinguishing thought disorder in 207–9; indicators of 91; inkblots 38 9
Schizophrenia Index (SCZI) 91–3
schizophrenia spectrum 195–200
Schretlen, D. J. 251
Schuldberg, D. 44, 172, 174, 272
scores, borderline-level thought disorder scores 231–2
scoring Comprehensive System (CS) 82–93
scoring examples of disordered thinking 28
Scoring the Rorschach: Seven Validated Systems 65–6
scoring Thought Disorder Index (TDI) 67–72
Scroppo, J. C. 238

SCZI (Schizophrenia Index) 91–3; borderline disorders 231
Seamons, D. T. 251
secondary psychoses: borderline disorders 227–35; dissociative disorders 238–40; OCD (Obsessive-Compulsive Disorder) 240–2; trauma 235–8
Segal, H. 140
selectivity 151
self-awareness 182
self-certainty 182
self-experience, disordered thinking and 158–60
self-monitoring 21, 22, 136
self-reflectiveness 182
semantic memory system 135–6
SevCog (Severe Cognitive Codes) 96, 185
Sewell, K. W. 251
Shakow, D. 196
Sheerer, M. 174
Shenton, M. E. 197, 200–1, 210
Shentoub, V. 128
Sherman, M. 249
signs of thought disorder 109
Silberman, E. K. 212
Singer, H. K. 88, 210, 213
Smith, K. 157–8, 261, 267
social cognition 183
social insight 183
soft signs, disordered thinking 228
Solovay, M. R. 197, 200, 210
source monitoring 22, 136
special content scores, CS (Comprehensive System) 88–9
Special Scores 198; CS (Comprehensive System) 87–8, 90–1, 98; R-PAS (Rorschach Performance Assessment System) 98
specificity and sensitivity of thought, malingered psychosis 254–7
speech: disorganized speech 15, 125–6; impoverished speech 117–18; thought disorder 12–14
speech disorder 13
Sprafkin, Q. R. 249
Sprock, J. 212
St. Peter, S. 233
Stage I Rorschachs 175
stilited speech 133
Stone, M. H. 228
Stopek, S. 208
Strauss, J. S. 206

structural deficiencies 208
structural shifts 208
Stuart, J. 233
Sugarman, A. 232
Sullivan, H. S. 152
superstitious beliefs 153
suspecting malingering 248–50
syllogism 146
symbiosis/separation 233
symbolic equation 140
symbolic interpretation of concrete images 150
symbolic interpretation of shading or color 150
symbolic responses 49–50
symbolization 54–5
symptom dimensions 194

tangentiality 132
TAT 233
Tausk, V. 139
Taylor, M. A. 15
TCI (Trauma Content Index) 236
TDI (Thought Disorder Index) *see* Thought Disorder Index (TDI) 2, 172; early-onset schizophrenia 266; mania 209; schizoaffective disorder 200
TDI 4-card sets 105
tendency scores, Thought Disorder Index (TDI) 67
testing, reality testing 9–10
testing of limits, assessing awareness 186–7
testing situations, interpersonal dynamics 184
theory of mind (ToM) 18, 183
thinking problems 16
Thomas, E. A. 267
Thought and Language Index (TLI) 15
Thought and Perception Composite (TP-Comp) 95
thought disorder 2; borderline psychopathology 229–34; continuums 19; deciphering 43; defining 11–12; distance from inkblots 43–4; distinguishing in schizophrenia and mania 207–9; disturbances 17; formal thought disorder 15–17; history of 12; issues in assessing 27–9; language 12–14; positive and negative 14–15; psychosis and 10–11; signs of 109

Thought Disorder Index (TDI) 2, 65–6; background of 66–7; clinical considerations 78–9; FABCOMs (fabulized combinations) 77; factor-analysis studies 74–5; INCOMs 77; normative base 73–4; reliability 72–3; scoring 67–72; validation studies 75
thought disorder scores 156
TLC (Scale for the Assessment of Thought, Language, and Communication) 13–14, 145; categories of formal thought disorder reflecting disorganization 132–3
TLI (Thought and Language Index) 15, 109
To Whom and When component, disordered thinking 18
ToM (theory of mind) 18, 22, 183
Total TDI score 68, 73
toxic etiology, psychotic phenomena in children and adolescents 263
toxic psychotic state 217
toxicology screenings 217
TPAS 105–6
TP-Comp (Thought and Perception Composite) 95
traditional psychological perspectives, illogicality 149–51
trance logic 239
trauma 235–8
Trauma Content Index (TCI) 236
trauma imagery 236
trauma-induced disorders, children/adolescents 269–70
traumatic thought disorder 236–7
TRAUT system 103–5
Trief, P. 249
TTD (traumatic thought disorder) 236–7
Tuber, S. B. 157

UHR (ultra-high-risk) 214
uncoded verbalizations 128–9
underincorporators 173
unusual verbalizations, CS (Comprehensive System) 83–5
Urist, J. 234

vagueness 48–9, 69, 118, 171–3
validation studies, Thought Disorder Index (TDI) 75
van der Kolk, B. 237
variables 54–56

Vaskinn, A. 183
VC (verbal condensations) 128
verbal fragmentation 129
verbal incoherence (VI) 128
verbal productivity 207
verbal slips 127
verbalization 43
verbalization responses, disorganization 127
verbalizations, uncoded verbalizations 128–9
VI (verbal incoherence) 128
Viglione, Don 93–4, 235, 252, 254, 270
visual pseudoperceptions 229
von Domarus, Eilhard 47, 146
VP (peculiar verbalizations) 127–8
VQ (queer verbalizations) 127–8

Wahlberg, K. E. 77
WAIS (Weschler Adult Intelligence Scale) 30, 67, 230
wandering away phenomenon 88, 100
Wechsler tests 230
Weighted Sum of Six Cognitive Codes (WSUMCog) 95–6
Weiner, I. B. 16
Weiner, Irving 82, 139, 147, 173, 184–5, 280; conceptualizing thought processes 130–1
Weingartner, H. 212
Weiss, R. 240

Werner, H. 152
Weschler Adult Intelligence Scale (WAIS) 30
Westen, D. 233
Wetzler, S. 201, 210
What dimension 17–18
When and With Whom 189
Where dimension 18
Why dimension 18–19
Wilson, A. 201, 210
Winnik, H. Z. 240
Winokur, G. 211
Within Card Perseveration 87–8
Wolf, E. 158
word approximations 133
word play 72
word-finding difficulty, Thought Disorder Index (TDI) 69
working memory 21
WSUM6 91, 199; dissociative disorders 239
WSUMCog (Weighted Sum of Six Cognitive Codes) 95–6

Yalof, J. 272
Yorozuya, Y. 216
young children, and the Rorschach 154–5
Yung, Allison 214

Zd (Processing Efficiency) 173
Zmuda, Bob 163–4